New World Cities

New World Cities

Challenges of Urbanization and
Globalization in the Americas

. . . .

EDITED BY

JOHN TUTINO & MARTIN V. MELOSI

University of North Carolina Press Chapel Hill

The University of North Carolina Press has been a member
of the Green Press Initiative since 2003.

Library of Congress Cataloging-in-Publication Data
Names: Tutino, John, 1947– editor. | Melosi, Martin V., 1947– editor.
Title: New World cities : challenges of urbanization and globalization
    in the Americas / edited by John Tutino and Martin V. Melosi.
Description: Chapel Hill : University of North Carolina Press, [2019] |
    Includes bibliographical references and index.
Identifiers: LCCN 2018031798| ISBN 9781469648743 (cloth : alk. paper) |
    ISBN 9781469648750 (pbk : alk. paper) | ISBN 9781469648767 (ebook)
Subjects: LCSH: Urbanization—Political aspects—America. | Globalization—
    Political aspects—America. | Globalization—Social aspects—America. |
    America—Civilization. | America—Politics and government.
Classification: LCC HT153 .N49 2019 | DDC 307.76097—dc23 LC record
    available at https://lccn.loc.gov/2018031798

Cover photos (clockwise from upper left): *Aerial View of Mexico City with Revolution Monument* (© iStock.com/UlrikeStein); Montreal (City of Montreal Archives, VM94-B269-034); Santa Marta and Botafogo, Rio de Janeiro (© Ratão Diniz); Houston, *Hurricane Harvey Impacts* (© iStock.com/Karl Spencer).

For our daughters:
Adria Melosi McDonald and Gina Melosi
Gabriela Tutino and María Tutino Mejía
metropolitan women leading us into the twenty-first century

Contents

Maps and Tables

Acknowledgments

This book has been a long time coming, and many have contributed along the way. The idea began in conversations between Bryan McCann and John Tutino in the common area of the Georgetown University history department. We were colleagues coming from different backgrounds in studies of Brazil and Mexico, converging in seeing urbanization as an essential focus if history is to address the twenty-first century. We agreed that a comparative project should span the hemisphere—and we needed a co-leader grounded in North American urbanization. Tutino proposed Martin Melosi, who quickly accepted. The three of us consulted to recruit Matthew Gutmann, Mark Healey, Michèle Dagenais, George Sanchez, and Joseph Pratt into the group.

We shared preliminary papers and began stimulating conversations in a first workshop held at Georgetown University in March 2009, sponsored by the Americas Initiative. There, Matthew Gutmann presented a powerful paper on Mexico City in the 1990s. His presentation and his conversation did much to shape our work, even though the demands of becoming a dean at Brown University blocked his continuing participation. Erick Langer, Katherine Benton-Cohen, and John McNeill chaired, commented, and led discussion in three lively sessions. They helped us see our way forward. Kathleen Gallagher, administrator of the Americas Initiative from its founding to her recent retirement, once again did everything needed to bring together scholars from across North America in sessions that seemed effortless—thanks to her exceptional efforts. Jane Tutino integrated a lively dinner gathering that helped turn a group assembled (mostly) as scholarly strangers into collegial friends.

We gathered a second time at the University of Houston in March 2010, sponsored by the Center for Public History. We reassembled without Matt Gutmann, an unfortunate loss, and with the addition of Joseph Pratt, a real gain. Kathleen Brosnan, Susan Kellogg, and Natalia Milanesio brought their diverse perspectives as discussion leaders. Our essays are better for their contributions. Staff from the Center for Public History—program coordinator Kristin Deville and graduate assistant Julie Cohn (now Dr. Julie

Cohn)—made the event go off like clockwork, which they have done so often. Thanks also to Carolyn Melosi for the excellent dinner party held in honor of our guests from around the United States and Canada. Her skills as a chef and social integrator sent us forward to continue our work in the best of cheer.

Funding from the Americas Initiative and the Institute for Global History at Georgetown University, and from the Center for Public History at the University of Houston made the workshops possible, providing the impetus for producing and publishing *New World Cities*. The Americas Initiative has continued to support the project through the process of manuscript preparation.

As our authors worked to shape and reshape analyses and essays over the years, Brandon Proia of the University of North Carolina Press saw value in our efforts to focus on cities across national and scholarly boundaries. Thanks to his efforts, our conversations will widen. Early on, Elizabeth Chavez, then a graduate student at Georgetown, chased down endless and often daunting demographic materials to construct the tables that sustain the comparative analysis in Chapter 1. We have all benefitted from her efforts. More recently, Eric Gettig, a rising scholar working at the intersection of U.S. and Latin American history (focusing on energy, economic challenges, and revolution in twentieth-century Cuba) took on the task of final preparation and streamlining of the manuscript. He has accelerated the project. And at the end, Rodolfo Fernández, a historian of urban Monterrey, Mexico, brought his sharp bilingual eyes to final proofs. Our endeavor has been a most collaborative process. Thanks to all.

New World Cities

· Introduction

Urbanizing History in Globalizing Times

· ·

JOHN TUTINO

The world became urban in the twentieth century. Across the Americas, growing majorities concentrated in metropolitan centers; economic and political power and possibilities focused there, as did educational chances, medical services, and cultural opportunities. Most of the world followed a parallel path, sharing in an urbanization driven in large part by the global population explosion that accelerated after 1950. Together, demographic acceleration and urbanization fueled the widening economic, social, and cultural interactions called globalization by century's end. Yet these historically transcendent transformations have barely begun to impact thinking about contemporary history. The first question is why. The more important challenge is to bring the urban experience—better, the diversity of urban experiences—to the center of histories that aim to understand the roots of key contemporary problems, in the process opening conversations about ways forward in a globalizing world in which some prosper and so many struggle.

The slow recognition among historians (and others) of the transforming importance of the rise of urbanization is understandable. Historical ways of thinking developed and became an academic perspective in times defined by the rise and spread of nation states. Political processes that are mostly national have long shaped scholarly and popular historical thinking—with larger interactions seen as international and local ramifications as just that: local. It is time to revise such emphases. As the twenty-first century began, dominant economic processes were global in unfathomably complex ways. Social life concentrated in metropolitan regions that were in no way local. Centered on nodes of power, they tied large, complex, diverse regions—and millions of people—to global powers and processes. Politics remained mostly national—and lamented as incapable of shaping global economic processes or serving the needs of changing metropolitan regions. Yet national states and their politics still focus historical analyses and most conversations about how to make urbanizing lives more livable in a globalizing world.

Our goal is to bring urbanization and the rise of globalization to the center of a new historical vision. We recognize that nations matter, as do their politics, but our explorations of six New World cities—Mexico City, Rio de Janeiro, Buenos Aires, Montreal, Los Angeles, and Houston—suggest that globalization shapes metropolitan lives more than national policies, and that urban politics often shape city lives as much or more than national processes. We hope to broaden conversations about how urbanization in times of globalization has generated burgeoning cities concentrating dynamic opportunities and enduring inequalities, and how diverse ways of popular participation drew benefits to people struggling to get by—with real yet limited successes.

Three key studies help define the challenges we aim to address. In *The Global City*, Saskia Sassen emphasized that great cities are the ruling centers of power in the new world of globalization—reproducing within their expanding populations the polarizing inequalities that mark the world they rule. She argues that we must recognize that while nations continue to organize politics and shape the languages in which we debate power and prosperity, increasingly people, social processes, and cultural engagements concentrate in vast metropolitan areas. Primary economic processes are global, shaped by urban networks more than by national boundaries, while most people live in complex metropolitan zones.[1]

In *Power and Plenty*, Ronald Findlay and Kevin O'Rourke take a long historical view to see how the twentieth century brought a fundamental transformation of the world economy. The commercial capitalism that shaped the world before 1800 was polycentric—integrating a world of diversity. The industrial capitalism that rose to rule the nineteenth century concentrated power, industry, and prosperity along a North Atlantic axis from northwest Europe to the northeast United States—while a vast rest of the world turned to selling raw commodities and buying finished goods. That world collapsed in wars and depression from 1910 to 1950, giving way (after diverse experiments in national development) to a new globalization that focuses financial power in leading cities from Europe, across North America, to Asia, disperses production to wherever resources are accessible and labor is cheap, sustains consumption in affluent and middling neighborhoods around the world—while poverty, insecurity, and marginality proliferate everywhere, in differing proportions.[2]

Now, in *Capital in the Twenty-First Century*, Thomas Piketty has mobilized vast quantitative data to document that nineteenth-century industrial capitalism generated mounting concentrations of wealth and power, even in favored centers of power and prosperity. He shows that such concentrations gave way to a greater sharing only in the decades of global depression, world war, and cold war from 1930 to 1970. And he details how the new globalization is again accelerating accumulations of wealth, property, and power.[3] Piketty argues that such rising concentrations cannot be sustained, either because they will eventually undermine economic dynamism or because they will provoke escalating and eventually disruptive opposition among the growing numbers facing prejudiced lives in diverse regions. He dreams of global policies to promote redistributions, but fragmented national political domains preclude such attempts. We are left to engage "Piketty's dilemma": how to preserve the productive dynamism of globalization yet distribute its products in ways that serve the needs of the unprecedented numbers of people now concentrating in vast metropolitan regions.

Globalization, urbanization, and economic concentrations seem poised to persist—despite recent political promises and programs proclaiming renewed nationalism. The democratization promoted as the way to shared participation and effective redistribution increasingly delivers theatrical promises and sows divisions. While the powerful still rule and take concentrating wealth, many in the middle struggle to hold bits of promised prosperity, and diverse majorities gain little. For too many, moments of political promise lead quickly to disillusion. It is time to look beyond national political theatrics. Our studies explore processes that create wealth, concentrate power, and limit justice and welfare in six expanding New World cities caught in a globalizing economy. We seek to understand the links between urbanization and globalization, diverse combinations of prosperity and poverty, and the ways popular groups have mobilized to make their lives, their neighborhoods, and their cities more livable.

Our six cities (again, Mexico City, Rio de Janeiro, Buenos Aires, Montreal, Los Angeles, and Houston) all link important regions and/or nations to a globalizing world. None are primary centers of global finance. All are marked by sharp concentrations of wealth and power, with populations shaped by racial/ethnic/religious diversities that often become divisions. All have seen popular movements make meaningful gains, none enduring or transforming enough to limit rising concentrations and the spread of lives struggling with marginalization. There is much to explore and understand in these six cities. Other New World cities would bring different perspectives. We focus on the Americas because taking on the diversity of the world is impossible in one volume, because New World cities have led the urban surge, and because they share enough common history to make their differing experiences, challenges, and responses illuminating.

The Century of Urbanization

Around 1900, most cities across the Americas and the world were centers of power and trade, ruling and integrating mostly rural and agricultural societies. Cities were urbane, places of prosperity and sophistication, surrounded by majorities working the land. Where there were industries, they were as likely to be in towns surrounded by agricultural hinterlands as in major cities. In the United States and Canada, most rural people were seen as farmers, selling crops to sustain cities and industries, locally and globally, while holding a bit of self-sufficiency. Across Latin America, they were *campesinos*, country people—pejoratively, peasants—often struggling to feed themselves while laboring seasonally at commercial estates that fed cities and supplied global commodity trades. Rural people lived caught up in powerful capitalist networks, yet they appeared separate, at times honored as independent, too often maligned as rustic. With all their diversity, rural peoples remained the great majority across the Americas and the world as the twentieth century began.

Urbanization accelerated after 1900, to reach unprecedented concentrations with the global population explosion after 1950. In 1900, Mexico City was home to about 500,000 people in a nation of fewer than 14 million; by 2000, the city approached 20 million in a nation nearing 100 million. In Brazil, Rio de Janeiro had 800,000 and São Paulo 200,000 inhabitants in a nation of 17.5 million in 1900; by 2000 they had grown enormously and reversed roles: São Paulo concentrated 18 million and Rio 12 million of Brazil's 170 million people. In the United States, industrialization brought greater urban concentrations in the nineteenth century; in 1900, New York included over 4 million and Chicago nearly 2 million of the nation's 75 million people; by 2000, metropolitan New York approached 18 million, while Los Angeles with nearly 12 million had replaced Chicago as the second city in a nation of 275 million. The rise of megacities led a broader urbanization across the Americas, creating nations with growing urban majorities. As the twentieth century ended, the United States and Canada formed the most urbanized region of the prosperous "first" world. Latin America was the most urban region of the world. Much of Asia and Africa retained (shrinking) rural majorities in 2000, yet they are following the Americas in accelerating urbanization. If the Americas led global urbanization, the hemisphere is a good place to begin comparative analysis of pivotal developments and challenges.[4]

Explosive population growth leading to unprecedented urban concentrations brought new dimensions to traditional human needs: How would such numbers be fed, housed, schooled, and cured? Could millions of new city dwellers, often migrants from countrysides near and far, find sustaining work? And unprecedented infrastructure needs loomed: water and sewer services were essential to everyday survival and long-term public health; daily mobility demanded streets and highways, trolleys and subways. Only complex power grids could keep cities in motion. Such infrastructure was (and is) exceptionally costly, and along with education it is usually a public expense.[5] Meanwhile, the concentration of millions of people—rich and poor, old residents and new migrants, often racially, religiously, and ethnically diverse—in close urban quarters raised new challenges of social coordination. Were caring social workers or stern police and hard prisons the solution? The tendency has been to rely on the latter, but any response demanded revenues. Urban expansion created unprecedented human needs and brought soaring public costs. Difficulties meeting them have challenged cities everywhere.

Our group set out to explore the challenges of explosive urbanization and the gains and limits of popular politics during the twentieth century in six cities across the Americas. Some are very old: Mexico City was founded in the 1300s; others relatively new: Houston was hard to call a city before 1900. All six remained pivotally important to key regions, large nations, and the world after 1950. All faced surging populations; all struggled to provide jobs, infrastructure, and services; all generated popular movements demanding better—usually with enough success to make cities more livable—while preserving enduring ways of power and inequity.

We focus on Western Hemisphere cities to control the larger historical complexities of comparative analysis. All six developed within the Americas' long history of European rule, cultural influence, and global economic incorporation, beginning in the sixteenth century. We excluded the hemisphere's richest and most powerful cities, notably the New York–Washington metropolitan axis. Our goal is to explore how burgeoning cities of pivotal importance, limited power, and changing, often uncertain prosperity have faced the challenges of explosive growth and popular politics in the Americas' favored north and struggling south.

We began with questions: How should we understand the challenges of building huge new urban concentrations? How did cities' differing social ways and ethnic relations shape life and politics? How did popular groups press their needs? To what extent did they find success? By choice we assembled authors bringing diverse analytical approaches to study different cities in several nations: some focus on infrastructure and environment, others on economies and neighborhoods of informality and illegality, others on migration and labor, race and ethnicity. All deal with urban politics—the public domains where power engages the populace. Most linked several of these issues. We saw no gain in imposing a common vision; we aimed to learn from each other and discover where our analyses converged and where we diverged. With our diverse approaches we recognize two underlying emphases: the economic challenges of building huge urban conglomerations, and the possibilities and limits of popular politics.

Urbanizing Twentieth-Century History

The twentieth century brought unprecedented changes and challenges to every aspect of life across the globe. Devastating world wars separated by a deep economic depression shaped the decades before 1950. Cold War competition between the United States and the Soviet Union structured the decades after 1950, shaping and constraining regional conflicts and revolutionary confrontations—until the collapse of Soviet power and an apparent U.S. hegemony announced new times of globalization. During a long mid-century transition, the United States promoted global capitalism while the Soviet Union pressed state socialism. Their rivalry marked an era, beginning with revolutions in Mexico and Russia in the 1910s, accelerating in the Depression of the 1930s, and continuing during World War II and the reconstructions and decolonizations that followed, in which most states pursued dreams of national development, whether capitalist, socialist, or mixed. The fall of the Soviet Union beginning in the 1980s, however, unleashed a capitalist globalization as national development projects collapsed almost everywhere. A moment of euphoria imagining a U.S. triumph soon gave way to recognition that globalization was ruled by no nation, and its impact on state powers and everyday lives would be immense, unpredictable, and beyond control of any state or coalition.

The globalization that accelerated during the Cold War, challenged national development projects, and ruled the world by the 1990s cannot be understood separately from the demographic explosion and rapid urbanization that simultaneously shaped the era. From 1800 to 1900, the world's population grew from 1 billion to 1.6 billion, a 60 percent rise in a century. By 1950, global population reached 2.6 billion, more than a 60 percent increase in fifty years—and urbanization began to rise amid wars and a depression. Then world population soared past 6 billion by 2000, more than doubling in another fifty years. That population explosion fueled the rapid shift to globalization and urbanization that now shapes the world.

Across the Americas, growing majorities now live in cities, with large concentrations in major metropolitan areas. As the twentieth century ended, a third of all Argentines lived in metropolitan Buenos Aires; 20 percent of all Mexicans negotiated life in greater Mexico City—the largest urban concentration in the hemisphere. In Canada, 27 percent lived in two dominant urban zones, Toronto and Montreal; in Brazil, São Paulo and Rio de Janeiro held 17 percent of the population in a larger, growing, and dispersed nation. And in the United States—the nation with the largest population and the most widely dispersed cities in the hemisphere—New York, Chicago, Los Angeles, and Houston combined to concentrate 15 percent of nearly 300 million people.[6]

The challenges of employing, educating, feeding, and housing the soaring populations concentrating in megacities shaped the second half of the twentieth century—while public, political, and scholarly conversations usually focused elsewhere. Demographic acceleration was not separate from the wars and economic opportunities of the age. Population growth was unleashed by antibiotics and other lifesaving medications developed during World War II and swiftly diffused by a globalizing medical capitalism (and socialism) soon after.[7] A new industrial agriculture (capitalist and socialist) integrated mechanization, chemical fertilizers, herbicides, and pesticides to feed unprecedented numbers.[8] That celebrated green revolution rapidly increased food production while radically decreasing employment in agriculture.[9] The productive triumph pressed rural people off the land, driving growing numbers to cities in search of new lives. After 1950, urbanization was more rapid than the unprecedented population growth that fueled it.

Most scholars and other analysts of the decades after World War II have emphasized the Cold War, its political ramifications, and the simultaneous social and cultural debates about race and ethnicity, gender and equality. They are pivotally important issues—that must be understood in the context of spreading urbanization and accelerating globalization. Fortunately, a few key scholars have focused on the urban transformation and its unprecedented challenges.

Saskia Sassen, a sociologist, again plays a pivotal role. She produced a series of works showing how key metropolitan centers rule networks of cities that organize a globalizing world. She focuses on what she labels global cities, metropolitan pivots of financial, organizational, and technical power that coordinate the global system: New York, London, Paris, Frankfurt, Tokyo (and recently Beijing). They concentrate the rich and powerful as well as diverse middle classes, along with growing populations that include many migrants seeking opportunity, yet often struggling as insecure and informal service and sales workers. To those who ask how global capitals flourish while they make less and less (as production disperses across the globe to find cheap labor), Sassen answers: they produce wealth by integrating the system—they make money. She adds that the leading global cities rule and integrate larger networks of cities. Primary global centers interact to reinforce each other's power, even as they compete for primacy. They link to other metropolitan nodes in the developed, developing, and desperate worlds to promote and integrate globalization. Sassen emphasizes that the urban engines of global power generate wealth, opportunity, and deepening inequities within their metropolitan regions, across nations—and around the world.[10]

In *Planet of Slums*, historian Mike Davis drives readers to confront the dark sides of global urbanization, detailing the rise of cities of desperation in the Global South.[11] He brings us to burgeoning settlements concentrating poverty, marginality, informality, and powerlessness across Africa, Asia, Latin America, and the Islamic world. Yet Davis recognizes that the megacities of marginality expanded in good part because they became places of limited opportunity, drawing millions who faced even lesser chances in small cities, dying villages, and mechanizing fields. He argues that development programs promising cures for rural desperation and urban marginality have repeatedly failed, notably because they bring more labor-saving integration into global capitalism. Labor-saving production empties rural regions of work, driving people to cities; there, labor-saving ways of production tap into slums' "comparative advantage" of plentiful, cheap, and often desperate labor. The cities may prosper, yet too many people face deepening inequities and lives of entrenched insecurity. Davis adds that popular political movements, rarely finding conditions approaching democracy in cities of desperation, mostly claim marginal gains. He details a city-centered world of concentrating power and expanding slums laden with desperation, a world unlikely to change but for an unimagined cataclysm.

In many ways, our city histories reflect the contrasting but not necessarily contradictory visions of Sassen and Davis. Both see the new megacities as places gathering huge populations while generating internal contradictions. Sassen focuses on cities of power and prosperity as nodes integrating global production. Davis insists that we also think about cities of desperation and argues that prevailing ways of globalizing production fuel contradictions and thus cannot cure them. We aim to integrate their visions and questions while exploring the histories of three cities of modest power and some shared prosperity in the Global North—Montreal, Los Angeles, and Houston—and three cities concentrating power and desperation in the Global South—Mexico City, Rio de Janeiro, and Buenos Aires.

We also take up Davis's challenge to look at popular political movements. Have they empowered poor and marginal urban dwellers? Have they brought meaningful access to power and/or gains in prosperity? On those questions, South African urban analyst Edgar Pieterse has sought a third way to understand the politics of urbanization.[12] Building on Sassen's insight that urbanization will persist and continue to concentrate power, opportunity, and inequality, and accepting Davis's conclusion that most development programs exacerbate inequities, Pieterse insists that there is a way forward—a political way. To sketch his complex argument: if global, national, and metropolitan actors committed to welfare and justice for urban majorities will work to promote rights to decent lives for all, and if they will interact openly and creatively with people in slums who show a remarkable readiness to mobilize to demand infrastructure, services, and ways of survival—then, with long effort, the lives of the least fortunate in an urbanizing world of enduring inequity may become more livable.

Our studies share with Pieterse the view that popular movements have made urban lives better—and can continue to do so. Still, they have rarely led to effective access to power, thus they have had little impact on the larger trajectories that build inequities into urban societies. Rather, our histories suggest that, by different means in differing cities, popular movements have gained just enough to make urban lives bearable—ultimately operating to keep an urbanizing and globalizing world on its current path of polarization.

There are voices that see more promise, if a few obstacles can be removed. In *Welcome to the Urban Revolution*, Jeb Brugman acknowledges global urbanization as a transforming development. His revolution, however, is not a popular rising but urbanization itself, an inexorable process of change to which people must adapt in cities from Toronto to Mumbai. He recognizes urban problems but sees them easily fixed by freeing entrepreneurs and markets from political constraints.[13] Economist Edward Glaeser focuses on the United States in *Triumph of the City*. He waxes lyrical about the creativity and prosperity of cities, downplaying contradictions and desperations. Like Brugman, he sees the poverty locked in parts of even the most prosperous cities. But for Glaeser, better urban planning—the opposite of free markets—is the cure.[14]

In *The Metropolitan Revolution*, Bruce Katz and Jennifer Bradley also focus on the United States. They take much from Sassen, notably that networks of cities now organize the United States and the world. They recognize that deep crises continue to challenge U.S. cities, crises they attribute to dysfunctional national and state politics. They see a revolution coming—not an inevitable technological-market revolution like Brugman's, but a revolution led by people challenging established powers. Yet the Brookings scholars' revolution is "leader driven," promoted by mayors, corporate and university leaders, civic organization, and NGOs: "tens, if not hundreds, of thousands of leaders who collectively steward their places, guide their regions, and co-produce their economies." Katz and Bradley celebrate alliances among civic leaders, planners, and entrepreneurs, and argue that success requires sovereign metropolitan regions.[15] An integration of metropolitan regions to break jurisdictional fragmentations and enable coordination among leaders for more effective politics and planning might well bring gains. Is there no role for mobilized popular communities in forging change to make cities more livable?

Not surprisingly, recent views from Latin America see darker prospects. In *El tamaño del infierno—The Dimensions of Hell*—Arturo Alvarado Mendoza set out to study crime and violence in Mexico City as urban expansion reached its peak while globalization accelerated under NAFTA in 1994, followed by turns to more democratic rule in the city in 1997 and in the nation in 2000. He found that crimes of violence and property remained low through the economic collapse of the 1980s and into the early 1990s. They nearly tripled from 1994 to 1999 with the turn to NAFTA, a quick economic collapse, the deindustrialization of the city, and the rise of an ever more informal urban economy. With democratization came a rapid increase in policing, and crime fell back—to hold at nearly twice the levels prevailing before the transition to NAFTA.[16] Mendoza shows that globalization brought the hemisphere's largest metropolis losses of secure employment; the spreading of lives of marginality left millions to live at too often violent intersections of informality and illegality to survive. Democratization and new policing—both imperfect—reduced crime, but left violence a corrosive presence in insecure metropolitan lives. To blunt claims of Mexican incapacity, Mendoza emphasizes that violent crime in Mexico City held a middle range among New World megacities—with Washington, Houston, Los Angeles, and New York well ahead in social morbidity. He emphasizes that studies of politics, justice, and policing must be set in the context of the insecurities and inequities entrenched by globalized urbanism—everywhere.

All these studies recognize that the world is now urban, and that urbanization has transformed every aspect of contemporary life. They differ in their evaluations: some see utopian promise, others entrenched devastations—the best recognize enduring contradictions. They also differ in their understanding of popular participation: some see great promise, others destructive interventions; the clearest recognize possibilities and limits. All acknowledge the importance of globalization in shaping cities; none focus on cities' differing, changing, often contradictory insertions in a globalizing capitalism that Piketty shows is built to continue, even deepen, the polarizations all see and lament. To understand better, we need historical analyses integrating accelerating urbanization, the rise of globalization, and the politics of power and participation that have contested the shape of cities and the welfare of their peoples in the twentieth century.

Unprecedented population growth and urban concentrations have become key emphases among environmental historians aiming to understand the transformations of the second half of the twentieth century. In *The Great Acceleration*, John McNeill and Peter Engelke explore how population explosion and urban concentrations mixed with Cold War conflicts and competitions between capitalism and socialism to promote ways of life that demanded vast quantities of energy, generated vast amounts of pollution, threatened health in unprecedented ways, and raised questions about the sustainability of prevailing development models (capitalist, socialist, and then globalizing). They focus on the challenges faced by states, societies, and peoples along an east-west axis across the Northern Hemisphere, the primary domain of global power, to raise new perspectives and pivotal questions.[17]

New World Cities, we believe, offers a complementary vision. We focus on a north-south axis, linking cities of greater power and prosperity to others concentrating poverty, marginality, and inequities. We understand the importance of energy and environment (an emphasis in the chapter on

Houston), yet we focus more on changing economic possibilities, on diverse mixes of power and exclusion, and on the possibilities and limits of political movements seeking wider distributions of opportunity and basic welfare. Can new ways of participation promote justice for diverse and often fragmented majorities? Going forward, an integration of analyses that recognize changing economic openings and limits while focusing on energy and environment and on politics, participation, and justice will bring more complex understandings of how the late twentieth century begat the challenges of the twenty-first. Analyses of other north-south axes (the gains from studies linking European and African cities quickly come to mind) will surely bring additional perspectives and new questions. What we all must share is the recognition that our globalizing world, with all its energy, environmental, social, and political challenges, is set in metropolitan conglomerations.

Globalization, Urbanization, and Popular Participation in Six New World Cities: A Preview

Our group first generated the six case histories. Workshop discussions made it clear that all our cities faced rapid demographic growth, limited economic possibilities, and scarce infrastructure and services while tied in varied and changing ways to global economic networks. The group challenged me to develop a framework that would place our cities in the context of their engagements with a changing world economy. A second workshop allowed us to discuss the framework and revised versions of our urban histories— leading to further refinements. The chapters that follow begin with the framework, aiming to allow an integrated reading of the city histories that form the core of our analysis. An understanding of how and why six different cities and their diverse peoples lived distinct variants of common historical processes is our goal. Martin Melosi's epilogue synthesizes our contributions and shapes questions for continuing conversations.

Chapter 1 sets "The Americas in the Twentieth-Century World." It outlines the technological and economic innovations that drove accelerating population growth and urbanization from the 1940s to the 1970s, and the turn to globalization that followed. It argues that under globalization, cities and their metropolitan regions became central to production and social relations. It sketches the origins and evolution of our six cities as capitalism and the Americas developed before 1900; it focus on how they engaged the twentieth-century world in different ways. All once claimed pivotal roles in global capitalism: Mexico City from 1550 to 1810, as silver drove global trade; Rio from 1700 to 1900 as Brazilian gold and then coffee fueled Britain's rise; Buenos Aires and Montreal as pivots of export economies serving British eminence from 1870 to 1930; Los Angeles and Houston as centers of energy and industry driving the rise of the United States from 1940 to 1980. Notably, all but Houston faced a fall from global eminence before 2000, while all lived the challenges of explosive urbanism after 1950. The opening chapter offers comparative insights on globalization, uncertain prosperity, falls from eminence, and their impacts in six cities facing common challenges with diverse prospects and populations.

We offer the six city histories in the order they claimed global importance and then fell from eminence. The sequence emphasizes the gains of economic centrality and the relative prosperity it brought, and the challenges that have come when times of economic demise mixed with population explosion.

We thus begin with Mexico City, the oldest of our cities and the largest metropolis in the Americas in 2000. My study of "Power, Marginality, and Participation in Mexico City" (chapter 2) notes the city's rise to eminence as the pivot of the global silver economy in the eighteenth century and its fall to struggle as the capital of a nation mired in "underdevelopment" in the nineteenth. Urbanization accelerated as the economy struggled, creating a divisive mix of prosperity and marginality before 1900. An early twentieth-century revolution drove a turn to national development in Mexico; the capital city continued to grow as industrialization brought new work that never proved enough to employ growing numbers. Neighborhoods of insecurity and lives of informality grew along with industrial development after 1950 until everything crashed in the 1980s. An oil-driven debt crisis forced a turn to globalization that drove industry and employment from the city. Insecurity, informality, violence, and illegality marked the metropolis as NAFTA shaped new links to the United States and the world. The city struggled to provide infrastructure and services; people with scarce incomes built neighborhoods—and the city—with combinations of hard work, neighborhood movements, and political demands. Power, prosperity, and opportunity for the few mixed with marginality, poverty, and exclusion for the many as the metropolis passed 20 million people.

Rio de Janeiro became the capital of Portuguese Brazil in the eighteenth century, the largest city in any Atlantic slave society. In the nineteenth century it gained new eminence as the capital of Brazil, linking a nation grounded in coffee and slavery to Britain's rising industrial power. But with the end of slavery and monarchy in 1888–89, Rio became a city of growing population yet diminishing economic and political importance. Informalities began to mark city life. When Brazil tried national development under Getúlio Vargas from the 1930s, industry focused on São Paulo; the founding of Brasília as the national capital in the 1950s sent much government work from Rio to the new city in the interior. Rio's population continued to grow as its economic prospects waned from the 1960s through the turn to globalization in the 1980s and afterward. In chapter 3, "The Arc of Formality in Twentieth-Century Rio de Janeiro," Bryan McCann focuses on the city's long struggles to build housing and neighborhoods. He shows how formal and informal development were inseparable in a city of limited resources; how popular movements claimed gains for favela families; and how under late-century globalization, pervasive informality created spaces for destructive, often violent illegalities—notably gangs linked to international drug cartels. Popular movements rose during midcentury decades, demobilized under military rule after 1964, reemerged to challenge that rule, and struggled to stay effective under late century democratization. They made real gains for families struggling at the margins—but never blunted prevailing patterns of power, exclusion, and corrosive violence.

Buenos Aires was a small port at the edge of Spain's South American empire until in 1776 it became the capital of a new viceroyalty, a port linking Andean silver to the Atlantic world. It grew rapidly to 1810, then lived decades of political conflict and economic reorientation, to emerge after 1870 as the thriving capital of Argentina, sending wool and hides, meat and wheat to sustain British industries and consumers. Around 1900, the city drew throngs of Spanish and Italian immigrants to a city celebrated as prosperous and cosmopolitan. But with the fall of British industrial eminence in the Depression of the 1930s followed by the rise of agricultural production across the globe after World War II, Argentina and its leading city struggled to hold their roles in the world economy and to keep their celebrated prosperity. In chapter 4, "Boom, Echo, and Splinter," Mark Healey explores three eras of growth and challenge in Buenos Aires: expansion with prosperity and transatlantic migration to the 1930s; continued growth with internal migration—and some politically forged shared prosperity—as Argentina turned to national development through the 1960s; then the fragmenting challenges that came with military rule and early globalization in the 1970s—and continued under the democratization and accelerating globalization that followed. Healy finds successes of urban development and popular politics, with limits, until military rule and globalization mixed to constrain popular movements and unleash new concentrations of power and prosperity—leaving the poor to struggle without effective voices even as electoral openings returned.

Montreal too was a small port at the edge of empire until it became a major city funneling key materials to British industries and cities in the late nineteenth century. It too struggled in the Depression, found ways to benefit during World War II—to face new difficulties and opportunities in the postwar decades. In chapter 5, "Montreal in the Twentieth Century," Michèle Dagenais follows the expansions and challenges of Montreal from its late nineteenth-century boom, though midcentury adaptations, to the challenges of globalization. She focuses on the city's character as a bilingual, bicultural metropolis, long ruled by Anglo-Protestants while Franco-Catholics were the working majority. Over time, other migrants (Italians and diverse Europeans early on, newcomers from around the world in recent decades) brought new challenges and a new multicultural city. Dagenais shows how the economic difficulties of the 1960s came with a rising francophone nationalism that brought new political and social adaptations, how globalization brought new economic challenges to an enduring industrial base, and how new and more diverse immigrant communities brought new political movements and social adaptations that continued to hold modest prosperity while facing new polarizations.

Los Angeles began as a small town at the edge of Spain's empire; after 1821, it became a northern outlier in an emerging Mexican nation—to be taken by war into the United States in the 1840s when gold promised California's first boom. The port grew as a city of agriculture, oil, and film before World War II; it expanded in population, geography, and importance by adding defense industries during the war and the Cold War that followed. It then faced waves of boom and bust from the 1980s, when key industries left as the population still grew in times of globalization. In chapter 6, "Generations of Segregation," George Sanchez focuses on how racial and ethnic separations began early, deepened during and after World War II, faced challenges when civil rights movements found political traction, yet persisted through decades of globalization and electoral openings. He explores how intersections of powerful political and economic interests used evolving segregation to limit popular gains in a political system often offered as a model. Los Angeles developed as a city of dreams and contradictions.

Many will be surprised that Houston emerges as the "success story" in our exploration of New World cities facing late twentieth-century globalization. In their analysis of the Texas metropolis as "Energy Capital and Opportunity City" (chapter 7),Martin Melosi and Joseph Pratt trace many of the same issues faced in other cities, with notable parallels to Los Angeles: origins as a port for agricultural products around 1900, the rise of petroleum production and refining before World War II, growth during and after the war thanks to energy demands, then the development of Cold War space industries and dynamic new medical centers. Houston too faced racial and ethnic segregation, labor conflicts, and deep environmental difficulties linked to its dominant industry. It negotiated those challenges to emerge as the pivot of a global energy industry in the era of globalization, drawing resources to sustain infrastructure, services, and a modestly shared prosperity. Two conclusions drawn from Houston shape our comparative visions: economic prosperity facilitates dealing with all other problems, and prosperity is set in large part by cities' changing participations in an increasingly global economy.

In the epilogue, Martin Melosi links our perspectives and city histories to a larger domain of urban-focused studies, notes commonalities and divergences in our approaches and conclusions. Most important, he generates questions for ongoing scholarly, policy, and public research and discussion. He explores our common yet differing approaches to cities as expanding ecological spaces, our understanding of urban ties to a globalizing world as city economies changed in distinct yet parallel ways, and our convergence in addressing questions of formality and informality, legality and illegality—questions everywhere in play, yet without precise definition (perhaps because they aim to separate the inseparable). He shows that popular groups everywhere pursued politics that demanded more livable cities—in different ways, with diverse outcomes, always making gains, nowhere blunting basic patterns of inequity and exclusion. Most important, Melosi emphasizes that *New World Cities* has opened questions that require continuing exploration if we are to understand how the twentieth century set foundations for a thoroughly urban and deeply uncertain twenty-first.

Our studies remind us that metropolitan regions cannot control their roles in the world economy. They make us ask: Can nations, even powerful and relatively prosperous nations, reshape power and prosperity in a globalized world? Can political leaders, national or urban, work to maximize the employment, infrastructure, and services available to their constituents in an economy that extends beyond borders to the far reaches of a world of polarity, inequity, and uncertainty? Piketty emphasizes that there is no "natural" tendency toward shared distributions in capitalist globalization; the ruling trend is toward concentration. Our studies suggest that when sharing has happened, it has been limited and in response to popular movements of diverse kinds. Where economic prospects and revenues were strongest, participation has focused on electoral politics—in diverse ways. Politics often took on hues of black and white in Houston, demands for African American, Mexican American (and other Latino) rights in Los Angeles, an emphasis on francophone Catholic rights in Montreal. Still, access to roles in government brought little enduring change in questions of distribution and justice. Where economic prospects and urban revenues were more constrained, popular politics took direct aim at labor rights, as in Buenos Aires, and at neighborhood infrastructure and services, as in Mexico City and Rio de Janeiro. Again, there were often immediate gains (and some persistence in Buenos Aires thanks to Peronist power), but movements for labor rights and neighborhood development often faded when limited gains came—and new electoral politics diffused popular power in time of globalization.[18]

Key questions remain. Are there ways to improve the economic prospects of growing metropolitan centers and widen the distribution of benefits? The enduring platitude that good policies and institutions will bring shared prosperity seems a fading "truth."[19] Our histories suggest the reverse: prosperity sustains at least limited sharing, enables stronger institutions, perhaps limits corruption, and rewards policy initiatives. Thus we return to our fundamental question: Can the unprecedented productive potential of globalization be turned to limit concentrations and share its wealth more widely—globally, in nations, and across metropolitan regions? Can elections serve popular interests effectively? Can neighborhood movements sustain energies after immediate goals are reached? Can just legal systems and more secure formal employment and services shape urban lives without closing the spaces of everyday creativity forged by necessity in cities of informality?[20]

To engage such questions, we must study the intersections of a changing global economy with national and metropolitan ways of production, distribution, and political participation. Studies of governance, law, and the challenges of corruption must be set in the context of the larger, often intractable difficulties grounded in a globalizing economy. We must understand the underlying importance of economic concentrations and inequities, their links to urban illegalities and profit taking in government—and their grounding in legally (and illegally) structured powers of capital in production and politics everywhere. Only such analyses will explain the concentrations of power and wealth that ground the inequities that shape our globalizing world. Only such understanding can inform debates on how to limit concentrations, open effective popular participations, and in time, perhaps, distribute capitalism's bounty more widely and in sustaining ways.

Notes

1. Saskia Sassen, *The Global City: New York, London, Tokyo* (Princeton, NJ: Princeton University Press, 2001); she broadened her vision to other urban centers in *Cities in a World Economy* 3rd ed. (Thousand Oaks, CA: Pine Forge Press, 2006).

2. Ronald Findlay and Kevin O'Rourke, *Power and Plenty: War, Trade, and the World Economy in the Second Millennium* (Princeton, NJ: Princeton University Press, 2007).

3. Thomas Piketty, *Capital in the Twenty-First Century*, trans. Arthur Goldhammer (Cambridge, MA: Harvard University Press, 2014).

4. These figures derive from the tables in chapter 1; perhaps the best overview of the importance of global urbanization in the twentieth century is J. R. McNeill, *Something New Under the Sun: An Environmental History of the Twentieth-Century World* (New York: Norton, 2000).

5. On the importance of urban infrastructure, see Martin V. Melosi, *The Sanitary City: Urban Infrastructure in America from Colonial Times to the Present* (Baltimore: Johns Hopkins University Press, 1999) and *Precious Commodity: Providing Water to America's Cities* (Pittsburgh: University of Pittsburgh Press, 2011).

6. See chapter 1, Tables 1.4–1.5.

7. This is a key emphasis of William McNeill's classic *Plagues and People* (New York: Anchor, 1977).

8. Population, urbanization, and industrial cultivation are emphasized in McNeill, *Something New Under the Sun.*

9. The social consequences of this disjunction for rural peoples are powerfully analyzed by Angus Wright in *The Death of Ramón González: The Modern Agricultural Dilemma*, rev. ed. (Austin: University of Texas Press, 2005).

10. Sassen, *The Global City* and *Cities in a World Economy.*

11. Mike Davis, *Planet of Slums* (London: Verso, 2006).

12. Edgar Pieterse, *City Futures: Confronting the Crisis of Urban Development* (London: Zed Books, 2008).

13. Jeb Brugman, *Welcome to the Urban Revolution: How Cities Are Changing the World* (New York: Bloomsbury, 2009), 55, 132.

14. Edward Glaeser, *Triumph of the City: How Our Greatest Invention Makes Us Richer, Smarter, Greener, Healthier, and Happier* (New York: Penguin, 2011).

15. Bruce Katz and Jennifer Bradley, *The Metropolitan Revolution: How Cities and Metros Are Fixing Our Fragile Politics and Broken Economy* (Washington, DC: Brookings Institution Press, 2014), 3, 8.

16. Arturo Alvarado Mendoza, *El tamaño del infierno: Un estudio de sobre la criminalidad en la Zona Metropolitana de la Ciudad de México* (Mexico City: Colegio de México, 2012), 90. The key graph on the trajectory of crime is on page 90. To emphasize that Mendoza is not an isolated radical, it is notable that his long project was funded by the MacArthur Foundation, the Tinker Foundation, and the European Union.

17. John McNeill and Peter Engelke, *The Great Acceleration: An Environmental History of the Anthropocene since 1945* (Cambridge, MA: Harvard University Press, 2014).

18. This is a key conclusion of Bryan McCann in *Hard Times in the Marvelous City: From Dictatorship to Democracy in the Favelas of Rio de Janeiro* (Durham, NC: Duke University Press, 2014).

19. Stephen Haber et al., *Mexico since 1980* (New York: Cambridge University Press), holds to the emphasis on law and institutions, while documenting the strictures imposed by Mexico's constrained participations in the world economy.

20. For illuminating comparative analyses of informalities in Latin American cities, see Brodwyn Fisher, Bryan McCann, and Javier Auyero, *Cities from Scratch: Poverty and Informality in Urban Latin America* (Durham, NC: Duke University Press, 2014).

1 The Americas in the Twentieth-Century World

Challenges of Urbanization and Globalization

JOHN TUTINO

Rapid urbanization reshaped lives across the Americas and the world during the second half of the twentieth century—a transformation at the heart of the accelerating transnational integration we call globalization. Cities everywhere faced trying challenges: soaring population growth, limited economic possibilities, difficulty providing employment, infrastructure, and services to burgeoning numbers—and the pressures of popular groups demanding better. The voices promoting globalization in the 1990s promised economic growth and shared prosperity. Growth has proven uneven, prosperity rarely shared. As the dream became realities shaped by concentrating wealth, uncertain popular gains, and widening insecurities, new challenges have arisen—often political, too often violent. The promise, power, and creativity of globalization concentrate in great cities. So do too much poverty and marginality, political frustration, and social violence. As the twenty-first century began, the vastly expanded population of a rapidly integrating world increasingly lived in cities defined by deepening polarizations. Great metropolitan regions concentrate power and promise—and burgeoning populations facing dependence and poverty, marginality and exclusion.

If we recognize that the inequities of globalization and the inequities of urbanization came together in one historical transformation, we must work to understand their inseparable dynamics if we are to begin to think about a world—and cities—of more shared prosperity, real justice, and effective participation. The inevitability of inequities is often emphasized. Yet our studies and many others show that some cities have generated greater opportunities for more of their people while others seem to promulgate desperation. The question is: how have cities found more or less success building economies, sharing limited wealth, providing essential services, and responding to popular demands?

This chapter offers an outline of the history of the Americas and our six cities as they developed within a changing global economy, focusing on twentieth-century transformations. It provides a framework for understanding the economic, infrastructural, social, and political challenges faced by New World cities, thus providing a context for analyzing the popular participations that aimed to address them with often real yet always limited successes.[1] The goal is to open conversations linking global processes, urban challenges, popular politics, and everyday lives.

Globalizing History

In recent decades, understandings of the long trajectory of global economic history have changed radically, enabling more complex visions of the nineteenth-century industrial revolution and the recent turn to globalization—contexts essential to analyzing contemporary urbanization. After a long era in which most analysts presumed an inevitable rise of the West, meaning Western Europe and its Anglo-American offspring, a new global history is taking shape. Scholars now recognize that China and South Asia led global production and centered world trades around 1500. The incorporation of the Americas, their silver and sugar, and the trades they stimulated after 1550 drove a long era of commercial integration in which European primacy was a late development. Only after 1800 did an industrial capitalism led by British textiles (grounded in a parallel expansion of slave-based production of raw cotton in the U.S. South) take center stage. Mechanized production concentrated in northwest Europe and the northeastern United States, pressing the rest of the world to sell raw materials and buy finished wares. A long nineteenth century (1800–1930) saw Western dominance grounded in industrial production, expanding global trades, consolidating national states in Europe and the Americas, and new empires that enabled European penetration of Africa, South Asia, and the Islamic world.[2]

Yet the world built in the nineteenth century began to crack in the early twentieth. After 1910, the industrial hegemons pummeled each other in the Great War, while revolutions in Mexico and Russia looked for new routes forward. The Great Depression of the 1930s broke the first industrial world economy. Another World War and a global Cold War sent nations across the globe in pursuit of national development focused on local resources, production, labor, and markets. In capitalist and socialist variants, visions of national industrialization offered utopias in which all would share in benefits gained only by a favored few in the long century of Anglo-led industrial capitalism. National development spread industrial ways across the world between 1930 and 1970. The model remained Western: promoters of development, capitalist and socialist, presumed the primacy of Western ways. Claims of Western cultural and institutional primacy, promoted by Max Weber in the late nineteenth century, were reformulated after World War II by Walt Rostow, Douglass North, and others offering formulas for national success.[3] Promoters of socialism adapted Karl Marx's equally Western vision in recipes for socialist development.[4] Into the 1980s, presumptions of Western primacy in technological innovation and economic success were everywhere—tied to promises that if they were adopted, all could prosper.

We will never know whether the mid-twentieth-century promise of national development and shared welfare was a possible dream or an impossible utopia. Beginning in the 1960s and culminating in the 1980s, nations pursuing national development faced mounting debt crises that forced "structural adjustments"—simply said, they could not fund national development, capitalist or socialist; few, if any, could keep promises of popular welfare. Endless ink blamed bad planning and too much populism, too much commitment to popular welfare (conceding that the model had failed in its proclaimed goal of shared prosperity). Our studies of the challenges of urbanization suggest that whatever the quality of nations' and cities' planning and the effectiveness of their politics, global processes were fundamental to beginning and then bringing down national development projects—at least in the Americas.

The rise of industrial capitalism after 1815 concentrated industrial production and imperial power in Britain, sustained by a United States that supplied slave-made cotton—and in time used its continental resources to become a competitor after 1870. Facing a United States with resource advantages, Britain and France (and to a lesser extent Germany and Italy) tried to compete by expanding empires in Africa and South Asia. Accelerating competition among European powers led after 1910 to war in Europe and revolutions in Mexico and Russia.[5] That decade of conflict led to global depression in the 1930s, global war in the 1940s, and a global Cold War from the 1950s through the 1980s. During the latter era, nations everywhere sought internal development while the U.S. and the U.S.S.R. competed for global hegemony.

The Depression-era collapse of global industrial capitalism and its leaders in Britain and the United States turned states and entrepreneurs across the Americas inward, but capital was scarce for national projects. The coming of World War II led the U.S. and Britain to seek economic support from Latin American allies like Brazil and Mexico, energizing their economies in the short term, holding out promises of support for development in a post-war era of capitalist freedom. But capital and technology were hard to gain in Latin America during the war. And afterward the U.S. and Britain concluded that the best way to support capitalist freedom in the face of the socialist challenge was to rebuild European allies and subsidize former foes Germany and Japan, while insisting that Latin American allies live—meaning find capital—in open markets. Credits built in Latin Americans' favor during the war funded brief years of development and some shared prosperity in the late 1940s. The exhaustion of credits made national development radically more expensive in the 1950s, just as Latin Americans faced unimagined population growth.[6]

Suddenly exploding populations and the rapid expansion of urban centers created needs and costs beyond the capacity of Latin American national projects, just as they faced scarce and expensive capital. As long as the Cold War persisted, and especially after the Cuban Revolution brought its challenge to the Americas, national development projects and promises of shared welfare were kept alive, notably in the credits advanced by the U.S.-promoted Alliance for Progress. Contradictions mounted as debts increased and repeated crises brought stabilizations that imposed the costs on working majorities. Meanwhile, rapidly expanding populations concentrated in burgeoning cities to become ever more disillusioned as employment, education, infrastructure, and effective participation proved scarce. Some turned to radical visions. Regimes in Brazil, Argentina, Chile, and elsewhere turned to military power and authoritarian rule to prevent radical transformations.[7] Population explosions and rapid urbanization came with national development crises and political closures.

Mexico City, Rio de Janeiro, and Buenos Aires all grew enormously after 1950; population explosions, economic growth with limited employment, infrastructure challenges, and service deficits were everywhere. After 1960, all faced more authoritarian polities (in Mexico without full military rule) that promised shared welfare and hinted at future democratizations. Deepening contradictions defined urban lives in the late decades of national development.

The same era saw the United States engage in wars, cold and hot, while promoting the rise of a Western Europe-U.S.-Japan axis that set foundations for a new capitalist globalization.[8] The immediate goal was to counter socialist challenges from Eastern Europe and the Soviet Union to revolutionary China and then Cuba. The intersection of national development and globalization favored U.S. cities like Los Angeles and Houston after World

War II. But when the end of socialist competition unleashed globalization in the 1980s, they too faced new challenges: Los Angeles struggled while Houston rose to new heights. The United States and its cities fared better than Latin American nations and urban centers as national development turned to globalization. Canada and Montreal lived a middle ground, prospering in times of national development, struggling less in the shift to globalization. Cities across the Americas faced parallel yet distinct challenges as their hugely expanded populations engaged globalization. A better understanding of their experiences and outcomes is our goal.

The trajectory from national development through demographic explosion and rapid urbanization to globalization has not brought simple success or failure to cities and nations. As Saskia Sassen and Mike Davis emphasize in contrasting ways, the urban successes of New York, London, and Tokyo saw concentrations of power and prosperity mix with growing populations of poverty and marginality. The failures of marginality often defined by the barrios of Mexico City, the favelas of Rio de Janeiro, and the slums of Mumbai came in cities also concentrating important powers and populations of prosperity. Before examining the changing roles of New World cities in a world shifting from national development to globalization, it is important to explore why polarizations have proliferated everywhere—in cities of power and prosperity, poverty and marginality.

The Great Contradiction: Labor-Saving Production Encounters Life-Saving Medicine

To understand the persistence of deepening polarizations, we must turn to the long rise and expansion of the labor-saving technologies that rose with industrial capitalism in Britain around 1800, spread with capitalist and socialist national development projects, and deepened in the turn to globalization. And we must see how they intersected with the live-saving, population-expanding medical advances that developed during World War II and spread across the globe soon after. Underlying modern economic—and urban—growth since 1800 has been the invention and proliferation of ways of production that combine machines and nonhuman energy to maximize output and minimize employment—long celebrated as "labor saving," now euphemized as promoting "productivity" and "efficiency." While such technologies have a long history, they began to reshape global developments when Britons applied water and then coal and steam power on a large scale to cloth and other production based on machines designed to "save" labor—

to produce more, at lower cost, employing fewer people, at lower wages if possible. Such technologies defined nineteenth-century industrial ways, spread with national development, and now proliferate in global networks of energy, communication, and transportation linked to machines that make almost everything.[9]

Labor-saving technologies are not socially neutral. Nor is their social impact universally determined.[10] They claimed the center of economic development first in England, an island with a small population and limited resources (except coal) that aimed to rule global textile production by drawing resources and selling products across the world. For such a project, labor was arguably scarce and thus expensive in England; perhaps it needed to be saved. Labor-saving production might benefit the majority of Britons, especially once unions could organize to promote worker interests.[11] The impact on the millions of South Asian artisans who had previously made most of the world's cotton cloth was arguably different.[12] The consequences for the slaves who labored intensively under coercion to produce the essential raw cotton were blatantly different.

The same technologies that undermined production in India and saved labor in England drove an expansion of slavery (by no means labor saving) in the southern United States to supply cotton to British mills after 1800. Machines soon enabled a competing cloth industry in the northeast U.S. Over decades, mechanization expanded to steam transportation on waterways and rails, to diverse industries, and eventually to agricultural harvesting. Labor-saving technologies allowed a United States with continental resources (taken from Native Americans and Mexicans) and a sparse population to grow economically and eventually to compete with Britain in the world. In the nineteenth-century United States, labor-saving technologies enabled a balance of agricultural and industrial interests to develop with relatively shared prosperity—once slavery ended, unions organized to defend workers' rights, and populists rose politically to promote farmers' welfare.

Given their centrality to nineteenth-century models of power and prosperity, labor-saving technologies held at the center of capitalist and socialist prescriptions for national development in the twentieth century. Every nation, capitalist or socialist, aimed to adopt labor-saving ways to promote industrial production and (promoters argued) the general welfare. To compete with established centers, new industries had to adopt equally productive and cost-saving techniques. So mechanized production powered by fossil energy spread across the Americas and the globe in projects of national development, profiting national elites and treasuries.

Yet reports of spreading unemployment, deepening inequalities, and growing populations locked in marginality seemed everywhere. Projects of national development widened the use of labor-saving technologies in societies where labor scarcity was not a problem—and scarce employment often was. Mexico is a classic example. Brazil and Argentina are less clear—their overall populations remained sparse in contexts of continental resources; still, growing urban populations needed sustaining work. All promoted labor-saving industrialization from the 1930s, increasing production while curtailing employment. In the 1950s and into the 1960s, national projects in a world of Cold War competition allowed unions and welfare politics to cushion exclusions in the United States and Canada, Mexico, Argentina, Brazil, and beyond. The promise of industrial development with labor-saving technologies found believers in worlds seen as developed and underdeveloped, even among those who recognized the challenges of enduring, often deepening inequities.

The diffusion of labor-saving production in projects of national development came just as the world faced a sudden population explosion. Developments during and after World War II were pivotal to both. The war and its Cold War aftermath accelerated the promotion of national development. The war also brought the development of penicillin and other antibiotics to save soldiers in the field. Afterward, a globalizing pharmaceutical capitalism brought life-saving drugs to people across the Americas and the world. Complemented by vaccination programs and urban water and sewer projects where resources allowed, there is little debate that widely and easily available antibiotics were the primary stimulus to global population expansion from the 1950s.[13] The benefits to families that saw children live longer and healthier lives cannot be questioned. What have not been examined sufficiently are the intersections between the life-saving and labor-saving technologies that merged to reshape the world beginning in the 1940s and 1950s.

An exploration of developments at the intersection of U.S. and Mexican history from the late nineteenth century to the aftermath of WWII provides an illuminating case study—with global ramifications. The United States pioneered the mechanization of agriculture to tap the potential of the great Mississippi basin in the late nineteenth century. Railroads and steamships moved grain across long distances, and mechanical harvesters allowed expanded production with few hands. Less recognized, the cordage essential to bind mechanically harvested crops was supplied by a rapid expansion of henequen production by large numbers of Mayan hands on estates that spread across Mexico's Yucatán peninsula. Labor-saving production was not labor saving everywhere. Growing populations in U.S. and European cities were fed by labor-saving production on the U.S. Great Plains—sustained by an expansion of poorly paid and at times coerced labor in Yucatán.[14]

In the same era, from 1890 to 1910, large growers raising sugar and wheat in basins around Mexico City adopted labor-saving ways. The turn to industrial sugar refining and mechanized wheat harvesting increased profits in basins where growing populations of villagers faced land shortages and loss of harvest wage work. A generation without access to land or work fueled Zapata's revolution from 1910 to 1920.[15] The revolution provoked a redistribution of land to rural communities in the 1920s and 1930s, pacifying the countryside, enabling rural families to feed themselves, and sustaining new population growth.

Land reform beneficiaries fed their families first, failing to generate surpluses sufficient to feed an expanding Mexico City. In response, during World War II the Mexican government (lobbied by U.S. Vice President William Wallace, son of the founder of Pioneer Seeds) welcomed Rockefeller Foundation funding and scientists led by Norman Borlaug. They developed the "green revolution" by adapting to Mexico the mix of mechanization, hybrid seeds, and chemical fertilizers and pesticides developed to promote production and profit in U.S. agriculture. Combined with Mexican government irrigation projects, the program brought rising commercial harvests, first in wheat, then in maize.[16]

The green revolution enabled Mexico to feed the rapidly growing urban population concentrating in Mexico City after WWII. That urban explosion came from the mix of industrial development focused on the city, the growing numbers kept alive by medical advances, and the flood of people forced off the land by green revolution technologies—which seemed all the more necessary to feed unprecedented urban throngs. Soon, rapidly rising populations in the United States, Mexico, and elsewhere stimulated a search for new means of population control.

From the 1950s, U.S. pharmaceutical corporations invested in exploration and research in Mexico seeking the herbal ways in which Mexican women historically limited reproduction, aiming to turn folk remedies into scientific methods of birth control. In the 1960s, the companies promoted those methods widely and profitably in the United States, and family sizes decreased.[17] The same remedies were not marketed widely and effectively in Mexico—with many explanations offered: Did Catholic prohibitions limit marketing? Did a regime known for limiting Church power prefer a growing population? Did women in a society of widespread poverty and rampant insecurity see children as essential to household sustenance and their only support in old age—and thus wait until they knew that most of their children would live before they adopted birth control? The latter is confirmed by the rapid decline in birth rates from the 1980s. The rapid spread of antibiotics and the delayed adoption of birth control drove an unprecedented population explosion fed by green revolution technologies that drove people off the land and to the cities—where labor-saving production kept work and incomes scarce.

The Mexican experience offers the clearest case—because both the green revolution and the development of birth control focused there—of the forces that shaped urbanization after 1950 across the Americas. The five nations and six cities examined here all experienced the mix of life-saving capitalism that induced population growth, and labor-saving capitalism, both industrial and agricultural, that increased production, sustained populations, yet limited employment. All faced rapid population growth between 1940 and 1970—decades of national development that were also seed years of globalization. Mexico grew the most at 145 percent, followed closely by Brazil at 126 percent. Argentina and Canada found a middle ground, at 95 and 88 percent, respectively—still huge expansions in only three decades. The United States grew by a substantial but limited 55 percent as it led the capitalist world in war and reconstruction. All five nations faced real challenges, but it is notable that those with the strongest economies saw less population growth. All were committed to life-saving and labor-saving capitalism; all allowed room for labor organization and welfare programs to cushion inherent inequities. The acceptance of contraception came early to the United States, helping limit population and contradictions there.

The decades from 1970 to 2000 brought the demise of national development goals and their limited commitments to labor rights and social welfare. The same period saw the rise of a globalization that continued to promote life-saving and labor-saving technologies, and made contraception more widely available, while political leaders everywhere undermined labor rights, wages, and social programs. Populations continued to grow, if at slowing rates: Mexico and Brazil continued to lead, at 106 and 82 percent, respectively; Argentina still held a middle ground at 55 percent; Canada at 39 percent joined the United States at 38 percent in slowing demographic expansion. Our six cities also continued to expand—at differing and generally slowing rates (except for Houston).

All faced uncertain incorporations into globalization while facing challenges providing employment and infrastructure, education and services to
their populations. Demographic growth sustained by life-saving medicine
underlies the urban challenges of the late twentieth century; the spread of
mechanized cultivation fed the cities and sent growing numbers without
work in the country in search of new lives in the cities. The continuing per-
fection of labor-saving technologies combined with hard turns against
labor rights and welfare programs kept workers plentiful and cheap almost
everywhere. Inequities deepened in increasingly urban societies.

The dream of modernization that marked decades of national development promised shared prosperity to those who followed correct recipes for
national industrial growth (capitalist or socialist). The utopia of globalization promised universal gain to those who bought neo-liberal prescriptions:
open markets and expanding trade. Both models generated economic
growth and deep inequities. But national development from the 1930s to the
1970s came with commitments to popular welfare grounded in state policies
and organizations that aimed to protect and represent workers—and in the
United States to support farmers, in Mexico to help rural communities.

With the turn to globalization in the 1980s, labor-saving production
spread as populations still rose and concentrated in cities. Commitments to
popular welfare receded, except in election-year rhetoric. States trimmed
budgets for infrastructure, education, and services; nations aimed for competitive advantage with "cheap and flexible labor." Organizations serving
and representing workers weakened or collapsed under state pressures, industry assaults, and a frustrating inability to generate the benefits they
aimed to provide. Underlying the turn against workers and popular welfare
was an accelerating turn to high-tech labor-saving ways in times of population growth. The resulting social challenges concentrate in megacities
laden with inequities.

Making the World an Urban System

As Saskia Sassen emphasizes, under the reign of globalization, cities organize life as much or more than nations. Globally integrated networks of cities
shape the world economy, regional social relations, and global cultures.
National states still make laws governing bounded polities, but no economy,
social order, or cultural conversation is contained within national bounds.
A small number of pivotal cities rule the generation of wealth and the

creation of opportunity for people with essential education and key skills. The capitals of globalization—New York, London, Tokyo, Frankfurt, Beijing— anchor metropolitan areas favored with solid infrastructures and strong institutions of education, medical care, and citizen participation. They also generate inequalities, especially among migrants streaming in hoping to find opportunity for themselves and their children. Financial, corporate, and government powers, top universities, museums, and theaters all mix in their centers or key suburbs, dazzling newcomers and visitors.[18]

Still, neighborhoods of poverty, insecurity, and illegality remain, often in enclaves the prosperous aim to avoid. At the edges of global capitals (and other prosperous cities), suburbs offer refuge to middle-class families working to keep basic comforts and to find chances for their children. These global hubs lead and integrate larger networks of first-world cities—where secondary financial powers and integrating institutions offer opportunity to populations still relatively prosperous. Such cities also offer education to middle classes and those aiming to join them, while they too spawn suburbs, draw poor migrants, and generate polarizing inequities.

The megacities of the other world, most in the Global South, are equally integral to globalization. They too concentrate financial power while serving as pivots of exchange and distribution, tying surrounding regions to the global economy. They too provide opportunities for bankers and merchants, skilled professionals and service providers. They too build educational and medical institutions. Yet they rarely generate solid employment, income, or services for more than small parts of their burgeoning populations. The megacities of the other world operate as subcapitals of finance, education, medical care, and more, ruling often desperately poor hinterlands. They include enough wealth and power, enough opportunity for the educated and the skilled, enough education and medical care, and enough hard labor, service work, and market chances to draw growing numbers of insecure, often desperate peoples, replicating within their expanding metropolitan zones the polarities of power and prosperity that shape the world.[19]

The urbanizing world forged in the later twentieth century thus divides into first-world cities—global capitals and their network of secondary centers, all concentrating power, opportunity, prosperity, and political participation, all drawing migrants and generating inequalities—and other-world cities—equally pivotal centers concentrating dependent power, limited economic opportunities and political participation, and burgeoning populations of often desperate migrants and their children. The megacities of the other world tie vast regions of often marginal and mostly insecure people to

MAP 1.1 Major cities of the Americas. Credit: Bill Nelson.

a globalization that profits a few, favors a few more, yet is prejudicial toward many and limits their participation. At first glance, our studies compare three leading secondary cities of the first world (Los Angeles, Montreal, and Houston) with three megacities of the Global South (Mexico City, Rio de Janeiro, and Buenos Aires). As we shall see, a closer look reveals greater complications and more complex contradictions.

Other urban networks, better, subnetworks fold into this primary pattern. Martin Melosi and Joseph Pratt led a group analyzing energy cities, including energy capitals like Houston and dependent centers such as Tampico.[20] Our inclusion of Houston brings the two networks and their essential interactions into view. A second global network links key urban-suburban centers of high-tech innovation. In the United States, Boston and Austin, Seattle and Silicon Valley come to mind—tied to key centers in Japan and South Asia. Energy capitals and high-tech centers organize elements of global prosperity. Another subnetwork links cities that concentrate production grounded in the wages of poverty. Along the border that integrates the United States and Mexico, Ciudad Juárez holds a pivotal place in hemispheric production, drawing poor workers, mostly women, to work at low wages in a city of few services, constant insecurities, and enduring violence.[21] Cities concentrating production and desperation now proliferate in Asia and elsewhere. They too are essential to the world economy, shaping key urban centers in ways profitable to businesses that rule production and prejudicial toward many who work for so little.

A New History of the Americas

In a world of urbanizing globalization, power, and prosperity, poverty and marginality are everywhere—in England and the United States, China and India, Brazil and Mexico. Cultural explanations cannot dominate understandings of successes, limits, and failure in such a complex world. Historical analyses grounded in geography and demography, production and trade, and looking carefully at state power, political participation, and popular mobilizations must come to the fore. Culture sometimes forges key unities, too often promotes debilitating divisions, regularly rises to justify power, and too often is mobilized to "explain" subordinations grounded in powerful exploitations. Culture matters—as one among many forces shaping an urban world.

History must aim to integrate power and production, social relations, and cultural conversations in integrated analyses of changes over time. Our six cities arrived at the twentieth century by diverse historical routes, with legacies that would shape their possibilities in a new century of unprecedented change. In 1800, Mexico City was a key center of global finance and trade; Rio de Janeiro and Buenos Aires were leaders of Atlantic trade; Montreal and Los Angeles were small towns with agricultural hinterlands; Houston had not been founded. By 1900, Mexico City and Rio struggled to rule complex nations facing difficult changes. Buenos Aires was a celebrated city of prosperity welcoming European immigrants, with Montreal on a similar path. Los Angeles was a rising city tying southern California to the rest of the United States, Mexico, and Asia. Houston was a small cotton port.

To understand their histories into and through the twentieth century, we must set our cities in a new history of the Americas in the world. New World history is usually seen as beginning in conquest and continuing through centuries of colonization. Led by the United States in 1776, Americans made nations out of colonies, enabling the U.S. rise to hemispheric and then global hegemony, while Latin America grappled with underdevelopment. Conquest, colonization, nation making, and linked questions of state, society, and culture shape a prevailing historical vision. It is a vision that matters, illuminating key issues and patterns of change. That emphasized, long and changing process of global integration and the late rise of urbanization suggest that ecological trajectories mixing geographic foundations and environmental changes, demographic trajectories, and evolving ways of production linked to global processes were equally important in making the Americas.

Unique to the Western Hemisphere, three demographic regimes have shaped the history of the Americas since 1500: disease-driven collapse from 1492 to 1650;[22] slow uneven growth from 1650 to 1950;[23] and explosive expansion after 1950.[24] Those distinct demographic regimes linked in complex ways with three eras of New World incorporation into global capitalism. The radical depopulation approaching 90 percent of indigenous peoples (who lacked immunities to smallpox and other Old World diseases) opened resources and made producers scarce from 1500 to 1650, followed by a slow recovery from 1650 to 1800. That era of collapsing and then sparse populations shaped the New World's incorporation into the global commercial networks and European empires that shaped founding centuries of commercial capitalism (1550–1800). In a founding divergence, the silver economies of Spanish America adapted by granting land rights and self-rule to indigenous communities, while the plantation economies along Atlantic shores brought throngs of Africans bound to labor as slaves. Both were adaptations to founding intersections of depopulation and economic opportunity: The former shaped Mexico City and its early silver economy; the latter marked Rio de Janeiro and Brazil's plantation economy.

New World nation making (1770–1830) and the hemisphere's incorporation into a new industrial capitalism (1800–1930) came with slow but steady population growth marked by rising imports of enslaved Africans until 1850 and growing flows of European migrants who came through the nineteenth century and into the twentieth. Numbers of producers and consumers increased while pressures on resources rose. The expansion of slavery (by growth, not immigration after 1807) led the Anglo-Americans to Texas in the 1830s; the Mexican-American War of the 1840s brought the U.S. acquisition of Los Angeles, which drew diverse migrants for the next century and more. Throughout the long century of industrial capitalism from 1800 to 1930, economic power and industrial production focused in Britain and the northeast United States, while all our cities focused on supplying commodities and buying finished products.

The decades of national development (1930–70) saw all our cities turn to promoting local industries (only Mexico City had a strong nineteenth-century start). All aimed to prosper in integrated national economies—in nations with distinct resource endowments and economic chances. All made industrial progress while population growth remained limited; all faced unprecedented struggles when populations exploded and urbanization accelerated after 1950. The stresses and the markets created by that historic urbanization proved pivotal to the rise of globalization after 1980. The population explosion made resources scarce and left people desperate for work and ways to survive, driving them to cities. The globalizing economy took advantage of labor-saving technologies to curtail employment, earnings, benefits, and workers' rights almost everywhere. Contradictions deepened everywhere.

Mexico City: From Silver Capitalism to National Capital to Pivot of Globalization

The global trades that fueled early commercial capitalism began in the sixteenth century as the Americas faced a radical depopulation. Europeans seeking power, profit, and religious hegemony arrived around 1500 bearing smallpox, plague, typhus, and other maladies unknown in the hemisphere. By 1600, indigenous populations had fallen nearly 90 percent, decimating native states and communities, facilitating European rule while leaving the continent with few people. It was amid demographic collapse that after 1550 rising silver economies began to tie highland regions becoming Spanish America to Europe and China. Mexico City, founded as the capital of the Mexica (Aztec) state in the 1300s, was rebuilt in the sixteenth century as the capital of New Spain, a center of government, finance, and commerce in times of depopulation, rising silver production, and emerging global trades. Until 1650, it was the second city of the Americas, after Potosí, the leading center of Andean silver mining.[25] After 1650, as immunities spread among native survivors and populations stabilized, the center of silver production shifted from the Andes to New Spain. In the eighteenth century, Mexico City became the leading city of the Americas, a pivot of government, finance, trade, crafts, and education. Its population passed 100,000 as it managed the soaring silver production that stimulated trade across the globe and wars among European contenders to power and profit.[26]

From 1810 to 1820, popular insurgents in the Bajío, the leading region of mining, irrigated cultivation, and cloth making in the Americas, took down the silver economy that for centuries had given New Spain a key role in global trade. When Mexico became a nation in 1821, Mexico City's economic importance to the Americas and the world had collapsed; still, its population grew, slowly until about 1850 and more rapidly after. An expanding United States took advantage of Mexico's difficulties, claiming the latter's north as a new West, a region of vast mineral, agricultural, and energy potential.[27]

Amid political divisions, leaders dreamed of economic reconstruction. Conservatives promoted national industries, which began in the 1840s and grew through the century—always limited to national markets. Liberals dreamed of a cotton export economy—an opportunity lost when Mexico abolished slavery in 1829 and Texas seceded in 1836. Mexican prospects were radically reduced when the United States took its vast northern territories by war in the 1840s. French occupation and Maximilian's imposed empire in the 1860s slowed economic growth—but not Mexico City's expansion. From the 1870s, Mexican liberals back in power paid U.S. contractors to build a rail network that tied Mexico and its capital to the United States. As hub of the rail network, commercial pivot, and political capital, Mexico City oversaw a new economy mixing established national industries and new exports. The city grew, a few prospered and many struggled with marginal lives, while rural communities grappled with growing populations, concentrating lands, and diminishing chances to labor as mechanization set in.[28]

Around 1900, Mexico City remained the political capital and commercial pivot of a nation still struggling to find a solid economy in the world of industrial capitalism. Mexican industries were limited to local markets. Agricultural resources had been stripped of great potential in the Mexican-American War (1846–48). The historic silver economy, facing a rush to the gold standard by the Atlantic powers, was taken over by the Guggenheims and other U.S. capitalists by 1900. Rising henequen exports from Yucatán provided cordage for mechanical harvesters in the Mississippi basin. And along Mexico's Gulf coast, U.S. and British wildcatters began to build the world's first oil export enclave. Mexico was bound to United States, dealing secondarily with Britain and other European powers. Its economy was notably industrial yet still mostly agricultural, focused on internal markets while export enclaves were pivotal to profit and state revenues. A center of industry and crafts, commerce, transport, and government, Mexico City had 500,000 people around 1900. It had grown 500 percent in a century of uncertainty, yet remained much smaller than New York or Latin American leaders Rio de Janeiro and Buenos Aires.

Marked by sharp inequities within, the Mexican capital was surrounded by rural communities with growing populations facing land shortages and scarce access to paid labor. They took advantage of a national political crisis in 1910 to drive a revolution that lasted a decade and shaped Mexico's twentieth century. In the 1920s, Mexico City became the first of our cities to lead an attempt at national development. If the revolution was famously agrarian, the regime that claimed power pursued export revenues in the context of a national capitalism (despite socialist rhetoric). To pacify the countryside, it implemented and then limited an agrarian reform delivering land to rural communities. To promote national development, it tapped U.S. capital and markets while trying to limit their dominance, a difficult challenge. In times of political reconsolidation and socioeconomic change, Mexico City grew to a million people by 1930. Export revenues fell and then collapsed in the Depression.[29] From 1934, led by President Lázaro Cárdenas, Mexico pursued policies that mixed agrarian reform, industrial promotion, and labor rights—and oil nationalization in 1938.[30]

World War II brought new opportunities to Mexico's regime of national development—opportunities that reveal how globalization grew within projects of national development. With U.S. funding and technical assistance, Mexico's government promoted irrigation and agricultural industrialization. The green revolution helped feed Mexico City and other urban areas.[31] The United States drew Mexican men to its fields and factories to

TABLE 1.1 Population of Mexico City compared to Mexico

Year	Mexico National Population (millions)	Mexico City Population (millions)	Mexico City Percentage of National Population (%)
1900	13.6	0.5	3.7
1910	15.2	0.7	4.6
1921	14.3	0.9	6.3
1930	16.6	1.2	7.2
1940	19.7	1.8	9.1
1950	25.8	3.1	12
1960	34.9	5.1	14.6
1970	48.2	8.6	17.8
1980	66.8	13	19.5
1990	81.2	15.3	18.8
2000	99.1	18.4	18.6

Note: Mexico City population from 1900 to 1960 is for the Federal District; for 1960 to 2000, it includes the metropolitan area as it expanded into the surrounding state of Mexico.

Credit: Tables generated by Elizabeth Chavez, confirmed by María Edith Pacheco Gómez Muñoz, *Ciudad de México, Heterogénea y Desigual* (Mexico City: Colegio de México, 2004), cuadro III.2, 88.

support World War II and its postwar revival via the Bracero Program. Mexican officials promoted joint ventures linking Mexican and U.S. capital in auto making, pharmaceuticals, and other industries, proclaiming national development while tying Mexico and Mexicans to the United States. As the center of government, new industries, and a rising middle class, Mexico City's population reached 2 million in the 1940s and 5 million by 1960.[32] For many, Mexico became a model of national development, praised as the "Mexican miracle." Others saw a regime proclaiming national development while welcoming U.S. capital, claiming to be revolutionary while focusing on controlling labor and rural producers. In the city and across the nation, the economy boomed while the majority still struggled.

Urban growth was a challenge. Migrants fleeing the green revolution filled the city. Thanks to penicillin and other life-saving cures, healthier generations led to soaring urban concentrations. Although national production (with labor-saving technologies) grew at celebrated annual rates of 5 to 8 percent, it could not provide jobs, education, infrastructure, and services to meet the needs of a city that grew from 5 million in 1960 to 13 million by 1980. The economic uncertainties of the 1960s were eased by the oil boom of the 1970s, only to give way to debt-induced collapse in the 1980s, when much of the city literally fell in the 1985 earthquake. Global bankers seconded by a self-proclaimed "revolutionary" regime led Mexico to embrace globalization in the 1980s and NAFTA in 1994. Mexico City lost industry while it reconsolidated as a pivot of financial power and services tying Mexico to the United States and the new global economy. Its population approached 20 million by 2000. Describing Mexico City as a pivot of contradiction in the new world economy might be an understatement.[33]

Rio de Janeiro: From Capital of Empire and Slavery to City of Dreams and Despair

Sugar and slave economies shaped the Atlantic Americas from the sixteenth century, flourishing first in northeastern Brazil. Cities were few and small, including Rio de Janeiro, founded as a southern outpost in the 1560s. After the sugar economy waned, ceding to new Caribbean producers after 1650, Rio rose to eminence when gold (mined by slaves) was found in interior hills in the 1690s. A key port linking Brazil to Portugal, sending gold that fueled Britain's commercial rise, Rio was designated the capital of Brazil in the 1760s. With 60,000 people, it was the largest city in Atlantic America around 1800, a place of power grounded in slavery.[34]

After 1790, revolutionary slaves in Saint Domingue—then the richest Atlantic plantation economy—ended French rule, founded Haiti, and broke plantation production of sugar and coffee.[35] Markets opened for sugar in Brazil's northeast (and in Cuba, too) and for coffee in the hills above Rio. Suddenly favored economically, Rio and Brazil bought soaring numbers of enslaved Africans, a trade that continued (despite legal prohibitions after 1830) to 1850. Rio consolidated its importance as the capital of a Brazilian empire from 1822, gaining power and population by leading the world's first great coffee export economy, sending the slave-grown stimulant to people facing industrialization in Britain and the United States.[36]

In 1900, with 800,000 people, Rio de Janeiro was the largest city in Latin America, though well behind New York in terms of hemispheric leadership. As a political capital and economic pivot of an empire long grounded in coffee and slavery and tied to Britain, Rio had prospered and grown through the nineteenth century. But when slavery and empire fell together in 1888–89, economic primacy shifted toward São Paulo, which drew European immigrants to keep coffee thriving in the countryside while the city began to industrialize.[37] Still, by 1920, Rio had over a million people while São Paulo remained half its size. Brazil's exports still mattered in British and European markets, and Rio remained the metropolis that linked them.

With the Depression, coffee exports and prices collapsed and Brazil turned to national development. São Paulo had a head start, having used coffee earnings to begin local industries. It increasingly challenged the primacy of Rio, economically and politically. The rivalry was pivotal to the fall of the Old Republic and the rise of Getúlio Vargas in 1930. He ruled Brazil's attempts at national development until 1945, and again from 1950 to 1954. His evolving regime tried to mediate between Rio and São Paulo, blocking a revolt by the latter in 1932, paying closer attention to the industrial city's interests afterward. He negotiated with politically strong but economically weakened export elites, promoted industry in São Paulo, and godfathered labor relations by providing reasonable wages and benefits when possible, while always inhibiting workers' political independence. With the outbreak of World War II, demand for exports improved, and Vargas convinced the United States to build a steel complex at Volta Redonda in exchange for an alliance that gave the Allies access to strategic resources like rubber and landing strips for flights to North Africa. Again, war linked national development to global integration.[38]

Brazil made real gains in industry and a broad commercialization in decades of national capitalism. Rio gained some industry and grew to 2.4 million people; São Paulo flourished and all but caught up, with 2.2 million by 1950. But the postwar decline in export markets, scarcities of capital, and costly access to technology brought a deepening inability to balance the interests of export elites, industrialists, and labor. Vargas was ousted by a coup in 1945, returned to office by election in 1950, and left finally by suicide in 1954. As São Paulo rose economically, it chafed under Rio's rule. The creation of Brasilia as a new national capital in the interior diminished the centrality of Rio but solved little. Rising conflicts in the workplace, across the countryside, and in regional and national politics led to military rule in 1964. A brutal closure of social mediation, political negotiation, and policy space allowed generals to work between landed elites and industrialists, while excluding labor, the rural poor, and growing communities of urban desperation. The generals drove Brazil through its final years of national capitalism, then opened the way to globalization when they left power in the 1980s. During the decades of national development, as antibiotics saved lives and mechanization cut rural labor needs, migrants flooded from a desperate northeast to burgeoning cities. Rio grew from 3.3 million in 1960 to

TABLE 1.2 Populations of Rio de Janeiro and São Paulo compared to Brazil

Year	Brazil National Population (millions)	Rio Population (millions)	Rio Percentage of National Population (%)	São Paulo Population (millions)	São Paulo Percentage of National Population (%)	Urban Total (millions)	Urban Total Percentage of National Population (%)
1900	17.4	0.8	4.6	0.2	1.2	1	5.8
1910							
1920	30.6	1.2	3.9	0.6	2	1.8	5.9
1930							
1940	41.2	1.8	4.4	1.3	3.2	3.1	7.5
1950	51.9	2.4	4.6	2.2	4.2	4.6	8.9
1960	70.2	3.3	4.7	3.8	5.4	7.1	10.1
1970	93.1	7.1	7.6	8.1	8.7	15.2	16.3
1980	119.1	9	7.6	12.6	10.6	21.6	19.3
1991	146.8	9.8	6.7	15.4	10.5	25.2	17.2
2000	169.6	10.9	6.4	17.8	10.5	28.7	16.9

Note: Empty fields for 1910 and 1930 indicate the absence of census data due to the infrequency of censuses during these periods.

Credit: Elizabeth Chavez.

9 million by 1980, becoming famous for its favelas, neighborhoods of poverty marked by informality and marginal opportunity.[39] São Paulo grew faster, from 3.8 to 12.6 million.

After 1980, as Brazilians struggled for and claimed redemocratization, rapid globalization saw Rio face economic collapse while adding 3 million people. Formal work and infrastructure were scarce; informality and illegality increasingly shaped production and construction, politics and policing. São Paulo added 4 million people in the same era. Its industrial base did not fully collapse, but adaptation to globalization left it, too, to grapple with unemployment, informality, illegality and crime. Can Brazil find new economic importance as population growth slows, begin to address urban challenges, and build a shared prosperity? Vast landed, mineral, and petroleum resources, a surviving industrial base, and political forces at times open to discussing popular welfare suggest a chance. Most signs favor industrial São Paulo. The 2014 World Cup and the 2016 Olympics could not turn the economy and neighborhoods of Rio around. Can uncertain petroleum production, the most labor saving of all industries, bring broad prosperity to a city of so many millions? The protesters who mobilized in 2013 and since have seen little gain. The party of Lula (Luiz Inácio da Silva) and Dilma (Rousseff) that dreamed of addressing popular needs has been ousted from power. Lula is jailed. Rio joins Mexico City as a once-leading New World city searching for a way to sustain a burgeoning population.[40]

Buenos Aires: From Aspiring Port to American Paris to Splintering Metropolis

Like Rio de Janeiro, Buenos Aires was also founded in the late sixteenth century. It was set on the Río de la Plata, at the Atlantic edge of Spanish South America, to stop the smuggling of Andean silver. For centuries, the small port lived by profiting from the smuggling it limited. In 1776, the Spanish regime attempted an ill-fated reconstruction aiming at reviving a flagging Andean silver economy (as New Spain soared). Buenos Aires became the capital of a new viceroyalty that included the Potosí mines. Silver began to exit legally through Buenos Aires—just as the great Andean insurgencies led by Túpac Amaru disrupted everything in the 1780s. Still, Buenos Aires expanded as Andean peoples were pacified and modest silver exports revived. It boomed when the Haitian revolution drove a revival of slave-based production in Brazil. Grazers on the pampas found new markets for salt beef to feed slaves there, and growing numbers of the bound Africans diverted from Haiti came to Buenos Aires to serve as town craftsmen and rural herders. The booming port's population approached 60,000 people in 1800.[41]

The wars that took Buenos Aires out of Spain's empire after 1810 led to decades of political conflict before Argentina consolidated as a nation with Buenos Aires as its capital in the 1870s. The port city's power in those long conflicts and its eventual rule of the nation were grounded by the continuing expansion of livestock production and the later rise of staples agriculture on its rich hinterlands. In addition to feeding Brazilian slaves, pampas grazers and growers increasingly sent beef and wool, and then rising harvests of wheat, to feed Britain's growing throngs of industrial workers and city dwellers.[42]

As the twentieth century began, Buenos Aires boomed as the capital and economic hub of Argentina, drawing millions of European immigrants as it became (in the minds of many) a great metropolis leading a modern and increasingly prosperous nation, its glorious center compared to Paris. The terminus of a rail network that served the rich pampas and the port where ships loaded grain and meat (now refrigerated) to feed Britain and Europe, Buenos Aires soon surpassed Rio as the largest city in Latin America, reaching 2 million as World War I began, 3 million by 1930. As long as Britain held a lead role in industrial capitalism, Buenos Aires remained one of the Americas' leading cities. Landed elites and export merchants ruled, but there was enough prosperity to offer employment to residents and waves of immigrants, build a splendid city center, and provide basic services to growing neighborhoods. In 1916, an oligarchic polity opened to broader electoral participation, though many immigrants, not yet citizens, remained outside. World War I brought export earnings, new industries, and new labor conflicts. Still, exports and immigration, urban prosperity and sociopolitical stability marked Buenos Aires and Argentina to 1930.[43]

As in so many New World regions, the Depression took down the export economy that had sustained Buenos Aires and Argentina. It did not immediately end their relative prosperity in the Americas. A 1930 military coup ousted elected Radicals (an urban middle-class party), enabling export elites to negotiate the Depression. Continuing (if reduced) export earnings helped expand nascent industries; Buenos Aires became a key market for local beef and grain, cloth and wine. The prosperity built in earlier decades brought the economy through the Depression, and World War II revived demand for Argentine exports. Neutrality during the war (the result of large Italian and Spanish populations and a preference to avoid dependence on the U.S.) aimed to keep markets open. A dearth of imports from historic suppliers favored expansion of national industry. After the war, demand for grain to feed Europe in reconstruction rose, while credits for supplies sent to wartime Britain paid for machinery to continue industrial expansion.

The war and the postwar boom were the context for the national capitalist project of Juan Perón, minister of labor from 1943, president from 1946 to 1955. From his rise to 1950, he promoted national industry and helped labor gain rising earnings, new benefits, and cultural respect. It was not an industry-labor alliance but a regime mediating between them, allowing both to prosper—unequally, of course—and keep export elites in check. As long as export earnings held strong and credits funded industrial investment, industrialists prospered, workers gained, and growing middle classes in Buenos Aires drove a widening consumer culture. In 1950, with 5 million people, Buenos Aires remained the largest, most prosperous city in Latin America, its infrastructure and services still serving the basic needs of a growing population.[44]

Everything seemed to turn against Argentina in the 1950s. Exports fell as European agriculture revived and mechanized production expanded global harvests. Argentine credits in England ran out, and the United States focused on investing in Europe and Japan, rebuilding its allies and adversaries in the recent war. It had no interest in aiding an Argentina that had been neutral in the war and accused of Fascist sympathies—a way to malign a nonsocialist Peronist regime that promoted national industry and labor and would not become a U.S. client (as Mexico and Brazil did behind sharpened nationalist rhetoric). No longer able to balance industry and labor while quieting export elites, Perón tried to promote industry, check landed elites, and call workers to sacrifice—that is, to work for less. He fell in 1955. The economy prospered with fewer benefits for the majority into the 1960s. Then Argentina fell into political crisis, social conflict, and military rule.

Argentina began to parallel Brazil, first trying to maintain national capitalism with an iron fist, then turning to globalization. By the 1970s, Argentina was becoming "underdeveloped." Buenos Aires, once a celebrated and prosperous metropolis, faced challenges long familiar to Mexico City and Rio. The city that led the Southern Hemisphere through most of the twentieth century continued to grow with the standard mix of health gains, mechanization, and migration from the countryside. Metropolitan Buenos Aires had over 8 million people by 1970, nearly 12 million by 2000. It fell behind Mexico City and São Paulo, while paralleling Rio's slowing demographic growth combined with persistent economic, infrastructural, and social challenges. Buenos Aires became an other-world metropolis increasingly marked

TABLE 1.3 Population of Buenos Aires compared to Argentina

Year	Argentina National Population (millions)	Buenos Aires Population (millions)	Buenos Aires Percentage of National Population (%)
1895	4	0.7	17.5
1914	7.9	2.1	26.6
1938	—	3.7	—
1947	15.9	4.8	30.2
1960	20	6.7	33.5
1970	23.4	8.5	36.3
1980	27.9	9.8	36.1
1991	32.6	11.1	34
2001	36.3	11.8	32.5

Credit: Elizabeth Chavez, revised with data in M. Healey essay.

by poverty, informality, and growing illegality after 1980—even as its center announced the glories of times past.[45]

Montreal: From River Port to Atlantic Pivot to Multicultural Metropolis

Montreal began in the seventeenth century as a French outpost on the St. Lawrence River, set to send furs gained by trade with native peoples to Europe. When Britain took Canada in the Seven Years' War of 1756–63 (its one clear gain in a pivotal global conflict), Montreal became a pivot of British trade in a still Franco-Catholic society—a francophone city ruled by an Anglo economic elite. Through the nineteenth century, it rose to importance by channeling produce of the Canadian interior out the St. Lawrence to England. Montreal's history parallels that of Buenos Aires in important ways—with a slower start, on a smaller scale, and with the advantage of stronger ties to Britain and the United States.

With about 300,000 people in 1900, the island city on the St. Lawrence was the primary port and processing center for a vast hinterland sending grain, timber, and mineral ores to British and Atlantic markets. Set where interior rails met ocean shipping, Montreal began to industrialize by processing exports in the mid-nineteenth century; new consumer industries diversified the city's economy in the twentieth. Like Buenos Aires, Montreal's export trade, relatively shared prosperity, and solid infrastructure survived the Depression and held strong during World War II and the postwar revival.

They survived, however, by different means. Argentina stayed neutral, pursuing national capitalism with broadening distribution under Perón. Canada joined the Anglo-American alliance in war and the Cold War, gaining better access to capital and export markets throughout. Into the 1950s, Canada prospered and Montreal remained its largest city with over 2 million people.

Then Montreal lost primacy as Canada's pivotal link to the world. In the late 1950s, the St. Lawrence Seaway let ocean ships pass by to Toronto and Great Lakes ports. Montreal's trade fell; its role as Canada's first city ended. Toronto grew as the national center of finance, industry, and more—passing Montreal in population in the 1970s. And as Montreal's economic and urban primacy in Canada faced challenge in the 1960s, French separatist culture and politics rose in the province of Quebec. Montreal remained the leading city and least francophone place in Quebec. Anglo-Protestant elites there had long ruled business and mediated complex ethnic politics. Economic decline weakened that establishment as employment, services, and infrastructure became scarce. The Franco-Catholic majority felt exclusions more sharply. Separatist demands led to conflictive, sometimes violent politics. Montreal in the 1960s seemed to face challenges parallel to those in Buenos Aires, framed in a distinct linguistic-nationalist context.

Still, Montreal continued to grow. Canada took in European immigrants long after the United States closed its borders (except to Mexicans) in the 1920s and Argentina ceased to be a destination of promise in the 1930s.[46] Facing decline in the 1960s, Montreal's economy did not collapse. While public debate focused on national and cultural independence for Quebec, Montreal led a new model of "national development" within Canada's turn to globalization. Negotiating the political and ethnic challenges of being a bilingual, bicultural city in a deeply francophone province within a mostly anglophone nation, Montreal protected key industries and promoted urban development to keep opportunities for a diverse population. For the province of Quebec, such a Montreal brought needed prosperity; for Canada, it helped keep Montreal and Quebec in the nation. Ethnic nationalism found gains even as its ultimate claims were blocked. As the twentieth century ended, Montreal was Canada's second city, with nearly 3.5 million people. It prospered and struggled, incorporating diverse immigrants with new political inclusions. Shared prosperity, however, became a challenge as industry remained limited, services proliferated—and too many services were poorly remunerated, insecure, and too often demeaning. Like all our cities, twenty-first century Montreal faces uncertain opportunities and rising challenges.[47]

TABLE 1.4 Populations of Montreal and Toronto compared to Canada

Year	Canada National Population (millions)	Montreal Population (millions)	Montreal Percentage of National Population (%)	Toronto Population (millions)	Toronto Percentage of National Population (%)	Urban Total (millions)	Urban Total Percentage of National Population
1901	5.4	0.3	5.5	0.2	3.7	0.5	9.2
1911	7.2	0.5	6.9	0.4	5.5	0.9	12.4
1921	8.8	0.6	6.8	0.5	5.7	1.1	12.5
1931	10.4	0.8	7.7	0.6	5.7	1.4	13.4
1941	11.5	0.9	7.8	0.7	6.1	1.6	13.9
1951	14	1.5	10.7	1.3	9.3	2.8	20
1961	18.2	2.2	12.1	1.9	10.4	4.1	22.5
1971	21.6	2.7	12.5	2.6	12	5.3	24.5
1981	24.3	2.8	11.5	3	12.3	5.8	23.8
1991	27.3	3.1	11.4	3.9	14.3	7	25.6
2001	30	3.4	11.3	4.7	15.7	8.1	27

Note: Urban total indicates two cities combined; figures for 1901–1941 for cities; 1951–2001 for metropolitan areas.
Credit: Table compiled by Elizabeth Chavez; data on 1991 and 2001 from M. Dagenais.

Los Angeles: From Spanish Outpost to City of Dreams to Uncertain Globalization

Los Angeles was founded as an outpost of New Spain as its silver economy drove north in the 1770s. Taken by war into the United States in the 1840s, it grew first by supplying the gold economy that drove U.S. westward expansion into California in the 1850s, later by sending citrus and other warm-weather crops east by rail to growing urban-industrial consumers across the United States.[48] A small city of 100,000 in 1900, it grew in the early twentieth century with waves of migrants from Europe, the U.S. East and Midwest, Asia, and increasingly from Mexico.

Los Angeles often seemed the quintessential American city of the twentieth century—in both the national and hemispheric senses of being American. Yet its role in the United States, the Americas, and the world changed over the decades. As California agriculture shifted from wheat to citrus, cotton, and vegetables, it supplied local demand and rising exports—most sent east by rail. Oil production rose to sustain local needs and growing exports, increasingly sent across the Pacific to Asia. A famously benign climate promoted immigration and tourism—and drew moviemakers. Military bases promoted port development and related industries, including aircraft production. By 1930, Los Angeles had 2 million people. When the Depression hit, export prices dropped and Mexicans were pressed back to Mexico— while the Midwest dust bowl sent new throngs westward. California survived the Depression better than most U.S. regions, poised to thrive as World War II began.

For the United States, that conflict began and ended in the Pacific. In metropolitan Los Angeles, shipbuilding, aircraft factories, and other war industries expanded, along with manufactures linked to them. Petroleum demand and production grew, too, as did agriculture. When Depression-era migrants from eastern regions were taken into the military, Mexicans were called back by the Bracero Program and opportunities to labor in fields, factories, and everything in between. During the Depression, World War II, and the Cold War that followed, the movie industry prospered, promoting visions of Los Angeles as the essence of the American Dream. By 1950, it was the third largest city in the United States, with 4 million people (and closing in on Chicago for second place).[49]

Into the 1960s, agriculture and industry, petroleum and media production prospered. "L.A." seemed synonymous with the promise of America. But not all was well. During World War II, misnamed "zoot suit riots" saw

TABLE 1.5 Populations of New York, Chicago, Los Angeles, and Houston compared to the United States

Year	U.S. National Population (millions)	N.Y. Population (millions)	N.Y. Percentage of National Population (%)	Chicago Population (millions)	Chicago Percentage of National Population (%)	L.A. Population (millions)	L.A. Percentage of National Population (%)	Houston Population (millions)	Houston Percentage of National Population (%)	Urban Total (millions)	Urban Total Percentage of National Population (%)
1900	76	4.5	5.9	1.8	2.4	0.1	0.1	–	–	6.4	8.4
1910	92	6.4	7	2.4	2.6	0.4	0.4	0.1	0.1	9.3	10.1
1920	105.7	7.7	7.3	3.1	2.9	0.8	0.8	0.1	0.1	10.6	10
1930	122.8	9.9	8.1	4.2	3.4	2	1.6	0.3	0.2	16.4	13.4
1940	131.7	10.6	8	4.2	3.2	2.4	1.8	0.4	0.3	17.6	13.4
1950	150.7	12.3	8.2	4.9	3.3	4	2.7	0.7	0.5	21.9	14.5
1960	179.3	14.1	7.9	6	3.3	6.7	3.4	1.1	0.6	27.9	15.6
1970	203.2	16.2	8	6.7	3.3	8.4	4.1	1.7	0.8	33	16.2
1980	226.5	15.9	7	6.8	3	9.5	4.2	2.4	1.1	34.6	15.3
1990	248.7	16	6.4	6.8	2.7	11.4	4.6	2.9	1.2	37.1	14.9
2000	281.4	17.8	6.3	8.3	2.9	11.8	4.2	3.8	1.4	41.7	14.8

Note: Urban total indicates four cities combined.

Credit: Elizabeth Chavez.

military men beating Mexican American youths. In the summer of 1965, riots in Watts reminded locals and the world that many African Americans had come to Los Angeles. They too saw the dream, or at least the promise—and learned that deep inequities remained. Soon it became clear that Cold War defense industries had driven much of Los Angeles' expansion. As the world changed, metropolitan Los Angeles—with 10 million people by 1980—faced new challenges.

The economic dynamism of Los Angeles faded in the 1980s. Agriculture remained but faced global competition; oil wells still pumped, but new fields and the great energy centers were elsewhere (notably Houston); aircraft and defense industries left, often for cheaper labor. Movie and television industries remained but often produced elsewhere, searching for cheaper costs—even as they promoted an image of a thriving (if violent) Los Angeles. Migrants continued to come, now from Mexico, Central America, and Asia. The metropolitan population approached 12 million in 2000, far exceeding Chicago and other contenders for second place in the United States. In the early 1990s, one analyst called Los Angeles the "capital of the third world"—not just for its growing Mexican, Central American, and Asian populations but also for the rising inequities and widening violence grounded in an economy in which a few prospered, growing numbers worked as poorly paid service workers, and too many struggled at the margins. The repeated crises of the California economy in recent decades remind us that the City of Angels, like so many Latin American cities, ended the century facing population growth, economic decline, widening polarities, and new ways of production and life, many grounded in informality and illegality.[50]

Houston: From Cotton Port to Energy Metropolis

Houston began in the fight to take Texas out of Mexico in the 1830s and was named for a hero of that war of secession. It was set as an inland port to ship slave-grown cotton to British textile mills. Taken into the United States by war in 1848, its cotton export economy continued to expand. Houston joined Texas in the Confederate secession of 1861, again defending cotton and slavery. It remade links to Mexico during the Civil War, working with merchants in Monterrey to relabel cotton as Mexican and ship it out on the Rio Grande to supply both British and Union mills, keeping Texas and the western Confederacy economically afloat—while helping sustain the industrial economy that brought Union victory in 1865. After the war, Houston revived as a cotton port as growers turned to black, Mexican, and Anglo sharecroppers to keep production growing.[51] In 1900, Houston remained a small Gulf port shipping cotton from the surrounding coastal plains.

It ended the twentieth century as the most prosperous of our six cities—a world city, the pivot of the global energy economy. It grew with oil discoveries along the Gulf coast, rising to 300,000 people as the Depression began and 400,000 at the outbreak of World War II. Like Los Angeles, Houston gained major stimulus in World War II. Petroleum fueled the U.S. and Allied war machines; oil production and refining spawned related industries, while cotton cultivation flourished on fields dotted with drilling rigs and producing pumps. During and after the war, Houston drew migrants, white and black, often from the U.S. South. The Cold War fueled a space race, which brought a Space Center and related industries to Houston. And as petroleum production, refining, and transport made environmental challenges a part of everyday life, the development of leading medical centers famous for cardiac and cancer care was a worthy response—good for health, the urban image, and a more diversified prosperity.

From the 1960s, Houston rose to become the global capital of petroleum and petrochemical production and refining, engineering, and services. The great multinational oil corporations—Exxon-Mobil, Shell, and BP—kept headquarters elsewhere, but the coordination of production, refining, and technological development concentrated in Houston. In 1980, the city had nearly 2.5 million people; by 2000 it approached 4 million. It is the only one of our six New World cities that retained a strong base of production and a broad base of well-paid labor as the twentieth century ended. Its global importance and population growth have continued into the new century. In 2010, Houston's metropolitan population approached 6 million, up 50 percent in a decade. Like Los Angeles, growing numbers arrive from Asia and especially Mexico—with Houston drawing on a new city-to-city migration tapping the often skilled and entrepreneurial population of Monterrey, Mexico, as it fell from industrial eminence under globalization via NAFTA. Houston prospers and grows, yet still faces challenges in providing infrastructure and education, in orchestrating a politics of complex ethnic diversity, and in facing the environmental threats inherent in the power and pollution of its petroleum and petrochemical economy. New informalities and illegalities in migration and employment spread.[52] The inevitable question in the context of our other cities' histories of rise and demise (and current low petroleum prices): can Houston's dynamism and relatively shared prosperity persist?

From National Development to Globalization: Comparative Perspectives

All our cities began the twentieth century as centers of trade, processing, and transit in the economy of industrial capitalism focused on Britain, western Europe and the eastern United States. Their relative power and prosperity reflected their greater or lesser importance in that economy: Buenos Aires and Montreal flourished; Mexico City and Rio struggled; Los Angeles and Houston were just emerging. All were ports except Mexico City, which was the hub of a rail network linking it to ports and border crossings. It also stood apart as the inland capital of a nation of limited agricultural potential, emerging industries, and uncertain export prospects as silver declined while copper and petroleum, henequen and coffee rose.

All our cities grew demographically in the last decades of industrial capitalism—generally in proportion to their economic importance. From 1900 to 1930, Buenos Aires, already the largest of our cities, grew five times over; Montreal, smaller, nearly tripled; Mexico City and Rio about doubled; Los Angeles and Houston, starting small, grew rapidly—the first becoming a major city of 2 million, the latter a growing port and petroleum processor of 300,000. During the final decades of global industrial capitalism, cities generally grew in relation to their economic prospects as suppliers of key industrial centers and consumers of their products.

National development got an early start in Mexico, enabled by a precocious nineteenth-century industrial start, driven forward by revolutionary promises of shared prosperity followed by the collapse of the export economy in the 1920s. The turn inward was accelerated there and elsewhere by the Depression that began in the United States and took hold of the hemisphere from 1930. As old industrial centers in Europe and the United States collapsed, all our cities faced a decline of exports and their earnings; all saw new industries as the way forward. World War II reinforced the trend as Los Angeles and Houston industrialized in support to the war effort; the rest of our cities aimed to build industries to supply local markets as the belligerents focused on war materials. After the war, all tried to sustain and expand their industries. The United States aimed to rebuild consumer industries and reclaim export markets amid Cold War challenges. Los Angeles and Houston boomed. But after brief postwar growth spurts, our Latin American cities (and francophone Montreal) struggled in the face of a resurgent U.S. industrial hegemony. Promises of national development rose everywhere, yet the United States focused on

TABLE 1.6 National and urban population growth: five nations and six cities

Nation and City	Real Increase, 1900–1950	Real Increase, 1950–2000
Mexico	12,200,000	73,3000,000
Mexico City	2,600,000	15,300,000
Brazil	34,500,000	117,700,000
Rio de Janeiro	1,600,000	8,500,000
Argentina	11,900,000	20,400,000
Buenos Aires	4,100,000	7,000,000
United States	74,700,000	130,700,000
Los Angeles	3,900,000	7,800,000
Houston	700,000	3,100,000
Canada	8,600,000	16,000,000
Montreal	1,200,000	1,900,000

Data compiled from Tables 1.1–1.5 from this book.

rebuilding a capitalist alliance among its formers allies and opponents from Europe to Japan. Latin America and its leading cities faced mounting difficulties and rising debts from the 1950s.

The era of national development was a time of rapid change in the global economy. From the Depression of the 1930s, through the war and postwar period of the 1940s, through a changing Cold War from the 1950s through the 1970s, all our cities worked to industrialize, all saw populations grow, first steadily, then rapidly. Meanwhile the global context shifted from favorable to national projects in the Depression, uncertain during the war and its immediate aftermath, to debilitating in Latin America (and to a degree in Montreal) as the Cold War intensified. And it was during the times of Cold War pressures that our cities' populations grew most rapidly. A comparative survey is revealing.

Mexico City expanded ten times over from 1930 to 1980 as the political, financial, commercial, and industrial pivot of a national project that began early and by the 1950s was touted as a model. From the 1930s, Mexico promoted a capitalist populism that called for national industry with broad redistributions; after 1940, it tied itself to U.S. markets, capital, and technology. Gaps widened between promise and performance, prosperity and poverty. Political stability grounded in a regime of corporatist mediation held even as sporadic protests faced rising repressions. After World War II, Mexico City boomed while it struggled to provide employment, infrastructure, and services to an exploding population. Informalities and illegalities became a way of urban development. The later decades of national development brought expanded industry, constrained organized labor, and broadened the middle classes while inequities deepened. The government pressed a nationalist vision, while tying development to U.S. capital, technology, and markets. Contradictions were everywhere.

Los Angeles grew five times over from 1930 to 1980, first as a hub of western U.S. development, then as a center of wartime production—stimulated by wars both hot and cold. Like Mexico City, it drew migrants from a rural Mexico facing population explosion and agricultural mechanization. For decades it seemed favored at the intersection of strong national development and emerging globalization—with energy and defense industries in the lead. Yet as its economy soared, persistent segregations constrained the distribution of benefits. The Watts riots of 1965 in which black Angelenos expressed their anger with life in the city preceded the 1968 conflicts at Tlatelolco in Mexico City (mostly a middle-class student protest) by three years. When the late century surge of globalization undermined L.A.'s industrial base, it too saw informalities and illegalities proliferate as the metropolis sustained segregations and exclusions.

During the same period of national development, Montreal tripled from a less populous start. Operating inside the Anglo-American sphere of power and prosperity, the bilingual, bicultural city was tied to the Allied war effort, building war industries and sending soldiers. After the war, Canada retained favored access to British and U.S. capital and markets, enabling Montreal to prosper until the St. Lawrence Seaway—built to facilitate global integration—ended the port's primacy in Canada's economy. It was in the face of that challenge that dislocations spread and social challenges rose in the movement for francophone nationalism—difficulties cushioned by the city's "limited" population growth.

Argentina's insistence on neutrality during the war did not inhibit radically its ability to sell exports to Britain or to develop local industries. But after the war the global agricultural revival limited Argentine exports and earnings as wartime credits vanished. U.S. ire with Péron's independence and pro-labor policies inhibited access to capital and technology. Still, politics grounded in mobilized unions and urban neighborhoods sustained development with meaningful distributions in Buenos Aires into the 1950s— one moment when popular politics brought real gains. Still, workers and consumers began to struggle as capital shortages and falling export earnings—both tied to U.S. policies favoring its northern hemisphere alliance in Cold War times—inhibited Argentine industries and generated rising debts while falling urban incomes cut consumption and limited internal markets.[53] That Buenos Aires' population also "only" tripled from 1930 to 1980 limited the dislocations that came with postwar difficulties.

Mexico City and Los Angeles, Buenos Aires and Montreal all gained new industries and some prosperity during the first decades of national development—times defined by the Depression, the world war, and the early postwar years. All faced difficulties and dislocations when the United States pursued a nascent globalization as the Cold War entrenched and escalated after 1950. All faced population growth that if extreme could exacerbate dislocations (as in Mexico City) or limit them if moderate (as in Montreal and Buenos Aires).

Our other two cities appear to be at opposite extremes—within broad shared trends. Long the pivot of an export economy tied to Britain, Rio de Janeiro's economic role was assaulted by the Depression. World War II brought some relief, as the city remained the national capital. But through the Depression and into wartime, industrial dynamism belonged to São Paulo, which rose to national economic and demographic primacy by 1960. No longer the national capital after the founding of Brasília, Rio faced demographic explosion in times of economic and political demise. The population grew from about 1.5 million in 1930 to 9 million by 1980, increasing six times over as its economy corroded. Rio's favelas began to define the desperation of so many cities labeled "third world." Informality and illegality became ways of urban development in a city that could neither afford nor contain explosive urban growth.[54]

Houston, in contrast, became an energy center during the era of national development, preparing it to soar with globalization. It struggled during the Depression, but with World War II and the Cold War, both national capitalism and nascent globalization favored the Bayou City's mix of petroleum, medicine, and space economies. The newest of our cities grew from 300,000 in 1930 to 2.4 million in 1980—expanding six times over, in parallel with Los Angeles and Rio. But the latter grew as its economy collapsed; Los Angeles first grew and then faced dislocations, in part due to the concentration of the global petroleum economy in Houston. The Texas energy metropolis expanded outward and found resources to build infrastructure and provide basic services—while slowly dealing with a racially divided politics to give black Houstonians a voice in the city and in the nation that depended on it for energy. There were limits to popular gains, and Houston remained a segmented if less segregated metropolis. Still, the rise of African-American Congresswoman Barbara Jordan to national eminence in the 1970s revealed emerging possibilities in a city of solid prosperity.

After 1980, national development projects collapsed (except in rhetoric) as globalization encompassed the world, the hemisphere, and our six cities. All continued to grow in population, though rates began to slow. Populations grew whether cities prospered, stagnated, or declined. All but Houston faced industrial collapse; employment became scarce, poorly paid, and often informal, insecure, and even illegal. Globalization deepened the urban contradictions inherited from decades of national development—except, perhaps, in Houston. It cured them nowhere.

In 1980, Mexico City was the second largest metropolis by population in the Americas, trailing only New York. With sudden insertion into globalization, its industry collapsed, leaving a city of services—financial, commercial, governmental, household, etc.—that tied Mexico to the United States and the world while generating deepening inequities of income. Another 5.5 million people brought the metropolitan total to nearly 20 million by 2000, passing New York as the Americas' largest conglomerate while marginality, informality, and social violence spread.

Globalization after 1980 also brought industrial decline to Los Angeles, a shift toward a service economy, and new polarities—while it held some economic strength as a pivot of trade linking Asia, the United States, and Mexico. By 2000, it had added another 2 million people, bringing its metropolitan total to near 12 million, by population the second city in the United States. It too faced enduring inequities, rising crime, and persistent economic uncertainties.

Rio's struggles, rooted in a long economic decline, continued while migrants still poured in from an even poorer Brazilian northeast. The fight against military authorities in the 1970s and 1980s mobilized urban neighborhoods, which made gains in services and rights. Yet deficits in infrastructure and employment remained daunting; illegalities and informalities remained ways of development and survival. Rio also added 2 million people in the two decades of corrosive globalization. By 2000, it approached 11 million, far behind São Paulo's 18 million. Rio and its favelas still defined urban desperation. The promise of the new century has mostly benefited São Paulo—and that city too faces fundamental urban challenges.[55]

The demise of Buenos Aires began in the 1960s. From 1980 it faced industrial collapse and a search for a place in a globalizing world economy. Prior success proved a liability. Mexico and Brazil (and Mexicans in Los Angeles) offered the world cheap labor; Buenos Aires had become middle class and relatively prosperous during the export boom and under Peronist national development. The legacies of Peronist labor power blocked an easy turn to an economy of cheap labor. Yet such labor began to arrive as migrants from Andean highlands came to the port, which grew from under 10 million in 1980 to nearly 12 million in 2000—another 2 million added in times of globalizing dissolution. Buenos Aires developed new neighborhoods of marginality, while political conflicts rooted in demands to sustain prosperities spread.

Montreal also struggled economically after 1980, while growing from 2.8 to 3.4 million people by 2000. Slower population growth limited urban challenges. So did Canada's ability to adapt to the new global economy via the 1987 Canada-U.S. Free Trade Agreement that opened markets for its industrial, energy, and agricultural exports. The province of Quebec spent resources to sustain the economy centered on Montreal, while national authorities in Ottawa recognized that unless Montreal and Quebec kept some prosperity, a return to Franco-Catholic nationalism could (and periodically did) rise. So Montreal sustained key industries and solid prosperity while it balanced anglophone and francophone political interests, incorporated diverse newcomers, and remained a city often praised even as it struggled to offer employment, infrastructure, and services in an ever more multicultural metropolis. The impact of the recent shift to an uncertain service economy remains to be seen.

Of all our cities, Houston prospered most after 1980. Its pivotal roles in the economies of energy and medical care served vital interests in the new globalization. Drawing migrants from Mexico and across the world, Houston's population "only" grew from 2.4 million in 1980 to 3.8 million in 2000, fueling dynamism while limiting dislocations in a context of economic strength. Houston's demographic surge came after 2000; its nearly 2 million people expansion in a decade brought the energy metropolis to nearly 6 million in 2010. That it remained smaller than all our cities but Montreal while building a leading role in the energy economy of globalization enabled Houston's continued provision of employment, infrastructure, and services, while it attracted streams of migrants. Yet Houston also lives with the inequities, escalations of crime, and the informalities and illegalities that have emerged everywhere with globalization. It also faces the ongoing environmental challenges inherent in its energy economy and location in hurricane prone coastal lowlands.

The histories of our six cities in the twentieth century make it clear that urban prospects have been shaped in fundamental ways by their shared yet differing experiences in the rise and fall of national development projects, rapid population growth, and the turn to globalization. The underlying constant was population growth as global medical capitalism kept children alive and mechanized, chemically dependent agriculture fed them. Yet that sustaining agriculture drastically cut the labor needs of cultivation, driving throngs to the cities. Simultaneously, the dominant models of development, national and then globalizing—promoted by corporations, states, and global institutions—called for accelerating mechanizations of industry, transportation, communications, and more. Technological virtuosity increased production and profits while curtailing employment, leaving more and more work unskilled, insecure, and informal. The intersection of population explosion, mechanized cultivation, and technological innovation created an urbanizing world shaped by concentrating power, profit, and prosperity—grounded in poverty, insecurity, and marginality.

The contradictions shaped by urban population explosions, growing production, and limited employment and remuneration defined life in cities and across the Americas in the twentieth century. At different times and places, broadly shared prosperity was possible—in Buenos Aires around 1900, Los Angeles in the 1950s, and Houston around 2000. But the sharing was always limited, never certain, nor inevitably enduring—note Buenos Aires after 1960 and Los Angeles from the 1980s. Mexico City seems to always remain pivotal to Mexico and the world, always finding some economic dynamism, yet always unable provide shared prosperity in the face of an exploding population. There was a certain consistency in that, as with Montreal's ability to prosper modestly and distribute reasonably through times of prosperity, decline, and revival. So, too, there is a sad consistency in Rio's struggles with a long economic demise, leaving shared prosperity a dream repeatedly shattered. Common challenges of soaring populations, limited employment, and constrained remunerations shaped all our cities as they lived the turn from national development to globalization. Different national resources, differing insertions in the globalizing economy, distinct social compositions, and differing political ways meant they all experienced those challenges differently.

The Promise of Informality, the Challenge of Illegality, the Costs of Incarceration

All our cities faced burgeoning populations after 1950, thanks to the benefits of global medical advances. Thanks to mechanizations, all faced challenges providing employment, infrastructure, and services—to varying degrees reflecting differing participation in the world economy. And everywhere, deficits in employment, infrastructure, and services were met by informal and sometimes illegal ways of work and trade, transport, housing, and neighborhood development. People have done what the formal economy and institutions of government have not—to the extent they could. Creating income and markets, building houses and neighborhoods outside of formal and legal channels are not signs of simple failure. Such efforts highlight popular creativity in the face of economic exclusions and institutional failures. Sadly, limited formal economies and ineffective institutions of political participation and justice not only elicit creative informalities, they open spaces for destructive, often violent illegalities.

In important ways, Mexico City and Rio de Janeiro were built by creative informalities in the twentieth century. Throngs with no legal rights to land, limited access to infrastructure and services, and minimal incomes used what little they had—mostly hard work, scavenged materials, and informal organization—to build houses and neighborhoods, barrios and favelas. Parallel efforts were present, if less dominant, in all our cities. The constructive gains were real, but where urban economies and neighborhoods operate outside the realm of the state regulations, the weakness or absence of sanctioned employment, services, and policies has invited a proliferation of economies outside the law. Drug cartels are infamous examples, yet development schemes in which lands are sold without title, then defended by vigilantes, are also problematic. The lines between the formal and informal, the legal and illegal become blurred. Crime is embedded in everyday lives. Yet crime is in the eye of the beholder—and in the text of the law. A person stealing to feed a family commits a crime, as does another defending a home built without title—as did the developer who sold the land without title.

We easily label the first a criminal; we wonder how to describe the second; we often see the third as merely corrupt. Yet the corrupt developer and his political allies profit from an informal capitalism outside the law; those who steal to eat or fight to hold untitled homes struggle to live under a capitalism that pushed them aside. Among the powerful, illegality is often called corruption; among people struggling to survive, it becomes crime. Measurement is uncertain, yet both appeared to grow in the late twentieth-century mix of globalization and urban expansion. Crime and corruption mark too many lives in cities that are struggling economically. And while illegalities in cities of desperation create profit for some and life chances for more, they too often generate violence that plagues the lives of the poorest, most desperate people. That is the clear message of Janice Perlman's classic studies of Rio de Janeiro's favelas and Arturo Alvarado Mendoza's recent documentation of crime and violence in Mexico City as it deindustrialized under NAFTA.[56]

In a probing study of crime in São Paulo as it transitioned from national development under military rule to globalization with a democratic opening, Teresa Caldeira kept a comparative eye on Los Angeles. She saw that crime rose in both cities as the twentieth century ended. In both, the prosperous withdrew into gated, often guarded enclaves—leaving crime to plague majorities struggling to find work. In both, there were calls for police to secure the cities.[57] But in São Paulo, a burgeoning city trying to find its way as military rule waned and globalization changed the economic rules and realities, resources were scarce. Police set out to fight crime, but there were no funds to build a costly system of courts to judge and prisons to isolate those deemed criminal. The result was informal and illegal police violence assaulting presumed criminals. Streets and plazas became more violent, while the prosperous built and reinforced walls of self-incarceration.

Los Angeles saw infamous incidents of police brutality, taken too often as unfortunate aberrations. As globalization drove polarization and exclusion, the city, county, and state found resources to expand the police, courts, and prisons. As the economy shed good paying jobs and crime spread, the state created steady employment in service of "security." Criminals were locked away and income went to those who provided safety in the public space. Better prosperity, grounded in stronger participation in the world economy, enabled Los Angeles to contain criminals and reinforce shared prosperity among those who served the law. The "carceral state," however, created jobs but did not produce goods. In time, funding the carceral regime became difficult as California's economy struggled with globalization. As police forces and prison populations have grown—and grown costly—the challenge of funding the state's education system has deepened.[58]

Los Angeles and Houston, the most prosperous of our cities in the era of national development, the former facing challenges, the latter still strong in times of globalization, are in carceral states. California and Texas keep vast prison systems that hold disproportionate numbers of racial and ethnic minorities, notably men of African ancestry, in ultimate segregation. Informality, illegality, and violence have everywhere accompanied urban explosions in times of globalization. In poorer nations and cities, coercion and violence remain informal and illegal; in more prosperous regions and urban centers, they are more formal, legal, and institutionalized.

In all our cities, from desperate Rio de Janeiro to prosperous Houston, globalization with population explosion has brought difficulties in creating employment, infrastructure, and services. Polarity deepens, and informality and illegality, criminality and violence expand. In interview after interview with Janice Perlman, the people of Rio's favelas see direct links between vanishing employment, scarce opportunities in the legal economy, and proliferating violence. Living that fundamental relationship, they see it more clearly than most scholars and policy analysts. Rio's favela dwellers long believed that self-help, political mobilization, schools, and democracy would improve their lives and those of their children. For decades they claimed real (if limited) gains, only to see economic prospects vanish, replaced by a drug economy that promotes violence.[59] Neither petroleum production nor celebrated international events have rebalanced life in the city arguably facing the greatest challenges in the Americas.

The Promise and Limits of Popular Participation

Meanwhile, the people are proclaimed sovereign. They are promised meaningful lives and political participation. Facing inequities, exclusions, and informalities, people in all our cities have mobilized to seek services, prosperity, and political influence. And everywhere, popular movements made gains, often gains essential to making cities more livable for a growing population. Rarely have they brought more than modest benefits; nowhere have they altered trajectories toward concentrating power, deepening polarization, and widening marginalities under the globalization that accelerated as the twenty-first century began.

Although important in all our cities, popular participations differ. They change as challenges change. When the twentieth century began, electoral participation was limited everywhere. Over time, women, more men, and racial/ethnic minorities were allowed to vote. In the United States and Canada, electoral rights persisted throughout and slowly expanded. In Mexico, they remained in law but were limited by a postrevolutionary regime that controlled elections at the highest level while it allowed and limited participation through corporate representation for peasants, workers, and middle sectors. In Brazil and Argentina, limited electoral systems also tried corporate representation in decades of national development; then military regimes closed everything as national development faltered, politics polarized, and globalization began. Finally, late-century globalization saw "democratic openings": to elections in Argentina, Brazil, and Mexico; to francophone rights in Montreal and Quebec; to minority rights in the United States. Have electoral openings enabled effective assertions of popular rights and goals in megacities of deepening inequity?

Our authors see real, limited, and varying gains everywhere. None joins the chorus of those who preach the need for Latin Americans to perfect their democracies (that is, electoral regimes), primarily by better policing, more effective courts, and more prisons—the rule of law. The roles and social consequences of judicial and carceral institutions need to be analyzed and debated, not presumed. Our studies join Perlman in seeing wider access to good employment with steady incomes, better infrastructures and services, and greater openings for popular movements, the key concerns in urban neighborhoods. Better police and effective courts are valued too, as complements to better jobs and income, services and education.

Too often, globalization and its divergent economic outcomes, its concentrations of wealth, and proliferations of poverty and marginality are accepted as givens. Among those who see such economic trajectories as set and their inequities unchangeable, fair elections coupled with solid carceral regimes become a model for urban and national governance. Effective elections may deflect more radical movements; fair courts and strong prisons may improve social control. But without real increases in and better sharing of opportunities and incomes, solid infrastructures, and accessible education and medical services, they will not lead to meaningful gains in the lives of struggling urban majorities.

Elections, of course, are not the only—nor always the primary—way popular groups press their goals. Through the twentieth century, the people of Mexico City faced a regime that controlled elections and limited self-rule in the national capital. Still, they found ways to make claims that were not controlled by the regime that orchestrated so much. They took to the streets, plazas, and government offices to demand rights and services, gaining enough to make neighborhoods more livable. But small successes brought exhaustion and demobilization. The celebrated electoral opening of 2000 came as globalization locked in polarities. Divisive elections ruled by money and media followed. Lives of insecurity marked by violence continued; disillusion reigned. Now, Andrés Manuel López Obrador, a former mayor of Mexico City who broke with the national political establishment, has won election to Mexico's presidency. Popular hopes have risen again. Can the people of Mexico and its capital metropolis escape the constraints of globalization? Time will tell.[60]

Mexico City offers a clear case of trajectories evident elsewhere. Labor politics, popular mobilizations, and ethnic movements occurred in all our cities, sometimes punctuated by riots and often facing official repression. During the midcentury decades of national development they often made real gains, most notably in Peronist Argentina. Yet the prospect of popular gains brought the military to power first in Brazil and then in Argentina; Mexico's once inclusive authoritarian regime became ever more closed and at times repressive; The United States and Canada saw conservative reactions.[61] Across the Americas and our cities, late century democratization has come with declining labor rights (as cheap, flexible, poor, and insecure labor is declared a good in a globalizing world) and limits on urban movements, whether focused on ethnic rights or services and survival.[62] Elections have become rituals of participation financed and shaped by powers beyond popular control. Disillusion with electoral democracy reigns to a greater or lesser degree in all our cities.

The effectiveness of elections in promoting popular interests is uncertain and debated. Our urban histories cannot resolve that question. We focus on how differing ways of popular mobilization brought real yet limited gains. In Mexico City and Rio de Janeiro, our poorest and most polarized cities, informal movements demanded infrastructure and basic services— and made gains. Families deep in informal economies, building homes without titles and permits, have organized to win streets and sewers, schools and transit services. They made the least favored of neighborhoods more livable. They built their cities, yet remain poor and marginalized. In once prosperous Buenos Aires, labor power and urban movements sustained some shared prosperity while Mexico City and Rio de Janeiro faced the collapse of the promise of nation development. In more prosperous Montreal, Los Angeles, and Houston, groups facing religious-linguistic, ethnic, or racial exclusions demanded political rights and access to services. They too made gains, yet segregations and marginalization persist. Nowhere have popular movements altered the trajectories of globalization and urbanization as they intersect to concentrate wealth, deepen inequality, and spread marginality. Popular movements arguably have gained just enough to make cities more livable, while sustaining globalization and urbanization. Cities became a bit more viable for struggling families and excluded minorities. By their efforts, they have survived—and sustained the dominant model of global urban development. Power and profits continue to concentrate; inequities deepen while exclusions and insecurities proliferate.

Piketty's dilemma remains, grounded in a world defined by unprecedented demographic pressures, accelerating urbanization, and entrenched global integrations. In diverse and too often fragmented ways growing populations demand better. Our histories of six New World cities probe their diverse historic challenges, emphasizing intersections of globalization, urbanization, and popular movements, aiming to understand the world we face, and wondering if we can do better.

Notes

1. For the period before 1800, see John Tutino, *Making a New World: Founding Capitalism in the Bajío and Spanish North America* (Durham, NC: Duke University Press, 2011). On the transformations of 1750–1870, see Tutino, "The Americas in the Rise of Industrial Capitalism," in *New Countries: The Americas in a Changing World, 1750–1870*, ed. Tutino (Durham, NC: Duke University Press, 2016), 25–70.

2. On early Asian primacy and the late rise of Europe, see Kenneth Pomeranz, *The Great Divergence: China, Europe and the Making of the Modern World Economy* (Princeton, NJ: Princeton University Press, 2000); and Prasannan Parthasarathi, *Why Europe Grew Rich and Asia Did Not: Global Economic Divergence, 1600–1850* (Cambridge: Cambridge University Press, 2011). On the role of the Americas, see Tutino, *Making a New World*. On the long nineteenth century, see C. A. Bayly, *The Birth of the Modern World, 1780–1914* (Oxford: Blackwell, 2004). For a synthesis of this new vision, see Ronald Findlay and Kevin O'Rourke, *Power and Plenty: Trade, War, and the World Economy in the Second Millennium* (Princeton, NJ: Princeton University Press, 2007).

3. See Max Weber, *The Protestant Ethic and the Spirit of Capitalism* [1905], trans. and ed. Stephen Kolberg (Oxford: Blackwell, 2002); W. W. Rostow, *The Stages of Economic Growth: A Non-Communist Manifesto* (Cambridge: Cambridge University Press, 1960); and Douglass North and Robert Paul Thomas, *The Rise of the Western World: A New Economic History* (Cambridge: Cambridge University Press, 1976).

4. Marx, a German, based his analysis of economic history and model for future prosperity on the experience of the British industrial revolution—which he admired, but for its capitalist power and social exclusions.

5. The role of imperial competition in leading to World War I and of that war in setting off the Russian revolution are well known; on the role of the war in the Mexican revolution, see Friedrich Katz, "International Wars, Mexico, and U.S. Hegemony," in *Cycles of Conflict, Centuries of Change: Crisis, Reform, and Revolution in Mexico*, ed. Elisa Servín, Leticia Reina, and John Tutino (Durham, NC: Duke University Press, 2007), 184–210.

6. This fundamental constraint was detailed by Samuel Baily in *The United States and the Development of Latin America, 1945–1974* (New York: New Viewpoints, 1976)—a vision drowned by promoters of national development.

7. See Jeffrey Taffet, *Foreign Aid as Foreign Policy: The Alliance for Progress in Latin America* (New York: Routledge, 2007) and the Latin American case histories in this book.

8. This is emphasized in John McNeill and Peter Engelke, *The Great Acceleration: An Environmental History of the Anthropocene since 1945* (Cambridge, MA: Harvard University Press, 2014).

9. This is a focus of McNeill and Engelke, *The Great Acceleration* (without the emphasis on labor saving).

10. The essential study is Edward Baptist, *The Half Has Never Been Told: Slavery and the Making of American Capitalism* (New York: Basic Books, 2016).

11. See David Landes's pioneering book *The Unbound Prometheus: Technological Change and Industrial Development in Western Europe from 1750 to the Present* (Cambridge: Cambridge University Press, 1969). See also Robert Allen's recent *The British Industrial Revolution in Global Perspective* (Cambridge: Cambridge University Press, 2009).

12. See Parthasarathi, *Why Europe Grew Rich*. On the global development and consequences of British industrialization of cotton cloth, see Sven Beckert, *Empire of Cotton* (New York: Knopf, 2014).

13. See William McNeill, *Plagues and People* (New York: Anchor, 1977); and John McNeill, *Something New Under the Sun: An Environmental History of the Twentieth-Century World* (New York: Norton, 2000).

14. The link between U.S. mechanization and Yucatecan production is clear in Gilbert Joseph, *Revolution from Without: Yucatán, México, and the United States, 1880–1924* (Cambridge: Cambridge University Press, 1982).

15. See John Tutino, *The Mexican Heartland: How Communities Shaped Capitalism, a Nation, and World History, 1500–2000* (Princeton, NJ: Princeton University Press, 2017), ch. 9.

16. Cynthia Hewitt de Alcántara, *Modernizing Mexican Agriculture: The Socioeconomic Implications of Technical Change* (Geneva: UN Research Institute for Social Development, 1976); Angus Wright, *The Death of Ramón González: The Modern Agricultural Dilemma* (Austin: University of Texas Press, 1990).

17. Gary Gereffi, *The Mexican Pharmaceutical Industry* (Durham, NC: Duke University Press, 1983); Gabriela Soto Laveaga, *Jungle Laboratories* (Durham, NC: Duke University Press, 2009).

18. Saskia Sassen, *The Global City: New York, London, Tokyo* (Princeton, NJ: Princeton University Press, 2001).

19. The dark view of Mike Davis in *Planet of Slums* (London: Verso, 2006) is complicated by the city histories here; by the studies in Brodwyn Fisher, Bryan McCann, and Javier Auyero, eds., *Cities from Scratch: Poverty and Informality in Urban Latin America*, (Durham, NC: Duke University Press, 2014); and by Edward Murphy, *For a Proper Home: Housing Rights in the Margins of Urban Chile, 1960–2010* (Pittsburgh: University of Pittsburgh Press, 2015).

20. Martin Melosi, Joseph Pratt, and Kathleen Brosnihan, eds., *Energy Capitals: Local Impact, Global Influence* (Pittsburgh: University of Pittsburgh Press, 2014)

21. See, for a powerful example, Devon Peña, *The Terror of the Machine: Technology, Work, Gender, and Ecology on the U.S.-Mexican Border* (Austin: University of Texas Press, 1997).

22. Alfred Crosby, *The Columbian Exchange* (Westwood, CT: Greenwood Press, 1968) remains the classic synthesis.

23. John McNeill, *Mosquito Empires* (New York: Cambridge University Press, 2010) explores the second stage of New World demographic history, focusing on tropical lowlands.

24. William McNeill, *Plagues and Peoples*, shows how medical advances led to the recent population explosion.

25. On silver capitalism and Mexico City, see Tutino, *The Mexican Heartland*, ch. 1–2; on Potosí, see Jane Mangan, *Trading Roles: Gender, Ethnicity, and the Urban Economy in Colonial Potosí* (Durham, NC: Duke University Press, 2005).

26. See Tutino, *Making a New World* and *The Mexican Heartland,* part 1; on the city before the conflicts of independence, see John Tutino, *Mexico City, 1808: Power, Sovereignty, and Silver in an Age of War and Revolution* (Albuquerque, NM: University of New Mexico Press, 2018).

27. See Alfredo Ávila and John Tutino, "Becoming Mexico: The Conflictive Search for a North American Nation," in *New Countries*, ed. Tutino, 233–277. See also Tutino, *The Mexican Heartland,* part 2.

28. This is a sketch of the more complex analysis in Tutino, *The Mexican Heartland,* part 2.

29. For an overview of the revolution, see Alan Knight, *The Mexican Revolution: A Very Short Introduction* (New York: Oxford University Press, 2016). For my interpretations, see Tutino, *The Mexican Heartland*, ch. 10–11.

30. On Cárdenas, see Adolfo Gilly, *El Cardenismo: Una Utopía Mexicana* (Mexico City: Cal y Arena, 1994), and Nora Hamilton, *The Limits of State Autonomy: Post-Revolutionary Mexico* (Princeton, NJ: Princeton University Press, 1982).

31. See Hewitt de Alcántara, *Modernizing Mexican Agriculture.*

32. On Mexico City during and after World War II, see Emilio Coral Garcia, "The Mexico City Middle Class, 1940–1970," Ph.D. dissertation, Georgetown University, 2011.

33. Louise Walker, *Waking from the Dream: Mexico's Middle Classes After 1968* (Stanford: Stanford University Press, 2013).

34. On the rise of Rio, see C. R. Boxer's classic, *The Golden Age of Brazil, 1695–1750* (Berkeley: University of California Press, 1962). On the city at the end of Portuguese rule, see Kirsten Schultz, *Tropical Versailles: Empire, Monarchy, and the Portuguese Royal Court in Rio de Janeiro, 1808–1821* (New York: Routledge, 2001).

35. On Haiti, see Carolyn Fick, *The Making of Haiti: The Saint Domingue Revolution from Below* (Knoxville: University of Tennessee Press, 1990); Laurent Dubois, *Avengers of the New World: The Story of the Haitian Revolution* (Cambridge, MA: Harvard University Press, 2005); and Fick, "From Slave Colony to Black Nation: Haiti's Revolutionary Inversion," in *New Countries,* ed. Tutino, 138–174.

36. Kirsten Schulz, "Atlantic Transformations and Brazil's Imperial Independence," in *New Countries,* ed. Tutino, 201–231, outlines Rio's role in Brazilian independence; Richard Graham, *Britain and the Onset of Modernization in Brazil, 1850–1914* (Cambridge: Cambridge University Press, 1972).

37. The key study is Warren Dean, *The Industrialization of São Paulo* (Austin: University of Texas Press, 1970).

38. The classic study of politics in the era of national development in Brazil during the Vargas era is Thomas Skidmore, *Politics in Brazil, 1930–1964: An Experiment in Democracy* (New York: Oxford University Press, 1967). On São Paulo, see Joel Wolfe, *Working Women, Working Men: São Paulo and the Rise of Brazil's Industrial Working Class, 1900–1955* (Durham, NC: Duke University Press, 1992); Barbara Weinstein, *For Social Peace in Brazil: Industrialists and the Remaking of the Working Class in São Paulo, 1920–1964* (Chapel Hill: University of North Carolina Press, 1996); and Barbara Weinstein, *The Color of Modernity: São Paulo and the Making of Race and Modernity in Brazil* (Durham, NJ: Duke University Press, 2016). On Rio, the pivotal work is Brodwyn Fischer, *A Poverty of Rights: Citizenship and Inequality in Twentieth-Century Rio de Janeiro* (Stanford: Stanford University Press, 2008).

39. Janice Perlman, *The Myth of Marginality: Urban Politics and Poverty in Rio de Janeiro* (Berkeley: University of California Press, 1980) is the classic study of favela life.

40. See Janice Perlman, *Favela: Four Decades of Living on the Edge in Rio de Janeiro* (Oxford: Oxford University Press, 2010); Bryan McCann, *Hard Times in the Marvelous City: From Dictatorship to Democracy in the Favelas of Rio de Janeiro* (Durham, NC: Duke University Press, 2014); for comparisons to São Paulo, see Teresa Caldeira, *City of Walls: Segregation and Citizenship in São Paulo* (Berkeley: University of California Press, 2000).

41. On the growth of Buenos Aires in the late eighteenth century, see Lyman Johnson, *Workshop of Revolution: Plebian Buenos Aires and the Atlantic World, 1776–1810* (Durham, NC: Duke University Press, 2011).

42. See Jonathan Brown, *A Socioeconomic History of Argentina, 1776–1860* (Cambridge: Cambridge University Press, 1979).

43. On the rise of Buenos Aires, see the classic studies of James Scobie, *Revolution on the Pampas* (Austin: University of Texas Press, 1967), and *Buenos Aires: From Plaza to Suburb* (New York: Oxford University Press, 1975); see also José Moya, *Cousins and Strangers: Spanish Immigrants in Buenos Aires, 1850–1930* (Berkeley: University of California Press, 1998); and Diego Armus, *The Ailing City: Health, Tuberculosis, and Culture in Buenos Aires, 1870–1950* (Durham, NC: Duke University Press, 2011).

44. See James Brennan and Marcelo Rougier, *The Politics of National Capitalism: Peronism and the Argentine Bourgeoisie, 1946–1976* (University Park, PA: Penn State Press, 2009); and Eduardo Elena, *Dignifying Argentina: Peronism, Citizenship, and Mass Consumption* (Pittsburgh: University of Pittsburgh Press, 2011).

45. Carlos Waisman, *Reversal of Development* (Princeton, NJ: Princeton University Press, 1987); Luis Alberto Romero, *A History of Argentina in the Twentieth Century*, trans. James Brennan (University Park, PA: Penn State University Press, 2002).

46. On Montreal, see Annick Germain and Damaris Rose, *Montreal: The Quest for a Metropolis* (Hoboken, NJ: Wiley, 2000); on industry, see Robert Lewis, *Manufacturing Montreal: The Making of an Industrial Landscape, 1850–1930* (Baltimore:

Johns Hopkins University Press, 2000); on conflicts of the 1960s and 1970s, see Sean Mills, *The Empire Within: Post-Colonial Thought and Political Activism in Sixties Montreal* (Montreal: McGill-Queen's University Press, 2010); on environment, see Stephane Castonguay and Michèle Dagenais, *Metropolitan Natures: Environmental Histories of Montreal* (Pittsburgh: University of Pittsburgh Press, 2011).

47. For this analysis, I rely heavily on Michèle Dagenais's essay in this volume.

48. For a history of Los Angeles and its region before 1900, see Douglas Monroy, *Thrown Among Strangers: The Making of Mexican Culture in Frontier California* (Berkeley: University of California Press, 1993).

49. On Los Angeles to 1950, see Douglas Monroy, *Rebirth: Mexican Los Angeles from the Great Migration to the Great Depression* (Berkeley: University of California Press, 1999); Robert Fogelson, *Los Angeles: The Fragmented Metropolis, 1850–1950* (Berkeley: University of California Press, 1993); George Sanchez, *Becoming Mexican American* (Oxford: Oxford University Press, 1995).

50. For Los Angeles in recent decades, see David Reiff, *Los Angeles: Capital of the Third World* (New York: Simon & Schuster, 1990); Steven Erie, *Globalizing L.A.: Trade, Infrastructure, and Regional Development* (Stanford: Stanford University Press, 2004); Abraham Lowenthal, *Global California: Rising to the Cosmopolitan Challenge* (Stanford: Stanford University Press, 2009).

51. On slavery and the origins of independent Texas, see Randolph Campbell, *An Empire for Slavery: The Peculiar Institution in Texas, 1821–1865* (Baton Rouge: Louisiana State University Press, 1989); Paul Lack, *The Texas Revolutionary Experience: A Political and Social History, 1935–1936* (College Station: Texas A&M University Press, 1992). On the Civil War cotton trade, see David Montejano, "Mexican Merchants and Teamsters on the Texas Cotton Road, 1862–1865," in *Mexico and Mexicans in the Making of the United States*, John Tutino, ed. (Austin: University of Texas Press, 2012), 141–170. On postwar cotton, see Neil Foley, *White Scourge: Mexicans, Blacks, and Poor Whites in Texas Cotton Culture* (Berkeley: University of California Press, 1999).

52. On Houston, see Martin Melosi and Joseph Pratt, eds., *Energy Metropolis* (Pittsburgh: University of Pittsburgh Press, 2007), and their essay in this volume. On Mexican migration, see Rubén Hernández-León, *Metropolitan Migrants: The Migration of Urban Mexicans to the United States* (Berkeley: University of California Press, 2008).

53. See Elena, *Dignifying Argentina.*

54. The key works are Perlman, *Myth of Marginality* and *Favela.*

55. See McCann, *Hard Times in the Marvelous City*, and Caldeira, *City of Walls.*

56. See Perlman, *Favela*, and Arturo Alvarado Mendoza, *El tamaño del infierno: Un studio sobre la criminalidad en la Zona Metropolitana de la Ciudad de México* (Mexico City: El Colegio de México, 2012).

57. What follows is my interpretation of Caldeira's analysis in *City of Walls.*

58. For an entry into the growing literature on the carceral state, see Vesla Weaver and Amy Lerman, "Political Consequences of the Carceral State," *American Political Science Review* 104, no. 4 (2010): 813–833.

59. See Perlman, *Favela*, especially 148–263; for examples of quotes, see 136.

60. This is the focus of Tutino's essay in this volume.

61. For a powerful case of repression and the end of popular participation in Córdoba, Argentina's second city, as national development collapsed in the 1970s, see James Brennan, *Argentina's Missing Bones: Revisiting the History of the Dirty War* (Oakland, CA: University of California Press, 2018).

62. See the essays by McCann and Sanchez in this book.

2 Power, Marginality, and Participation in Mexico City, 1870–2000

· ·

JOHN TUTINO

Mexico City had lived six centuries of complex history, indigenous, imperial, and national, when it faced the population explosion that brought
unprecedented challenges after 1950. It had been capital of a Mesoamerican empire, pivot of global silver capitalism, center of a liberal national project, then leader of an experiment in national capitalism. The city was
home to more than 200,000 people before Europeans came in 1519. They
delivered diseases that cut the urban population—while carrying visions of
profit that led the city to rise again as Spain's North American capital, the
financial and commercial center of a silver economy that drove global trade
and brought the city back near 150,000 as the nineteenth century began.
Popular insurgencies and political wars took down silver capitalism and
Spain's empire after 1810, setting off a difficult century of nation making
and searching for a new economy while the capital's population grew past
500,000 as the twentieth century began.

The twentieth century escalated the challenges of being urban. By 2000,
the metropolis approached 20 million inhabitants in a nation of 100 million. The urban explosion created unprecedented needs for employment and
housing, food and water, sewage and garbage removal, transportation, medical care, schooling, recreation, and more. The people of Mexico City learned
and relearned that cities are places of power and production, of exchange,
education, and culture—and of work, marginality, and desperation. Opportunities were legion, yet chances to prosper, even to live comfortably,
never approached the needs of a soaring urban population.

The question is why. Historically, cities have concentrated power. In the
surge of twentieth-century urbanization they came to concentrate growing
throngs of the poor—many working, too many struggling in marginal lives.
Whatever the mix of power and poverty, prosperity and marginality, cities
are defined by dependencies. They cannot feed themselves and must draw
sustenance from outside, whether a nearby countryside or a global food

system. On a larger scale, cities depend on economies and infrastructures controlled by financial, business, and state institutions with powers tied to larger national and international networks. Thus cities are concentrations of power and population, defined by dependencies that too often result in marginal lives, conditions that both elicit and limit popular participation.[1]

To understand the trials of urbanization in twentieth-century Mexico City, we must explore the transformations provoked by rapidly growing concentrations of population and the challenge of providing sustenance and services to sustain them as the nation and the world changed. The city remained the political capital and economic pivot of a nation driven by liberal capitalism in a U.S.-led industrial world before 1910. Then, shaken by a revolution rooted in the countryside, the city led the search for a national capitalism from 1920 to 1980. When that possibility crashed, the sprawling metropolis faced the challenges of globalization. We must analyze political regimes and economic ways as they engaged a changing global system—and together shaped the life chances of Mexicans becoming ever more urban. Through the decades from 1870 to 2000, Mexico City always concentrated power, always generated prosperity for many, and always left too many to struggle in poverty. Political regimes, economic ways, and cultural conversations changed; the mix of power, marginality, and political contest that shaped the city endured—as it also changed.

During an era that began with the consolidation of liberal rule around 1870 and culminated in the triumph of neoliberal globalization after 1980, Mexico City was always shaped by combinations of law and illegality, formal economic ways and enduring informalities. Perhaps most revealing, the law often stimulated illegalities while the limits of the formal economy regularly provoked informalities. This history of the Americas' largest metropolis focuses on how liberalism in the world of industrial capitalism created urban concentrations and exclusions, how revolution and national capitalism could not reverse their rule, how neoliberal globalization deepened polarities—and how legality and illegality, formality and informality shaped the city and a politics in which the many pressed the few to demand—and sometimes gain—better lives.

City in a Changing World, 1300–1850

México-Tenochtitlan was founded on a small island in the lakes that center the highland Valley of Mexico, a refuge for a wandering warrior people seeking a place in the militarized politics of Mesoamerica. They built productive lake bed platforms called *chinampas* to feed a fortress that by 1500 was the largest city, greatest center of power and trade, and capital of the strongest polity in the Mesoamerican region of states, cities, and cultivating communities that extended from the Valley of Mexico west to the Pacific and southeast to Guatemala and Yucatán.[2] Still, Mexica power was far from absolute, contested by Tarascans to the west, Tlaxcalans to the east, and the state-free Chichimeca peoples who ruled the lands stretching far to the north. War was constant, shaping regimes and production, social relations, and religion.

In that world of conflict, the Mexica capital grew to 200,000 people. It drew sustenance first from rich nearby *chinampas*. As the city grew and its armies conquered neighboring and outlying city-states, México-Tenochtitlan took tributes in sustenance, labor, and luxuries from subject peoples. Militarized power backed labor drafts that built *chinampas*; armed might pressed battles to take tribute from conquered peoples. Surpluses were traded in markets, local and long-distance. Texts written by the powerful to legitimate Mexica power insisted that the militarized regime followed religious principles while protecting the lakes region and its rich production; the views of people working *chinampas* and outlying dry land have not survived.

In the sixteenth century, Iberians linked Mexico City to Europe and the wider world—and brought diseases that devastated native peoples, reducing their numbers by 90 percent in a century.[3] For decades from Cortés's landing in 1519 to the rise of silver and the consolidation of Spanish rule after 1550, illegalities and informalities were everywhere as newcomers aimed to rule and natives worked to adapt and survive. Only when silver linked New Spain to global trades did its profits and revenues enable an economic consolidation grounded in a new regime that promoted mining while consolidating surviving communities as landed indigenous republics— all orchestrated by authorities that mediated more than they regulated. Rebuilt as New Spain's capital, Mexico City revived as the administrative, judicial, financial, commercial, religious, and educational pivot of territories that by 1800 reached to San Francisco, California—and to Manila, the great entrepôt of Pacific trade. The city was smaller than in 1500—with perhaps 80,000 people around 1600 and 130,000 in 1800.[4] Still, it was a financial center of global importance, a key subcapital in Spain's empire, a place concentrating power and wealth—sustained by a mix of native communities, organized artisans, less formal barrios, and a floating underclass that carried the city's everyday loads and met its diverse needs for service.[5]

Imperial Mexico City drew sustenance from native communities reconstituted as indigenous republics. The Spanish regime granted them land and local self-rule to enable the survivors of smallpox and other diseases to recoup culturally—and to sustain the silver economy. As populations grew after 1700, the city depended more on the commercial estates that developed among the communities across nearby basins. Estate growers supplied the capital's markets, using workers recruited seasonally from nearby villages. All along, global trades in fine cloth and other luxuries announced the wealth and power of the city at the center of colonial administration and silver-driven trades. In times of sparse population and silver dynamism, military power receded as judicial mediation kept order after 1600. The Spanish regime promoted commercial dynamism, in good part by guaranteeing rights to land and self-rule to communities around the capital, and by mediating in court the conflicts that emerged. Informalities grew in city barrios and nearby rural communities; popular interests found limited voice in local councils and colonial courts.[6] There were moments of resistance, as in the Mexico City food riots of 1692.[7] Still, commercial dynamism and judicial mediations limited conflicts until Napoleon's 1808 invasion of Spain drew people to streets and plazas in contests that became militarized (while proclaiming popular sovereignties).[8] In 1810, insurgencies began north of the capital; a decade later they had taken down silver capitalism.[9]

In 1821, the city became the capital of a Mexican empire, giving way in 1824 to a federal republic. It lost rule over Central America, Cuba, and Manila. With the fall of silver, the resources that had sustained the city's economic prosperity and mediating powers were gone; it had little to offer distant provinces. Its political domains shrinking, the silver economy in crisis—Mexico City faced unprecedented challenges marked by endemic political illegalities and economic informalities that revealed an underlying shift to favor resilient popular communities.[10]

For decades after 1821, the capital was a focus of political conflicts and constant debates seeking an economic transformation. Many in the city believed the capital should rule the nation; many in the provinces insisted the capital existed to coordinate regional interests and links with the world. Liberals in the capital and the provinces promoted individual rights, private property, and free trade. Their opponents, often concentrated in the capital and other cities, preferred a nation keeping Catholic traditions— while they promoted a tariff-protected industrialization that took hold around Mexico City after 1840.

Mexico City, now a national capital set in a Federal District subject to national rule, faced new challenges. No longer a center of capital accumulation, finance, and revenues, it struggled to find its role in the nation and to sustain a growing population with uncertain economic prospects. City people watched regimes come and go; they kept up artisan production as guild regulations and protections ended; they dealt in neighborhood markets to buy food still produced by outlying commercial estates and indigenous villagers—the former struggling to profit, the latter newly assertive in post-independence decades. While political conflicts raged and the commercial economy struggled, communities around the capital retrenched on the land—making the city's dependence on the countryside clear to all. Did informalities spread in this time of uncertain and contested legalities? Perhaps. But the city pawnshops that were the primary source of credit and emergency assistance for working families remained regulated while local courts held on as the regular recourse of people facing disputes.[11]

City people did find new political ways. Crowds took to the streets to demand political participation in 1808, to support independence in 1821, and to proclaim Agustín de Iturbide emperor months later. In 1828, they rioted to help the popular mulatto Vicente Guerrero to power—and to destroy shops in the Parian, where the rich bought Asian and European imports in the plaza in front the former viceregal palace, now the seat of national government. They rose again in 1847 to resist the U.S. troops occupying their city—challenging the national leaders who fled to Querétaro to stand with them and defend the nation and the city. All this showed the interests, persistence, and adaptability of the city's peoples, their willingness to work in formal legal channels when they served popular needs, and their readiness to take to the streets when power threatened popular interests and made lives uncertain.[12] In times of political conflict and economic uncertainty, illegalities and informalities grew slowly. So did the city, from near 150,000 people at independence in 1821 to 200,000 in 1870. The Federal District, with growing industrial suburbs, reached 300,000.[13]

Liberal Development and the Legal Origins of Illegality and Informality, 1850–1910

The middle decades of the nineteenth century brought intense political, ideological, international, and social conflicts: defeat in war and the loss of vast lands to the U.S. in the late 1840s; the triumph of national liberalism in 1855; a civil war from 1858 to 1860 that blocked conservative resistance;

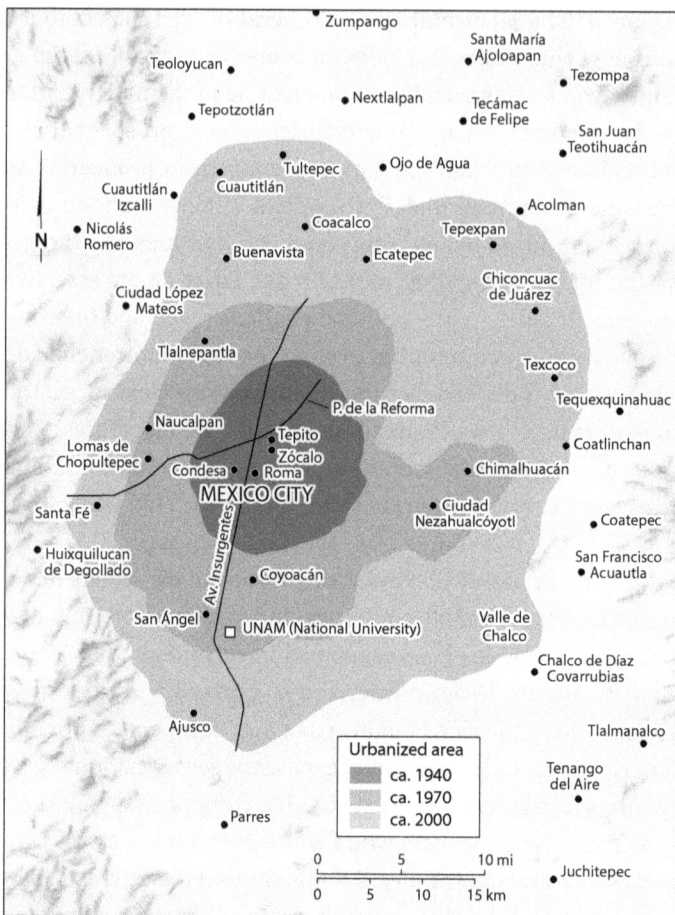

MAP 2.1 Mexico City. Credit: Bill Nelson.

French invasion in 1862 and the imposed empire of Maximilian from 1864 to 1867; the return of the republic in 1867—followed by a round of regional insurgencies by indigenous peoples resisting liberal privatization of community lands. While all that rattled national politics and commercial life, from the 1840s to the 1870s mechanized textile mills spread across the slopes south and west of the Mexico City center, tapping hydraulic power. Tacubaya, just west, emerged as a suburb where the archbishop, old colonial families, new immigrant merchants, and rising industrialists built country homes. The city became a metropolitan complex. Manufacturing suburbanized, drawing workers from the city center and outlying towns like Puebla and Querétaro. Artisans making cloth, clothing, shoes, and more still concentrated in the center near their customers.[14] The city and its economy found new dynamism amid political conflicts as uncertain legalities allowed informalities that could profit investors and draw workers too.

When liberals retook power, led by Benito Juárez in 1867, they continued to press visions of homogenized rights and laws, mandating the privatization of Church properties and indigenous community lands. Since the Cádiz Constitution of 1812, Spanish liberals had aimed to abolish corporate rights and limit church and community power. The Ley Lerdo of 1856, incorporated in the liberal Constitution of 1857, called for national privatizations. The Church and its conservative backers resisted, setting off the War of Reform (1858–60), leading Juárez to nationalize church properties and take the revenues for his embattled liberal state. Church properties were sold in the capital and suburbs like Tacubaya in times of conflict, enabling rich investors to buy properties that once generated revenues for clerical institutions, often schools and hospitals. Maximilian dared not alienate the buyers (and had no funds to repay them). When Juárez retook the capital in 1867, the alienation of Church holdings complete, his liberal state moved to end the land rights of indigenous communities, both rural and urban.[15]

The lands of Mexico City's native *parcialidades,* San Juan Tenochtitlan and Santiago Tlatelolco, would be privatized. The house lots of barrio families would become property of the residents; plazas and streets would pass to the city; open space would be auctioned to the highest bidder. No one surveyed lots or gave titles to the homes of the poor on once community lands. The city could not pay for legalization; liberals insisted that privatization could not wait. The result was a dual process. Larger, more valuable church and community properties passed to wealthy investors who could profit from rents, sales, and new urban subdivisions. The poor clung to lots and homes with uncertain rights. Liberal privatization accelerated both the formal urbanization that served the rich and comfortable and the informal urbanization that forced the poor to survive by self-help in contexts of legal uncertainty.[16]

Liberal leaders and ideologues insisted the goal was to promote widening ownership and a dynamic real estate market. Developers had other plans. As early as 1856, while the Ley Lerdo was still in planning, a consortium backed by the Martínez del Río banking group and led by the personal secretary of President Comonfort proposed a deal. They would contract to privatize all unclaimed, untitled land in the Federal District. They would draw straight streets and sell lots, but provide neither paving nor other services—and pay no taxes to a city left responsible for essential infrastructure. Investors would profit. The government would gain no income; services would depend on a regime with little revenue. The Lerdo Law preempted the project—allowing the Martínez del Río investors to buy privatized Church and community lands and promote urban development by similar, if smaller, schemes.[17] Liberal policies facilitated and legitimated city development that generated escalating inequalities around poles of profit and informality.

City residents mobilized to adapt and resist. Barrio families claimed homes and lots, defended plazas, streets, and markets, and worked to limit claims by outsiders—with limited success. Workers in new suburban industries and established downtown crafts joined political clubs and mutual aid societies, pressed demands for pay and working conditions, and periodically went on strike. They claimed the attention of leaders struggling to consolidate political power and gained limited concessions. But geographic and occupational divides between downtown artisans and outlying industrial workers, many newly in from the provinces and all facing an uncertain economy that kept jobs scarce and insecure, combined to set workers in competition with each other, inhibiting city dwellers' ability to find unity and claim enduring gains.[18]

Then, in the 1870s, politics stabilized, the national economy revived, and Mexico City continued to grow. Liberals now led by Porfirio Díaz consolidated an authoritarian regime that limited electoral participation. To the end of the nineteenth century, the city council was elected. But voting was in two tiers: 50,000 to 60,000 men might cast ballots to choose 400 to 600 electors—who then chose councilmen. It was a system ruled easily by a political machine with money, economic power, and presidential connections.[19]

Meanwhile, the capital grew as the pivot of a diversifying national economy. The 1870s saw rails connect Mexico City to the Gulf at Veracruz. The 1880s brought trunk lines to the U.S. border at Laredo and El Paso—reinforcing the centrality of the capital in the nation while connecting its economy to a world increasingly ruled by the United States, its capital, and its resources. Decades of dependent development would benefit Mexico City—or at least its capitalists and their favored allies. The population of the city more than doubled in the late nineteenth century; the Federal District that included growing industrial suburbs tripled. There were signs of a new modernity and prosperity: palatial homes and public buildings near the center, and a steam railroad that linked the center to the retreat at Tacubaya in 1858. By 1869, steam rail integrated most of metropolitan region, supplemented in the 1880s by horse-drawn trolleys in the center—all replaced by a growing network of electric trolleys around 1900.[20]

Factories moved downtown as steam and electricity allowed locations near markets and workers. New neighborhoods for the rich and the growing middle class stretched west and south along the elegant Paseo de la Reforma (celebrating liberalism), serving the wealthy and the comfortable; they came with names like Cuauhtémoc and Juárez (honoring indigenous leaders, pre-Hispanic and liberal), Roma and Condesa (asserting classic and noble ancestries). Fine neighborhoods got pavement, water, sewer, and lighting in deals between the city and developers. For liberals, entrepreneurs, and families in a small but growing middle class, life in the late-nineteenth-century city was worth celebrating.

But there was another Mexico City, less celebrated, expanding north, east, and south of the center. There, subdivision and settlement often preceded sanction. Sometimes, developers began with city sanction and obligations to provide services. Legality was uncertain; informality inevitable. When legalization came, it mostly recognized outcomes, legalizing developers' profits without providing clear titles or basic services to poor residents. Informality was thus sanctioned and set to endure in the lives of growing numbers.[21]

Tepito offers a case study. Privatization came to the once indigenous barrio after 1868, without surveys or titles. During the following decades, it underwent four subdivisions. Entrepreneurs bought up large sections at low cost from poor residents with uncertain titles. Developers got city permission to draw streets and plazas, set lots, and sell them with title to buyers. The city promised to pave streets; water, sewer, and lighting were left to future decisions. The land was privatized: entrepreneurs profited and many residents got titles—a single basic legality. But they owned plots on streets the city never paved (claiming lack of funds), access to water depended on artesian wells drilled in public spaces, there was no public lighting, and the unpaved streets doubled as sewers. The contrast with the new neighborhoods to the west was striking to those who would see.[22]

Still, the growth of neighborhoods without services was not just a calamity. Places like Tepito offered ways of survival for growing populations of the displaced and marginal poor. New industries concentrated in the city, along with transport, commercial, and government services. Tax revenues were never enough to pay for neighborhood services; employment never provided secure earnings to the urban majority. The proliferation of informality allowed ever more numerous marginal families to struggle to survive—sustaining the model of urban development that kept them marginal.

In the face of growing populations, rising landlessness (promoted by liberal policies of rural privatization and the beginning of agricultural mechanization) sent rural people to the city, men in search of labor, women to serve in prosperous households. More than 87,000 immigrants lived there in 1895, 151,000 in 1900, 142,000 in 1910—a decline revealing high death rates and that the city's promise was not being fulfilled.[23] Few newcomers found secure employment. Many survived in poor, marginal, informal neighborhoods like Tepito. Rents were cheap; vendors were everywhere—and as poor as their customers. Informal and insecure work and sales allowed a growing population to survive in urban marginality. By the early twentieth century, Tepito was famous for its unregulated markets. There one could buy food cheaply; cloth, clothing, and shoes were made and repaired. Tools and household goods were on every street corner, the price so low who would ask whether they were used or stolen? The market that was Tepito created a community of informality—condemned from without, a way of life within. It was a calamity and an opportunity for those whose nimble adaptations negotiated its insecurities. It was informal, unhealthy, and often illegal. Yet cheap housing, cheap sustenance, and cheap wares subsidized the formal economy—helping many paid paltry wages to survive, enabling those who paid such pittances to profit and proclaim their modernity.[24]

Not every neighborhood was Tepito or the celebrated Condesa. Expanding industries created new chances for some. As struggling households needed multiple earners to survive, employers drew women into the labor force, condemning their abandonment of families while using their numbers to keep wages low. For women and men on the margins of the middle class and at the heart of the working class, life brought enduring insecurities. It took multiple workers and incomes to sustain a household. A downturn, sudden unemployment, an illness that left one or more without work or with reduced earnings—so many things could threaten family life. We know of two responses. Pawning became a way to get funds when all else failed. Cheap jewelry, clothing, utensils, and other housewares could be left for cash and (hopefully) redeemed when times improved. It was a part of life for middling and working women in the city from the late imperial decades on. But in Spanish times, pawning was regulated. Even during the uncertain post-independence era, regimes struggling for stability and legitimacy limited interest rates. But with the triumph of liberalism, regulation ended in the 1870s. Interest rates rose as women continued to pawn to survive recurrent times of difficulty.[25]

The more social response was to organize. Women working in factories, as home workers in industry, as domestics, and as street vendors faced constant insecurities and low, often falling earnings. When they built mutual aid societies, they were honored. When they turned to charities for aid, they gained small rewards. When they demanded rights and higher pay, they were condemned.[26] Men also organized to seek better earnings and workplace rights. They too were condemned as radicals and repressed if they became too assertive. In the face of structural inequities and mounting insecurities, the ability to struggle informally allowed desperate people to claim small improvements. Their negotiations helped stabilize city life while their poverty subsidized a formal economy that profited a few, sustained the regime, and kept the city alive and growing while lives of marginality proliferated.

Meanwhile, the national power holders who ruled the city focused on one problem and engineered a solution to sustain the city on its trajectory of concentrating profit and proliferating poverty, marginality, and informality. The city was deadly. In 1900, the infant death rate was close to 400 per 1,000 live births; the overall death rate was almost 34 per 1,000 population. The city grew only by in-migration. Deadly diseases flourished in an unsanitary city, including tuberculosis, typhus, and typhoid. And death threatened everyone: the rich, the few in the middle, the poor and marginal. Something had to be done.[27]

Politically powerful men and public health practitioners saw two problems: filthy people and deadly water. Growing numbers lived in desperate poverty, crowded into *vecindades* (tenements) or hovels without access to clean water and with only the streets as sewers. These conditions resulted from a dearth of employment, from marginal wages and more marginal earnings in informal activities, and from the city's denial of basic services to poor neighborhoods, always blamed on scarce revenues. All that was built into a political economy structured to concentrate profit and power and to promote marginality—a liberal imposition of informality on the poor. Yet those who profited and ruled attributed popular filth to its victims: the people were filthy; if they would learn to live hygienic lives, the city would flourish. The people had to be educated to cleanliness.[28]

Yet, in 1896, only 14,000 of more than 300,000 people were in public primary schools. And 60 percent of all schoolchildren were in the first year, after which most were drawn away to join desperate searches for family sustenance.[29] The men who ruled the city had no ability to alter the place of Mexico and its capital in a North American economy that kept most Mexicans poor and many desperate. They had no interest in altering political and economic structures that favored the few and constrained the majority. They invested little in educating the people they condemned as filthy. They were ready to attack the problem of deadly water: that could be profitable, improve health for everyone, and preserve the city's structures of power and inequity.

The challenge of water came with the city's location in a basin without natural drainage. The Mexica built dikes to control the lakes around the capital, gaining protection, transportation, and rich *chinampa* cultivation. The silver capitalists of New Spain tried to drain the lakes, aiming to control the floods that periodically threatened their capital. They had little success.[30] The expansion of the city's population from 150,000 to over 500,000 in the nineteenth century exacerbated the problem of dirty, disease-bearing water. The waste of half a million people flowed in open gutters and rough streets to the San Lázaro canal east of the center, then to broad but shallow Lake Texcoco, which colonial drainage had lowered just enough to serve as a vast cesspool. Most days the canal and the lake stank as they took effluent from the city. When great rains brought floods, as in 1886, the cesspool backed up and returned the sewage to the city.

Here was a problem Porfirian elites were ready to solve. Public health experts demanded a remedy. Engineers designed a great canal, tunnel, and outflow channel to drain Lake Texcoco, taking its putrid waters out of the valley, through the Mezquital basin just north, to the Tula and Pánuco rivers, eventually to reach the Gulf of Mexico. To build the project—to save the city—they took loans from London bankers and let a contract to Pearson and Company, a British capitalist close to the regime. In 1900, the new *desagüe* was inaugurated to great fanfare; in 1903, new sewers fed the drainage project. The problem of deadly waters seemed solved.[31]

Underlying challenges remained. To fund sewers and drainage, the regime imposed a 400,000-pound sterling loan floated in London on the Mexico City council in 1890. The debt translated to about 12 million pesos—two-thirds of all city revenues during the previous decade. Yet the city only received about 8 million pesos as bonds were discounted to draw British investors even as it owed the full 12 million pesos, plus interest. Debt service took 40 percent of annual city revenues. Then national authorities cut another 40 percent from those revenues in 1896, ending the city's right to tax the food, building materials, and other goods entering its markets.[32]

The tax cut lowered consumption and construction costs, but how was the city to pay the debt for the *desagüe* and provide other services, from clean drinking water to schools?

One answer was clear. Where revenue-generating services like electric power, public lighting, and electric trolleys could be let to consortiums of German, British, and Canadian capitalists, they became ways to promote contract capitalism and urban modernity.[33] Services that brought little or no revenue—pavement, water, health care, education—were marginalized along with the people they served. Profit flowed to Pearson, to British bankers and bondholders, to international consortiums that electrified the metropolis—and to the small clique of Porfirian capitalist-managers who collected "fees" of hundreds of thousands of pesos to facilitate the *desague* and other deals. Then, in 1903, with the sewer and drainage project done and the city council facing a huge unpaid debt, the national regime proclaimed that the "independent" city government had failed. The elected council was reduced to a consultative role; the governor of the Federal District, long a presidential appointee, would rule.[34]

The council had failed, but not because it was independent, representative, or imaginably democratic. The Porfirian regime appointed the city's governor and built a political machine that controlled the council. It forced debts on the council and cut its revenues. Then it announced the council had failed. What could have been built with the profits paid to Pearson, with the more than 20 million pesos paid to British investors for a loan that delivered but 8 million pesos? Not to mention the millions more invested in monuments: to Columbus, who linked the Americas to global capitalism, to Cuauhtémoc, who defended the city from Spanish conquest, to Hidalgo and others who fought for independence, to Juárez and the liberal privatizing reformers of the nineteenth century—a contradictory mix that ideologized the contradictions of the regime and the city.[35]

By 1910, a modern city was in place, marked by the contradictions of liberal capitalism. Power concentrated in the hands of political entrepreneurs, facilitating profit taking by global investors and consolidating mass urban marginalization grounded in scarce employment, poor wages, absent services, and limited access to schooling—all legitimated by monuments to modernity and "compensated" by irregular neighborhoods and informal housing, production, and markets. The rich and powerful flourished, and a small but growing middle sector of managers, merchants, and professionals gained new roles and comforts. They lived in new neighborhoods with the best services along the Paseo de la Reforma, where monuments proclaimed the greatness of the city and the nation. The majority struggled to live in equally new neighborhoods north, east, and south of the center, far from the monuments—and with few services except for drainage canals that flushed the city's effluent by the penitentiary at San Lázaro—newly built to proclaim the penalties for men who might protest. Participatory city government, always limited to facilitate the rule of the few, was pronounced a failure and ended.

Revolution and the City, 1910–1940

When the Díaz regime collapsed in 1910–11, Mexicans faced a decade of revolution and decades more of reconstruction. The conflagration began in the failure of the authoritarian liberal regime to solve the problem of succession as Porfirio Díaz approached eighty years of age. The political crisis revealed the failure to incorporate emerging middle sectors and industrial workers—many in Mexico City—into political life. Political conflict became a revolutionary confrontation when rural communities south of the capital entered the fray to pursue their own goals. Liberal land privatizations had concentrated limited holdings while population grew and estates began to mechanize. A generation of men desperate for land while facing scarce chances at labor joined Emiliano Zapata in an insurgency that challenged liberal capitalist power.[36]

During the decade of revolution, city residents organized to demand rights, while rural insurgencies made sustenance scarce and uncertain. Most urban people stayed at work, uncertain observers as social revolution surrounded them and political warriors descended from the north. Mexico City lived the revolution; its diverse residents tried to shape it as they could. But they could not make a revolution.[37] Lives locked in dependent insecurity generated deep frustrations that led to organizations, petitions, strikes, and riots. Dependence on wages and purchased food, definitional of city life, prevented insurgencies like those in rural regions, where rebels could take the land, revive subsistence production, and sustain guerrilla movements for years.[38] The revolution that began Mexico's twentieth century was famously agrarian—close by the city, but never of the city.

Inside the city, years of revolution brought heightened political conflicts, economic and social insecurities, and continued population growth. Between 1910 and 1921, the nation lost almost a million people, many to revolutionary violence, most to devastating influenza in 1918. Yet the capital added 200,000 residents as people sought refuge from conflict and disease all around. The city grew in times of political stability and economic growth; it also grew in times of civil war and economic difficulties.[39]

Throughout, urban growth generated social polarization. Rhetoric could change; city workers might be courted, even mobilized to fight when possible. But ultimately the victorious Constitutionalists led by Venustiano Carranza aimed to consolidate a new regime and deliver as little as possible to city workers and residents.[40] Claiming revolutionary sympathies, they could not publicly blame the working poor for the challenges of city life. In 1916, engineer and Constitutionalist intellectual Alberto Pani saw the social polarization and endemic disease that still plagued the city; he blamed "the sickening corruption of the upper classes and the destitution of the lower classes."[41] In 1917, recognizing that a "Constitutionalist revolution" had to allow basic political participation, President Carranza sanctioned the election of the Mexico City council. The Federal District governor remained a presidential appointee.

The 1920s brought continuing political conflict, the revival of the export economy, and a slow turn toward national industrialization. The city continued to grow, still without resources to provide basic services. Chapultepec Heights—later known as Lomas de Chapultepec—became the elegant new neighborhood for "revolutionary" elites, with parks, paving, and the best electric, water, and sewer services. Elsewhere, new subdivisions for growing throngs seeking a chance in the city profited those who sold the land, in most cases without services. The poor continued to adapt to the city by self-help, competing in a newly politicized environment to claim the limited resources of a "revolutionary" regime. In 1928, Álvaro Obregón, angling to return to the presidency for a second term, proclaimed the city council corrupt and city services as failing. He proposed to end council rule and again submit the capital to presidential power. Obregón was reelected, then assassinated; his successors renationalized city government. The city population passed 1 million as it lost even limited self-rule. Meanwhile, self-proclaimed radicals descended on the city from the United States and across the world, building an imagined city of promise grounded in a revolutionary utopia set in unseen rural communities, while they rarely visited the urban barrios of marginality so close by.[42]

The Depression crashed export markets; external capital became scarce. Under President Lázaro Cárdenas (1934–40), Mexico turned to internal development, both agricultural and industrial. Cárdenas responded to agrarian mobilizations by accelerating land distribution to pacify rural people, facilitating production for sustenance, and drawing many villagers to the regime as staunch supporters. The same reform cut the commercial estate cultivation that had fed the city since colonial times. Meanwhile, Cárdenas promoted national industry, building on nineteenth-century precedents, concentrating new factories and consumers in Mexico City. Cárdenas's political consolidation favored industrial workers with union rights and rising wages—again in exchange for political support.[43] The parallel promotion of rural self-sufficiency, industrial development, and labor rights brought regime consolidation and a structural disjunction deepened by population growth and continuing urban expansion.

Land reform and labor benefits gave working families incentives to have children and new means to feed them. Programs of irrigation, sanitation, health care, and education—limited but real—promoted health. From 1921 to 1940, the national population rose by nearly 40 percent; Mexico City and the Federal District doubled. Rural communities with new land fed growing families, limiting the surpluses sent to city markets while urban population rose. City people wondered who would feed them and supply the industries that promised employment.

The question was how to respond and who would participate in shaping a response. Political ideals remained democratic, promising electoral rule. Yet electoral rights had ended in Mexico City as it came to include 10 percent of the nation's population by 1940. The challenge of stabilizing postrevolutionary rule during a global depression led to new ways of participation. Rural communities demanded land; commercial growers resisted. The regime promoted industry while workers demanded union rights and rising remunerations. Regional interests cut across (and often against) national goals and challenges. In that vortex, Cárdenas built a regime that was authoritarian at the top, corporatist in great confederations of peasants, workers, and entrepreneurs, inclusive in its goal of drawing every major interest into a state-mediated domain where goals could be negotiated, interests balanced, and oppositions mediated—yet ultimately controlled. Participation was never equal: land reform beneficiaries and industrial workers were drawn into sectors of a state-ruled party (the PNR, the PRM, then the PRI) that mixed limited representation with deepening controls; entrepreneurs organized national chambers and gained access to the heights of power free of party controls. Despite an anticlericalism that alienated many, Cárdenas's political consolidation succeeded. Mexico proved the most stable regime in Latin America during the rest of the twentieth century.

Yet it was a regime designed to deal with the challenges of an agrarian revolution in a still rural country aiming to industrialize—before explosive urbanization began. Rural villagers gained land, organization, and ways to participate in the regime. They were favored in the 1920s, constrained in the 1930s, and increasingly controlled from the 1940s. Industrial workers gained rights, benefits, and better wages in the 1930s; they too faced new controls from the 1940s. Entrepreneurs gained support for industrialization in the 1930s even as they faced constraints from a regime working to pacify peasants and benefit workers. From the 1940s, capitalist goals shaped a regime set in power and ready to contain popular pressures and participation.

In Mexico City, the new regime offered fragmented participation. With no independent government for the city or the Federal District, politics focused on national authorities and the party they led. Entrepreneurs found representation through chambers of commerce and industry; organized industrial workers pressed interests through unions and a national labor confederation (CTM). The often antagonistic and always unequal participation of industrialists and workers facilitated industrial concentration in the city and allowed limited address of worker concerns. The huge peasant sector (CNC) of the party-regime had a small role in the city. It did keep the countryside mostly at peace and in production, focused more on rural sustenance than supplying city markets. Growing middle sectors later found representation in a new popular sector (CNOP); their dependence on the state for employment and education kept them dependent and also fragmented.[44] The rising numbers of newcomers who flocked to the city found employment scarce; they settled in old neighborhoods like Tepito or new barrios on the fringes with little voice in the regime that ruled the city and the nation.

Metropolitan Mexico: National Development and Explosive Urbanism, 1940–1980

After 1940, everything seemed to change. The regime that set its revolutionary credentials in 1938 by nationalizing the oil industry joined the United States as a staunch ally in World War II, sending commodities, workers, and soldiers to sustain U.S. power in the fight for global hegemony. From the war until 1980, Mexico would struggle to balance economic nationalism with growing integration with the capital and markets of the United States. With that integration came access to penicillin and other antibiotics promoted to save soldiers during World War II. After the war, these medicines came to Mexico, cutting death rates and setting off a population explosion. The nation grew from under 20 million in 1940 to nearly 70 million by 1980. Urban population growth was more explosive: metropolitan Mexico City expanded from fewer than 2 million people in 1940 to 13 million in 1980. For families with healthier children and longer lives, new medicines were a blessing. For a regime claiming to be revolutionary and promising welfare to all in a capitalist world under U.S. hegemony, the burgeoning population concentrating in the cities was a daunting challenge.

The political system built by Cárdenas did provide effective if limited participation and mediation in times of change. The regime allowed representation to leading entrepreneurs and organized labor, forging a populist model of development while the regime concentrated industry in Mexico City. When middle sectors grew in the 1950s, the party-state created the popular sector to engage their interests, in limited and controlling ways. Political conflicts rose in the 1950s and 1960s, yet were generally contained. The regime coerced when its power seemed threatened, yet it preferred to co-opt, mediate, and constrain, and it usually succeeded. In the context of the conflicts prevailing across Europe and Latin America, Mexico seemed a model of stability from 1940 until the crisis of 1968—and even the latter proved limited.[45]

Governance was not the first challenge in Mexico City. A rapidly expanding population had to be fed. The agrarian reform essential to ending revolutionary mobilizations had delivered land to villagers whose first interest was to feed their families. They increased production and consumption, had more children, and fed them too. Land reform limited the surpluses sent to urban markets while promoting the population growth that sent migrants to the city. The government pressed villagers to form cooperatives and use chemical fertilizers and pesticides, hoping to generate surpluses. But villagers knew what they wanted from their revolution: autonomy of sustenance and community life, not new, costly, and market-dependent ways to send produce to city consumers. Villagers kept their produce at home and sent their children to the city.[46]

Development planners, promoters of industry, and city people began to see the revolution and its agrarian reform as failures. The regime found a way forward: green revolution. From the start, that program of scientific, mechanized, chemical, often irrigated, and always commercial agriculture focused on urban sustenance. During World War II, Mexican officials, the U.S. government, and the Rockefeller Foundation allied to bring scientists to Mexico to develop hybrid seeds that when combined with chemical fertilizers, herbicides, and pesticides would generate soaring yields on irrigated lands. The early work focused on river bottomlands in the northern regions favored with government irrigation projects and new roads—and far from villagers adamant about their right to land and to consume its produce. The scientists focused on wheat, the staple of the urban middle and upper classes; they left maize, the base of life for the Mexican majority, for later. As a program of agricultural productivity and city sustenance, the green revolution was a great success—bypassing once-revolutionary villagers to feed growing populations. A new capitalist agriculture would feed burgeoning cities.[47]

With the regime consolidated, urban participation constrained, and a new economy of city sustenance begun, the way opened for economic development. From the 1930s through the 1970s, that meant industrialization to make consumer goods for a growing national population. It was an immense challenge in which Mexico had a limited advantage in its nineteenth-century industrial start and in revolutionary nationalist rhetoric. During the Depression, when U.S. industry collapsed, and World War II, when it turned to sustain the military, Mexico found solid industrial expansions to serve growing markets at home—mostly in rising cities. But after the war, as Mexican capital, resources, and markets proved limited while U.S. capital and industries flourished and sought new markets, Mexican industrialization became a project laden with contradictions. Borrowed capital created debts; rural poverty limited markets; protected markets generated inefficiencies; political commitments to organized labor increased costs.[48]

Still, Mexican industries concentrated in Mexico City and flourished for a time. As the city grew more rapidly than the nation, the government promoted investment and infrastructure in the capital; so did leading banks. The national transportation network focused there, a legacy of nineteenth-century rail construction reinforced by twentieth-century road building. Energy resources focused on the city, with petroleum piped from the Gulf coast to suburban refineries. People also concentrated in the capital. Before 1970, permanent migration to Mexico City paralleled temporary migrations to the United States. By that year, the capital area included nearly half of Mexican industrial production and related services. Almost 60 percent of transportation activities focused there, easing access to national markets. The great metropolis held 40 percent of the nation's urban population and an equal share of its nonagricultural production. The capital region was home to nearly 20 percent of Mexico's total population—and to twice its share of industrial investment, output, and related activities.[49]

How could city people not prosper? Government spending on infrastructure reinforced business investment in industry and services to concentrate the most dynamic economic activity in Mexico City. Migrants followed. The concentration of people in the metropolitan zone was only exceeded by the concentration of power and production there. Yet for the majority, life in the city remained a series of everyday challenges.[50] While investment in infrastructure to facilitate production boomed, investment in infrastructures of daily life lagged. The provision of water and drainage, electricity and education remained scarce in barrios home to growing numbers of workers, vendors, and domestics, and the migrants who joined them.

Why? The easy answer is that private and public investment always focused on profit and production, both concentrated in the capital by the regime and the capitalists based there. People pouring into the metropolis and competing for ways to survive could fend for themselves. Their poverty and desperate availability to work for minimal earnings facilitated infrastructure projects and economic expansion; they subsidized national and urban development with low wages and self-help initiatives. There is truth in that understanding; it is a fair description of the trajectory of Mexico City since 1940. But it is only part of the history we need to understand.

The challenge of building a metropolis that grew from 2 million in 1940 to 13 million by 1980 was unprecedented. The regime always knew the importance of providing services: water, sewers, paving, electricity, schools, and more. It funded such infrastructure, but never on pace with explosive urban expansion. Officials insisted that failures were due to lack of funds. Critics responded that politicized powers made choices. Both were (and are) right. National and city officials made politicized choices with persistently insufficient financial resources.

Mexico faced population explosion and extreme urban concentration with structurally deficient economic resources. There were economies of scale and real savings in focusing economic and infrastructure investment in one metropolis. That drove development in Mexico City, drawing a burgeoning population and creating escalating needs for the infrastructure and services essential to urban life. But the regime had few resources left to fund such investment. So it planned, promised, and fulfilled promised plans in limited ways, after 1950 often financed by foreign borrowing. A metro electric rail was finally built; water and sewer works came sooner or later—all funded by loans that fueled cycles of debt crises. The promise of petroleum in the late 1970s led to more borrowing for investment and infrastructure. When the price of crude fell in 1981, Mexico could not pay. Yet important infrastructure was built, and urban neighborhoods did gain schools and services—before everything collapsed in the 1980s.[51]

While many unfortunate decisions were made, the fundamental problem was structural: how to accelerate economic activity to sustain a population that kept multiplying and to pay for unprecedented urban expansion. Investment in production came first, investment in city life second. The brief dream of oil in the late 1970s and the borrowing and building frenzy it provoked revealed the enormity of the challenge; those who led the regime took it on (politically, or course) when they believed they had resources. They soon learned that they did not—that they could not pay to build the livable city they imagined and residents demanded.

All this was negotiated in a political environment of limited participation. The national regime, authoritarian at the top, corporatist in organization, inclusive within limits, and participatory in controlled ways, ruled the Federal District that included Mexico City and the core of the metropolitan population. The president appointed the head of district government; as a result, urban movements had to address national officials. The corporatist organizations that structured participation in the national regime had unequal roles in the city. Chambers of commerce and industry easily promoted entrepreneurial interests via national and city officials. The national labor confederation (CTM) included industrial workers across the metropolis, but it represented them as workers in industries that extended across the nation. As the decades passed it controlled laborers more than it represented them. And it rarely addressed the questions of neighborhood services that shaped workers' lives outside the factories. The national peasant confederation (CNC), pivotal to implementing land reform, pacifying the countryside, sending limited services to rural communities, and holding the regime's base, was not a factor in the city.

The popular sector (CNOP), organized in the 1950s to allow a growing middle class of government bureaucrats and others to gain corporate representation, did focus on Mexico City. But most of its members depended on government employment. Beyond the bureaucrats, middle-class interests proved fragmented.[52] Ultimately, growing middle sectors were key beneficiaries of midcentury developments even as they struggled to remain middle class. They lived an enduring contradiction: depending on the government for education, on its bureaucracy and allied industries for employment, they sought consumer lives modeled on the United States—lives often beyond reach. Most held Catholic principles that cut against the secular ways promoted by the regime.[53] In that bind, Mexico City's middle sectors rarely found ways to press their interests.

The result was a city of constant mobilization, organization, and negotiation, but little representation capable of shaping long-term policies. The city gained limited benefits from a national government that understood how much of the nation lived and worked in the metropolis and that its legitimacy required basic urban viability. Still, as the city grew beyond control, many neighborhoods remained settlements where families struggled in poverty, insecurity, and worse.

In that context, and following long traditions, many of the poorest and most desperate of people took development into their own hands. Barrios built with sanctioned illegality, defined by economic insecurity, and shaped by informalities in housing and services made self-help a way of life—and the base of political mobilizations, negotiations, and pacifications that shaped the chances of millions. Such developments were not new. Land subdivisions of uncertain legality, sanctioned by the powerful, and profiting a few had led to neighborhoods without services and lives locked in informalities in Tepito and other barrios north and east of the center since the liberal privatizations of the 1860s. As people in Tepito carried on near the city center, struggling to incorporate throngs of new rural migrants in the 1940s and after, its history of informality and illegality leavened with self-help was replicated on an unprecedented scale in Ciudad Nezahualcóyotl in the 1960s and 1970s.

Nezahualcóyotl—Neza in everyday city-speak—occupies a vast flat expanse of the drained Lake Texcoco, just east of the airport, outside the Federal District in the state of Mexico.[54] Settlement began informally in the 1950s; perhaps 30,000 people squatted by 1960. The state set regulations requiring subdivisions to provide basic services: paved streets, water, sewer, and electricity. In 1963, Nezahualcóyotl became a municipality. Well-connected interests gained rights to establish large subdivisions. They sold lots to people desperate for a stake in the city, and the population exploded. Former residents of the city center came in numbers equaled by migrants from outlying states. In 1970, Neza had over 500,000 residents, by 1980 over a million.

New subdivisions were sanctioned but rarely gained legally mandated services. Residents got lots on streets that were literally lines in the sand. A few wells provided water, electricity was scare and irregular, and sewage removal was informal. Everything flooded in the annual rainy season. Titles were uncertain: granted by developers who did not live up to the terms of their original ownership. Lots changed hands informally. The construction of Nezahualcóyotl was the essence of sanctioned illegality. People came in astonishing numbers. Sanctioned illegality created neighborhoods and lives shaped by structural informalities—informalities that offered at least marginal opportunities for people facing lives without secure work, regular sources of income, or access to the regime's corporatist structures.

As population concentrated in Mexico City, secure and remunerative employment remained scarce. Labor-saving technologies shaped urban industrial growth; labor-saving cultivation drove rural people to the city and fed them there. A few at the top profited, more in the middle prospered, industrial workers found secure work with solid incomes, while a burgeoning urban majority struggled in the face of scarce work, limited infrastructures, and sparse services.

For millions, neighborhoods like Nezahualcóyotl became a solution. There one could buy a house lot for very little and build a home with family labor and neighbors' help, using materials bought or scavenged as circumstances allowed. The constant arrival of newcomers created economic openings, however small: a woman could make food to sell to neighbors building makeshift homes; others could make or repair clothing, or help with childcare for the few away at regular jobs. A small entrepreneur could sell tools and hardware; another could repair cars that barely ran; others could tap electric lines for themselves and neighbors. Building a city without services, a city of sanctioned illegality and structural informality, allowed desperately poor, insecure, and dependent people to use what little they had—a house lot, work, self-help, and neighborly assistance—to build new lives.

The tradition of mobilizing local efforts coordinated among neighbors to make the best of structural subordination has a long history in rural Mexico. Urban neighborhoods like Tepito and Nezahualcóyotl allowed (and required) city people facing insecure dependence to use what they could to seek small improvements in desperate lives. Cooperation building homes and neighborhoods led to organization to demand that the city, new suburban municipalities, and the developers they sanctioned live up to obligations to provide pavement and drainage, electricity and lighting, water and sewer services, education and health care, and title to lots. The rise of informal organizations demanding services across the city is well known and deeply studied.[55] If effective as an organizer and skilled in engaging local authorities and the party-state, a leader could help gain real benefits for the neighborhood. Many an organizer also found a job in the party or the government, usually away from the original organized neighborhood. Along

the way, neighbors might gain pavement or better water service, longer electric lines, perhaps a school or a clinic—undoubtedly an improvement, yet
never sufficient to resolve underlying difficulties.

An urban politics of organized informality allowed leaders real opportunities and neighborhoods real gains—just enough to keep focus on the
fight for limited improvements and away from any challenge to the regime
or the ruling model of development. Sanctioned illegalities and structured
informalities, usually portrayed as key problems of urban development,
were pivotal (if limiting and polarizing) solutions to the inherent contradictions of capitalist urbanization in a capital-dependent and resource-poor
city and nation in times of explosive population growth. They provided favored entrepreneurs ways to profit; they offered government officials ways
to negotiate popular discontent; they gave millions of struggling city dwellers ways to take what little control they had and make life a bit better. Informality became a central, structural characteristic of the political economy
of the capitalist megacity in a context of limited state resources and constrained economic opportunity—for the nation, the metropolis, and the
people of the barrios. By the early 1980s, Nezahualcóyotl was becoming a
city with services and a settled, if still poor, population. Meanwhile, marginal neighborhoods sprang up farther out, as economic and political crisis
again struck the nation and the metropolis.

Globalizing the Megametropolis, 1980–2000

During the 1960s and 1970s, Mexico faced mounting international debts,
deepening internal inequities, and rising protests among once-favored
sectors, including workers and students now angered by political exclusions. A brief oil export boom created new hope after 1976. Yet it was fueled
by more debt, so when oil prices dropped in 1981 another crash brought
deep recession and challenges to every aspect of Mexican politics and development in the 1980s.[56]

Mexico City's metropolitan challenges contributed to the crisis. Funds
borrowed internationally had built metro lines and water and sewer projects; when oil revenues plummeted debts could not be repaid. City people
who had lived the difficulties of unequal and underfunded development
faced deeper unemployment, declining wages, and delayed services in the
"lost decade" of the 1980s. They turned even more to informal ways of work,
trade, and politics; street venders were everywhere, hawking anything and
everything. Then the 1985 earthquake assaulted the city center, prosperous

enclaves like Condesa and Roma, and working barrios east and south. Apartments, schools, and hospitals collapsed; tens of thousands died, with many thousands more left homeless and unemployed, living in tents and rough shelters in parks and boulevard medians.

In the face of the quake's destruction, the responses of the national regime and the city government it controlled were inadequate, both limited and late. People who had built much of the city by self-help did not hesitate. Young men came independently to devastated neighborhoods, crawling through rubble to rescue survivors. Neighbors pitched in to provide food, clothing, and shelter. Every observer—local, national, and international—concluded that the regime had failed while the people persevered. The system—formality—was condemned; informality and independent action were honored as the saving response that allowed the people of the city to show their strength and solidarity.

There was truth in that understanding but not the whole truth. Much of the infrastructure the regime had built—pressured by neighborhood organizations, to be sure—survived the quake, enabling the celebrated informality that led the response to destruction and the beginning of reconstruction. The metro (costly in part because it was built to survive earthquakes) kept running under crushed neighborhoods and collapsed medical complexes, allowing people to move to survive. Electricity, water, and sewer services faced disruptions but continued in most of the city. In the rush to condemn the regime, its role (however slow, political, and pressured) in building the infrastructure essential to keeping informality and everyday life possible was lost.

What followed is well known. The ever more authoritarian party-regime and its model of national industrial development had lost legitimacy in the face of the 1981 economic crash, as the United States led the world in a rush to globalization. Mexico joined the General Agreement on Tariffs and Trade early in 1985, ending the dream of national industrialization, opening a weak and deeply indebted economy to the power of international capital and the competition of world trade. Poverty and marginality were already entrenched and set to proliferate as the quake struck.

In its wake, there was talk of a democratic opening, but the regime clung to authoritarian power to force trade liberalization and the privatization of state enterprises, generating unemployment to cut costs and pay international creditors—policies euphemized as "structural adjustment." The regime blocked the challenge of Cuauhtémoc Cárdenas, son of the president who had built the regime of national development in the 1930s, guaranteeing the "election" of Carlos Salinas as president in 1988. In office, with the party-regime intact, Salinas broke the power of the unions that had gained at least limited benefits for favored industrial workers.[57] He ended the right of rural communities to *ejido* lands in 1992, opening rural Mexico fully to the winds of world markets, completing the commercialization driven for decades by the green revolution—again accelerating migration to Mexican cities and into the United States.

Having broken the organized power of Mexican workers and villagers (long under siege to be sure), Salinas proposed and negotiated NAFTA, the North America capital and trade block implemented as 1994 began. It aimed to free the movement of capital and goods across borders within North America, linking the Mexican economy to the U.S. and Canada. It aimed to limit the movement of people across the same borders. Yet the legal integration of the economies brought unemployment and displacement across Mexico, stimulating a surge of migration that drew millions of Mexicans into new domains of sanctioned illegality (as employers profited from their work) and informality (as undocumented migrants struggled to live in the shadows) across the United States. Mexicans displaced by globalization rebuilt lives and communities when and where they could.[58]

Only after NAFTA locked in the neoliberal transformation, the PRI engineered another victory in 1994, and Mexicans endured the economic collapse that followed did the regime respond to demands for democratic participation with an electoral opening. The Federal District finally elected a mayor and council in 1997; national democracy was proclaimed in the celebrated opposition win in the presidential election of 2000. Still, the district gained self-government only after half the metropolitan population lived beyond its borders. Formal participation via elections shaped by money and media came only after growth and jurisdictional fragmentation guaranteed that popular voices would be divided and of limited effect.

What did globalization bring to Mexico City and its people? Industry had concentrated there when its role was to produce for Mexican consumers. In the new neoliberal model, the city lost industry and the secure, well-paid union jobs it sustained. To survive in a globalizing world, industries had to serve export markets; new *maquiladoras* stretched along the U.S. border, employing young women for low wages, few benefits, and without union rights. Mexico City shifted to a service economy focused on government, finance, and commerce, A few prospered while most faced poverty and insecurity, whether in formal retail and service employment or in the vast informal sector of self-employment and street vending. Still, the metropolis continued to grow: from 13 million in 1980 to over 15 million in 1990, to approach 20 million by 2000. The city had to accommodate nearly 7 million new people as its economy restructured to maximize informal, low-wage, insecure ways of production.[59]

Why did the city keep growing as its economy collapsed and faced a transformation that limited opportunities for the working majority? In part, population growth resulted from the coming of age of the expanding generations who built the city from 1950 to 1970. Thanks to longer lives, growth continued even as birth rates fell from the 1970s and plummeted in the 1990s. People struggling to survive in the metropolis had smaller families. But small families were ever more numerous and reinforced by continuing arrivals from the countryside. With NAFTA promoting free trade in agriculture (and the U.S. subsidizing its corporate farmers), Mexicans began to rely on staples from U.S. industrial farms. Rural Mexicans migrated north to harvest those crops for low wages or to Mexico City, hoping for a chance in the metropolis.[60]

So the city kept expanding, its people locked in transnational dependency as growing numbers faced marginal lives. Amid a shift from national development and authoritarian mediation toward neoliberal globalization with electoral democratization, metropolitan expansion continued as it had since the nineteenth century: concentrating wealth, power, and comfort; proliferating marginality and informality; leaving families to build neighborhoods through local organization, political mobilizations, and constant, often desperate self-help.

The histories of Ajusco in the 1980s and Valle de Chalco in the 1990s illustrate much. The Sierra de Ajusco rises majestically at the southern end of the basin that contains Mexico City. As 1970s urban development filled the plain below with universities, businesses, and shopping centers along with rich, middle-class, working, and marginal neighborhoods, Ajusco loomed just beyond. It was the last unsettled space in the Federal District, a forested upland close to opportunities for employment and transit links to the wider metropolis. Everyone wanted to settle in Ajusco: the air was cleaner, the forests refreshing, the views spectacular. People rich and poor were ready to invade or buy lands held by land reform communities or the heirs of estate owners. The law prohibited community sales, yet many were ready to profit as urban sprawl came to lands of little agricultural value. Officials opposed expansion in Ajusco. They knew how difficult and costly it would be to provide roads, water, and sewers in rugged highlands; in times of new environmental concern they argued that settlement in Ajusco would cut the forests that made oxygen for an oxygen-thin basin and disrupt the recharge of aquifers needed to sustain the entire metropolis. Ajusco was set aside as an ecological preserve.[61]

Once again, the law created illegalities that became the basis for negotiations among the regime, the powerful, and the desperate poor. Early settlements and attempts to enforce environmental restrictions came in the late 1970s, during the debt-accelerated oil boom that fueled a sense among officials and the populace than anything was possible. Private landlords and community leaders sold land to settlers who got titles that were at best uncertain and often fraudulent. Rich settlers bought official acquiescence and essential services. The destitute banded together to build homes, rough streets, and schools, and to string electricity, to truck in water, even build schools. They mobilized against government attempts to restrict their access, arguing that the ecological ban aimed to keep Ajusco for the rich. They knew the history of city settlement from Tepito to Nezahualcóyotl. Politically connected developers with uncertain rights sold land with minimal services to desperate buyers. Once profits were taken and settlers entrenched, the latter mobilized to defend their occupation and build houses and neighborhoods. Sooner or later, usually later, authorities "regularized" land titles (often increasing profits for developers paid a second time to create clear titles). Officials responded slowly to demands to pave streets, to bring electric, water, sewer, and drainage services, to build schools and medical clinics—in long-contested processes that consolidated neighborhoods and demobilized exhausted residents.

When oil boom turned to debt crisis in the early 1980s, the sequence played out again in Ajusco, with a new environmental language shaping public debates, and little else. Neither a struggling national regime nor city officials had the resources or the political power to change a now-standard process: titles were regularized, often allowing landlords to sell a second time. Settlers stayed in ecological preserves; minimal services slowly came. The government finished and staffed settler-built schools; city programs offered work with political constraints to once-independent community leaders. The slow provision of services was punctuated by festivals celebrating national glories, while globalization reshaped the city and nation. As the national state coped with the turn to neoliberalism and city officials grappled with earthquake damage, Ajusco saw developers profit from illegality while settlers built communities by mobilizing informalities. One key difference shaped Ajusco: the wealthy also coveted its uplands. They too negotiated crisis, illegality, and informality to set their own, often-gated communities not far from entrenched marginal neighborhoods. They look down together at the city below, sharing a unique vantage as neighbors in a polarizing metropolis.

As Ajusco consolidated in the 1980s, settlement surged east toward Valle de Chalco.[62] A first look would suggest they were very different metropolitan fringes. Ajusco was an upland forest coveted by the poor and the prosperous; Valle de Chalco was a dried lake bed southeast of the city, left to the desperate because no one with resources would settle there. Still, there were parallels. Both began with uncertain, often illegal land sales, both generated settler mobilizations that demanded legalization and services, both were built mostly by settler sweat, and in the end, both gained just enough state support to consolidate marginal lives and demobilize popular pressures.

As the last major settlement in the metropolis as the twentieth century ended, Valle de Chalco grew in revealing ways. As national and urban population growth slowed, a majority came from already urbanized zones, including Neza, where services were in place and rents too high for the poorest families. In Valle de Chalco, they could buy a lot and own a piece of the city. They knew they would begin without services, without schools, and far from employment and transit. But they could own a bit of land and build a home with discarded materials and hard work. They could demand water, electricity, and schools from a government promoting privatization and promising to benefit every Mexican—even those building new slums in the dusty lake bed along the highway to Puebla, one of the most visible sites in the nation.

Young men and women starting families went to work; both often joined the economy—a few traveling outside to gain employment, many entering the informal economy that grew again to service the poverty of a new fringe city approaching 300,000 in the early 1990s. They wanted land, the chance to work, and schools for their children. As at Ajusco, settlers endured hardships for a chance at education for the next generation. They knew it was the only way ahead in a de-industrializing metropolis in a globalizing world. Their visibility and their mobilizations got the attention of the Salinas administration as it promoted NAFTA in the early 1990s. The president, promising a new Mexico with the levers of the old authoritarian state, was undermining union power, ending rights to community land, and shrinking programs of social assistance. He insisted that private enterprise would bring prosperity; he knew it would not reach Valle de Chalco any time soon. So he created the National Solidarity Program, targeted at Mexico's most desperate communities, with Valle de Chalco its demonstration site in the metropolis.

National Solidarity brought electricity, water, schools, and medical services more rapidly than usual, but not pavement or sewers. Employment came more slowly. Most production remained in the informal sector; most families worked long hours, juggling childcare with endless work on a dusty urban plain that still flooded dangerously in 1996 when rain came in torrents. Valle de Chalco, like its predecessors, got just enough services to stabilize marginality. Political activity waned, refocused on the fragmented electoral politics of an urban municipality in the state of Mexico at the fringe of a metropolis centered in the Federal District. Meanwhile, families struggled to gain income from marginal participation in a mostly informal economy and hoped that education would offer their children a road forward. Too often, their struggles were marked by gendered violence: young fathers raised to patriarchal presumptions but living without means to provide for families in traditional patriarchal ways hit wives struggling to contribute to household income and thus challenging patriarchal presumptions. Sometimes wives and mothers hit back; too often, fathers and mothers struck children. People locked in marginal lives at the margins of the metropolis, lacking economic opportunities and political openings to better their prospects, lived with everyday violence in family households struggling to survive.[63]

Valle de Chalco did not represent the entire metropolis in 2000. It is important to recognize that as desperate marginality replicated itself there, older neighborhoods from Tepito to Neza to Ajusco consolidated basic services and more bearable ways of urban life.[64] Many city people found meaningful gains in important aspects of their lives. The city has become healthier. The death rate that held at 34 per 1,000 in 1900 fell to under 13 in the 1950s, when antibiotics began to have their effect, and then to less than 5 per 1,000 by 1995. The infant death rate fell from 400 per 1,000 live births in 1900 to 28.5 in 1990, and 22.5 in 1995. Infants lived, and people lived much longer—accounting for most population growth since 1950. Once it was clear that their children would live, women had smaller families. Birth rates that held at 43 per 1,000 to 1970 fell under 24 by 1995. Women had an average of six children in 1970, and only two or three by the 1990s. Population growth slowed from 5.9 percent annually in the 1940s to 5.3 percent in the 1970s, to 4.2 percent in the 1980s—to 1.4 percent from 1995 to 2000. Migration from the countryside keeps the city growing, though at much slower rates than previously. Meanwhile, basic education has become widely available: boys in the city on average complete ten years, girls nine—well above the national averages of 7.5 and 7 years.[65]

Life-preserving medical care, mostly through easy access to pharmaceuticals, is a real gain for city people and the base of the population growth that challenged every other aspect of their lives. Authorities have struggled to provide water and sewers, pavement, electricity, and education to serve burgeoning numbers. Yet over time, in response to neighborhood mobilization and with enormous subsidies from desperate residents' self-help efforts, most of the metropolis gained basic services. Given the enormity of the population growth and its metropolitan dispersal, the accomplishment is impressive.

Yet the metropolis remains a place of deep and enduring inequalities. Extending west from the historic center, the institutions that integrate the city into a globalizing world stretch along the Paseo de la Reforma (the boulevard honoring liberalism now serves neoliberalism). The visitor passes the Bolsa (stock exchange), the old U.S. embassy, and the local headquarters of global banks and brokerages all around. Past Chapultepec Park with its monuments to Mexico's past (the museum dedicated to pre-Hispanic peoples; the monument to the *niños héroes*, cadets who died rather than submit to U.S. invasion; the castle where Spanish viceroys and the tragic Maximilian lived), Reforma's extension rises to reach Santa Fe, the new edge city where the Mexican offices of multinational corporations mix with elegant residences, new universities, posh shopping centers, and a new U.S. embassy complex. A highly visible, unimaginably rich part of Mexico City has become a booming global center.[66]

The old historic center is rebuilding, providing housing for professionals and others in the middle class, and refurbishing many remnants of Mexico's past. The pre-Hispanic Templo Mayor sits between the seventeenth-century cathedral and the palace, once viceregal, now national, that remains the seat of national government. The center proclaims a persistent Mexican nationalism while the city has become a conduit of globalization. Middle-class neighborhoods like Condesa and Roma, built as adjuncts to Porfirian prosperity, crushed in the 1985 earthquake, are now rebuilt as places where the young and hip aim to live and party near globalizing power.[67]

Stretching south along Insurgentes, the avenue honoring the rebels who began Mexico's war for independence, the city's diversity also shines: the intellectual promise of Coyoacán not far from the wealth of San Ángel; the old and prestigious National University near the new and prestigious

Colegio de México; pharmaceutical makers along the Calzada de Tlalpan, just east, with hospitals everywhere. With important overlap, neoliberal Reforma stretches west from the center to link Mexico to the world; the more national Insurgentes stretches south to attend to the medical and educational needs of the city and the nation. Along that long southern stretch of the city, diverse middle- and working-class barrios have consolidated to allow always challenging yet ever more bearable (in Spanish, *soportable*) lives for growing numbers.

Near the National University, in an enclave surrounded by prosperity, Santo Domingo began with land invasion—founded in illegality and forged in years of informality. As lives became more settled and the city changed, families adapted. They became smaller, and in the struggle to sustain them men and women adapted patriarchal ideas as women gained income and men devoted more time and care to their children—especially their sons. Through the 1980s and 1990s, the people of Santo Domingo, like so many others, pressed efforts demanding services and democratization. They made real gains—for their neighborhoods, their children, and the city.[68] The question remains: with basic services and new electoral government, can people in neighborhoods like Santo Domingo continue to influence the powers that rule? Can they find lives beyond struggles for daily survival, energized by hope for their children?

There is evidence that gender norms and family relations are changing, if slowly, across the metropolis. As the economy turned from industry to services, middling and poor families had to send multiple earners to work. More and more women work for income—among the poorest, children work as well. In middle sectors, where women with education gain solid incomes that make everyday life better and increase their children's opportunities, men—especially younger men—have begun accepting more egalitarian households. Among those working to get by day to day, where women's earnings often are small, informal, and insecure, men—even younger men—adapt reluctantly. They accept the necessity of women as earners, but often aim to retain patriarchal prerogatives in daily life. Among the most desperate, as in Valle de Chalco, violence remains too common in families struggling to make lives in the city.[69]

In the late 1990s, as neoliberalism took hold, unemployment proliferated, marginality spread outward, and democracy remained an uncertain promise, a wave of violent crime took the streets of Mexico City. Muggings, robberies, kidnappings, violent assaults, and homicides nearly tripled to reach new heights and fan rising fears. As the wave peaked, armed guards seemed everywhere, offering new employment to those ready to risk their lives to protect others' property and prosperity. With democratization in the Federal District in 1997 and in the national government in 2000, followed by a new time of economic expansion, crime waned in the metropolis—dropping back to a level still nearly twice what it was before the turn to globalization via NAFTA mixed deindustrialization with the spread of informality, insecurity, and marginality.[70]

The metropolis entered the twenty-first century learning to live with recently reduced, yet still historically high, levels of crime. A newly expanded presence of police forces, public and private, aimed to protect city powers and people from crime, yet too often lived in symbiotic engagements with criminal elements—some organized, many informal, all structurally entrenched in the globalized city.[71] Meanwhile, drug cartels forged a dynamic new economy built on illegality and violence in producing zones near the Pacific and transshipment areas along the U.S. border—a structural illegality driven by unabated demand for marijuana, cocaine, and opioids in the United States. People in Mexico City abhor that violence and quietly appreciate that it has not focused on their metropolis.

Along the way, a celebrated democratization came to the city. The people in the Federal District now vote for a mayor and assembly, along with local delegation officials. Formally renamed La Ciudad de México, the residents of the long dependent district have gained a level of political autonomy backed by an urban constitution to negotiate uncertain times. Yet more than half the people of the metropolis live in the state of Mexico. As urban growth and sprawl continue, people live with a fragmented electoral politics, voting for local leaders and national deputies, some for a state governor, others for the head of city government. All can vote for president—in elections not all believe are free of the influence of power and manipulation (as when Mexico City leader Andrés Manuel López Obrador, then of the opposition PRD, lost the presidency in 2006). Still, electoral politics have claimed the public space while the informal mobilizations long essential to gaining city services have waned. Do elections offer new, more meaningful participation and ways for struggling families and communities to better their lives? Or do they deflect popular energy to domains controlled by established institutions and ruled by power and money?

Of course, only parts of peoples' struggles to survive in the city—important domains of infrastructure and education, services and policing—are shaped in the political arena. The financial institutions concentrated along Reforma and in Santa Fe transmit the power of global financial centers, tying Mexico and its metropolis to a neoliberal world. They coordinated the shift of Mexican industry and agriculture to serve the United States; they rule Mexicans' access to food and other goods from the U.S. and across the globe via Walmart and other distributors. The bankers, financiers, lawyers, accountants, and publicists who tie Mexico to the world rule a commercial-service economy that brings them great wealth while structuring the limited chances for prosperity and survival available across the metropolis. There is no participatory representation in the structure and implementation of globalization.

A more formal commercial-service economy stretches south along Insurgentes and parallel boulevards named Revolución, Universidad, and Tlalpan. It sells education, medical care, and consumer goods to a growing middle class. That metropolitan middle sustains the transnational economy, the national government, and the national subsector of the global economy. Its participants and their families are often prosperous, usually comfortable, yet rarely secure. They cannot approach the wealth of their neighbors who directly serve global integration.

A less prosperous, sometimes formal, often informal service economy is everywhere. It includes retail clerks and restaurant staff to serve the transnational sector and the metropolitan middle class. It includes innumerable street venders, repairmen, and women who clean homes and watch others' children. It is a growing sector, probably including a majority in the metropolis, mixing formal work for marginal wages with informal activities that define lives of marginality. In this spreading service economy, people just survive. They serve the sectors above them, literally by providing inexpensive goods and services, structurally by surviving in such deep poverty that they hold down wages and expectations—keeping Mexico "competitive" in a world economy racing to concentrate power and profit while generating poverty and insecurity.

In the 1980s and 1990s, Mexicans in general, and often led by the people of Mexico City, rose in emphatic movements demanding an effective democratization that many believed would be the first step toward greater social justice. They gained much, including the end of one-party rule and new electoral participation.[72] Yet there were sharp limits to their gains, notably in realms of economic opportunity and social justice.[73] The spike of crime and violence was contained at the cost of expanding forces of social coercion. Again, this time on a national scale yet with Mexico City in the lead, popular efforts claimed important yet limited gains—and then faced exhaustion. Popular exertions receded, enabling the continuing concentration of wealth and power, built on enduring inequities and injustices, and marked by persistent corrosive violence and limited efforts at police containment.[74]

Into the Twenty-First Century

The largest and most powerful city in Mesoamerica in 1500, then the largest and most globally important center in the Americas in 1800, Mexico City began the twentieth century as a national capital struggling to find a role in a world of industrial capitalism ruled by the United States. A decade of revolution set the city and nation in search of a more national capitalism after 1920. In the process, the nation accelerated the adoption of labor-saving industrial and agricultural practices, while the population soared thanks to the gains of medical capitalism. Mexico's burgeoning capital experienced a population explosion, while industrialization limited employment. Later, globalization via NAFTA drained the city of industrial work, leaving a service economy marked by lives of insecurity and marginality—while the population continued to grow. In this long history, urban communities turned repeatedly to self-help and local mobilizations to make lives minimally sustainable in the face of deepening inequities shaped by dependent insecurities. Popular efforts made the city more livable, yet never threatened the concentrations of power that were political and industrial in times of national capitalism, then political and financial under globalization.

From the 1990s, neoliberal development via NAFTA deepened polarizations, while electoral democratization dampened popular mobilizations.[75] Marginality, informality, illegality, and violence spread. When promised jobs did not come to Mexico, Mexicans trekked to the United States. As the legal investment of international capital did not make Mexicans prosperous, illegal capital taken in U.S. drug markets backed by guns bought in U.S. arms markets combined to make Mexico more violent. Millions in the diverse and unequal neighborhoods of the Mexico City metropolis continued to struggle for decent lives. They resisted migration to the United States and avoided the worst of the drug wars. Can globalizing capitalism and a Mexican regime that serves its interests find the will, ways, and means to enable such resilient people to claim more secure, prosperous, sustainable lives?

As the twenty-first century began, a brief moment of cooperation between newly elected presidents Vicente Fox and George W. Bush (whose foreign policy experience as Texas governor focused on Mexico) brought conversations about turning NAFTA from a pact freeing capital and trade to a more European-style union that might free people to move and work as they saw best for their families. However promising or improbable, the possibility of a deeper union closed when the September 11, 2001, attacks on the institutions and symbols of globalizing finance and military power in the U.S. turned the global hegemon inward and fueled a rising xenophobia. Soon, the U.S. government pressed Mexico's leaders to undertake a "war on drugs"—while the United States did nothing to curb the demand that drove the drug economy, sold arms to the Mexican military (legally and formally), and armed the transnational cartels (often illegally and surely profitably). Mexico was blamed for the U.S. drug crisis and maligned as violent while the economy of drug production, transportation, marketing, and consumption carried on unhindered.[76]

Then, in 2008, the U.S. economy crashed. A financial bubble built as the U.S. invaded and occupied Iraq burst, sending waves of unemployment and insecurity across North America that soon struck Mexico and its capital. In 2009, the H1N1 swine flu emerged in Mexico and spread globally—striking Mexico City hard, closing the city for weeks. Again, Mexico and Mexicans were maligned in the U.S. media as the cause of plaguing problems, until it became evident that the virus had jumped from swine to humans at a U.S. owned and operated hog operation east of the capital. Suddenly, an understanding of the complexities of globalization became the order of the day. The flu scare passed. The U.S. government bailed out the global financiers and the economy of North America revived slowly through difficult years. Concentrations of wealth, proliferations of insecurity, and corrosive violence carried on as Mexico City resumed its uncontrolled expansion.

As crisis waned and the mix of concentrating wealth and insecurity continued to mark North American lives, many in the United States looked again to scapegoat Mexico and Mexicans. Donald Trump won the presidency in 2016 arguing that breaking NAFTA and blocking migration from Mexico would make life better for those pummeled by U.S. deindustrialization and the corrosion of middle-class lives. Under Trump's presidency, nationalist rhetoric shapes politics as economic integration keeps economics and lives inseparable. Concentrations of wealth and power continue apace in both nations; both generate growing populations grappling with lost dreams and new insecurities. People in the United States, on average, live materially better lives than most Mexicans, whose low wages still subsidize transnational profits and middle-class consumption. Frustrated U.S. voters complain of cars made in Mexico costing U.S. jobs, and of Mexicans coming to the United States to labor in fields, yards, restaurants, and construction projects. Such visions mask more complex realities. Mexicans assemble cars made of U.S. parts. Mexicans work in U.S. fields, hired by U.S. corporations who rule the food production that sustains the United States, Mexico, and much of the world. Meanwhile, avocados, tomatoes, strawberries, and more grown in Mexican fields by Mexican hands profit U.S. corporations delivering fresh food to consumers across North America. Walmart profits selling food, clothing, appliances, and more to U.S. and Mexican consumers equally dependent on global supply chains. Is separation surgery possible in 2018? Can anyone foresee its consequences?

Mexico City, 2017–2018: Boom, Concentration, and Marginality

I returned to the city in March 2018, six months after the earthquake of September 2017, ten years after the global crash of 2008–09, four months before presidential elections might change Mexican politics—or not. Political conversations in the media and on the streets were all about candidates and corruptions—endless debates that have led to little meaningful change in the lives of people in the city and across the nation. Politics seemed structured to generate stalemate.

Patterns of concentration and marginality persist. The skeletons of new skyscrapers under construction again mark the Paseo de la Reforma and the boulevards stretching south, built to accommodate the needs of international financial, commercial, legal, and service enterprises. Wealth and power build their monuments, with the latest electronic security to ensure that only the right people enter. Yet scattered nearby, structures left shaken by the latest quake stand sealed off and unrepaired. Fine restaurants serve international fare to those who can pay, while on the nearby sidewalks vendors sell the foods of everyday Mexico. Vendors claim a marginal living; customers eat quick lunches they can afford. And the vendors and their customers appear favored among the ragged, often disabled men and women who beg on street corners and at subway entrances. On the trains, more vendors hawk cheap wares, from combs to gum to pirated movies and music. Displaced youth are joined by fathers and sons, mothers and daughters all aiming to claim bits of income. Above, on the streets, every intersection is patrolled by men and boys washing windshields, claiming a few pesos to stay alive in a city of riches and scarcity.

People facing dearth and insecurity do what they can to live. The September 19, 2017, earthquake, fortunately, was a pale facsimile of its catastrophic 1985 predecessor. Still, the quake shook everyone—literally—and hundreds of deaths and thousands of collapsed buildings took a real toll. As in 1985, city and national authorities lacked the resources and organization to respond. The people did not hesitate. Young men risked death to dig out survivors; everyone aided the injured, fed the hungry, keeping neighborhoods and the city alive. The people who built the city with their own hands will not let it crumble.

In the face of election theatrics, popular voices also still demand to be heard. On March 6, 2018, a parade of indigenous peoples stretched for blocks along the Paseo de la Reforma, passing the monuments to global capitalism on their way to the national palace. Thousands carried banners demanding justice for disappeared students, rights for native peoples, and affordable food and energy, gasoline and diesel, for all. As life urbanizes, indigenous peoples concentrate in the capital. Their needs parallel those of the multicultural poor: jobs with fair earnings; health care, education, and other services for families and children; and basic food at affordable prices. A poster placed in metro rail cars revealed the authorities' response: announcing that city people speak fifty-five of Mexico's sixty-eight indigenous languages, they call for public recognition of native linguistic rights— without addressing the scarcity of jobs, income, and services that plague all the urban poor, the scarcities that focused the demands of the marchers in the streets.

The polarizing trajectory of Mexico City in a globalizing world persists. Power concentrates, people in the middle juggle to hold prosperity, and vast numbers struggle to survive and sustain families and communities in the face of dependence, insecurities, and marginality. Corrosive violence still marks too many lives. In that context, Andrés Manuel López Obrador won a sweeping victory in the July 2018 presidential elections. He promised an economy that serves the people along with social justice, political participation, and a reduction in social, political, and cartel violence. The question remains: when inaugurated can AMLO with his broad base of political and popular support effect such change in the city he once led as mayor and the nation he has a mandate to transform? The political will is clear. Yet the metropolis and nation that share a name remain locked into a global economy built to entrench polarities. In the coming years, Mexico and its capital will offer a test case of the possibilities and limits of life under urbanizing globalization.

Notes

1. This relationship is a central emphasis of John Tutino, *The Mexican Heartland: How Communities Shaped Capitalism, a Nation, and World History, 1500–2000* (Princeton, NJ: Princeton University Press, 2017). That study along with Enrique Cárdenas Sánchez, *El largo curso de la economía Mexicana: De 1780 a nuestros días* (Mexico City: Fondo de Cultura Económica, 2015) provide essential context and orientation for this analysis. Chapter 13 of *The Mexican Heartland* on "Building the Metropolis: Mexico City, 1940–1970" contributed much to my development of this larger overview of the long challenges faced by people in Mexico's capital city.

2. See Inga Clendinnen, *Aztecs* (Cambridge: Cambridge University Press, 2000); Ross Hassig, *Trade, Tribute, and Transportation: The Sixteenth-Century Political Economy of Mexico* (Norman: University of Oklahoma Press, 1985; and Ángel Palerm, *Obras hidraúlicas prehispánicas en el valle de México* (Mexico City: INAH, 1973).

3. This analysis follows Alfred Crosby's classic *Columbian Exchange* (Westport, CT: Greenwood Press, 1972).

4. On the reconstruction of the city under Spanish rule, see Barbara Mundy, *The Death of Aztec Tenochtitlan, the Life of Mexico City* (Austin: University of Texas Press, 2015).

5. This overview of Mexico City in the era of silver capitalism synthesizes Tutino, *The Mexican Heartland*, Part 1, in the context of Tutino, *Making a New World: Founding Capitalism in the Bajío and Spanish North America* (Durham, NC: Duke University Press, 2011).

6. My views of the seventeenth-century city are shaped by J. I. Israel, *Race, Class, and Politics in Colonial Mexico* (Oxford: Oxford University Press, 1975); Louisa Hoberman, *Mexico's Merchant Elite: Silver, State, and Society, 1590–1660* (Durham, NC: Duke University Press, 1991); and Brian Owensby, *Empire of Law and Indian Justice in Colonial Mexico* (Stanford: Stanford University Press, 2008).

7. Natalia Silva Prada, *La política de una rebelión: Los indígenas frente al tumulto de 1692 en la ciudad de México* (Mexico City: Colegio de México, 2007).

8. See John Tutino, *Mexico City, 1808: Power, Sovereignty, and Silver in an Age of War and Revolution* (Albuquerque: University of New Mexico Press, 2018).

9. John Tutino, "The Revolution in Mexican Independence: Insurgency and the Renegotiation of Property, Production, and Patriarchy in the Bajío, 1800–1855," *Hispanic American Historical Review* 78, no. 3 (1998): 367–488.

10. On Mexico's emergence after silver capitalism, see Tutino, *Mexican Heartland*, ch. 6.

11. Personal communication from Louise Walker, based on her new research on life in the city.

12. See Sonia Pérez Toledo, *Los hijos del trabajo: Los artesanos de la ciudad de México, 1780–1853* (Mexico City: Colegio de México, 1996); and Luis Fernando Granados, *Sueñan las piedras* (Mexico City: Ediciones Era, 2003).

13. The decades of early national struggles are detailed in Tutino, *The Mexican Heartland*, ch. 6–8.

14. See Carlos Illades, *Hacia la república del trabajo: La organización artesanal en la ciudad de México, 1853–1876* (Mexico City: Colegio de México, 1996); Mario Trujillo Bolio, *Operarios fabriles en el valle de México, 1864–1884* (Mexico City: Colegio de México, 1996); Sergio Miranda Pacheco, *Tacubaya: De suburbio veraniego a ciudad* (Mexico City: UNAM, 2007); and Claudia Agostoni, *Monuments of Progress: Modernization and Public Health in Mexico City, 1876–1910* (Calgary: University of Calgary Press, 2003).

15. See Jan Bazant, *The Alienation of Church Wealth in Mexico: Social and Economic Aspects of the Liberal Revolution, 1856–1875*, trans. Michael Costeloe (Cambridge: Cambridge University Press, 1971).

16. Ernesto Aréchiga Córdoba, *Tepito: Del antiguo barrio de indios al arrabal* (Mexico City: Ed. Uníos, 2003).

17. Miranda Pacheco, *Tacubaya*, 88–95.

18. This synthesizes Aréchiga Córdoba, *Tepito*; Illades, *Hacia la república del trabajo*; and Trujillo Bolio, *Operarios fabriles*.

19. Ariel Rodríguez Kuri, *La experiencia olvidada: El Ayuntamiento de México, política y gobierno, 1876–1912* (Mexico City: Colegio de México, 1996).

20. Miranda Pacheco, *Tacubaya*, 145–165; Rodríguez Kuri, *Experiencia olvidada*, 151–174.

21. Rodríguez Kuri, *Experiencia olvidada*, 92–96.

22. This is detailed in Aréchiga Córdoba, *Tepito*.

23. Agostoni, *Monuments of Progress*, 24.

24. Aréchiga Córdoba, *Tepito*, is the key source. For a new study of the historical roots of Tepito's black market, see Andrew Konove, *Black Market Capital: Urban Politics and the Shadow Economy in Mexico City* (Oakland, CA: University of California Press, 2018).

25. Marie Eileen Francois, *A Culture of Everyday Credit: Pawnbroking and Governance in Mexico City, 1750–1920* (Lincoln: University of Nebraska Press, 2006).

26. Susie Porter, *Working Women in Mexico City: Public Discourses and Material Conditions, 1879–1931* (Tucson: University of Arizona Press, 2003).

27. Agostoni, *Monuments of Progress*, 67, 115–153.

28. Agostoni, *Monuments of Progress*, 27, 75.

29. Rodríguez Kuri, *Experiencia olvidada*, 143.

30. See Vera Candiani, *Dreaming of Dry Land: Environmental Transformation in Colonial Mexico City* (Stanford: Stanford University Press, 2014).

31. Agostoni, *Monuments of Progress*, 115–153, details the triumph. For a new analysis of Mexico City's water challenges from Porfirian times into the postrevolutionary decades, see Matthew Vitz, *City on a Lake: Urban Political Ecology and the Growth of Mexico City* (Durham, NC: Duke University Press, 2018).

32. Rodríguez Kuri, *Experiencia olvidada*, 118–123, 128–133.

33. Rodríguez Kuri, *Experiencia olvidada*, 151–215.

34. Rodríguez Kuri, *Experiencia olvidada*, 14, 72–78.

35. Rodríguez Kuri, *Experiencia olvidada*, 130; Agostoni, *Monuments of Progress*, 77–114.

36. On the revolution around the capital, see Tutino, *The Mexican Heartland,* ch. 9–10.

37. On the city in revolution, see John Lear, *Workers, Neighbors, and Citizens: The Revolution in Mexico City* (Lincoln: University of Nebraska Press, 2001); Pablo Piccato, *City of Suspects: Crime in Mexico City, 1900–1931* (Durham, NC: Duke University Press, 2001); and Katherine Bliss, *Compromised Positions: Prostitution, Public Health, and Gender Politics in Revolutionary Mexico City* (State College: Pennsylvania State University Press, 2002).

38. Tutino, *The Mexican Heartland,* ch. 10.

39. See chapter 1, Table 1.1.

40. Lear, *Workers, Neighbors, and Citizens.*

41. From Pani, *La higiene en México* (1916), cited in Agostoni, *Monuments of Progress,* 149–152.

42. On political economy, see Sergio Miranda Pacheco, *La creación del Departamento del Distrito Federal: Urbanización, política, y cambio institucional* (Mexico City: UNAM, 2008); on the radical utopia, see Mauricio Tenorio Trillo, *I Speak of the City: Mexico City at the Turn of the Twentieth Century* (Chicago: University of Chicago Press, 2013).

43. On Cárdenas and the post-revolutionary regime, see Nora Hamilton, *The Limits of State Autonomy: Post-Revolutionary Mexico* (Princeton, NJ: Princeton University Press, 1982); and Adolfo Gilly, *El cardenismo: Una utopía mexicana* (Mexico City: Cal y Arena, 1994). On post-revolutionary industry, see Susan Gauss, *Made in Mexico: Regions, Nation, and the State in the Rise of Mexican Industrialism, 1920s to 1940s* (University Park: Pennsylvania State University Press, 2011). On the limits of Cárdenas's power, see Ben Fallaw, *Religion and State Formation in Post-Revolutionary Mexico* (Durham, NC: Duke University Press, 2013).

44. Diane Davis, *Urban Leviathan: Mexico City in the Twentieth Century* (Philadelphia: Temple University Press, 1994) remains a key study.

45. See Luis Medina, *Hacia un nuevo estado* (Mexico City: Fondo de Cultura Económica, 1995); and Elisa Servín, *Ruptura y oposición: El movimiento henriquista, 1945–1954* (Mexico City: Cal y Arena, 2001).

46. Guillermo de la Peña, *A Legacy of Promises: Agriculture, Politics, and Ritual in the Morelos Highlands of Mexico* (Austin: University of Texas Press, 1982); and Arturo Warman, *We Come to Object: The Peasants of Morelos and the National State,* trans. Stephen Ault (Baltimore: Johns Hopkins University Press, 1980).

47. The classic study is Cynthia Hewitt de Alcántara, *Modernizing Mexican Agriculture: Socioeconomic Implications of Technical Change* (Geneva: UN Research Institute for Social Development, 1976).

48. See Tutino, *The Mexican Heartland,* ch. 11.

49. On the concentration of industry in Mexico City, see Gustavo Garza, *El proceso de industrialización en la ciudad de México* (Mexico City: Colegio de México, 1985). On road building, see Benjamin Fulwider, "Driving the Nation," Ph.D. dissertation, Georgetown University, 2009.

50. This is powerfully illustrated for the 1950s in Oscar Lewis, *The Children of Sánchez* (New York: Knopf, 1961).

51. Davis, *Urban Leviathan*, shows how city infrastructure projects built debts that helped crash the system.

52. This understanding of city politics depends on Davis, *Urban Leviathan*.

53. My understanding of the middle class relies on Emilio Coral, "The Mexico City Middle Class, 1940–1970: Between Tradition, the State, and the United States," Ph.D. dissertation, Georgetown University, 2011; and Louise Walker, *Waking from the Dream: Mexico's Middle Classes After 1968* (Stanford: Stanford University Press, 2013).

54. Carlos Vélez-Ibañez, *Rituals of Marginality: Politics, Process, and Culture Change in Urban Central Mexico, 1969–1974* (Berkeley: University of California Press, 1983); Fernando Palma Galván, *La participación social en la planeación de desarrollo urbano: Caso Nezahualcoyotl, Estado de México* (Mexico City: UNAM, 2007).

55. See Vélez-Ibañez, *Rituals of Marginality*; Wayne Cornelius, *Politics and the Migrant Poor in Mexico City* (Stanford: Stanford University Press, 1975); and Susan Eckstein, *The Poverty of Revolution: The State and the Urban Poor in Mexico* (Princeton, NJ: Princeton University Press, 1977).

56. See the essays in Elisa Servín, Leticia Reina, and John Tutino, eds., *Cycles of Conflict, Centuries of Change: Crisis, Reform, and Revolution in Mexico* (Durham, NC: Duke University Press, 2007); Walker, *Waking from the Dream*; and Stephen Haber et al., *Mexico Since 1980* (New York: Cambridge University Press, 2008).

57. Dan LaBotz, *The Mask of Democracy: Labor Suppression in Mexico Today* (Boston: South End Press, 1992).

58. See Rubén Hernández-León, *Metropolitan Migrants: The Migration of Urban Mexicans to the United States* (Berkeley, CA: University of California Press, 2008; and Rubén Martínez, *Crossing Over: A Mexican Family on the Migrant Trail* (New York: Picador, 2002

59. See Peter Ward's superb synthesis, first published in English in 1989, then revised and updated in Spanish as *México megaciudad: Dearrollo y política, 1970–2002* (Zinacatepec: El Colegio Mexiquense, 2004), supplemented on production and labor by Edith María Pacheco Gómez Muñoz, *Ciudad de México, heterogénea y desigual: Un estudio sobre el mercado de trabajo* (Mexico City: Colegio de México, 2004).

60. For a critical long-term view of the green revolution, see Angus Wright, *The Death of Ramón González: The Modern Agricultural Dilemma* (Austin: University of Texas Press, 1990).

61. See Keith Pezzoli, *Human Settlements and Planning for Environmental Sustainability: The Case of Mexico City* (Cambridge: Massachusetts Institute of Technology Press, 1998).

62. This brief synthesis depends upon Daniel Hiernaux, "La expansión metropolitana y las estructuras regionales: El Valle de Chalco el la actualidad," in *Entre lagos y volcanes: Chalco Amecameca, pasado y presente*, ed. Alejandro Tortolero, vol. I (Zinacatepec: Colegio Mexiquense, 1993), 575–598; Alicia Lindón Villoria, *De la trama de la cotidianidad a los modos de vida urbanos: El Valle de Chalco* (Mexico City: Colegio de México, 1999); and Martha Rebeca Herrera Bautista and Patricia Molinar

Palma, *En el silencio de su soledad: La reproducción de la violencia intrafamiliar* (Mexico City: Juan Pablos, 2006).

63. This is my reading of the research and analysis reported in Herrera Bautista and Molinar Palma, *En el silencio de la soledad*.

64. See Emilio Duhau, "The Informal City: An Enduring Slum or a Progressive Habitat?" in *Cities from Scratch: Poverty and Informality in Urban Latin America*, ed. Brodwyn Fisher, Bryan McCann, and Javier Auyero (Durham, NC: Duke University Press, 2014), 150–169.

65. Olga Lorena Rojas, *Paternidad y vida familiar en la Ciudad de México* (Mexico City: Colegio de México, 2008), 81–83

66. See Saskia Sassen, *Cities in a World Economy*, 3rd ed. (Thousand Oaks, CA: Pine Forge Press, 2006).

67. See David Lida, *First Stop in the New World: Mexico City, the Capital of the Twenty-First Century* (New York: Riverhead Books, 2008).

68. This is explored in detail in Matthew Gutmann, *The Meanings of Macho: Being a Man in Mexico City* (Berkeley: University of California Press, 1996) and *The Romance of Democracy: Compliant Defiance in Contemporary Mexico* (Berkeley: University of California Press, 2002).

69. On historic patriarchy, see Steve Stern, *The Secret History of Gender* (Chapel Hill: University of North Carolina Press. 1996); and Tutino, *Making a New World*. On patriarchy and family violence in Mexico City, see Gutmann, *Meanings of Macho*; Herrera Bautista and Molinar Palma, *En el silencio*; and Rojas, *Paternidad*.

70. Arturo Alvarado Mendoza, *El tamaño del infierno: Un estudio de sobre la criminalidad en la Zona Metropolitana de la Ciudad de México* (Mexico City: Colegio de México, 2012). The key table is Cuadro 2, 90.

71. This, too, is detailed in Alvarado Mendoza, *El tamaño del infierno*.

72. For a synthesis, see Guillermo de la Peña, "Civil Society and Popular Resistance: Mexico at the End of the Twentieth Century," in *Cycles of Conflict*, ed. Servín et al., 305–345.

73. Enrique Semo, "The Left in the Neoliberal Era," in *Cycles of Conflict*, ed. Servín et al., 346–362. Semo offers a scholarly insider's analysis of the demise of the revolutionary option and the limits on popular power in the electoral domain.

74. This is also emphasized by Pezolli, *Human Settlements*.

75. In *Hard Times in the Marvelous City: From Dictatorship to Democracy in the Favelas of Rio de Janeiro* (Durham, NC: Duke University Press, 2014), Bryan McCann details how electoral democratization constrained popular movements.

76. See Sam Quiñones, *Dreamland: The True Tale of America's Opiate Epidemic* (New York: Bloomsbury Press, 2015). It focuses on social disintegration in the U.S., transnational production and marketing, and the limited responses of U.S. authorities, deemphasizing cartels to explore drugs and violence on both sides of the border.

3 The Arc of Formality
in Twentieth-Century Rio de Janeiro

・・

BRYAN McCANN

Rio de Janeiro has always been ahead of the curve, although not always in the best ways. Rio has led the developing world through several traumatic urban transitions. The contrast between stately public buildings in cosmopolitan business districts and sprawling, unserviced slums nearby became unmistakably evident in Rio earlier than it did in places like São Paulo and Buenos Aires, for example, where self-built housing for the poor was for the most part pushed farther to the periphery. Rio's political powers experimented both with localized eviction and then large-scale favela removal projects a generation ahead of their peers in places like Lima and Mexico City. Partly as a result, residents of such neighborhoods learned to mobilize as communities and activate political networks to protect their urban stake sooner than their counterparts across Latin America. And planners in Rio de Janeiro turned to slum upgrading and titling programs as attempted solutions to the problems of informality well before planners in cities like Mumbai and Johannesburg. Early manifestations of such programs date from the 1940s in Rio de Janeiro, and they became the decisive urban strategy beginning in the 1980s. As a result, Rio has been a laboratory for urban trial and error in the Global South. Consequently, close investigation of Rio's history in this regard illuminates both local and global transitions.

At every stage of Rio de Janeiro's twentieth-century history, development in the formal sector—like the creation of new neighborhoods by private developers, publicly funded infrastructural expansion, and the construction of factories—triggered growth in what we now describe as the informal sector—primarily consisting of housing built by the people who intended to occupy it, without recourse to any legal registry, and work done off the books, beyond the reach of labor law. This parallel relationship has been neither equivalent nor steady. Instead, a staggered arc of formalization stretched across the twentieth century, with formality rising over the first five decades of the century, reaching a peak under the military dictatorship in the 1960s and 1970s, and then giving way to new manifestations of informality as democratization came with globalization in the 1980s and beyond.

In the second decade of the twenty-first century, employment in the formal sector has once again started to rise, slowly and haltingly. In the housing sector, informal growth continues to outpace formal development, notwithstanding new legislation and policies designed to incorporate existing informal housing into the formal sphere. These recent trends give some basis for hope, but do not mark a departure from Rio's longer history of conjoined formal and informal growth. Analysis of the way that growth unfolded over the course of the twentieth century provides the necessary context for any analysis of Rio's current policies, as well as their opportunities and limitations.

In the nineteenth century, most labor happened outside formal labor codes, and a significant portion of urban housing was unregistered in any property deeds. Formalizing measures began in the first decades of the twentieth century as Rio consolidated its transition from imperial court to capital of the new republic founded in 1889. They picked up speed and gained new inflections during the turn to national development in the 1930s, under Getúlio Vargas's Estado Novo in the 1940s, and then continued through the populist democratic years and the military dictatorship that followed in 1964. Both employment and housing were largely formalized during this span. Heavy industrial enterprises, including those in Rio's construction industry, developed a close reliance on the state and vice versa, ensuring that most of the region's growth in employment and housing would fall within the state's purview.

Yet even at its high-water mark in the 1960s, rising formalization never contained informal growth, and deliberate attempts to eradicate informal labor and housing always created new informalities. With redemocratization in the 1980s, the informal sector burgeoned and formality retreated. The resurgence of informality had three primary causes. First, Rio de Janeiro deindustrialized—a clear parallel with Mexico City as both faced the new globalization—and jobs that disappeared from the formal industrial sector were partially replaced by irregular work in the informal service sector. Second, popular movements against favela eradication and against crackdowns on informal commerce found proponents in the newly pluralistic electoral arena. Over time, these popular movements and their political representatives proved generally successful in warding off renewed threats of eviction or suppression. But they proved unsuccessful in guaranteeing full protection under the law. Instead, they reinforced the informal sector, in ways that offered some opportunities to the urban poor, while also imposing some costs upon them. Third, over the course of the 1990s, Brazil, following global patterns evident across the Americas, pulled back on the reins of state intervention. As a result, many new economic ventures, both productive and predatory, grew outside the formal sphere.

At every stage, the trajectory of informality responded to large-scale economic transitions and local social mobilization. Rio industrialized less during the decades focused on national development, and then deindustrialized under globalization, because other Brazilian cities, like the municipalities on the periphery of metropolitan São Paulo, produced more efficiently and established strategic connections to national and international consumers. Having lost its status as the national capital to Brasília in 1960, Rio de Janeiro progressively lost political leverage on a national scale. Hemispheric shifts in production, consumption, and marketing, similarly, projected Rio de Janeiro as a tourist destination while shifting manufacturing and industrial production elsewhere.

Meanwhile, despite deindustrialization, Rio continued to draw migrants expelled by drought, population growth, and the mechanization of agriculture from other parts of Brazil, and this expanding urban population required employment and housing. The city's economy, oriented increasingly toward tourism and a middle-class real estate sector, proved incapable of responding to these needs. The city's political structure proved only slightly more accommodating, largely consigning the urban poor to clientelistic roles, negotiating political support for city council members and state representatives. In return, they received minimal infrastructural investment and, less frequently, some access to public employment. More commonly, they were granted mere tolerance for their presence and their manifold strategies of eking out a living in the city. Almost inevitably, both this presence and the labor strategies that went with it failed to conform to modernist housing and labor codes that envisioned a more orderly, disciplined city. As a result, the urban poor were largely consigned to informality of housing and labor.

Whenever the political context allowed, the urban poor mobilized to demand infrastructure, services and employment. These periodic mobilizations regularly revived hopes of a more democratic and inclusive city, and have yielded important gains. (The massive protests of 2013, initially triggered by rising bus fares, are a recent example.) They too, however, have become part of the way the city reproduces itself, of the way the formal versus informal divide may shift expressions but continues to perpetuate itself.

The persistence and renewed expansion of the informal sector came as a surprise to many *cariocas*, who assumed that favelas and *camelôs*, or sidewalk vendors, were aspects of the premodern city that would be subsumed and replaced by the modern city. In recent years, *cariocas* have had to grapple with the unavoidable recognition that these phenomena are more prominent than ever, and that the idea that an imagined formal city would gradually overtake its informal counterpart may have been obscuring the way the *real* city works. What in Rio's urban DNA has driven the long cycle of push and pull between formal and informal that underlies much of the city's economy and its patterns of occupation? Why has attempted formalization always driven renewed informal expansion? And how can a consideration of these questions move us beyond a limiting binary perspective of formal versus informal, toward a greater appreciation of the way Rio actually functions?

Over the last decade, such questions have given rise to a renewed attempt to "formalize" Rio. In some cases, this involves the salutary practice of recognizing long-standing informal practices and making them legal—renewing attempts to confer property title on long-standing favela residences, for example. In others, it involves a crackdown on informal employment that overlooks the way that such employment responds to and reflects deep needs within the city. When attempts at formalization ignore the needs served by informal methods, they tend to fail. Predictably, this most recent wave of formalizing energy has created winners and losers and provoked strong mobilization in response. It has not fundamentally altered the way the city functions.

This chapter seeks to explore the historical development of those urban functions through close analysis of a series of episodes, each marking a key transition in the relationship between formal and informal spheres over the twentieth century. The goal is to capture the political, juridical, and social importance of this legal distinction while at the same time illuminating the underlying logic of the *real* city that required both formal and informal sectors. I will concentrate on land rather than on labor. These two sectors are closely related: favela residents are far more likely to work in the informal sector than are residents of formal neighborhoods. This was true in 1950 and remains true in the twenty-first century. But patterns of land use are both easier to identify and more decisive to Rio's political and cultural life.

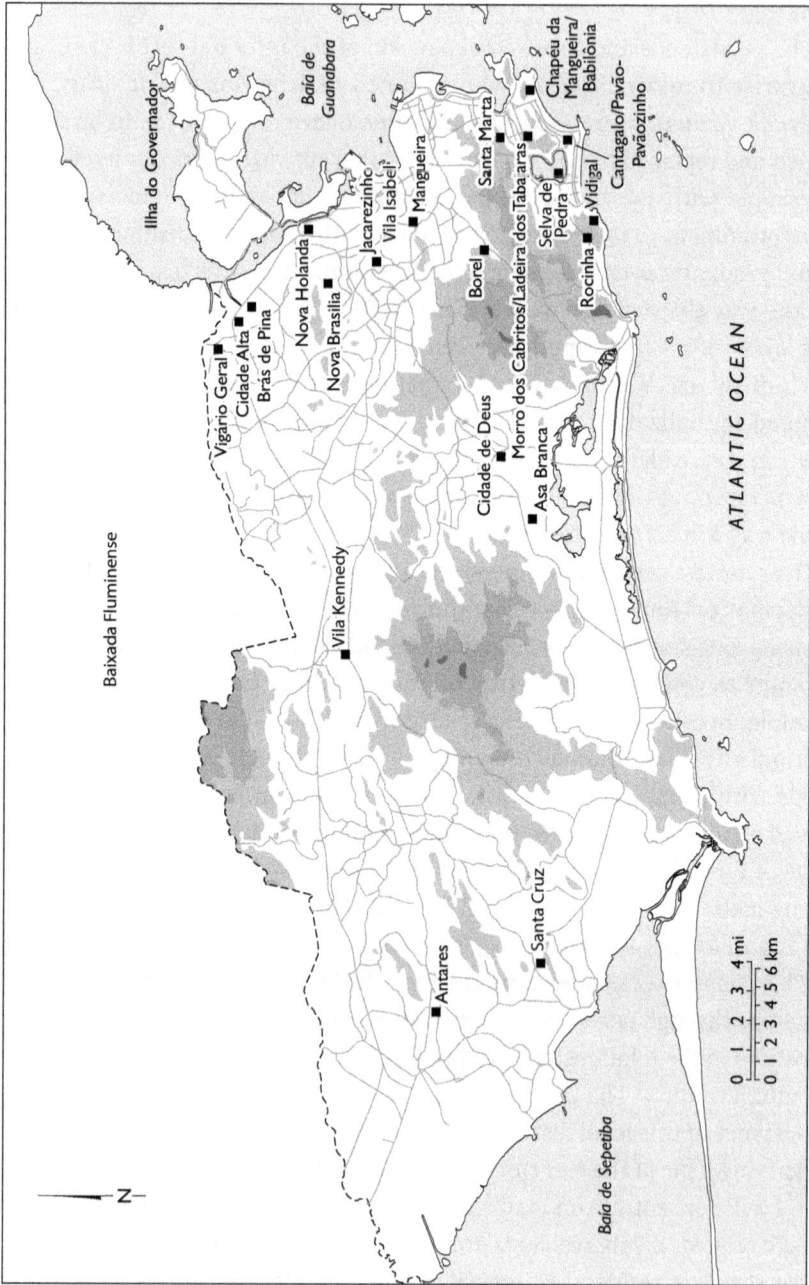

MAP 3.1 Rio de Janeiro. Credit: Bill Nelson.

The relationship between favela and *cidade* has shaped the way both *cariocas* and outsiders have understood Rio for most of the last century. This chapter traces the evolution of that relationship, exploring the ways in which urban land has been distributed, categorized, and reformed. A complete narrative of this relationship would be prohibitively long: instead, I will focus on key moments illustrating broader transformations.

The formal/informal divide has been extensively theorized, investigated, and criticized.[1] The most simplistic formulations of this division suggest that the mere act of regularizing informal property will set off a virtuous cycle that will vastly improve the lives of the urban poor.[2] Numerous failed titling programs—including several discussed below—have shown this is easier said than done. More starkly, programs that have merely delivered title without also upgrading infrastructure and improving employment and educational opportunities have failed to improve the lives of the urban poor significantly.[3] Nevertheless, the idea of erasing informality by simply handing out property titles remains popular at the level of political discourse.

This popularity has triggered a scholarly backlash, suggesting that the formal/informal division is largely an abstract theoretical concept that obscures more than it reveals and should be abandoned.[4] There is something to be said for this: in Rio, most dramatically, central favelas in the early twenty-first century do not fit any traditional definition of urban informal communities. Their buildings are made of brick and mortar, some rising seven stories high. They have functioning water, electricity and sewage networks, regular trash pickup, public schools, and a vibrant blend of commerce and residential housing. All of these features are more precarious than those in neighboring middle-class neighborhoods, but are in many cases superior to those in far-flung formal neighborhoods.[5]

These central favelas also have thriving informal real estate markets, and both residents and outside developers have been able to play those markets as a form of savings and investment, and to use favela "property"—not recognized in the eyes of the law, but acknowledged by the surrounding community—as collateral for loans, including those from formal businesses.[6] This undermines one of the most prominent arguments about the burdens of informality—that it prevents the urban poor from using their stake in their own homes as a form of investment and collateral.

When used in simplistic ways, the category of informality can also become a way of criticizing the poor and working-class citizens for practices largely ignored among the wealthy. Extensive irregular building and occupation practices in middle-class neighborhoods—the penthouse built with no permit and in violation of building codes, the clandestine sewage pipe, and so on—are rarely discussed as a matter of public policy or scholarly inquiry, and when noted at all are seen as individual violations rather than systemic problems.

Given these caveats, does legal informality in Rio de Janeiro still matter? Did it ever matter? Or have these favelas been undergoing a process of consolidation not recognized before the law but nonetheless characterized by the same features of improvement and diversification undergone by working-class suburban developments, for example?

My contention is that legal informality has mattered and continues to matter. It is not the decisive characteristic shaping the lives of Rio's favela residents, but it is one crucial and consistent factor in the marginalization of favela residents from the guarantees of the rule of law. It has played a key role in leaving favela residents vulnerable to systemic police brutality and criminal turf occupation. And it continues to mark favelas as a terrain apart from, or considered in opposition to, the regular city. For these reasons, this chapter concentrates on the way informal development has unfolded in relation to trends and initiatives in the formal sector.

When looked at in the hemispheric context of this volume, this importance becomes clearer. As these chapters reveal, the relationship between informality and inequality is by no means perfectly consistent. High inequality can coincide with high rates of formality, as in Los Angeles. Even in the Latin American cities, informality and inequality are not always directly proportional, as formalization without inclusion can penalize the working poor. But informality has been one decisive way in which inequality in these cities is maintained and codified. In Rio de Janeiro, in particular, it has often been the means of ceding a place and a role to the working poor without granting them the protections of full citizenship.

Streetcars and Railways

Expansions and retractions in formality and informality have followed transitions in Rio's larger economy and labor structure. Throughout the colonial period and most of the nineteenth century, slavery and its link to tropical commodity export constituted a dominant perverse formality. Abolition and the decline of coffee planting in the province of Rio de Janeiro brought many rural migrants—most of them former slaves and descendants of former slaves—to the burgeoning city in the late nineteenth century. Through 1960, Rio remained the national capital and also a secondary industrial pole, lagging well behind São Paulo in that regard, but nurturing light-industrial sectors large enough to provide expanding formal employment. The capital moved to Brasília in 1960, around the same time that Rio's industrial sector began a long decline, and Rio shed formal jobs. The tourism industry expanded to fill this vacuum, but many service-sector tourist-industry jobs remained in the informal sector.

Over the course of Rio's long arc of formalization, the shape of the city and the function of its parts changed dramatically. Like the exchange of energies between the formal and informal sectors, this spatial evolution happened in fits and starts. In the closing decades of the nineteenth century, streetcars and railroads pulled the city in new directions, with contrasting implications. Streetcar lines were built primarily by private foreign investment on the south side and near north side of the city. They made practical a new kind of baronial urban life, melding the comforts of subtropical gardens with rapid connections to the commercial center. The grand homes of the south zone provoked the competitive aspirations of rising merchants, stimulating the growth of less imposing homes, filling in the avenues of these growing neighborhoods.[7]

They also required the labor of an extensive servant class, many of whose members settled either in *cortiços*, or tenements, or built their own housing on nearby hillsides. The destruction of many of the tenements in modernizing reforms of the early twentieth century played a key role in the establishment of self-built housing for the urban poor on Rio's hillsides, as evicted tenants looked to the hills for refuge. Within the first decade of the twentieth century, a diverse collection of property claimants ranging from inheritors of colonial land grants to local strongmen were collecting rents from these hillside settlers.[8]

In the near north side neighborhood of Vila Isabel, streetcar capitalists worked closely with real estate developers to plot out subdivisions along the tracks, drawing upwardly mobile families, most of whom had at least one breadwinner working downtown every day. These neighborhoods were Rio's first *loteamentos*, or planned subdivisions.[9] As in the south zone, a middle-class population generated a demand for working-class service labor. And as in the south zone, this would be filled by mobile workers left to carve out a residential niche, usually by buying or renting hillside lots from *grileiros*, or property claimants with dubious legal rights.[10]

The railroads stretched farther north and west. Brazil's first railroad, the Estrada de Ferro Dom Pedro II, built in the mid-nineteenth century, connected Rio with farmland north of the city in the Baixada Fluminense

(Fluminense Lowlands).[11] That growing metropolis gradually devoured the farms—by the 1930s, many had been sold off to or claimed by new developers of the periphery, who divided them into lots and resold to individual families. They represented a new kind of subdivision, often characterized by dubious legal title and lacking basic services. By midcentury most of these peripheral zones had become *loteamentos irregulares*, or irregular subdivisions. Like favelas, they were usually not part of formal property registries. But their individual plots would literally lay the groundwork for a gradual process of incorporation into the formal sphere that would slowly separate them from the fortunes of favelas.[12]

Subsequent rail lines were created to facilitate industrial growth. The Leopoldina line generated industrial development north and east of the city, serving a burgeoning textile sector, as well as cigar, furniture, and a range of other factories. Some factory owners took advantage of tax subsidies to build housing for their workers, but the quantity of workers quickly overwhelmed the supply of housing. By the 1930s, many factories allowed workers to construct their own shacks on ample back lots.[13] Several of these became the nuclei of enduring informal settlements in the north zone. The growth of rail and streetcar lines in the late nineteenth and early twentieth century thus facilitated the rapid expansion of the usable terrain of the city, and in doing so established patterns of linked formal and informal growth across the metropolis.

Strategies for Modernity, Ideas of Tradition

Engineer Francisco Pereira Passos served as Rio's mayor from 1902 to 1906, years marked by ambitious projects inspired by Georges-Eugene Haussmann's overhaul of old Paris in the mid-nineteenth century. Like Haussmann, Pereira Passos sketched broad avenues flanked by majestic buildings. His team gutted swathes of the center to make this possible. The resulting thoroughfares gave parts of downtown Rio cosmopolitan flair: the showcase central plaza, bordered by an ornate opera house and a grand National Library fulfilled aspirations of Parisian grandeur. Even at the time, however, it was widely observed that Pereira Passos's reforms created islands of glittering modernity surrounded by a chaotic urban sea, lacking any plan for housing the growing ranks of the urban poor.[14]

The unpredictability of judicial decisions regarding urban terrain reflected this preference for ad hoc solutions. Property law was a reflection of struggles carried out on the ground, rather than a set of codified principles.

Brazil's republican-era constitution provided for limited rights of *usucapião*, or adverse possession, recognizing the property interests of settlers who had improved land for at least thirty years. But the *usucapião* rights of the urban poor were rarely upheld in court. Public lands (including those that had "devolved" to public ownership when original grantees failed to improve them) were generally deemed unsusceptible to adverse possession. In disputes over private land, judges were as likely to rule in favor of absentee claimants rather than uphold principles of adverse possession.[15]

These judicial trends were important in framing the formal/informal divide, but largely irrelevant in determining the actual occupation of land. Most settlers never considered filing a legal claim. In practice, occupation was determined through the constant struggle between the will of local strongmen who often had financial interests in irregular occupation, the manipulation of the police by these same strongmen and absentee owners, and the sheer persistence of residents themselves.

Bairro and Favela Grow Together

Favela growth proved to be a key component of Rio de Janeiro's modernization, rather than an aberration. The simultaneous and interdependent growth of the favela Morro dos Cabritos and the formal neighborhood Bairro Peixoto, in Copacabana, illustrate the way this worked out in practice. Throughout the nineteenth century, trekkers from downtown Rio reached the pristine beach of Copacabana via a rough trail over the hill separating the Botafogo neighborhood from the Atlantic. A small informal settlement on the Copacabana side of the hill emerged to serve this traffic. The opening of a tunnel through this hill in 1892 and the inauguration of a streetcar line connecting Copacabana to the center greatly eased travel and facilitated formal settlement. Residential settlement filled in beachside blocks first, while merchants developed lots closer to the tunnel. During these same years, the Brazilian navy built a hospital on the hill. Like the factories of the north side, the hospital generated both formal and informal settlement by employees around it.[16]

In 1938, Felisberto Peixoto, owner of a farm on the Copacabana side of the tunnel, donated his property to several charitable institutions, with the stipulation that they develop the real estate with single-family homes of no more than three stories. Over the course of the 1940s, a conglomerate created by the charities plotted the land and sold it to builders, creating the formal neighborhood of Bairro Peixoto. In these same years, the naval hospital relocated to the north side of town. Landlords with dubious claims occupied the land around the old hospital site, and rented lots to low-income residents. These informal lots became collectively known as the Favela Morro dos Cabritos. The growth of Bairro Peixoto and Morro dos Cabritos is a particularly clear example of a pattern of interdependent formal and informal growth that unfolded across the city.[17]

In other cases nearby, favela landlords were wealthy, esteemed members of *carioca* society, exploiting inherited land for steady profit.[18] This was a no-risk proposition—favela residents took on all the burdens of building their own homes and maintaining access. Landlords merely collected the rent, and either hired muscle to keep out interlopers or did the job themselves. As a result, many property owners developed a strong economic interest in the expansion of the informal sector.

Favelas were rarely "squatter settlements" in the precise sense of that term: only in exceptional cases were hillsides populated by residents who staked individual claims. Such settlements were not likely to endure, as they had no protection from more powerful interests. Instead, favelas were generally settled by renters who paid monthly fees to those who claimed property ownership.

Getúlio's Formalization and Its Unintended Consequences

Getúlio Vargas's rise to the presidency in the Revolution of 1930, and more ambitiously his initiation of the dictatorial Estado Novo in 1937, marked the initiation of large-scale attempts at the expansion of industrialization and formalization across the country. Rio, the capital city, would function as a test case for many Estado Novo reforms. Vargas's regime sought to extend formal workplace protections, construct a welfare state and increase the regulatory capacity of the federal government. These initiatives were hugely influential, winning Vargas working-class support and strengthening the central state.

But Vargas's reforms also created a rigid distinction between the formal and the informal that proved difficult to transcend. Vargas's 1937 Building Code for Rio de Janeiro, for example, set a high bar for legal construction. Under its provisions, all legal buildings required licensed architects and contractors, formal plans approved by the city, and inspection before habitation. Any construction that did not meet this high standard was illegal and thus subject to being razed. The exacting provisions of the 1937 code provoked protest across the social spectrum, from contractors and property owners as well as humble favela residents. Most of its requirements were never enforced—but the threat that they *could* be at any time kept favela residents insecure in their occupation.[19]

Vargas did seek to create new model housing for urban workers, in developments called proletarian parks. They consisted of long rows of barracks divided into individual family apartments, supplemented by health clinics, daycare centers, and schools. They exemplified the Vargas regime's commitment to uplifting the nation by training and harnessing the strength of its humblest citizens. But they also pointed out the unrealistic expectations guiding urban policy: the proletarian parks housed some 8,000 people. They were touted as models, but their real importance on the overall shape of urban housing was negligible.[20]

These same years witnessed the consolidation of a real estate sector, bringing together developers, investors, and pension institutes in ventures often mediated by the federal government. The Vargas regime imposed a Lei do Inquilinato, or Renting Law, in 1942, freezing property rents. This was initially imposed as a temporary measure, but it became difficult to repeal, enduring until 1964.[21] In practice, the law was toothless—families of means found ways to pay gratuities beyond fixed rents in order to gain preferential access to a dwindling supply of rental units. But this inconsistency in the application of the law did little to help working-class *cariocas*, as the rent freeze proved a strong disincentive to the production of popular housing in the formal sector. Developers dedicated their energy to commercial real estate and to construction of homes for sale.

Formal housing expanded rapidly but was targeted almost entirely at the middle class. Vargas's incentives for industrial production facilitated construction of multistory apartment buildings, but the apartments in new buildings were designed for purchase, rather than rental. Few Brazilians had access to bank loans for mortgages. Instead, most homebuyers borrowed the purchase price of a single-family home or apartment within family networks, a strategy that clearly barred those not already part of the propertied classes. Vargas's reforms included the creation of workers' pension institutes, jointly funded by employers and employees, and administered with strong state influence. The pension offered low-interest loans to workers, and some 25,000 families purchased homes through these institutes—a significant number, but small in proportion to the size of Rio's working class. The rent freeze, meanwhile, produced an artificial scarcity of rental apartments in the formal sector. Low-wage workers thus had little recourse but to look to informal housing.[22]

The 1937 Building Code and the 1942 Renting Law were examples of *leis que não pegam*—laws that do not stick, in the Brazilian parlance—but that nonetheless have far-reaching consequences. Each attempted to consolidate formality, bringing the real estate market more firmly within state regulation. In its own way, each proved a spur to greater development in the informal sector, and an obstacle to the legal protection of the precarious stakes of poor city dwellers. Designed to eliminate informality, they instead perpetuated it. Designed at least in part to protect the working class, they consigned the working poor to vulnerability.

Irregular Subdivisions

Both formal and informal settlement pushed the periphery of the city steadily outward. Vargas and his successors invested in drainage of surrounding wetlands. The result was a massive expansion of land suitable for settlement, much of it rapidly turned into irregular subdivisions. Property claimants often had no clear title to the land, the subdivided plots were often too small to be legally sold, and the subdivisions almost always lacked the infrastructure required for legal real estate transactions. Instead, new residents banded together to press for roads and services.[23]

In the populist democratic arena following the end of Vargas's Estado Novo in 1945, this process became systematic. Peripheral real estate developers sold off subdivided lots in several stages. The first lots were sold cheaply to working-class buyers who built their own homes. Once these initial residents reached sufficient density to pressure elected politicians for services in return for votes, their subdivisions began to improve. Developers then sold remaining lots for successively higher prices.[24]

Once residents of irregular subdivisions bargained for political protection, they rarely faced threat of removal, and gradually became part of the formal urban grid. Their residents faced neither the same social stigma nor the particular political limitations faced by favela residents. They evolved as an alternate zone—an important and largely ignored tangent to the dyad of favela and formal city.[25]

The Battle of Rio

In 1948, Carlos Lacerda, a city councilman and a rising politician with national ambitions, synthesized a growing anxiety about favelas with a series of newspaper articles entitled *"A Batalha do Rio"* ("The Battle of Rio").

Lacerda, a former communist student radical, had reinvented himself as a Catholic moralist and young leader of the União Democrática Nacional, an anti-Getulista party. Lacerda took a once-marginal political issue that had gradually been gaining greater political centrality and framed it in such a way that it appeared the most decisive of political challenges facing Rio: if the city failed to surmount the challenge presented by favelas it was destined for misery and chaos.[26]

Lacerda was deliberately incendiary; at the same time, the battle of Rio was not a figment of his imagination. The consolidation of a real estate sector linking developers and property agents with civil servants facilitated the expansion of the formal property grid. Investment capital in the sector, coupled with improved engineering techniques, prompted developers to set their sights on hillsides formerly deemed too steep for formal construction. In some cases, favela landlords quietly facilitated these projects by selling their stakes, making way for developers to begin the process of eviction.[27]

Residents of favelas targeted for eviction quickly became skilled in activating a network of alliances, starting with their own neighbors. They staged communal demonstrations, mobilized reporters to publish articles about their fate and bargained with clientelist politicians, trading votes in return for the delivery of minimal services. And they called on activist lawyers to defend them in court, investigating the often-dubious property claims of developers.[28]

This marked an important innovation in the evolving relationship between formal and informal. In order to secure their perch, even residents of informal neighborhoods needed to organize based on some kind of corporate identity. That organization did not bring them under the umbrella of the formal sphere, but it did give them entrance into the political arena, often winning them protection that partially offset continuing legal vulnerability.

Borel and the Fight Against Eviction

The favela of Borel is prototypical of this process. Borel occupies a steep hill above the formal neighborhood of Usina, the northernmost stretch of the larger district of Tijuca. In a pattern typical of the north side growth, workers from the cigarette and textile factories in Usina settled on the adjacent hillside, where they rented lots from local strongmen who claimed to represent the interest of absent property owners.[29]

By the mid-1940s, residents on the Borel hillside had reached sufficient density that they determined to stop paying rent to the current strongman, a Portuguese immigrant named Daniel Gonçalves. Not long afterward, Gonçalves sold his stake to Borel, Meuron Imóveis, a real estate company interested in developing the hillside. Borel, Meuron subsequently contracted to rent the hillside back to Gonçalves, an arrangement designed to create a paper trail that might substantiate its own shaky property claims. Late in 1953, Gonçalves stopped paying rent, and Borel, Meuron filed court papers to evict him and all his sub-lessees—the favela residents of Borel. Early in 1954, armed police gave residents four days to move to a new location farther north.[30]

The favela residents summoned reporters from the left-wing *Imprensa Popular*, leading to a flurry of favorable news coverage. Community leaders alleged that Gonçalves was a paid agent of Borel, Meuron, and that the lawsuit was contrived to produce an order of eviction. They enlisted the aid of Antoine Magarinos Torres, a communist lawyer who lived in nearby Tijuca. Magarinos Torres filed suit on behalf of the hill's residents, accusing the police of abuse of authority. Torres and community residents pressured a local judge to investigate, leading to the discovery that there was no legal eviction order. In April of 1954, hundreds of Borel's residents marched to city hall and the Federal Congress building—both in downtown Rio— demanding protection from eviction.[31] Community leaders and Magarinos Torres attracted the support of legislative allies, avoiding numerous attempts at eviction.

Borel's residents realized these victories were temporary. They created the União dos Trabalhadores Favelados (UTF), the Union of Favela-Dwelling Workers. Each of the three terms in the name was crucial—the UTF was intended to unite favela dwellers across the city, it recognized favela resident as a specific category, and it stressed that favela residents were also workers. The UTF galvanized local resistance movements and became a crucial link in a broader network, fostering connections between local leaders, lawyers, political representatives, and journalists.[32]

Getúlio Vargas's suicide in August, 1954, played a curious role in these developments. A massive outpouring of public grief in the wake of the suicide demonstrated the depth of popular Getulismo, not least among favela residents. Confronted with overwhelming evidence of Getulista passion, few officials, particularly elected politicians, were willing to risk anti-popular measures in the ensuing months. As a result, late 1954 through 1956 marked a high point for judicial decisions and legislation favorable to the interests of favela residents. Judges handed down a series of decisions demanding the expropriation of favela lands in order to stop proposed evictions. Federal legislators declared a moratorium on all favela evictions for a period of at least two years, beginning in September 1956.[33]

In 1955, federal congressmen voted to provide funding to the Cruzada São Sebastião, a new Catholic Church initiative created by Bishop Dom Helder Câmara to provide housing for the urban poor. Helder Câmara was in the vanguard of a trend toward politically engaged pastoral work that would flower as Latin American liberation theology in subsequent decades. The roots of that theology were already apparent in the bishop's strong advocacy of favela organization. Only the flurry of popular legislation in the wake of Getúlio's death could have brought initial funding to an organization like the Cruzada, designed to contest private property rights.[34]

In the same year, Rio's municipal government established the Serviço Especial de Recuperação das Favelas e Habitações Anti-Higiênicas (SERFHA), or Special Service for the Recuperation of Favelas and Anti-Hygienic Habitations. SERFHA was more technocratic than the Cruzada, but both were fueled by an emerging understanding of the favela as a solution to the housing needs of the urban poor.[35] Demographer and journalist Alberto Passos Guimarães played a key role in this transition. In 1953, Passos Guimarães published a short article in the *Revista Brasileira de Estatística*, an academic journal with a minuscule readership. Guimarães was an employee of the Instituto Brasileiro de Geografia e Estatística and had played a strong role in designing the 1950 census of Rio de Janeiro in order to count the favela population accurately. Guimarães's study counted approximately 170,000 favela residents in fifty-eight favelas, in a city of over 2 million people—a number far lower than some of the ominous speculative figures cited by Lacerda and his allies, but far outstripping the capacity of municipal or federal government to provide formal housing. Guimarães drew the simple and direct conclusion that urbanizing favelas would be more efficient than wiping them out and resettling their inhabitants, a task that would exceed the capacity of local government.[36]

The initial publication of Guimarães's article cannot have reached many readers—in the short term, his ideas found broader popular circulation through his writing and editing for the *Imprensa Popular*. In the long term, Passos Guimarães's article was to become a touchstone of Brazilian urban planning, and its early endorsement of favela urbanization a widely accepted starting point for reform proposals of a later generation. The divisions of space and their functions in place in the late 1950s would shape the evolving nature of the formal/informal divide. Favela residents were protected from private eviction proceedings but denied property title. More subtly, it was understood that only through collective mobilization could they bring improvements to their community.

The Guanabara Experiment

With the transfer of the capital to Brasília in 1960, the old Federal District of Rio de Janeiro became the tiny but pivotal state of Guanabara. Residents of the new state of Guanabara elected a governor for the first time in 1960. Carlos Lacerda won the election with a heated right-wing campaign that relied on characterizing Rio's favelas as a petri dish for communist agitation. Once in office, Lacerda put that rhetoric into action with an energetic campaign to raze favelas and remove their residents to distant housing projects.[37]

President John F. Kennedy and the architects of his hemispheric Alliance for Progress shared Lacerda's fear that Latin American poverty was a breeding ground for communist revolution. To contain that threat, Kennedy increased aid to Latin America, funding a wide variety of projects. Even in the case of Rio de Janeiro and its informal communities, these initiatives were far from monolithic: Peace Corps volunteers in the favelas often became the most influential advocates for urbanization. But no single Latin American politician was more effective than Lacerda at securing USAID funding, and he used it primarily to eradicate favelas and build suburban housing projects.[38] Lacerda selected highly visible communities near middle-class neighborhoods and tourist zones, in areas of immediate interest to private capital or the state itself.

Favela residents removed to new projects in distant suburbs soon found that reality failed to live up to Lacerda's promises. When the first families arrived, new residential units in Vila Kennedy, Vila Progreso, and Vila Aliança were skeletal. The shells of the single-family homes had been built, but in many cases provisions for water and electricity were either inconsistent or merely in planning stages. Streets were not paved; schools were not built and would not be for some time.[39] Although Lacerda's projects were intended as models, they gained a reputation as places to be avoided. This conviction bolstered a new wave of mobilization. Favela leaders banded together in a pan-favela organization, the Federação de Associações de Favelas do Estado de Guanabara (FAFEG).[40] The organization became a cause for Lacerda's concern and a target of suspicion for the increasingly restive anticommunist officers in Brazil's armed forces. The support of these officers for Lacerda would have dramatic consequences for Rio's favelas.

Removals Under the Dictatorship

Lacerda was the most active civilian in calling for the military overthrow of João Goulart's populist presidency in 1964. Lacerda strongly supported the coup in April of that year, and hoped to use his early alliance with the regime to rise to the presidency the following year. But his popularity in Guanabara was slipping rapidly, a decline that played a large role in the regime's decision to postpone presidential elections. Lacerda's handpicked candidate for his successor as governor of Guanabara lost the 1965 election to Francisco Negrão de Lima, a product of the Getulista machine who had made his peace with the military regime.

Negrão was a fierce political adversary of Lacerda but continued most of his urban policies. Like Lacerda, he expanded the network of highways and tunnels connecting the city center and the north side with the middle-class beach neighborhoods of the south sides. These projects subsidized the creation of upper-middle-class apartment buildings in the south zone, while obliterating working-class rental housing in the north zone.[41] Most favela residents fared even worse under Negrão tenure than they had under Lacerda, as the new governor accelerated favela removal.[42] The most notorious case was the favela Praia do Pinto, a dense conglomeration of wooden shacks clustered between a picturesque lagoon and the middle-class residential neighborhood of Leblon. One night in 1969 the entire favela went up in flames. Residents attributed the fire to arson, suggesting that off-duty police had done the dirty work in the interest of real estate speculators. State employees immediately removed the charred remains of the favela and trucked former residents to "triage" housing—state-owned barracks on the north side. Those able to pay monthly dues were housed in the new apartment blocks of Cidade Alta. Others were pushed farther out to the distant periphery.[43]

The area formerly occupied by Praia do Pinto was apportioned to military pension institutes and real estate conglomerates, who pushed through plans for a complex of middle-class high-rises. The new neighborhood became known as the Selva de Pedra—the concrete jungle. There could be no clearer example of a favela being uprooted to satisfy the demands of the expanding real estate sector.[44]

Informalization in the Housing Projects

The Guanabara years (1960–75) were the high-water mark for formalization in Rio de Janeiro. Eradication of the informal sector was Lacerda's primary goal. His successors were less committed to this goal ideologically but
continued his projects. The social costs of this expansion for the urban poor
were notoriously high. But this attempt to formalize the city never beat back
the currents of informal growth. Even Lacerda's projects generated their
own variations of informality. The housing projects created under Lacerda
and Negrão de Lima were administered by the Companhia de Habitação
(COHAB), Guanabara's state housing authority. After 1964, COHAB was
linked to the Banco Nacional de Habitação (BNH), or National Housing
Bank, a federal mortgage bank created by the military regime. The new institutions were part of an initiative to promote middle-class homeownership as part of a broader anticommunist strategy.[45] The BNH introduced
relatively low-interest home loans, but neither the BNH nor the state housing authority was in a position to subsidize mortgage loans permanently.
Residents of the new housing projects found themselves saddled with mortgages they could not pay. Many residents viewed the mortgages as a form of
rent, and did not feel obliged to pay if the landlord—the state housing authority, in this case—did not live up to its pledges. As promises of completed infrastructure, schools, and transportation went unfulfilled, many residents
stopped making their monthly payments. Many sold their homes on the irregular market—a process known as "ceding the keys" or "passing a house."[46]
Within a few years, the projects were characterized by high rates of mortgage
delinquency and irregular tenancy. Services declined further in response.
The housing projects, designed to be the antidote to the favelas, rapidly became new zones of entrenched informality. The military regime had set itself
the project of ending informality but in effect created new manifestations.

Brás de Pina

The trauma inflicted by favela removals outraged observers convinced that
removal was immoral, inefficient, and socially disastrous. These observers
included engaged scholars, clerics and lay assistants of the Catholic Church,
and favela leaders themselves. They also included an increasing number of
middle-class *cariocas*, who began to resent the kind of urban reorganization the removal policy served, one dedicated to construction of highways
and apartment blocks.

Opponents of removal began to look to a new experiment in favela urbanization unfolding in the neighborhood of Brás de Pina, a swampy low-
land settlement pressed between the city's north-side industrial belt and
Guanabara Bay. Partly in order to counterbalance his aggressive removals
on the south side, Negrão de Lima selected Brás de Pina as a showcase for
urbanization.[47] He created Codesco, the Companhia de Desenvolvimento
Comunitário, or Company for Community Development, and hired a team
of young architects to urbanize Brás de Pina, relying on the manpower of
the favela residents themselves. The architects saw their work as a radical
departure from modernist thinking. Rather than draft a grand, ambitious
project, they sought to enable local families to build the homes they
wanted.[48]

Carlos Nelson Ferreira dos Santos, one of the Codesco architects, found
the experience so transforming that it helped push him to earn a doctorate
in anthropology, where he wrote a thesis based on his experience in Brás
de Pina and other urban reform movements. Over the next twenty years,
Nelson would become one of the most compelling analysts of the place of
the poor in urban transformation, and an inheritor of the mantle of Alberto
Passos Guimarães.[49]

By 1970, the transformation of Brás de Pina from a muddy conglomeration of precarious shacks into a neighborhood of brick and concrete homes
connected to urban infrastructure was largely complete. Yet although that
transformation succeeded at the material level, it ran into legal obstacles.
Brás de Pina was denied the full status of formality: when Negrão de Lima
left office, Codesco was disbanded. State government, no longer interested
in the particular success of Brás de Pina, never followed through on delivery of property title to the residents.

Lessons of Brás de Pina

The Brás de Pina experiment demonstrated that urbanization of informal
housing was the most effective means of accommodating the urban poor.
The most constructive role for policy makers and implementers was to facilitate consolidation and ensure a path to full integration.[50] For a growing
cohort of scholars, Brás de Pina confirmed their conviction that urbanization could be accomplished efficiently. The British sociologist Anthony Leeds
led a seminar in his Copacabana living room to discuss these issues. Leeds's
gatherings united a group of young scholars just beginning their community fieldwork. Particularly influential in this cohort were Lícia Valladares

and Janice Perlman. Valladares was a sociologist who studied the experiences of favela residents resettled in distant housing projects. Publication of her findings later in the 1970s offered a devastating criticism of the hubris of the philosophy of social engineering that informed removal and relocation.[51] Perlman was a Peace Corps volunteer whose work in Rio's favelas persuaded her to pursue a doctorate in anthropology. Her work rebutting stereotypes of the dysfunctional favela and revealing the profound economic and social integration of favela residents later in the decade transformed the international debate on poor people's urbanization.[52]

The Slow Road to Redemocratization

By the late 1970s, this intellectual transformation invigorated and was in turn enriched by grassroots mobilization against the dictatorship. Favela residents were at the vanguard of the transition. In 1977, the residents of Vidigal, a favela perched on a hillside above Leblon, successfully resisted a removal attempt. Vidigal was a real estate speculator's dream, and its ability to hold off removal demonstrated that the alliance of the real estate and construction industries with local and federal governments had been weakened by the military regime's declining popularity. The regime could no longer risk brazenly anti-popular measures. Vidigal's victory effectively brought to an end the era of large-scale removal begun by Lacerda fifteen years earlier and began a wave of popular mobilization against favela removal.[53]

Over the next several years, popular mobilization reached a peak as tens of thousands of *cariocas* joined new neighborhood associations and constructed alliances bridging the gap between formal and informal spheres. This alliance proved decisive in the election of socialist Leonel Brizola as governor of Rio de Janeiro in 1982, in the first democratic elections for state office since 1960.[54] Brizola's election marked a sea change in the relationship between formality and informality—just as globalization took hold and neoliberalism began to argue against "excessive" state interventions. The weeks between his election and his inauguration brought a land rush on Rio's north side, as thousands of hopeful settlers erected temporary housing on public lands, allegedly with the slogan *"Invade, que Brizola legalize"*—invade and Brizola will legalize possession. These were truly squatter settlements—an anomaly in *carioca* history—and most did not last: once in office Brizola negotiated with community leaders and facilitated resettlement—in most cases within previously existing favelas.[55] But the episode demonstrated the prevailing understanding that Brizola, owing his election to the votes of favela residents, was not in any position to crack down on irregular occupation.

Brizola's Attempted Regularization

Brizola supported regularization of existing land tenure: he wanted to grant legal title to property to every family in the city. The goal was to take property ownership away from real estate speculators and irregular landlords and push it down the social scale to the working class and the urban poor. Doing so, however, required confronting not just the formal real estate sector but landlords in the informal sector. To add more complication, doing so also conflicted with the communitarian goals of many local leaders, who advocated collectivization of favela property, and warned that individual property titles would lead to gentrification and further marginalization of the poor.

Brizola unleashed his signature social program with great fanfare, dedicated considerable resources to it, and then watched it founder. Cada Família Um Lote, One Plot for Every Family, was an urban-titling program designed to extend the formal property grid over the entire state, beginning with the test case of the municipality of Rio de Janeiro.[56] Brizola charged teams of local leaders and city planners with creating community maps and censuses, planning to use them to confer legal title to current residents.[57] But Brizola's planners found it impossible to determine who held legal title to much of the city's terrain. Many favelas straddled public and private lands, complicating regularization.[58] The technical difficulties, however, were manageable. The waning enthusiasm of favela leaders for title regularization proved a greater obstacle.

Brizola's plan required continued popular mobilization. But as soon as Brizola guaranteed practical possession of urban turf, favela residents largely dropped out of the drive for regularization.[59] This reluctance had several causes. To begin, regularization would entail paying taxes on legal property, imposing costs when benefits were uncertain. The program had no mechanism for legalizing the common practice of renting, rather than owning, favela housing. Perhaps most importantly, community leaders invoked the threat of *remoção branca*—white removal, or veiled removal—suggesting that legalization would trigger gentrification, accomplishing through the market the removal that favela residents had successfully resisted.[60] As a result, One Plot Per Family fell short of its goals of regularizing favela property. Indeed, favela housing expanded dramatically during the mid-1980s.

Material standards of living in central favelas improved dramatically during Brizola's term. Granted implicit guarantees of possession, favela residents invested in their homes. Favelas expanded horizontally and vertically, cultivated more extensive commerce and greater services, and witnessed the growth of greater internal disparities in wealth. The informal sphere was becoming increasingly central to the city, characterized by parallel processes of development, organization, and diversification.

Criminal Turf Occupation

By the late 1980s, attempts to universalize formality through both top-down planning and broad-based community participation had failed. Informal land tenure increased dramatically—the most reliable studies now estimate that there are approximately 1,000 favelas in Rio, home to at least 20 percent of the population, or 2.5 million people in a metropolitan region of some 12 million residents.

Meanwhile, the nature of the relationship between formal and informal spheres began to change. Through much of the twentieth century, the favela served as a compromise solution for both the urban poor and the state. It offered the poor a precarious stake in the city, and it freed the state from the obligation of providing popular housing. As unsatisfactory as that compromise solution was, it met the interests of both the urban poor and government officials sufficiently to remain an important part of the urban landscape. Outsiders always had economic interests in the favela, as well. From the beginning irregular landlords profited from favela occupation. But in the last thirty-five years, those economic interests and their political influence have changed.

Over the course of the 1980s, as the world economy moved towards globalization, transitions in international drug-trafficking patterns—themselves responding to trends in international policing, specifically increased vigilance against direct shipment of cocaine from Andean nations to the United States—made Rio de Janeiro increasingly important as a transshipment node in the export of South American cocaine to Europe. The cocaine trade in both its local and international ventures was heavily reliant on illegal weaponry, fueling a parallel trade in illegal arms. Again, these transitions demonstrated the vulnerability of Rio de Janeiro's poor to hemispheric economic and political transitions far beyond their reckoning, much less their control.[61]

Drug and arms traffickers looked to Rio's favelas as safe havens for their operations. By the late 1980s, many of Rio's largest and most strategically located favelas were patrolled by local factions associated with expanding criminal networks. By the end of the decade these networks had acted decisively to take over favela turf.[62] In a few favelas, residents connected to state police and fire departments mobilized to drive out drug traffickers. By the early 1990s, a few of these groups had organized more coherently as defense militias, and had begun to create their own citywide network. Although the militias were created to fight *traficantes*, they quickly developed their own irregular economic interests, extorting payments from residents and businesses. Like the drug traffickers, the militias took over the favela turf where they operated, usually more openly, and were often applauded by local politicians for doing so.[63] *Traficantes* and *milícias* became parallel criminal networks using monopolization of political power within favelas to extract profit, and protecting their operations through political connections. By the mid-1990s, as a result, informality had ceased to be primarily a compromise solution between the urban poor and the state. It had become an investment strategy for expanding criminal-commercial networks.

Favela-Bairro and Beyond

In the mid-1990s, Rio Mayor César Maia sought to adapt to global neoliberal trends by pitching urban reform to international investors—in this case, the Inter-American Development Bank. Maia followed the example of Carlos Lacerda in pinning his hopes for urban reform on international funding, but followed the thinking of Alberto Passos Guimarães, Carlos Nelson, and Lícia Valladares in his planning. He hired urban planners who had studied under these key figures and aimed to put their ideas into practice on an unprecedented scale.[64]

With $600 million in initial funding—most of it from the IDB—they launched Favela-Bairro in the mid-1990s. The stated goal was integration of favelas into the surrounding city—to turn favelas into *bairros*, or typical urban neighborhoods. The program invested in upgrading projects in over one hundred favelas. Favela-Bairro hired teams of architects and social scientists, undertook extensive research projects and crafted sophisticated proposals. These projects were at least partially successful—expanded streets and public plazas, in particular, made valuable contributions to local infrastructure. But Favela-Bairro included no tools to bridge the legal gap between favela and city, nor any meaningful commitment to maintenance.[65]

Although extension of title to favela residents was a stated goal of Favela-Bairro, the goal was purely rhetorical. The program included no mechanism for titling and achieved no results in that regard. Indeed, the program co-incided with rising rates of housing informality, and its inflationary effects on informal rental markets probably contributed to them. The second and third versions of Favela-Bairro, from 2005 to the present, made several key improvements to the original program. They provided greater funding and mechanisms for maintenance of infrastructural projects, and exercised greater supervision over local programs. The second and third generations of Favela-Bairro offered more realistic goals and assessments of the program as a well-designed strategy for targeted urban upgrading within limitations imposed by the relative lack of federal funding.

The evolution of Favela-Bairro coincided with a new flexibility in approaches to regularization of urban property across Brazil, in the form of recognition of *Zonas Especiais de Interesse Social* (Special Social Interest Zones, or ZEIS). These Special Zones were made possible by 1980s legislation that legally exempted favelas and other low-income housing conglomerations from zoning and building codes in recognition of their crucial role in providing housing for the urban poor and working class. In 2001, the passage of a far-ranging federal law known as the *Estatuto da Cidade* (City Statute) began to open new possibilities for the meanings of the Special Zones. The City Statute gave municipal governments power to expropriate and regularize land based on its "social function"—a principle long set in Brazilian law, but rarely evoked in previous practice. The City Statute explicitly charged municipal governments with drafting and implementing plans to defend popular housing against real estate speculation.[66]

Since 2004, various Brazilian cities, Rio de Janeiro among them, have begun creating Special Zones in order to fulfill their obligations under the City Statute, using these not only to exempt self-built, low-income housing from building codes but to protect certain communities against removal and real estate speculation triggered by rising market values. Like Favela-Bairro, the Special Zones have brought limited gains rather than thoroughgoing transformations. In Rio, they have the enormous advantage of recognizing that the favela is a vital part of the city, not a perverse negation of it. But their very "special" nature continues to consign favelas to a different class of property law, one that makes it more difficult for individual homeowners to demand rights to other public investments, like infrastructure, schools, and health clinics.

The most striking and controversial innovation in favela policy has been the security strategy introduced in 2009 known as the Unidades de Polícia Pacificadora (UPPs), Pacifying Police Units. In the initial design of the program, each UPP occupied a favela or complex of favelas previously domi-nated by criminal networks. Each UPP began with a military occupation, transferring power to lightly armed community police once the favela was deemed "pacified." The UPPs have had an obvious downside: the occupa-tion that defines them is heavily military, reinforcing understandings of the favela as war zones cut off from the rest of the city. They have operated mostly in neighborhoods formerly dominated by *traficantes*, not those con-trolled by *milícias*, who continue to rely on allies within police ranks. The UPPs enjoyed a brief period of wide enthusiasm, then ran into inevitable difficulties. Several notorious cases of violence perpetrated by UPP officers, coupled with increasing resentment over marginalization of favela resi-dents, undermined support for the program both within and outside of favelas.[67] As Rio's overall economic and political fortunes declined after the 2016 Summer Olympics, the UPP model entered into noticeable decline.

From the standpoint of urban property regularization, one of the most interesting consequences of the new security strategy was that real estate values spiked in UPP neighborhoods, both in the favelas themselves and in the streets of surrounding neighborhoods.[68] The real estate boom was not limited to UPP neighborhoods. The 2014 FIFA World Cup and the 2016 Sum-mer Olympics heated up Rio's real estate market in both the formal and informal sectors. As in the past, new formal development associated with major events triggered informal growth, as well—in this case primarily in "clandestine" irregular subdivisions in the sparsely populated far western zone of the metropolitan region. At the same time, the mega-events brought a renewed wave of removal in favelas along new transit lines or in the path of Olympic development. As in the 1970s, residents of these communi-ties rallied to resist, mobilizing allied politicians and nongovernmental organizations. As in the 1970s, in some cases that mobilization was suc-cessful. But in other cases, even vigorous mobilization and the leverage of an extensive network of supporters failed to stop Olympic-related removal. These differential outcomes left no doubt that prospective real estate value was the determining factor. The return of capricious favela removal to the table as a political option was one of most pernicious aspects of Olym-pic development.

On a national level, the run-up to the Olympics coincided with one of the largest and most complex political scandals in Brazilian history, as investi-gations into kickbacks on government contracting led to the indictment of politicians from every major party. Fallout from the scandal eventually led to the impeachment of President Dilma Rousseff. Impeachment deepened entrenched partisan enmity and brought to power a cohort of old political hands deeply embroiled in the government contracting schemes. The ongoing investigations became a means of prosecuting partisan rivalry, leaving little hope that they would lead to an improvement in the transparency of administrative operations.

The implications for the city of Rio de Janeiro and its favelas were enormous. Former Rio de Janeiro State Governor Sérgio Cabral (2007–14) was one of the most prominent politicians caught up in the widening scandal (indeed, Rio de Janeiro's state scandal constituted a second front connected to but not contained by the national investigations). Cabral's term had coincided with Rio's boom years, as high oil prices, rising tourist revenue, and preparations for the mega-events flooded Rio with foreign investment. The fall of commodity prices, the poor planning of the mega-events, and the hangover left in their wake revealed the fragility of that growth. In April 2016, four months before the Olympics, an elevated bicycle path skirting the granite escarpments near Rio's most prominent beaches collapsed, killing two people and injuring several more. The bikeway collapse was symbolic of the development of the Cabral years: a great deal of flashy but poorly planned initiatives undertaken primarily to generate lucrative contracts, which fell apart under the first signs of stress.

Cabral himself was arrested on corruption charges, as was his wife. Rio's economic growth ground to a halt, with complex implications for favela residents. On the one hand, it slowed the impetus for favela removal. On the other hand, it made it more difficult for favela residents to find employment, as indices of formal employment, rising steadily since the early 1990s, retreated once again. And economic woes seemed only to intensify a backlash against policies emphasizing inclusion and consolidation of civil rights. As in most recessions, moreover, rent prices in both formal and informal sectors largely held steady while incomes dropped. The overall effect was decidedly negative. A window of opportunity for inclusionary local development slammed shut, with devastatingly little to show for it.

2018: State Violence, Popular Mobilizations, and an Uncertain Future

With the impeachment and removal from office of Dilma Rousseff in August 2016, former Vice President Michel Temer became president, and immediately swung to the right. Temer drastically cut government spending on social services. These cuts coincided with falling oil prices, the ongoing fallout from political scandal in Rio de Janeiro's state government, and a legacy of broken promises from the 2016 Summer Olympics, all of which hit the city of Rio de Janeiro hard. After years of progress, levels of violence began to rise again, with a particularly sharp spike in police shootings. The community policing initiatives of the UPP foundered in most favelas across the city, as police retreated to bunkers, emerging only with guns drawn, ready to fire. In Rio's favelas, the bad old days of the mid-1990s were back, in many cases with even greater intensity.

In February 2018, Temer imposed military intervention in Rio de Janeiro, placing Rio's police under military command. Since the end of the military dictatorship in 1985, military intervention in local security has been used sparingly and with mixed results at best. The notorious Operation Rio of 1994, for example, was characterized by military invasion of favelas, with tanks occupying major intersections and imposing severe restrictions on civil rights, but failed to reduce levels of violence appreciably, and had negligible long-term effects. Temer's eagerness to return to a tactic that had failed previously seemed driven more by his efforts to protect himself from continued political scandal endangering his own presidency than by commitment to improving security in Rio de Janeiro.

The situation took a catastrophic turn for the worse with the assassination of City Councilwoman Marielle Franco on March 14, 2018. Franco was an inspiring figure who defied every expectation for Brazilian politicians: she was a black, bisexual woman from the Maré Complex of favelas on Rio's north side. Although Franco's profile was unique for an elected politician, she grew out of a long tradition of powerful female leaders in Maré, and embodied that neighborhood's legacy of challenging inequality and confronting abuse and exploitation. One of Franco's key areas of activism was her leadership in the struggle to contain and investigate police violence. In the days before her death, she had specifically called for investigation into the brutal tactics of the 41st Battalion of the Rio state police, active in the favelas of the city's north side. The assassination of Franco, carried out by a gunman in the backseat of a car that had trailed her vehicle through downtown Rio, had all the characteristics of an extrajudicial assassination carried out by off-duty police.

Franco's death triggered a wave of revulsion and mobilization, with tens of thousands of citizens of Rio de Janeiro, of all classes, taking to the streets to call for investigation and prosecution and vowing to continue Franco's work. Franco's death showed in horrifically vivid fashion that the citizenship of favela residents remains constrained by long-standing patterns of abuse and violence. The mobilization in response to that death offers some hope of broad rejection of the recent return to militarized violence, and a commitment to recover the gradual but important improvements of the early twenty-first century.

Conclusion

The meaning of favela residence has changed enormously in the last forty years. Favela residents are no longer overwhelmingly consigned to marginality, and instead have seized the growing opportunities of Brazil's new democracy to achieve greater economic, educational and social mobility, and to demand continued public investment in urban upgrading. But informality continues to matter and to impose costs both on favela residents and on the broader city. The lack of access to the legal protection of property constricts the range of political action available to favela residents, leaving them with limited options for confronting criminal interest groups and weakening their ability to protect their communities from police violence and the threat of removal, for example.

In the mid-twentieth century, the corporatist organizing patterns of the Estado Novo conferred new political leverage on collectively mobilized favela residents. By the late twentieth century, collective representation had been distorted and undermined, and individual rights appeared farther off than ever—despite globalizing neoliberalism's promotion of the individual against the power of the state. Current developments emphasizing more flexible property and zoning legislation, municipal focus on popular housing, and improved security strategies offer reason for cautious optimism— despite current political turmoil. They have not fundamentally transformed the relationship between formal and informal development in Rio de Janeiro. Over the past century, legal informality created compromise solutions to the inadequacy of development in the formal sphere, without facilitating full legal inclusion of large percentages of Rio's poor and working-class citizens. Despite new wrinkles, that dynamic still defines the city's growth.

As ever, the options of Rio's working poor are shaped and constrained by local, national, and global trends. The loss of its status as national capital in 1960, deindustrialization in the 1970s and 1980s, and the transformation of Rio into a hub in hemispheric drug trafficking in the 1980s and beyond have all imposed challenges for Rio's residents, particularly for favela residents. The consolidation of Rio as a global tourist destination enriched real estate and service-sector titans, while often exacerbating challenges for the urban poor. Until recently, the tourist industry shunned the urban poor. The rise of favela tourism in the past decade makes a few favelas the site of exotic sightseeing, yet offers little benefit to local residents.

The history of Rio de Janeiro, for all its challenges, offers some support for Edgar Pieterse's understanding of the possibilities of urban mobilization. Residents of Rio's favelas in particular have seized the opportunity to mobilize and pressure political authorities whenever the political context allowed. To invoke John Tutino's formulation in this volume's introduction, "if global, national, and metropolitan actors committed to welfare and justice for urban majorities will work to promote rights to decent lives for all," then popular mobilization can yield important fruits. It is not likely to eliminate the formal versus informal divide that has long served as a proxy for inequality in Rio de Janeiro. But it may eliminate its worst consequences, bending the arc of formality toward inclusion, recognition, and protection of rights.

Notes

1. For a few of the key entries in the literature on informality, see Alejandro Portes, Manuel Castells, and Lauren Benton, eds., *The Informal Economy: Studies in Advanced and Less Developed Countries* (Baltimore: Johns Hopkins University Press, 1989); Alejandro Portes and Richard Schauffler, "Competing Perspectives on the Latin American Informal Sector," *Population and Development Review* 19, no. 1 (1993): 33–60; Martim O. Smolka and Ciro Biderman, "Measuring Informality in Housing Developments: Why Bother?" *Land Lines* (Lincoln Institute of Land Policy, April 2009): 14–19; Martim O. Smolka, Ciro Biderman, and Anna Sant'anna, "Urban Housing Informality: Does Building and Land Use Regulation Matter?" *Land Lines* (Lincoln Institute of Land Policy, 2008): 14–19; Ramiro Corso and Gustavo Riofrío, "Formalización de la propriedad y mejoramientos de barrios: bien legal, bien informal," Lima, Desco, Programa Urbano, 2006; Ann Varley, "The Relationship between Tenure Legalization and Housing Improvements: Evidence from Mexico City," *Development and Change* 18, no. 3 (1987): 63–81; Ann Varley, "Private or Public: Debating the Meaning of Tenure Legalization," *International Journal of Urban and Regional Research* 26, no. 3 (2002): 449–461; and Ananya Roy and Nezar Alsayyed, eds., *Urban Informality: Transnational Perspectives from the Middle East, Latin America, and South Asia* (Lanham, MD: Lexington Books, 2004). In addition to these titles, there are several think tanks and research groups that have produced extensive series of papers analyzing the question of informality from every conceivable perspective. Recommended among these are the Lincoln Institute of Land Policy in Cambridge, Massachusetts, the Land Tenure Center at the University of Wisconsin, Madison, and the Instituto de Pesquisa e Planejamento Urbano e Regional at the Universidade Federal do Rio de Janeiro.

2. Hernando de Soto, *The Mystery of Capital: Why Capitalism Triumphs in the West and Fails Everywhere Else* (London: Black Swan, 2002). De Soto's argument as presented in *The Mystery of Capital* is not simplistic and has many strengths, but it is journalistic and anecdotal. Its highly optimistic description of the benefit of titling, by itself, and interpretation of unequal development based primarily on titling practices, have inspired currents of thought that hail titling as the magic bullet of urban development.

3. See, for example, Smolka and Biderman, "Measuring Informality," and Corso and Riofrío, "Formalización de la propriedad."

4. For nuanced discussion of the competing positions in this ongoing scholarly debate, see Smolka and Biderman, "Measuring Informality," and Basudeb Guha-Khasnobis, Ravi Kanbur, and Elinor Ostrom, eds., *Linking the Formal and Informal Economy: Concepts and Policies* (New York: Oxford University Press, 2006), in particular the chapter by Alice Sindzingre, "The Relevance of the Concepts of Formality and Informality: A Theoretical Appraisal."

5. See Bryan McCann, *Hard Times in the Marvelous City: From Dictatorship to Democracy in the Favelas of Rio de Janeiro* (Durham, NC: Duke University Press, 2014), 19–42 for further analysis.

6. Mariana Cavalcanti, "S/Morro Varandão Salão 3 dorms: a construção social do valor em mercados imobiliários liminares," *Antropolítica* (Universidade Federal Fluminense, 2011); and Cavalcanti, "Do Barraco à Casa: tempo, espaço e valor(es) em uma favela consolidada," *Revista Brasileira de Ciências Sociais* 24 (2009): 69–80.

7. Maurício de Abreu, *Evolução Urbana do Rio de Janeiro* (Rio de Janeiro: Jorge Zahar, 1987); Christopher G. Boone, "Streetcars and Politics in Rio de Janeiro: Private Enterprise versus Municipal Government in the Provision of Mass Transit, 1903–1920," *Journal of Latin American Studies* 27, no. 2 (1995): 343–365. As Boone argues, private capital created the streetcars, but largely followed the preferences of federal and municipal government in establishing its lines and setting rates, indicating that the demographic patterns facilitated by streetcar development conformed to governmental expectations as well as the dictates of private profit.

8. Brodwyn Fischer, *A Poverty of Rights: Citizenship and Inequality in Twentieth Century Rio de Janeiro* (Stanford: Stanford University Press, 2008), 242–246.

9. Abreu, *Evolução Urbana*.

10. Manoel Gomes, *As Lutas do Povo do Borel* (Rio de Janeiro: Edições Muro, 1980).

11. Abreu, *Evolução Urbana*.

12. See Filippina Chinelli, "Os loteamentos da periferia," in *Habitação em Questão*, ed. Lícia do Prado Valladares (Rio de Janeiro: Jorge Zahar, 1980), 49–68; and Susana Mara Miranda Pacheco, "Produção e reprodução de loteamentos na periferia de Rio de Janeiro," M.A. thesis, Universidade Federal do Rio de Janeiro, 1984. The *loteamentos irregulares* became so predominant that the term *loteamento* itself came to imply irregularity: when *cariocas* speak of *loteamentos*, they are in the great majority of cases referring to *loteamentos irregulares*. See also McCann, *Hard Times*, 39–43, 61.

13. Gomes, *As Lutas.*

14. For background on Pereira Passos's reforms, their benefits, and social costs, see Jeffrey Needell, *A Tropical Belle Époque: Elite Culture and Society in Turn-of-the-Century Rio de Janeiro* (New York: Cambridge University Press, 1987); and Teresa Meade, *Civilizing Rio: Reform and Resistance in a Brazilian City: 1889–1930* (University Park: Pennsylvania State University Press, 1997).

15. For extensive, fine-grained analysis of the judicial battles of Rio's urban poor in areas of residential, labor, and criminal law, see Fischer, *Poverty of Rights.*

16. Bryan McCann, "Troubled Oasis: The Intertwining Histories of Morro dos Cabritos and Bairro Peixoto," in *Cities from Scratch: Poverty and Informality in Urban Latin America*, ed. Brodwyn Fischer, Bryan McCann, and Javier Auyero (Durham, NC: Duke University Press, 2014), 102–126.

17. McCann, "Troubled Oasis"; Mário Aizen, *Bairro Peixoto: O Oásis de Copacabana* (Rio de Janeiro: Prefeitura da Cidade do Rio de Janeiro, 1992), 39–44.

18. See the case of Eduardo Duvivier, analyzed in Fischer, *Poverty of Rights,* 242–246.

19. Maria Laís Pereira da Silva, *Favelas Cariocas, 1930–1964* (Rio de Janeiro: Contraponto, 2005), 51–55.

20. Marcelo Baumann Burgos, "Dos parques proletários ao Favela-Bairro: as políticas públicas nas favelas do Rio de Janeiro," in *Um Século de Favela*, ed. Alba Zaluar and Marcos Alvito, 3rd ed. (Rio de Janeiro: FGV, 2003), 25–60.

21. Pereira da Silva, *Favelas Cariocas,* 37–40.

22. Pereira da Silva, *Favelas Cariocas,* 37–40; Fischer, *Poverty of Rights,* 69, 245.

23. Luciana Correa do Lago, "O movimento de loteamentos do Rio de Janeiro," M.A. thesis, Universidade Federal do Rio de Janeiro, 1990; Pacheco, "Produção e repodução."

24. Carlos Nelson Ferreira dos Santos, *Processo de crescimento e ocupação da periferia* (Rio de Janeiro: FINEP/IBAM, 1982).

25. McCann, *Hard Times,* 39–43.

26. Lícia do Prado Valladares, *A Invenção da Favela: do mito de origem a favela .com* (Rio de Janeiro: FGV, 2005), 36–54.

27. Gomes, *As Lutas.*

28. Fischer, *Poverty of Rights,* 253–273.

29. Mariana Cavalcanti, "Of Shacks, Houses and Fortresses: An Ethnography of Favela Consolidation in Rio de Janeiro," Ph.D. dissertation, University of Chicago, 2007; Gomes, *As Lutas*; Fischer, *Poverty of Rights,* 282–285.

30. Gomes, *As Lutas,* 17; Nísia Verônica Trindade Lima, "O movimento de favelados de Rio de Janeiro: Políticas do Estado e lutas sociais, 1954–1973," M.A. thesis, Instituto Universitário de Pesquisas do Rio de Janeiro, 1989, 100–107; Fischer, *Poverty of Rights,* 284.

31. Fischer, *Poverty of Rights,* 284–290.

32. Lima, "O movimento de favelados." For painstaking research and innovative analysis of Borel's history, see Mauro Amoroso, "Caminhos do lembrar: a construção e os usos políticos da memória no Morro do Borel," Ph.D. dissertation, Fundação Getúlio Vargas-CPDOC, 2012.

33. Fischer, *Poverty of Rights*, 293–299.

34. Valladares, *A Invenção da Favela*, 75–78.

35. Marcelo Baumann Burgos, "Dos parques proletários ao Favela Bairro: as políticas públicas nas favelas do Rio de Janeiro," in *Um Século de Favela*, ed. Alba Zaluar and Marcos Alvito, 3rd ed. (Rio de Janeiro: FGV, 2003), 30–33.

36. Alberto Passos Guimarães, "As favelas do Distrito Federal e o recenseamento de 1950," *Revista Brasileira de Estatística* 14, no. 55 (1953): 250–278.

37. Américo Freire and Lúcia Lippi Oliveira, eds., *Capítulos da memória do urbanismo carioca* (Rio de Janeiro: Folha Seca, 2002).

38. Leonardo Benmergui, "The Alliance for Progress and Housing Policy in Rio de Janeiro and Buenos Aires in the 1960s," *Urban History* 36, no. 2 (2009): 303–326.

39. Lícia do Prado Valladares, *Passa-se uma casa* (Rio de Janeiro: Jorge Zahar, 1978).

40. Trindade Lima, "O movimento de favelados."

41. Mark Kehren, "Tunnel Vision: Urban Renewal in Rio de Janeiro, 1960–1975," Ph.D. dissertation, University of Maryland, 2007.

42. Mário Brum, "Cidade Alta," Ph.D. dissertation, Universidade Federal Fluminense, 2011.

43. Júlio César Pino, "Labor in the Favelas of Rio de Janeiro, 1940–1969," *Latin American Perspectives* 25, no. 2 (1998): 24–28.

44. Américo Freire and Lúcia Lippi Oliveira, *Novas Memórias do urbanismo carioca* (Rio de Janeiro: FGV, 2008), 115–116.

45. Portes, "Housing Policy," 8–10.

46. Valladares, *Passa-se uma casa*.

47. Carlos Nelson Ferreira dos Santos, *Movimentos urbanos no Rio de Janeiro* (Rio de Janeiro: Jorge Zahar, 1981).

48. Gilda Blank, "Experiência de urbanização de uma favela carioca: Brás de Pina," M.A. thesis, Universidade Federal do Rio de Janeiro, 1977.

49. Blank, "Experiência"; Santos, *Movimentos urbanos*.

50. The published version of Carlos Nelson's thesis is Santos, *Movimentos urbanos*.

51. Valladares, *Passa-se uma casa*.

52. Janice Perlman, *The Myth of Marginality: Urban Poverty and Politics in Rio de Janeiro* (Berkeley: University of California Press, 1976).

53. Mário Brum, "'O povo acredita na gente': Rupturas e continuidades no movimento comunitário das favelas cariocas nas décadas de 1980 e 1990," M.A. thesis, Universidade Federal Fluminense, 2006, 79–80; McCann, *Hard Times*, 1–18.

54. Brum, "O Povo," 106–108.

55. Rodolfo Moraes, "Intervenções governamentais sobre movimentos de invasões de terrenos urbanos: estudo de casos no município do Rio de Janeiro," M.A. thesis, Escola Brasileira de Administração Pública, FGV, 1988; McCann, *Hard Times*, 77–78.

56. Maria Sílvia Muylaert de Araújo, "As Práticas de Execução do Programa Cada Família Um Lote," M.A. thesis, Universidade Federal do Rio de Janeiro, 1988.

57. Muylaert de Araújo, "Cada Família Um Lote."

58. Michael G. Donovan, "Negotiated Land Reform in Action? The Case of Rio de Janeiro's Forum for the Regularization of Illegal Subdivisions," paper presented at Latin American Studies Association, Montreal, 2007, 13–14; Muylaert de Araújo, "Cada Família Um Lote." See also McCann, *Hard Times*, 85–90.

59. Muylaert de Araújo, "Cada Família Um Lote."

60. Author interview with Gibeon de Brito Silva, Morro do Chapéu Mangueira, 2004.

61. Elizabeth Leeds, "Cocaine and Parallel Polities on the Brazilian Urban Periphery: Constraints on Local Level Democratization," *Latin American Research Review* 31, no. 3 (1996).

62. See, for example, the three communities analyzed in Enrique Desmond Arias, *Drugs and Democracy in Rio de Janeiro* (Chapel Hill: University of North Carolina Press, 1996).

63. Wânia Amélia Belchior Mesquita, "'Tranquilidade' sob uma ordem violenta: o controle social da mineira em uma favela carioca," in *Vida Sob Cerco: Violência e Rotina nas Favelas do Rio de Janeiro*, ed. Luiz Antônio Machado da Silva (Rio de Janeiro: Editora Nova Fronteira, 2008), 227–249.

64. Adauto Lúcio Cardoso, "O Programa Favela-Bairro: Uma Avaliação," in *Seminário Programa Habitare—avaliação de projetos IPT em habitação e meio ambiente: assentamentos urbanos precários*, ed. Rose Marie Zenha and Carlos Geraldo Luz de Freitas (Rio de Janeiro: FINEP, 2002).

65. Bryan McCann, *Throes of Democracy: Brazil Since 1989* (London: Zed Press, 2009).

66. Solange Gonçalves Dias, "Regularização fundiária em Zonas de Especial Interesse Social," *Integração* 14, no. 53 (2008): 143–149.

67. For one officer's overview of the program and its use of the lessons of previous models, see Vadael Antero da Silva Filho, "A Polícia Militar e o Policiamento Comunitário: de Nazareth Cerqueira a UPP," Escola Superior da Polícia Militar, 2009. For a skeptical analysis by an urban activist, see "Unidades de Polícia Pacificadora: o que são, a que anseios respondem e quais desafios colocam ao ativismo urbano," *Passa Palavra*, June 25, 2010. For assessments of ongoing difficulties, see Rodrigo Serrano-Berthet, Flávia Carbonari, Mariana Cavalcanti, and Alys Willman, "Bringing the State Back into the Favelas of Rio de Janeiro: Understanding Changes in Community Life After the UPP Pacification Process," in *Sustainable Development Sector Management Unit Report* (Washington, DC: World Bank, October 2012); Marcelo Burgos et al., "O Efeito UPP Na Percepção Dos Moradores Das Favelas," *Desigualdade & Diversidade: Revista De Ciências Sociais da PUC Rio* 11 (August–December 2011); and Ignácio Cano, "Os Donos do Morro: Uma avaliação exploratória do impacto das Unidades de Polícia Pacificadora no Rio de Janeiro," *Fórum Brasileiro de Segurança Pública*, Rio de Janeiro, 2012.

68. Mariana Cavalcanti, "Threshold Markets: The Production of Real Estate Value between the 'Favela' and the 'Pavement,'" in *Cities from Scratch: Poverty and Informality in Urban Latin America,* ed. Brodwyn Fischer, Bryan McCann, and Javier Auyero (Duke University Press, 2014).

4 Boom, Echo, and Splinter

Citizenship and Growth in Greater Buenos Aires

• •

MARK HEALEY

For more than a century, the city and suburbs of Buenos Aires have contained a third of the population of Argentina, an extraordinary level of dominance even for a region where urban primacy is the rule. At the outset of the city's growth, the expansion of its metropolitan area became closely linked with the expansion of citizenship—understood as increasing political participation, social rights, and access to public goods. Yet over the course of the century, the urban periphery has gone from a crucible for transforming national politics to a space of division and abandonment. This chapter will explore why and how that took place, sketching the relationship between governance and citizenship in expanding Buenos Aires over the twentieth century. Pursuing a crucial insight from Adrián Gorelik about the changing "roles of the periphery" over this period, this chapter looks to deepen the conversation about the politics of urban growth in cities of the Americas. As the title signals, the growth of Buenos Aires can be conceptualized in three broad moments.[1]

First came a boom between 1887 and 1936, a period in which the city rapidly expanded outward and this expansion because a powerful avenue for social integration. This process of urban expansion accompanied the more dramatic expansion of Argentina's population due to immigration and of its economy thanks to agricultural exports and incipient industry. While both the expansion and integration were shaped by central power, neither was primarily directed from above. This chapter will argue that it was precisely the interaction between social protest and political mobilization on the periphery and municipal power at the center that drove the process of social integration.

Second came an echo of this earlier boom, a further expansion out beyond the limits of the federal capital between 1936 and 1976. Here too the expanding periphery was a key avenue to social ascent, closely linked to the broader and conflict-ridden process of industrial growth. Crucially, this echo of expansion took place outside the limits of the federal capital in a score of surrounding municipalities, and it involved primarily migrants from the Argentine interior rather than immigrants from Europe.

Third came the splintering of this integrative model, as a brutal military regime (1976–83) decisively turned against mobilized popular sectors and the broader industrialization project, devastating the suburbs even as it dramatically reshaped the center. Later democratic regimes failed to reverse this trend, and new modes of urban development, social policy, and local politics only sharpened social divisions and expanded the distance between periphery and center. Thus the periphery has gone from being a space of integration to a space of fracture, even as the political forms perfected on the periphery have been decisive in shaping urban and national politics in each period.

As this capsule overview suggests, the changes (and importance) of the periphery can only be understood in relation with changes in the "core" of Buenos Aires, the city proper. The importance and the contradictions of this relationship are suggested by the fact that, in Argentine usage, "greater Buenos Aires" is the term for the suburban area now holding 10 million inhabitants—but it does not include the nearly 3 million inhabitants of the city of Buenos Aires itself. Since 1880, the city of Buenos Aires has been a distinct jurisdiction, the federal district for the nation. By contrast, the suburbs are divided into twenty-five municipalities, widely varying in size, all part of the separate province of Buenos Aires. Six of the suburbs now have more than 1 million inhabitants. The split between the city and its suburbs has deepened, and even produced contrasting political forms, in the last thirty years. Since this split is crucial to the story of how the periphery went from playing an integrating to a fragmenting role, this chapter begins with the core, the city of Buenos Aires itself.[2]

From the Plaza to the Barrios, and Back Again, 1880–1936

Like other cities across the Spanish empire, Buenos Aires was established with a central plaza and a surrounding grid. Political power in the city and the country has resided on that plaza ever since. It is the location of the presidential palace, the national cathedral, the national bank, the most important government ministries—and the seat of municipal government. The plaza itself is the most resonant civic space in the country, target of all major rallies and demonstrations. This is the starting point of the city's subway system and the heart of the district known today as the *microcentro*.[3]

Even as the city was remade along neoliberal lines in the last thirty years, proximity to power remained so crucial that the most valuable area for new office space was the redeveloped former port, only one wide avenue away from the Casa Rosada.

The city and then the suburbs stretch out in concentric rings from this kilometer zero of the nation. Until quite recently, proximity to the center was roughly but unmistakably correlated with higher social standing. Yet Buenos Aires is very much a city of barrios, a vast expanse of neighborhoods with distinctive identities and social networks. As in the Chicago that was a laboratory for so much urban sociology and theory, the center retained its primacy even as the outskirts flourished. Indeed, key aspects of the politics and identity of the twentieth-century city were forged on the fringes.

Buenos Aires began as a strategic outpost of Spanish power, its port commanding the river system that drained the lower third of South America and provided an outlet for the rich lands of the Pampas. Always closely tied to the Atlantic World, it became the seat of the new Viceroyalty of the Río de la Plata in 1776 and, with the collapse of the empire, the capital city of the United Provinces of the Río de la Plata, first among equals. Its port made it the hub of booming exports of hides and salted meat, and the point of entry for all imports. But this primacy engendered overreach in its leaders and resentment among its rivals: for seventy years after breaking away from Spain, the place of Buenos Aires within the national order and the degree to which that national order was oriented toward the Atlantic World were motives for dispute and intermittent civil war. The issue was only finally resolved in 1880, when the city and province of Buenos Aires rebelled against a president from the interior. After the revolt was defeated, the victorious national forces split the city from the province it had commanded and turned it into an autonomous federal district ruled by nationally appointed authorities.

Throughout the turmoil, the port had remained the centerpiece of a dynamic export economy. After 1850, those exports dramatically expanded, in successive booms of mutton, cereals, and chilled beef that fueled rapid economic and demographic growth of the Pampas in general and the city of Buenos Aires in particular.

Up until this point, the growing city remained relatively compact, following the street grid and cultural patterns established by the Spanish. The elite remained near the plaza, with the popular sectors further out. After a yellow fever epidemic in 1871, however, the elite began to decamp to the north, establishing what would become a string of wealthy neighborhoods

TABLE 4.1 Population of Buenos Aires metropolitan area
and suburbs

Year	City	Suburbs
1869	176,787	—
1881	315,206	—
1895	661,198	—
1904	945,094	243,100
1914	1,575,814	486,281
1938	2,519,000	1,203,687
1947	2,981,043	1,785,500
1960	2,966,634	3,897,476
1970	2,972,453	5,563,579
1980	2,797,719	7,007,216
1991	2,871,519	8,225,715
2001	2,725,488	9,095,055
2010	2,891,062	9,910,282

Sources: Argentine Census Bureau (INDEC); César Vapñarsky, *La Aglomeración Gran Buenos Aires* (Buenos Aires: EUDEBA, 2010).

along the riverside. Impressive mansions went up along elegant boulevards, as the city began to refashion itself on the model of Paris—an enclave of Europe in the Americas. As many of the elite left the center, their homes were subdivided to rent to immigrants and the urban poor. Downtown grew denser, and its class composition changed. This created the city of the *fin-de-siècle*, a newly elegant, densely settled, and bitterly polarized place marked by increasingly violent protest and repression.[4]

The social makeup of the city, and country, was transformed after 1880 by mass immigration from Europe. The population of the federal capital expanded from 300,000 inhabitants in 1887 to just under 3 million in 1936. In fifty years, the city grew ten times in population and six times in built-up area. Most of this increase came from immigrants, who by 1914 were the majority of the city's population.

Within the city, a clear pattern of distinction developed between the wealthy and residential north and the poorer and industrial south. The northern neighborhoods began with the elite departure from the center. A string of settlements roughly paralleling the river contained most of the parks in the city and received the most state investment.

The southern tier, on the other hand, was centered on the Matanza-Riachuelo, the river that defined the city limits to the south. The original city port was located at its mouth and an industrial complex had grown up around it. Many of these low-lying neighborhoods frequently flooded. Over the coming decades, while an extensive flood-control program was implemented on the prosperous northern side of the city, the industrial south saw ambitious proposals but sparse results. What infrastructure investments came benefited industry, not the working neighborhoods.[5]

But the decisive space in the making of the modern city was the west. Here the periphery was opened up by the rapid growth of privately run transport networks: horse trams starting in the 1870s, then electric streetcars after 1895, and later subways and buses. The possibility of purchasing an inexpensive lot and building a modest home, often in stages and with one's own labor, meant that, as James Scobie put it, for workers "possessed of skills or savings, the road upward led toward the suburbs."[6]

This was a generation-long process by which empty fields and vegetable farms became first precarious and isolated homes, then scattered neighborhoods, and finally tight clusters of buildings along paved streets. This expansion took place almost entirely within city limits and, crucially, along a street grid that municipal engineers drew up between 1898 and 1904. The outline of the streets was largely determined at the outset, but actually building these visions was the joint work of speculators, homeowners, municipal institutions, and above all neighborhood associations. For a long time, the wealthy neighborhoods and political powers largely ignored the world of the outskirts, and the city defined itself in terms of grand boulevards and a booming port. But out on the periphery, in the struggle for services and improvements, sometimes coupled with the struggle for recognition and legal ownership, a new mode of politics was born.[7]

There had been a strong tradition of urban popular politics in nineteenth-century Buenos Aires, rooted in the independence struggle and finding expression by the 1850s in immigrant associations and political clubs.[8] But this tradition was largely eclipsed by the emergence of a powerful national state dominated by a narrow elite and the arrival of waves of immigrants with no political rights after 1880. Out of this tumultuous world there developed a powerful labor movement, with anarchists particularly prominent, and two reformist parties led by dissident elites and committed to mass politics: the Socialists and the Radicals. Already in 1904, a working-class section of Buenos Aires elected the first Socialist to a national legislature in the Americas. With the passage of universal (male) secret suffrage in 1912, these two parties would come to dominate municipal electoral politics.[9]

Modern Buenos Aires was made on the periphery. These two rival mass parties, Radicals and Socialists, were forged in the neighborhoods of the west and south, in a dense web of social and cultural institutions—party offices, neighborhood associations, libraries, social clubs, bars, cafes, sports clubs, and eventually parish churches.[10] The popular culture of the modern city grew out of this hardscrabble world of immigrant striving, or more precisely the complex interplay between the rough authenticity of the outskirts and the seductive sophistication of the center. One testimony to the power of this experience is the extraordinary number of soccer teams—and vast stadiums—in the neighborhoods of Buenos Aires. An indication of its national resonance is the fact that even today teams from the capital account for nearly all of the national first division.

The political culture of the city also emerged here, in the interaction between the neighborhood organization and mobilization required to obtain political recognition and municipal services, and the modernizing drive of the national government to remake the territory it controlled most intimately. It was especially important that this first cycle of expansion took place almost entirely within city limits and the grid municipal engineers had drawn up.[11] Here the peculiarities of Argentine federalism played a role: the federal capital and the national territories were the only places where national agencies could act directly, rather than through provincial administrations. This greater freedom of action, the desire to make the capital a showcase, and the political pressure for reform led federal agencies to provide services in Buenos Aires sooner and better than anywhere else in the country. There are many examples of this dynamic, from education to public health, but perhaps the most dramatic is in urban waterworks. After taking over a failed private concession in 1891, the federal government brought potable water and sewer service to the entire city, providing by 1914 a level of coverage within Buenos Aires that would not be achieved nationwide until the 1960s.[12] The boom development of the city in the late nineteenth and early twentieth centuries came in times of economic prosperity as the port funneled sustenance to industrial Europe. In that context, the local mix of political demands and coordinated planning led to a mostly legal and broadly formal urban expansion and widely available services—limiting the impact of prevailing inequities.

This expansive cycle of municipal politics had a curious relationship to national politics. Buenos Aires did not elect its own municipal executive, but it did elect city councilmen and national legislators, and from early on, these included some of the fiercest voices of dissent in government nationwide. In 1916, the Radical Party won the presidency in the first elections by universal (male) secret ballot, marking a dramatic democratic opening for country and city. Even after the military overthrew the Radical government in 1930, ending five decades of constitutional succession to install a corrupt Conservative regime, democratic institutions continued to flourish within city limits—and Socialists even won control of the city council. But the endurance of inclusive, relatively transparent, and highly mobilized politics inside the city after 1930 came to mark an increasingly sharp contrast with the fraudulent, repressive, and exclusionary politics outside it. As the city of Buenos Aires came to symbolize open politics, the neighboring province of Buenos Aires exemplified fraud. If the city had seemed like a laboratory of democratic citizenship for the nation, increasingly it became more like an isolated outpost, its social inclusion limited by its geographic exclusion.[13]

In 1936, just as settlement had covered nearly the entire area inside the federal district's boundaries, save a few low-lying areas along the Riachuelo, the city government launched a major infrastructure program to reassert the power of downtown. Symbolically aimed against the democratic and decentralizing reforms the Socialist and Radical parties had been pushing for decades, this program involved the large-scale renewal of the city's core, with the creation of an expanded entertainment district, the construction of the ten-lane-wide 9 de Julio Avenue through the middle of downtown, and the raising of the iconic obelisk at the key corner of the new avenue. By building a new parkway along the city's border, General Paz Avenue, the program also sharply drew the city's limits. This counteroffensive of "modernization without reform" incorporated cultural motifs from the barrios to reinforce the importance of the center and the limits of the city. It produced a distinctive synthesis, on the level of municipal identity and social inclusion, of the dense towers of downtown with the low-slung homes of the suburbs. But the social polarization that had waned within the city limits would live on outside it.[14]

After 1936, nearly all growth would take place outside the city limits, and there would be no organized effort to bring these areas under unified authority. Argentine cities, in contrast to many North American cities, faced powerful legal and political obstacles to annexing neighboring territory and expanding their reach. For the federal capital, these obstacles proved insurmountable, and after the early annexation of surrounding townships in the 1880s, city limits expanded no further. General Paz Avenue, the ring road along the city limits, would become "the material and symbolic border of the 'European city'" as the suburbs beyond drew new migration from Argentina's interior.[15]

The Making of Greater Buenos Aires, 1936–1976

By 1936, the city had already outgrown its borders and its suburbs contained more than a million people, a quarter of the metropolitan area population. The train lines out into the countryside provided the backbone for this growth. To the north, a commuter line along the coast linked together a series of bedroom communities that blended in to the wealthy northern neighborhoods of the city—complete with a competing horse track. To the west and to the south, other lines carried freight and commuters, enabling several small villages to become modest industrial suburbs and striving middle-class hamlets. Interspersed with these towns were a few summer retreats for the wealthy. Along the Riachuelo on the city's southern border, the dynamic was somewhat different. Here there already were industrial establishments on both sides of the river when the city limits were drawn.[16] Over time, the municipalities immediately bordering the Riachuelo on the provincial side became an area of lightly regulated expansion, burgeoning with factories, casinos, and working-class communities, all under the control of a brutal Conservative political machine. It was in the industrial dynamism and social deprivation of these new working-class communities, especially in the south, that Peronism would find its strongest support.[17]

When the military took power in 1943, overthrowing the fraudulent Conservative government, they promised a new era of social justice by authoritarian means. From early on, the reformist elements within the military regime, soon led by Secretary of Labor Juan Perón, promoted a broad array of new social policies focused on improving the working and living conditions of the majority, starting with industrial workers. These reforms won Perón ample support on the poorer fringes of the city, and not only there. When middle-class opposition forced him from office in October 1945, a demonstration by perhaps a million workers occupied the Plaza de Mayo and the city center to successfully demand his return. This upended the Argentine political system, forging an enduring link between workers, unions, and Perón. In a complex shift over the following year, Socialists and Radicals would lose much of their working-class support, with the Radicals becoming a more uniformly middle-class party and, eventually, the catch-all party of political opposition.

The October 17, 1945, protest was a decisive moment in the history of Buenos Aires, because its protagonists were workers from the outskirts, many young and recent migrants from the interior, and because their actions were focused on seizing the preeminent symbolic space in the republic—the Plaza de Mayo—and on ritually discrediting the urban institutions that embodied the national establishment. Here a different connection was established between the central plaza and the outlying barrios. From this point forward, Perón's success as leader would be built on his ability to take the streets, to fill the plazas, to generate a new form of mobilizing politics, but also to make concrete improvements in the daily lives of his supporters in outlying areas.[18]

Within the capital city, Perón's administration raised a few housing projects and built many governmental buildings. Outside the city, the Peronist government undertook one massive unified planning project in Ezeiza, just to the southwest. This was an ambitious attempt to open up a new southern approach to the city, building a new international airport, the city's first major highway, many housing projects, and a network of parks on the river floodplain. This signal intervention was notable for the central place it occupied in Peronist iconography and the disdain and mockery it drew from regime opponents.[19]

Important as government-built housing projects were as a symbol of Peronist policy, the most wide-ranging changes came through other means. Most importantly, by strengthening unions and expanding social policy, Peronist rule carried out a massive redistribution of income. It produced a "democratization of prosperity," which dramatically increased popular consumption and greatly expanded popular presence in the parks, plazas, and shopping areas once dominated by the elite. The conquest of the city did not involve destroying the older cultural institutions, but rather changing their meaning, as they were appropriated by new users to new ends.[20] This conquest did, of course, spark resistance. The revulsion at popular appropriation of urban space and the loss of social privilege would be key to the emergence of anti-Peronism and to future urban policy.[21]

Peronism pursued policies that transformed the city and particularly its suburbs. First, regime support contributed to dramatic industrial expansion. The factory belt was already concentrated in the south and on the fringes of the city—precisely where many workers in the October 1945 protests came from. After 1945, many factories remained within the federal capital, but the industrial center of gravity shifted into the nearby suburbs. While two-thirds of industrial jobs were inside city limits in 1947, two-thirds were outside city limits by 1960. Thus the most dynamic engine for job creation was just outside the capital.[22]

The second area of major changes was housing. Rents were frozen in 1943, and remained frozen under Peronist rule, even as inflation eroded their real cost. This policy was a boon to renters, who were nearly three-quarters of the metropolitan (city and suburb) residents. It was obviously less favorable to owners, who first ceased to invest in new rental housing and then sold off existing properties. The increase in real earnings for most workers, the expanded availability of inexpensive mortgages, and the passage of a condominium law that allowed buildings to be sold piecemeal combined to drive a rapid shift from renting to owning. By 1960, 58 percent of metropolitan residents owned their homes. Inside the capital, this process solidified middle-class neighborhoods—the social groups most passionately opposed to Perón were among its greatest beneficiaries—but outside city limits, it opened up new possibilities for workers.[23]

Public action furthered this process in several ways: the newly nationalized railroads kept commuter fares deliberately low, the nationalized banking system provided generous credit, and official policies favoring industrialization and unions created plentiful well-paying work.[24]

Of course, the combination of internal migration and industrial growth is a familiar theme across Latin American cities in these years, and certainly present in Mexico City and Rio de Janeiro. In all these cities, this was a moment of expansion on the periphery. But Buenos Aires was distinctive because it had already pioneered a model for social mobility through an expanding periphery, and this new moment built on that prior precedent. In contrast to peripheries elsewhere, in Buenos Aires the new suburbs were not spaces of legal informality: land was sold legally, neighborhoods were generally laid out according to a street grid, and though there certainly were fraudulent subdivisions, the vast majority of locals had clear title to their property. This was also a function of terrain: the flat land surrounding the city was far easier to divide up and build on than the complex topography of cities like Rio de Janeiro—not surprisingly, it was in low-lying and flood-prone lands where irregular settlements later clustered. The population of the suburbs grew by as much as 6 percent annually during this period, largely due to internal migration. Between 1947 and 1960, the suburban population doubled, and its percentage of homeowners rose from 43 to 67 percent.[25]

Yet public action was constrained in important ways. These years of robust growth took place under the auspices of Perón's Five Year Plan (1947 to 1952), which turned a general enthusiasm for the idea of planning into the specific requirement that municipalities develop a master plan. The city of Buenos Aires developed a plan, focused on a handful of demonstration projects which were not finished but did highlight the need for coordination across the metropolitan area. Planners and officials working for the province of Buenos Aires took up the call. As a result, in 1948 the national government for the first time recognized the existence of the metropolitan region, calling it the *"conurbano bonaerense,"* defined as the seventeen municipalities in the province of Buenos Aires which surrounded the federal capital (it would later be expanded to twenty-five). The government decreed that the municipalities should develop joint policies for growth, infrastructure, and housing, but did not provide any specific institutions or funding to do so.[26] And in the context of a federal political system that underrepresented the province of Buenos Aires within the national legislature and underrepresented the *conurbano* within the provincial legislature, locals had relatively few mechanisms to press for greater coordination or resources.[27]

Remarkably, at this moment of great enthusiasm for planning, municipalities placed almost no restrictions on land use. This marked a significant difference with the first phase of expansion. Instead of a range of neighborhoods developing in similar ways under a single municipal authority, outside the capital a far larger and more varied assortment of neighborhoods would develop under weak and competing municipal authorities. Loose land regulations were almost a condition of growth in this period: they made it possible for many workers to buy a piece of property, but they also ensured that more than a few of those properties would be in low-lying areas subject to flood, or far from any present or future infrastructure investments. Definitive numbers are not available, but all evidence is that suburban governments had a fraction of the capacity and funding of the capital—four decades later, they spent a fifth as much per capita.[28] They competed against each other to attract factories and lacked any meaningful regional coordination. There certainly were significant infrastructure investments in the *conurbano*—schools, hospitals, and sewers—but they were not part of an overall plan, unlike the capital, where the continuity of institutions and the focus of political pressure had produced more consistent results.

The key actors in this process were less municipal governments than the real estate interests who subdivided properties and the families who bought lots and then, in stages and with the help of neighbors and local groups, gradually built homes on them. Despite all the available open land around the city, building would quickly cover most of the terrain. Buenos Aires proper had an extensive network of parks, which largely dated from the early days of its expansion. In neighborhoods consolidated after 1910, very little space was reserved for parks, and this pattern would intensify in the suburbs outside city limits, as housing and later pavement would cover most of the available area.

Beyond the political limitations, the physical geography of this expansion also worked against coordinated planning. The first settlements were often located along rail lines, laid out with the familiar street grid, provided with pavement and basic infrastructure, and populated with the kinds of neighborhood associations and civil society institutions that had characterized the outer neighborhoods within city limits a generation earlier. But the greatest expansion came in between these settlements, in previously inaccessible land opened up by the new bus lines and ambitious speculators. These lots were sold off inexpensively, with no infrastructure, and buyers often built homes themselves in gradual stages. There was a flourishing of neighborhood associations and civil society institutions, as in the outer neighborhoods within the city limits a generation earlier. But resources were fewer and the scale far larger.[29]

The second expansion was far more dispersed than the first, in terms of physical location, social networks, and political governance. As water and sewer access show, far less infrastructure was provided. As late as 1972, potable running water was available to 100 percent of the city of Buenos Aires, but only 46 percent of the suburbs.[30]

Even so, this expanding world was held together by a shared hope for prosperity and two primary institutions—unions and, when it was legal, the Peronist Party.[31] To some extent, this institutional weakness was a deliberate choice on the part of the national (and provincial) government. The Peronist leadership were empowered but also deeply unnerved by their success in mobilizing labor, and many later policies could be seen as an attempt to tame the tiger Perón had unleashed. A robust set of metropolitan or regional institutions might produce another potential space of autonomy and contention. With Perón already jealous of the popularity of the governor of Buenos Aires, whom he eventually pushed out of office, there was little chance that his movement was going to favor such an initiative. After Perón's overthrow, various technical bodies were created to conduct regional planning, but persistent political instability and continuing growth hampered any effective coordination.

The dramatic social advances of 1946–55 were partly reversed by the military coup that overthrew Perón and the succession of unstable civilian and military regimes that followed over the next eighteen years. Still, the underlying spatial logic of peripheral expansion continued largely unchanged until 1976. Indeed, the persistence of this egalitarian space of achievement for common Argentines was a key reason why Perón retained political credibility in these areas during his long exile, and why workers showed the social confidence and political determination to repeatedly challenge the rule of factory bosses and the political system during the contentious sixties and seventies. But this rebelliousness sparked frequent military interventions, and a growing unease at the very existence of the industrial belt. As Metropolitan Buenos Aires grew far beyond the core during and after World War II and its economy faced wartime uncertainties, post-war opportunities, and then cold-war constraints, Peronist politics enabled a broad if contested and uneven distribution of earnings and services uncommon in other Latin American cities. Political mobilization could and did make a difference—for a time.

Three other factors evident even in the boom years suggested that this expansion with benefits contained the seeds of its own demise. First, however inexpensive self-built housing on the periphery was, it was not inexpensive enough for all. Thus, with massive migration from the countryside, one unanticipated effect of the shrinking of the rental market was the appearance of the first shantytowns in Buenos Aires. Calling into question the successful trajectory of urban integration so far, the "*villa miseria*" was the first sign of what would become a deepening structural crisis. Quite small at first, representing less than 1 percent of the population of the metropolitan area in 1955, the villas were subject to the usual mix of top-down proposals for eradication of shanties and for the reeducation and rehousing of residents. During the twenty years after the fall of Perón, a series of governments returned to the cause, as the villas continued to grow. In particular, villas developed substantially within the city of Buenos Aires. In an unexpected reversal of prior trends, they became a marker of the growing desperation of the housing situation. Government efforts failed to provide shelter for more than a fraction of those in the most desperate communities. A mix of brutality and neglect spawned the emergence of a *villero* movement.[32]

By the late 1960s, as political mobilization reached a crescendo, the *villeros* emerged as a powerful mobilized constituency, with a citywide coordinating body and strong allies among radicalized priests and students. Overwhelmingly Peronist, the *villeros* were an important constituency in agitating for his return in 1973, but their activism would soon make them targets of repression by right-wing elements within Peronism and especially by the military after the 1976 coup.[33]

Second, the military and civilian regimes after 1955 deepened the drive to industrialize, but tried to shift industrial growth elsewhere in the country. This was partly an attempt to compensate for regional imbalances in development, but it was also a strategy for undermining the power of Peronist unions. Most of the large-scale new industrial enterprises that opened in the sixties, from petrochemical plants to automobile factories, were located in the interior, especially Córdoba.[34] But after the attempt to make Córdoba a model backfired by 1969, producing massive strikes, the military tried to draw industry to poorer provinces of the northwest with tax incentives, a program even Perón embraced when he triumphantly returned to power in 1973. As this suggests, many powerful political actors were committed to shifting the center of gravity of industry away from greater Buenos Aires.[35]

Third, while the overall population of the capital core had not grown significantly—beyond the relative expansion of the *villero* population—the city itself had been transformed, with a dramatic rise in the number of automobiles and a replacement of much of the older low-story housing with new apartment towers. Buenos Aires was turning inward in some ways, becoming more residential and less industrial, a shift that would bring a new vision for the city and changing relationships with its expanding suburbs and the larger Argentine nation.

Rupture and Reinvention, 1976–Present

When the military seized power again in 1976, they embarked on a radical restructuring of Argentine society, beginning with Buenos Aires. Despite deep divisions within the military, all groups agreed on the need to eviscerate labor unions and the left. This was key to undoing the social equality and political participation which they blamed not only for a decade of unrest but also for three decades of political instability. They thus began on a wide-ranging campaign of terror to shatter the civil society that had supported Peronism.[36] At the same time, they launched upon a systematic attempt to reorder the Argentine economy and social landscape, calling their government the "Process of National Reorganization."

The architects of government economic policy aimed to weaken the power of unions, streamline industry, and encourage the growth of an unregulated financial sector. Lowered tariffs and an overvalued currency brought in a wave of imports, marking the beginning of a long process of deindustrialization. There were many inconsistencies in military policy, particularly between the proponents of market reforms and the advocates of authoritarian planning, but there were also several clear shared objectives. In few places was this so clear as in metropolitan Buenos Aires.

The dictatorship was the high point for planning in the city: this was when a uniform planning code was finally implemented, with the clear goals of cleaning up industry (by closing it or driving it out of the city), eliminating irregular settlements (in practice, any cluster of the poor the military could uproot), and encouraging denser and taller construction. The centerpiece of this effort was the new highways the military drove through the city. This radical "urban surgery," which ripped through several neighborhoods and displaced thousands, was accompanied by a hardline policy against irregular settlements. Paramilitary violence had already decimated leaders of the *villero* movement, and when the military came to power, they tore apart what remained of the movement and the communities it represented. During military rule, an estimated 200,000 people were ejected from the city of Buenos Aires, many simply dumped unceremoniously just outside municipal jurisdiction. The city expelled its poor, breaking apart the networks of activism and support they had forged. As the military mayor memorably put it, "Living in Buenos Aires is not a right but a privilege— not everyone deserves the city."[37]

Within the capital, a new geography of wealth and privilege emerged. The military lifted the rent control in place in varying forms since 1943, leading to mass evictions, a rapid rise in rents, and a boom in speculative new construction. Much of the debt run up during the early years of military rule went into grand projects, like a new state television complex, and private construction, especially residential towers. To turn Buenos Aires into a modern and orderly city, the military wanted to purge the unruly Peronist and industrial city of the recent past. They also laid the groundwork for the urban redevelopment that would flourish a generation later.

At the same time, the military regime destroyed the industrializing project that had been the motor of the suburbs. Whatever their fragmentation, those suburbs were held together by shared aspirations for a better life. As studies documented at the time, even many *villeros* were factory workers. The unions were a central institution in local social life, however threatened by the military, rank-and-file insurgency, and leftist challenges during these years. When the military unleashed its brutal attack, factory workers were the single hardest-hit group, and the industrial belt of Buenos Aires (along with Córdoba and Rosario) was a particular target for state terror.

As unions were crushed or sidelined, regime policies set the region on the long road to deindustrialization. The gutting of the industrial sector was not complete, as a dwindling number of factories survived. But industrial work lost its former role as the social anchor for communities. With the assault on popular politics, the breaking of unions, and the turn to neoliberal globalization, Buenos Aires and the Argentina it dominated joined the Latin American mainstream: urbanization promoted concentrated power and prosperity for the favored while marginality spread.

Outside of the capital, the military attempt at planning led to the implementation of a strict new law on subdivisions that brought the decades of legal self-construction to a close. Coming just as nearly all land in inner suburbs had been used up, the law drove up prices and pushed future attempts at self-building still further out from the city and, above all, onto land that was prone to flooding or held by irregular title. An ambitious military attempt to coordinate garbage collection and disposal for the city and suburbs, for example, created a ring of government-owned dumps circling the capital which soon became targets for irregular settlements. The full effects of this law only became evident with the return of democracy, but it decisively closed off the process of gradual integration that had characterized much of suburban development until this point. By blocking legal access to land without providing alternatives, the military regime set Buenos Aires down the path to rising levels of informality Brazilian cities had pioneered decades before.

Military rule also brought decentralization, as municipalities were given greater authority over their own budgets and planning. This laid the groundwork for future fragmentation, as the military proved less effective in increasing accountability than in weakening government capacity in social policy. One place where these effects can be seen is in land-use policy: the framework set out by the military would survive into democracy and enable the proliferation of fragmented development projects after 1989. Another clear example of the neglect that accompanied decentralization is infrastructure. Already by 1972, greater Buenos Aires was falling behind the rest of the province, much less the capital. By 1980, greater Buenos Aires had less running water service than any other province except for predominantly rural Misiones. By 2001, greater Buenos Aires ranked dead last in the country.

The expulsion of the *villeros* not only crippled activist networks in the city but also destabilized the suburbs they were sent to. Facing the arrival of thousands of *villeros,* and later of thousands of migrants from the impoverished interior, municipal governments had little capacity to help.

Dumped in relatively few places, and without any means of building stable shelter, the expelled groups tended to form new villas in the suburbs. While the suburbs had always had limited funds, heterogeneous populations, and often irregular patterns of growth, these exceptions increasingly became the norm, as the poor became a dominant group among local residents just as jobs and progress were slipping away.[38]

In some municipalities, particularly Quilmes and La Matanza in the south, these groups would eventually organize, and in the early years of democracy, seize lands for regularized settlements. These efforts would be aided by the progressive elements within the Catholic Church, a dynamic group, despite its relatively small place in the Argentine Church. In La Matanza, several groups of provincial migrants, evacuated *villeros*, and displaced local residents came together to seize lands next to Ciudad Evita, a landmark project from Perón's first administration which had subsequently become a middle-class neighborhood. Here the precarious but combative future came together with the orderly and iconic past: a regular street grid laid out by the illegal occupants of land next to the culs-de-sac in the shape of Evita's profile of the earlier project.[39]

Over the course of the dictatorship, familiar forms of social and political organization in the suburbs had broken down. One sign was the many land seizures, part of a broad wave of activism by a newly impoverished society. Another was a result of the 1983 democratic elections, the first legitimate election in forty years that Peronism did not win. This was due partly to the Peronist candidate's military ties, in contrast to the clean democratic break represented by his Radical Party rival. But it was particularly because the union-based political model of the past decades had broken down, and Peronism needed to find a new way to win.

This new path to victory would be pioneered on the periphery. Peronism remade itself, and recaptured a central role in local and national politics, by embracing the changes the military regime had wrought. Peronism was transformed from a worker's party based in unions into a clientelistic party of the poor.[40]

The decades after the return of democracy were shaped by cycles of economic crisis. First was the imaginative but failed strategy of the Radical administration of Alfonsín (1983–89) to overcome debt and restart growth, which spiraled into hyperinflation in 1989. This was followed by the radical free-market reforms of the Peronist administration of Menem (1989–99) which privatized many state assets and seemed for a while to spark sustained growth, but instead produced dramatically increased corruption, inequality, and unemployment, eventually leading to Menem's electoral defeat, a deep recession, a default on foreign debt, and the economic collapse of 2001–02. The brutal impoverishment that resulted was partly overcome by the export-led growth and increased social spending of the Peronist administrations of Duhalde (2002–3) and especially Néstor and Cristina Kirchner (2003–15).

Despite the dramatic shifts in political strategy, economic policy, and rhetoric between these administrations, a common thread was the increasing fragmentation of greater Buenos Aires as a social landscape and its increasing relevance as a political actor. There was a clear institutional reason for this. The new constitution ratified in 1994 introduced two changes of crucial impact on urban politics.

First, the city of Buenos Aires was for the first time made into a sovereign political unit with its own constitution and elected head of government, making it equivalent to a province. This would lead to considerable innovations in local government but also, and crucially, to a sharpening of political and social distinctions between the city and its suburbs in the province. Politics had been quite different on either side of General Paz Avenue for some time, but now that distinction would grow far deeper.

Second, the new constitution eliminated the electoral college, awarding the presidency to the winner of the direct vote count. The vast suburbs of Buenos Aires, so close to the media of the capital, now became even more important to winning power.

Alongside these shifts in political representation, the city and suburbs underwent significant social change, as several processes begun under the dictatorship accelerated and intensified. The city of Buenos Aires was in many ways the showcase of the free-market reforms of the 1990s, which sparked booms in office towers downtown and especially in residential towers across the city, a mode of speculative real estate development that would only intensify after the crisis of 2001–02. The suburbs followed a divergent path.

Viewed from the outside, the most familiar of these processes was the belated but swift incorporation of greater Buenos Aires into a U.S.-inspired suburbanization of the wealthy. The expansion of the highway network and the shifts in land-use laws enabled the rapid emergence of dozens of shopping centers and malls and—more importantly—hundreds of gated subdivisions, which in Argentina were called "countries." While there had been a small number of country clubs scattered across the *conurbano* for a long time—hence the term applied for the new developments—this was the first time the upper-middle and upper classes moved outside of the northern corridor. In a few cases, the new highways were also lined by new factories, as some of the new foreign investment flowing into the country in the 1990s established new facilities. But a far more characteristic feature of the suburban landscape were older factories that had shut down or, in a few poignant cases, been turned into malls.

The other transformation of the social landscape of the suburbs was the increasing presence and prominence of poverty. With unemployment rising during much of this period, and spiking in 2001–2, fewer were able to pursue the old dream of building their own house on a legal lot. The decreasing availability of land and increased restrictions created by the military law led to more land seizures, villas, and other forms of irregular occupation. Even when jobs slowly began to return after 2003, and the Kirchner administrations launched various programs to regularize titles, ease access to credit, and subsidize construction, a large and increasing percentage of the population lived in informal settlements.

Starting in the 1980s, but intensifying in the 1990s, it became increasingly important for communities to organize politically and to link up with party brokers in order to secure social assistance and a place to live. Such political connections had always been important but now became essential: they would be the backbone for the ability of Peronism to respond to social discontent and continue to win elections in the 1990s. As the social situation worsened and protests increased, this neighborhood organizing would give birth to the *piquetero* movement, that would prove a robust challenge to Peronists and their successors in the crisis years of the late 1990s and early 2000s. After the 2001 collapse, finding a way to incorporate protestors and to use neighborhood groups to distribute aid and stabilize communities became essential to any successful political project.[41]

Decades before, demands for services and the drive for recognition on the urban periphery had been a key laboratory of urban democracy, producing social integration within the city of Buenos Aires and an apparent model for future growth. With that model now broken apart, from the fractured landscape of the impoverished suburbs a new model of democracy would emerge. Imperfect as it was, it underscored the central place the urban periphery has had in forging Argentine citizenship. But the politics generated out of these protests and demands on the periphery proved far less robust and inclusive. And even as the periphery was being remade, its impoverished and sometimes violent landscape was becoming ever more strongly stigmatized by a more prosperous, more developed, and more self-governing city of Buenos

Aires. No longer seen as an imperfect extension of the city or even as the raucous hub of a slightly different national project (as in the midcentury years), greater Buenos Aires now was widely viewed from the city center as a site of danger, of degradation, and of unworthy citizens. When a new right-wing party won the mayoralty of Buenos Aires, it set about inventing a new mode of politics that would reduce the influence of the mobilized poor and the laboratory of the periphery. Once again, the center would try to reassert its primacy. Two successful terms in the mayoralty and a surprising victory in the 2015 presidential elections reveals the enduring power of this vision. But the history of the past century suggests that whatever the future path of development for the country, it will be powerfully shaped by patterns of citizenship forged in the suburbs of Buenos Aires.

Modern Buenos Aires was forged during the long export boom after 1880, a dynamic city with buildings and infrastructure reflecting ever greater ambitions. Expanding infrastructure and urban services received a generation of European migrants in a city of stark inequalities but increasingly lively civil society and possibilities for advancement. The Depression challenged the export economy the city commanded and led to a turn to national industry. A cluster of factories turned into a broad industrial belt. World War II brought new uncertainties with the emergence of Peronism, the intensification of the industrial project, and the disruption and breakdown of export markets. All the while, new streams of migrants came from the Argentine interior to drive continuing urban growth. In the face of changing and uncertain times, popular demands grounded in Buenos Aires's outer neighborhoods created and sustained a Peronist national project that kept alive a broadly if imperfectly shared urban prosperity unique in Latin America. Through the 1950s the metropolis carried on, maintaining prosperity and services that echoed once celebrated urban glories.

The mid-century echo came with contradictions that became conflicts and led to crisis in the 1970s. Politicized demands for popular welfare persisted while a changing world economy prejudiced the Argentine industrial project—challenges shared across the Americas. A changing Peronism worked first to secure and then to contain popular gains; then the military seized power and destroyed the popular mobilization long key to advancing broader welfare. The rupture guaranteed that the coming transformation would serve the powerful and marginalize the long assertive people of Buenos Aires, a metropolis still expanding as people arrived from an interior facing collapsing prospects for employment and income. Under military rule and even after a new "democratization" the once leading metropolis of South America faced a splintering of political possibilities, of urban development planning and processes, and of the economic gains that increasingly flowed to benefit a few—while so many faced poverty and insecurity. Buenos Aires came to share the deepening polarities that shaped most New World cities in the turn to globalization. Where once the outskirts of Buenos Aires had been a raucous space of aspiration, now they contained the largest concentrated areas of poverty in the nation. The neoliberals in power in 2018 seem poised to continue that splintering trajectory. Still, the history of Buenos Aires shows that change can come and that politics matter.

Notes

1. My framing of the three moments follows Horacio Torres, *El mapa social de Buenos Aires (1940-1990)* (Buenos Aires: Universidad de Buenos Aires, Facultad de Arquitectura Diseño y Urbanismo, 1995). My overall interpretation follows the suggestive essay on "Los roles de la periferia" by Adrián Gorelik, in *Correspondencias: arquitectura, ciudad, cultura* (Buenos Aires: SCA/Nobuko, 2011), 265–294.

2. On the complex relationship between the city and its suburbs, see Gabriel Kessler, "Prólogo," and Adrián Gorelik, "Ensayo introductorio: terra incognita" in *El Gran Buenos Aires, Historia de la provincia de Buenos Aires*, ed. Gabriel Kessler, vol. 6 (Buenos Aires: Edhasa/Unipe, 2015), 11–72.

3. For a suggestive recent history, see Silvia Sigal, *La plaza de Mayo: una crónica* (Buenos Aires: Siglo XXI, 2006).

4. See the map in Adrián Gorelik, *La grilla y el parque* (Bernal: Universidad Nacional de Quilmes, 1996), 15.

5. Antonio Elio Brailovsky, *Buenos Aires, ciudad inundable* (Buenos Aires: Capital Intelectual, 2010).

6. James Scobie, *Buenos Aires: Plaza to Suburb, 1870-1910* (New York: Oxford University Press, 1974), 159.

7. Luciano di Privitellio, *Vecinos y ciudadanos: Política y sociedad en la Buenos Aires de entreguerras.* (Buenos Aires: Siglo XXI, 2003), 105–148.

8. Hilda Sábato, *The Many and the Few: Political Participation in Republican Buenos Aires* (Stanford: Stanford University Press, 2001), especially 29–52; Gabriel Di Meglio, *¡Viva el bajo pueblo!* (Buenos Aires: Prometeo, 2008).

9. For an excellent treatment of the rise and fall of anarchists, see Juan Suriano, *Paradoxes of Utopia: Anarchist Culture and Politics in Buenos Aires, 1890-1910* (Oakland: AK Press, 2010). For an overview of municipal politics in this period, see Richard Walter, *Politics and Urban Growth in Buenos Aires, 1910-1942* (New York: Cambridge University Press, 1993).

10. Leandro Gutiérrez and Luis Alberto Romero, *Sectores populares, cultura y política: Buenos Aires en la entreguerra* (Buenos Aires: Sudamericana, 1995), especially 155–175.

11. Gorelik, *La grilla y el parque*, 126–148.

12. Osvaldo Rey, *El saneamiento en el area metropolitano: del Virreinato a 1993* (Buenos Aires: Aguas Argentinas, 2003), 31–50. See also Olga Noemí Burda de Ragucci, *El agua privada en Buenos Aires, 1856–1892: Negocio y fracaso* (Buenos Aires: Editorial Vinciguerra, 1997).

13. On Socialist initiatives, see Gorelik, *La grilla y el parque*, 337–356; on the relationship with national politics, see di Privitellio, *Vecinos y ciudadanos*, 183–205.

14. Gorelik, *La grilla y el parque*, 387–452.

15. Adrián Gorelik, "Buenos Aires Is (Latin) America, Too" in *City/Art: The Urban Scene in Latin America*, ed. Rebeca Biron (Durham, NC: Duke University Press, 2009), 68.

16. For an excellent overview of the early development of suburban Buenos Aires, see Charles Sargent, *The Spatial Evolution of Greater Buenos Aires, Argentina, 1870–1930* (Tempe: Center for Latin American Studies, Arizona State University, 1975), 93–106.

17. On corrupt machine politics in industrial suburbs, see Norberto Folino, *Barceló, Ruggierito y el populismo oligárquico* (Buenos Aires: Ediciones de la Flor, 1983).

18. On the protest, see Daniel James, "October 17th and 18th, 1945," *Journal of Social History* 21, no. 3 (1988): 441–461. On the broader social background, see Daniel James, *Resistance and Integration: Peronism and the Argentine Working Class, 1946–1976* (New York: Cambridge University Press, 1988), 7–41.

19. The definitive account of Peronist urban policy is Anahi Ballent, *Las huellas de la política: Vivienda, ciudad, peronismo en Buenos Aires, 1943–1955* (Bernal: Editorial de la Universidad Nacional de Quilmes, 2005), especially 127–152 on Ezeiza.

20. Juan Carlos Torre and Elena Pastoriza, "La democratización del bienestar" in *Los años peronistas, Nueva Historia Argentina*, ed. Torre, vol. 8 (Buenos Aires: Sudamericana, 2002), 257–312. On consumption and Peronism more broadly, see Eduardo Elena, *Dignifying Argentina: Peronism, Citizenship, and Mass Consumption* (Pittsburgh: University of Pittsburgh Press, 2011).

21. For a compelling account of how greater popular consumption (and access to public space) sparked anti-Peronism, see Natalia Milanesio, "Peronists and *Cabecitas*: Stereotypes and Anxieties at the Peak of Social Change" in *The New Cultural History of Peronism*, ed. Oscar Chamosa and Matthew Karush (Durham, NC: Duke University Press, 2010), 53–84.

22. Horacio Torres, *El mapa social de Buenos Aires (1940–1990)* (Buenos Aires: Universidad de Buenos Aires, Facultad de Arquitectura Diseño y Urbanismo, 1995).

23. Horacio Torres, "El mapa social de Buenos Aires en 1943, 1947, y 1960" *Desarollo Económico* 18, no. 70 (1978): 203.

24. Torres, *El mapa social de Buenos Aires*, 16.

25. Torres, "El mapa social de Buenos Aires en 1943, 1947, y 1960."

26. Horacio Caride, *La idea del conurbano bonaerense*, Instituto del Conurbano, Documento 14. (Los Polvorines: Universidad Nacional General Sarmiento, 1999), 29–35.

27. The imbalance favoring the small provinces was the fruit of the constitutional compromise that ended the nineteenth-century civil war, and it would become more

dramatic with the greater growth of Buenos Aires after 1880. The imbalance favoring the rural interior of the province of Buenos Aires over its industrial suburbs was the fruit of deliberate institutional design under Conservative rule, only partly improved during the Peronist government. On these dynamics generally in Argentine federalism, see Edward Gibson, ed. *Federalism and Democracy in Latin America* (Baltimore: Johns Hopkins University Press, 2004). For the institutional dynamics in Buenos Aires, see Gustavo Badia and Martina Saudino, "La construcción político-administrativa del conurbano bonaerense" in *El Gran Buenos Aires*, ed. Kessler, 103–128.

28. Nora Libertun de Doren, "Growth and Poverty in the Urban Fringe: Decentralization, Dispersion, and Inequality in Greater Buenos Aires," Ph.D. dissertation, Massachusetts Institute of Technology, 2007, 63.

29. An excellent overview of the dynamics of this process for two suburbs in the *conurbano* is provided in Diego Armus and Ernesto Bohoslavsky, "Vivienda popular y asociacionismo en la conformación del Gran Buenos Aires" in *El Gran Buenos Aires*, ed. Kessler, 6, 493–520.

30. Alieto Aldo Guadagni, "Aspectos economicos del saneamiento urbano en la Argentina" *Desarrollo Económico* 13, no. 52 (1974): 681, 684.

31. For the raucous world of labor politics in greater Buenos Aires after 1955, see James, *Resistance and Integration*, especially 88–134.

32. Hugo Ratier, *Villeros y villas miserias* (Buenos Aires: Centro Editor de América Latina, 1975).

33. See Alicia Ziccardi, "Villas miseria y favelas: Sobre las relaciones entre las instituciones del estado y la organizacion social en las democracias de los años sesenta," *Revista mexicana de sociología* 45, no. 1 (1983): 45–67; and Ziccardi, "El tercer gobierno peronista y las villas miseria de la ciudad de Buenos Aires (1973–1976)," *Revista mexicana de sociología* 46, no. 4 (1984): 145–172.

34. James Brennan, *The Labor Wars in Córdoba, 1955–1976: Ideology, Work, and Labor Politics in an Argentine Industrial City* (Cambridge, MA: Harvard University Press, 1994).

35. Libertun de Doren, "Growth and Poverty in the Urban Fringe."

36. James Brennan, *Argentina's Missing Bones: Revisiting the History of the Dirty War* (Oakland, CA: University of California Press, 2018).

37. Oscar Oszlak, *Merecer la ciudad: los pobres y el derecho al espacio urbano* (Buenos Aires: CEDES-HUMANITAS, 1991).

38. Oszlak, *Merecer la ciudad*, 36–71.

39. Denis Merklen, *Pobres ciudadanos: Las clases populares en la era democrática, Argentina 1983–2003* (Buenos Aires: Gorla, 2006).

40. Steve Levitsky, *Transforming Labor-Based Parties: Argentine Peronism in Comparative Perspective* (New York: Cambridge University Press, 2003); Javier Auyero, *Poor People's Politics: Peronist Survival Networks and the Legacy of Evita* (Durham, NC: Duke University Press, 1996).

41. See Gabriel Vommaro, "El mundo politico del conurbano en la democracia reciente"; and Maristella Svampa, "La irrupción piquetera: las organizaciones de desocupados del conurbano bonaerense" in *El Gran Buenos Aires*, ed. Kessler, 365–433.

5 Montreal in the Twentieth Century

Trajectories of a City under Strains

· ·

MICHÈLE DAGENAIS

The history of Montreal in the twentieth century has been defined by multiple, quite unique tensions. It can only be understood by considering interlocking local/regional, national, and international developments. The leading metropolis of a country undergoing rapid growth at the end of the nineteenth century, Montreal found itself one century later in a period of redevelopment and redefinition. Long the engine of the Canadian economy, it was the place where wealth, power—and poverty—concentrated. Now a regional metropolis, the city evolves at the intersection of its role as Quebec's primary metropolis and as the center of diverse networks linking the region to Canada, North America, and the world.

The locomotive of its development, the site where its wealth is concentrated, the home of regional and international migrants and cultural diversity, Montreal dominates the province of Quebec. For some, Montreal rules by its demographic weight alone—25 percent of the Quebec population, 48 percent when the entire metropolitan region is included. In 2000, the island of Montreal counted 1.8 million inhabitants, while the metropolitan region consisted of nearly 3.5 million.[1] At times, the city appears as a foreign body within Quebec, a place apart with a population considerably different from the rest of the province. The bastion of the British bourgeoisie during a long part of its history, Montreal was already very different socially and culturally from the rest of Quebec at the beginning of the twentieth century. The object of a long conquest on the part of French-speakers, it is increasingly defined as a multicultural city. The only large agglomeration in the province, Montreal is the place *par excellence* of superlatives: the most populated city, the most polluted, the poorest, the most cosmopolitan, and the most anglicized.

The differentiation of the metropolis in comparison to the rest of the province is not unique to Montreal or Quebec. From coast to coast, the major Canadian cities that dominate the provinces often differ from the smaller towns of their hinterlands, notably with regard to the racial composition of their populations.[2] This is the case of Vancouver, British Columbia. It is also the situation of Toronto, in Ontario, even though here the leading Canadian metropolis centers the most urbanized region of the country. In Montreal, however, the multicultural character of the population doubles as a linguistic issue. While the other large Canadian cities are predominately anglophone, two linguistic groups coexist in Montreal—French-speakers and English-speakers—and their demography and importance in the urban landscape have changed over time.

Montreal's identity has always been contested; no one group has ever managed to dominate and impose its symbolic power. Since the end of the eighteenth century, Montreal has been organized and structured around the presence of two majorities, French and English. This initial segmentation influenced the settlement of other groups, from the early nineteenth century onward. It led to the development of ethnic enclaves as a means of spatial and social organization for both minority and majority groups. Deeply rooted in Montreal's urbanity, this characteristic marked the history of the city throughout the twentieth century.

While the phenomenon of the ethnic enclaves often suggests segregation, in Montreal it has been a means of aggregation, enabling immigrants to settle in the city and adapt to a new milieu.[3] Throughout the century, however, the relationship of the enclaves to one another was transformed in power struggles between the two majority groups. Essentially defined by its bicultural character, the city of the "two solitudes," as it was referred to in the first half of the twentieth century, became multicultural and French after the Second World War, and then multiethnic and partially multilingual at the turn of the twenty-first century. The two dynamics, ethnicity and language, must be taken into account to understand the processes of segregation and aggregation, a recurring tension in the history of twentieth-century Montreal.

But what territory and which reality define the term "Montreal"? Does it designate the city itself or the city center, the island of Montreal, or the city-region—the metropolitan area as determined by the census?[4] The list of these terms indicates the successive growth of Montreal. Never completely confined to its administrative boundaries, the city inexorably developed by surpassing its limits: in nearby working-class outskirts in the middle of the nineteenth century, in the adjacent suburbs at the end of the nineteenth century, farther out during the second half of the twentieth century. Montreal has known diversified growth rates, sometimes more intense in the urban territory, sometimes greater in suburban territories.

In the twentieth century, the redrawing of Montreal's territorial boundaries redefined the dynamic between the center and the periphery in a radical manner. The tensions that resulted are one of the particularities of the social and political history of Montreal. Certainly, these tensions link to the relations between a city center and its suburbs, a characteristic of the histories of most Canadian and U.S. cities—and Buenos Aires, too. But in the Montreal case, territorial restructurings were also processes of reappropriation and construction of urban territories by different ethnic and linguistic groups. Understanding the spatial settlement of ethnic groups is therefore essential to exploring the complex dynamic through which the city of Montreal was formed and developed over time.

In this chapter, I examine the identities and spatial dynamics that shaped Montreal throughout the twentieth century following the patterns different groups adopted to integrate[5] into the urban landscape, as well as to appropriate certain areas, both in the city and its suburbs. Indeed, very early in the twentieth century, the ethnic enclave pattern spread to the suburbs surrounding Montreal. The suburbanization process, a geographic and social withdrawal from the urban core coinciding with social mobility, has been colored by ethnolinguistic questions. Capturing the interethnic dynamic of Montreal requires analysis of the city, the suburbs, and their changing interactions. Throughout the twentieth century, their profiles changed while their functions remained the same: people moved toward the suburbs once the city no longer served their interests—often finding new spaces to promote collective identities. In the following pages, I attempt to evaluate the effects of ethnic enclaves on the definition and cohesion of Montreal throughout the twentieth century on a citywide as well as a metropolitan scale.

The City of Solitudes

Situated in the middle of an archipelago, Montreal is built on an island at the intersection of two major rivers, the St. Lawrence and the Ottawa. The St. Lawrence flows by the south of the island city, draining the Great Lakes and much of North America. The Ottawa River comes from the northwest and divides to make the island: part meets the St. Lawrence west of Lake Saint-Louis before passing by the narrow corridor of the Lachine Rapids, at

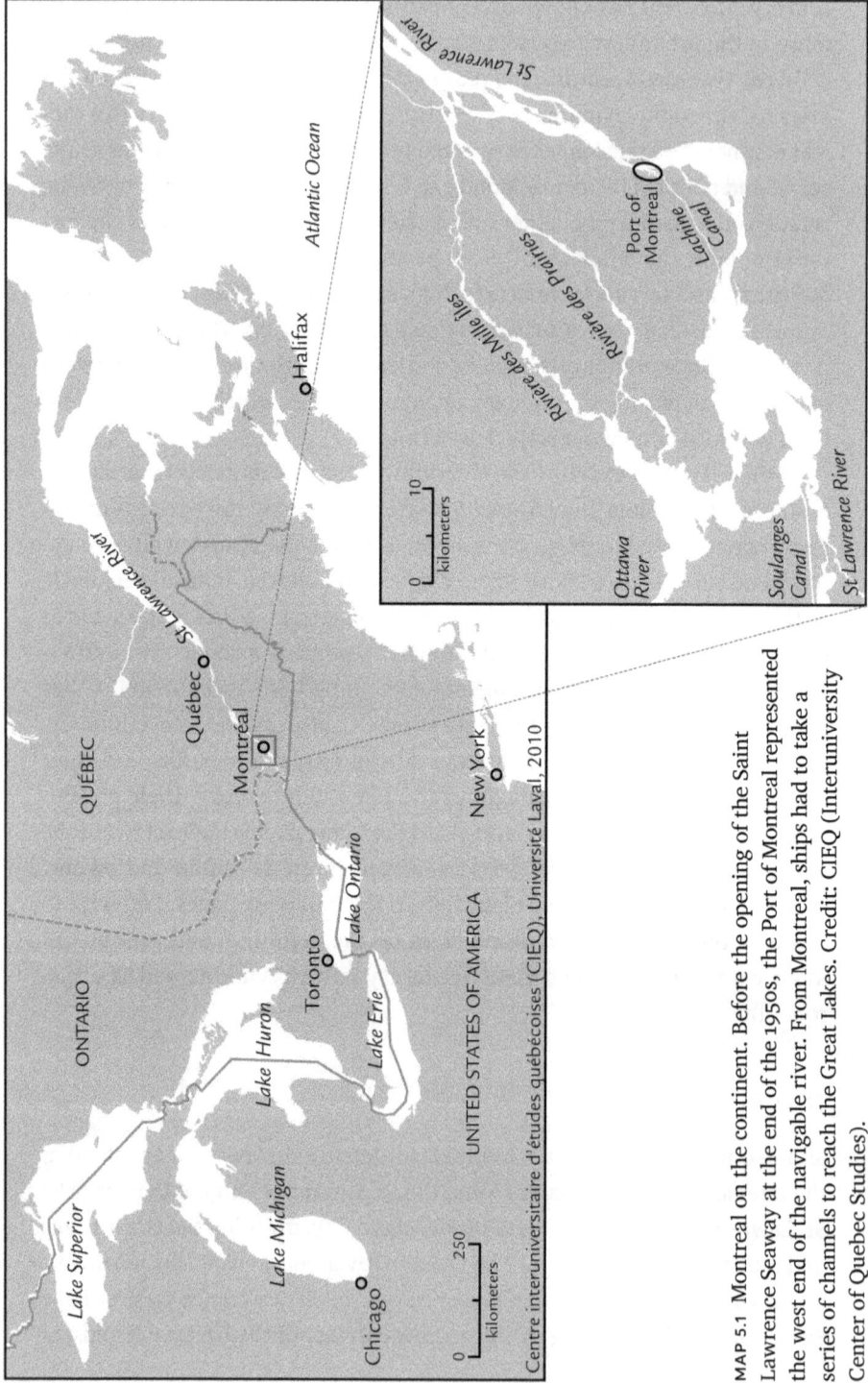

MAP 5.1 Montreal on the continent. Before the opening of the Saint Lawrence Seaway at the end of the 1950s, the Port of Montreal represented the west end of the navigable river. From Montreal, ships had to take a series of channels to reach the Great Lakes. Credit: CIEQ (Interuniversity Center of Quebec Studies).

the same height as the city. The rest of the Ottawa flows into the Lake of Two Mountains and becomes the Des Prairies River that makes Montreal an island, flowing by on the north until joining the St. Lawrence.

In every history of Montreal, the authors underline the importance of its particular geographic position, set at the origin of the city's development.[6] It was precisely its role as the breakpoint for cargo that led to the initial impetus for the economic growth of this city, founded in 1642. Starting in the eighteenth century, Montreal became an obligatory stop in the context of the fur trade. All the goods coming from the West and the Great Lakes had to be unloaded from the boats and transported by road around the Lachine Rapids all the way to Montreal, where they were transferred to ships bound for overseas markets. Goods coming from Europe, intended for the Northwest and the continental interior, had to reverse the process of transshipment.

The Golden Age of the City's Economy

In the nineteenth century, important infrastructure works consolidated Montreal's role as a hub of commerce, aiming to make the city a pivot of ocean, river, and land transport. Between 1820 and 1850, British authorities constructed a series of canals to encourage the territorial development of northern North America, including the Lachine Canal that removed one main obstacle to transcontinental navigation. From then on, commercial elites, mainly of British origin, worked to make Montreal a leading metropolis. They developed its role in trade, linking maritime and railroad transport. To this end, they undertook construction of an improved port in the middle of the nineteenth century. They already commanded the resources to seize the new opportunities of economic expansion created with the foundation of Canada in 1867. The new country developed with a growth strategy orientated along an east-west axis, emphasizing the colonization of the West and the integration of the various colonies making up British North America. The British elites developed an industrial sector that became the spearhead of the Montreal economy in the second half of the century.[7] The building of a transcontinental railway in the 1880s and the economic activity it stimulated accelerated Montreal's industrialization to serve growing internal markets.

At the turn of the twentieth century, Montreal was the uncontested metropolis of Canada. Described as the "city of wealth and of death," the city concentrated the great fortunes of the country, and also its poverty.[8] In 1901, there were 325,000 inhabitants, 20 percent of the population of Quebec. It was the most populous Canadian city, the second being Toronto with 209,000 residents.[9] Attracting residents from rural areas and immigrants from abroad, Montreal possessed a sizable pool of cheap labor. Thirty years later, the city totaled nearly 820,000 inhabitants and the island, one million. Montreal then represented 28.5 percent of the Quebec population.[10]

At the top of the social hierarchy, the Montreal business classes engaged in a variety of activities: commerce, finance, transportation, industry, and more. The manufacturing was relatively dispersed, having developed both heavy industry, in particular the railroad sector, and light industry (textiles, clothing, footwear, food, brewing). From before the end of the nineteenth century, Montreal and its suburbs produced 52 percent of the manufactured goods in Quebec.[11]

After the First World War, however, the foundations on which the Montreal bourgeoisie built its power began to weaken. Up to then, Montreal had relied on a geographical location that set the city at the heart of international trade, principally oriented toward Great Britain. When the United States started to play a more important role in Canadian economic life, the winds began to change. Toronto, situated as an extension of the U.S. Midwest, became favored. Its elite, looking to escape the power of the Montreal bourgeoisie, took advantage of the situation to increase their role in the control of trade. Though Montreal continued to dominate economically, Toronto increasingly disputed its supremacy. By the end of the 1940s, two competing metropolises characterized Canada.[12]

A First Segmentation of the Urban Space
in the Nineteenth Century

From the nineteenth century on Montreal expanded with the arrival of immigrants from overseas, as was the case in many New World cities from Canada and North America through São Paulo and Buenos Aires in South America. The ethnic diversity of Montreal is not unique. What has distinguished the city, however, is the presence of two major linguistic groups, anglophone and francophone, which have, since the end of the eighteenth century, evolved within relations defined by rivalries and compromises redefined over time. At first French-speaking and inhabited predominately by residents of French origin, Montreal diversified only after the British conquest, at the end of the Seven Years' War.[13] At the beginning of the 1830s, inhabitants of British origin were a majority, thanks to the arrival of a large cohort of immigrants from Ireland, Scotland, and England. Then, in 1871, Montreal was once again predominately French-speaking, and this group's numbers gradually increased until the middle of the twentieth century, when it represented nearly 68 percent of the population.[14]

Throughout the nineteenth century, four ethnic groups (French, English, Scottish, and Irish) coexisted in the Montreal urban landscape, divided into two linguistic blocs, as well as according to religious identification. On the French-Canadian side, the majority of the population was Catholic. On the English-Canadian side, the portrait was more diverse. While the majority of Montrealers of British origin was Protestant, the Irish divided between Protestants and Catholics. The cohabitation of all these groups resulted in frequent violent episodes, mainly in the first half of the nineteenth century, which in turn led to the "sharing" of spaces more or less clearly delineated between anglophone and francophone societies. In fact, at this time, the elites of the various ethnic groups agreed to establish separate institutional networks for their respective communities in an attempt to ensure stability and social peace. Each group developed its own spaces, institutions (churches, hospitals, schools, and philanthropic agencies), national societies and tools for cultural and social affirmation.

From the middle of the nineteenth century, the school system divided into two components, French Catholic and English Protestant. Yet the two school boards did not operate in an identical manner. In the French Catholic schools only French-speaking students or students seemingly inclined to adopt the French language and of Catholic faith were admitted. As a result, the clientele was fairly homogenous. The situation was different on the English side. Facing different denominations of Protestantism, the Montreal Protestant School Board tried to remain somewhat neutral so that all anglophones, including Irish Catholics, could be educated in its schools.[15] The two boards differed in terms of material resources as well. By law, financing came from the school tax, based on property values. As anglophones were wealthier than francophones, the Montreal School Board had more money than the Commission des Écoles Catholiques de Montréal, which affected the quality of its infrastructure.

Of course, neither group was socially homogeneous. While there was an Anglo-Protestant bourgeoisie, a non-negligible proportion of English-speakers belonged to the working classes. Likewise, among French-speakers,

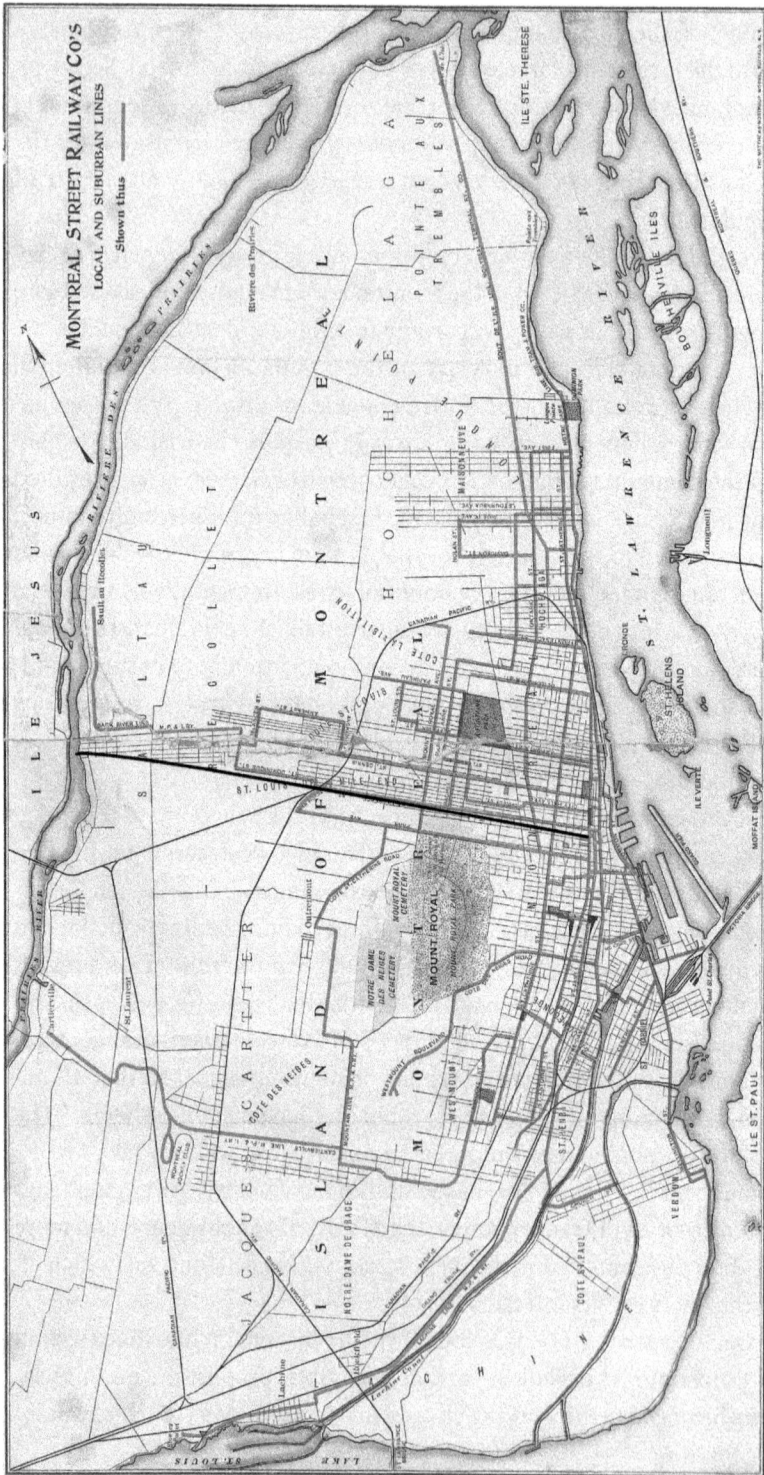

MAP 5.2 Montreal at the beginning of the twentieth century. Montreal Street Railway Company's local and suburban lines, 1915. Credit: Archives de la Ville de Montréal.

though the majority belonged to the working classes, the linguistic group also included economic elites. Moreover, at the top of the socioeconomic hierarchy, French- and English-speakers collaborated on various political and economic undertakings.

In the urban landscape, the dividing line between the two sociocultural worlds was the Saint-Lawrence Boulevard: the west side was predominantly English, the east mostly French. Such segmentation was repeated on a smaller scale in other areas: in the southwest, where there was an important industrial neighborhood, space was shared between the two linguistic groups, each with a tendency to live side by side. Spatial segregation did not completely prevent incidents of violence; still, the limited interactions between the two linguistic groups in most of areas in the city kept open conflicts rare in the first half of the twentieth century.

A Third Solitude

A third element emerged toward the end of the nineteenth century, consisting of immigrants of neither French nor British origin.[16] Although Montreal's port was the point of arrival for many immigrants all throughout the nineteenth century, rarely did they remain in the city, choosing instead to leave for south of the border where employment prospects were better. From the end of the nineteenth century on, however, in a context where the Canadian, and especially the Montreal, economy was more developed, immigrants were choosing to settle in Canada. The Montreal economy attracted a strong proportion of immigrants who started to change the face of the city. In the space of a few decades, their weight went from 5.3 percent of the population in 1901, to 10.7 percent in 1911, then to 14 percent in 1921 (see table 5.2).

The division of Montreal between anglophones and francophones strongly influenced immigrant patterns of settlement into the physical and sociocultural space of the city.[17] Arriving at the port of Montreal, at the end of Saint-Lawrence Boulevard, the immigrants moved up the street that divided English and French Montreal. It became the corridor by which immigrants first came into contact with the city. They settled on either side of the boulevard, developing their own enclaves, at first close to the city center and then toward the north as the city grew outward. Thus, the immigrants did not disperse throughout the city, but instead settled among one or the other of the majority linguistic groups. The long boulevard-corridor became a buffer zone that separated the two solitudes.

TABLE 5.1 Population of Montreal, 1901–2001

Year	City of Montreal	Island of Montreal	Census Metropolitan Area
1901	324,880	360,838	—
1911	528,397	554,761	—
1921	689,753	724,305	—
1931	818,577	1,003,868	1,023,158
1941	903,007	1,116,800	1,139,921
1951	1,021,520	1,320,232	1,395,400
1961	1,191,062	1,747,698	2,109,509
1971	1,214,352	1,959,143	2,743,208
1981	980,354	1,760,122	2,828,349
1991	1,017,666	1,775,871	3,127,242
2001	1,039,534	1,812,723	3,426,350

Sources: Paul-André Linteau, Histoire de Montréal depuis la Confédération (Montreal: Boréal, 1992), 85, 314, 460; Census of Canada, 1991; Census of Canada, 2001.

Impoverished Catholic immigrants, coming from rural areas or as workers, settled in French-speaking neighborhoods and sent their children to French Catholic schools. This was the case for the Italians and, to a lesser degree, the Ukrainians and the Polish. Nearly all of these newcomers lived in the east of the city, in the vicinity of the Saint-Lawrence Boulevard. The Italians formed the most important contingent. They established their own parish in 1911, Notre-Dame-de-la-Défense, situated in the north end of Montreal, on the outer edge of urban development, where they took advantage of being on the outskirts of the city to garden and raise sheep and poultry. They developed their own institutional network. Though Italian Montrealers sought to learn both French and English, they had more daily contact with francophones.[18]

The immigrants coming from northern Europe, Germany, Scandinavia, and various eastern European countries integrated into the Anglo-Protestant community. Since they dispersed throughout the west end of the city, their presence seems to have been negligible. Nevertheless, their numbers were significant. We can estimate that in predominately British neighborhoods, such as Notre-Dame-de-Grâce or Mont-Royal (in the Côte-des-Neiges area), close to 30 percent of inhabitants were born abroad. Thus, anglophone areas were more heterogeneous than their francophone counterparts.

A third group, the Jewish community, associated with neither franco-phones nor anglophones. By far the largest contingent of immigrants, Jews were nearly 6 percent of the Montreal population in 1911, while Italians were only 2 percent. In Montreal, the Jewish community carried over the rich institutional life developed elsewhere: synagogues, schools, charities.[19] More than any other community, this group added to the institutional divisions put into place by the French and the English. Their geographic concentration led to political representation at three levels of government (municipal, provincial, and federal) from the interwar period.

The Jewish community formed a very cohesive community in the first half of the twentieth century. They preferred a separate Jewish school board; the government refused, so most Jewish children were educated in English Protestant schools. The community settled in between English and French Montreal, residing along the Saint-Lawrence Boulevard where a large number of garment factories were found. At first workers, then artisans, and eventually small business owners, Jews lived near their workplaces. Dozens of synagogues built in this part of the city contributed to the identification of the neighborhood with the Jewish community. Economic success also distinguished the community; some of its members, once financially established, migrated northwest, to the Côte-des-Neiges and Outremont neighborhoods, and later to Côte-St-Luc, which became a suburb after 1945.

Thus, more than ghettoization based on wealth, religious identification and linguistic proximity led to the dynamic of segregation/aggregation. Both cemented the cohesion of communities. In Montreal, groups did not have much choice; as educational and social institutions were under Church control, religious identification was obligatory. This contributed to the continual creation of ethnic enclaves, as migrants arrived to Montreal. Furthermore this dynamic reinforced the existence of the two major communities, French-Canadian and English-Canadian.

Partially real, partially symbolic, this bifurcated inscription into space and the cleavages of the social landscape served as the foundation of the two solitudes metaphor. Enunciated by the writer Hugh MacLennan in his 1945 novel in order to describe the political reality of Canada, the metaphor was inspired by what he discovered upon his arrival to Montreal in the 1930s and described as follows: "It had, so far as I knew no counterpart anywhere on earth . . . . Here, the two cultures of Canada, without even planning it, had evidently decided that the best way to coexist was to ignore the existence of one another . . . . Yet Montreal was perhaps the politest city in the world then."[20]

It was in this context that immigrant communities came to be understood as a third solitude, as a world apart evolving according to its own traditions. This simplistic and schematic manner of conceiving of the groups making up Montreal society and their inscription into the urban landscape, reinforced the two solitudes, considered homogeneous blocs, but also contributed to the marginalization of minority groups during the first half of the twentieth century.

But the effects of the third solitude on the equilibrium between francophones and anglophones were not neutral. Firstly, it must be underlined that the majority of immigrants adopted English. By doing so, they significantly contributed to the demographic maintenance of the English-speaking community because at the time, especially between 1901 and 1941, the percentage of Montrealers of British origin declined, going from 33.7 percent to 20.3 percent. Meanwhile, the francophone population gained ground, going from 61 percent in 1901 to 66.3 percent in 1941 (see table 5.2).[21]

The increase in francophones was the result of a series of factors: rural exodus to Montreal from many regions in Quebec, the annexation to Montreal of francophone suburbs, and finally, the considerable migration of the British toward suburbs in the west end of the island. However, even though French-speakers were more numerous, the powerful British minority dominated. The latter owed its position to its control of economic activity and big business. Until the 1950s, Montreal remained dominated by the English and defined by the metaphor of the two solitudes, ignoring more or less the existence of what has been called the third solitude.

Urban Sprawl on the Island

Coinciding with the diversification of Montreal's population, the dynamic between the two solitudes extended beyond the adjacent suburbs. By the end of the nineteenth century, Montreal exploded. The phenomenon was not so much the result of overpopulation within the city, but instead a territorial expansion that responded to various needs. Industrial suburbs were born primarily due to the actions of entrepreneurs in search of space and territory where the bylaws were less strict than in the city, in order to establish even larger businesses. Also, the elites' desire to live among themselves led to the creation of bourgeois suburbs around Montreal. Sim-

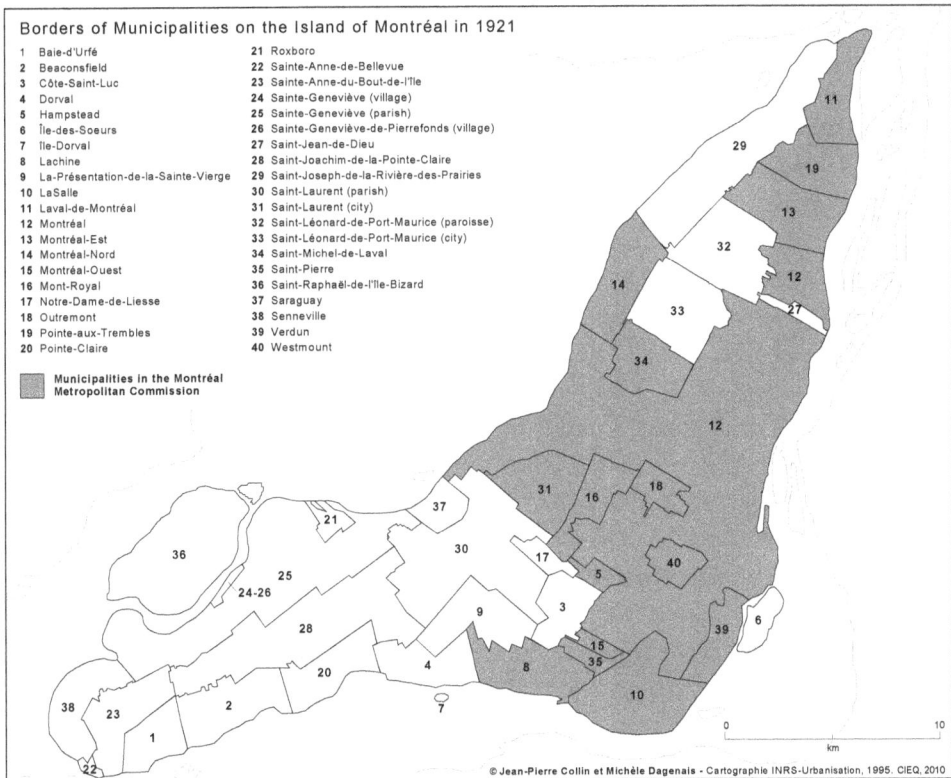

Borders of Municipalities on the Island of Montréal in 1921

1 Baie-d'Urfé	21 Roxboro
2 Beaconsfield	22 Sainte-Anne-de-Bellevue
3 Côte-Saint-Luc	23 Sainte-Anne-du-Bout-de-l'Île
4 Dorval	24 Sainte-Geneviève (village)
5 Hampstead	25 Sainte-Geneviève (parish)
6 Île-des-Soeurs	26 Sainte-Geneviève-de-Pierrefonds (village)
7 Île-Dorval	27 Saint-Jean-de-Dieu
8 Lachine	28 Saint-Joachim-de-la-Pointe-Claire
9 La-Présentation-de-la-Sainte-Vierge	29 Saint-Joseph-de-la-Rivière-des-Prairies
10 LaSalle	30 Saint-Laurent (parish)
11 Laval-de-Montréal	31 Saint-Laurent (city)
12 Montréal	32 Saint-Léonard-de-Port-Maurice (paroisse)
13 Montréal-Est	33 Saint-Léonard-de-Port-Maurice (city)
14 Montréal-Nord	34 Saint-Michel-de-Laval
15 Montréal-Ouest	35 Saint-Pierre
16 Mont-Royal	36 Saint-Raphaël-de-l'Île-Bizard
17 Notre-Dame-de-Liesse	37 Saraguay
18 Outremont	38 Senneville
19 Pointe-aux-Trembles	39 Verdun
20 Pointe-Claire	40 Westmount

Municipalities in the Montréal Metropolitan Commission

© Jean-Pierre Collin et Michèle Dagenais - Cartographie INRS-Urbanisation, 1995. CIEQ, 2010

MAP 5.3 Montreal and its suburbs. Credit: CIEQ (Interuniversity Center of Quebec Studies).

ilar to many other cities at the time, the borders of Montreal were redefined by the dual process of the annexation of small cities and the creation of suburbs.

In Montreal, these dynamics were colored by the rivalry between francophones and anglophones, leading to the creation of new enclaves beyond the municipal borders. The rapid growth of the francophone majority in the last few decades of the nineteenth century and the ascension of a new French-speaking commercial bourgeoisie led to the birth of a francophone political elite whose influence increased throughout the period. The direction of Montreal life, which up until this point had been shared via the tradition of alternating English- and French-speaking mayors, shifted in favor of francophones.[22] Their greater control over municipal management came at a time of rapid population growth, which provoked the continual expansion of services and greater budgets.

Wealthy English-speakers founded other suburbs as the city became increasingly French-speaking: Westmount, Montreal West or Hampstead, and Outremont stand out. Anglophone elites viewed their suburbs as places for community affirmation and means to protect their interests.[23] At the time, the development of public transportation (tramways and trains) facilitated the expansion of the inhabited territory around Montreal, on and beyond the island.[24] On the west end of the island, Lachine, Verdun, and Lasalle expanded. In addition, a few suburbs came into being near the bridges: on the south shore near Saint-Lambert and Greenfield Park, at the exit of the Victoria Bridge, and near Longueuil, at the end of the Jacques-Cartier Bridge.

The city of Montreal itself grew by annexing the surrounding municipalities; many knew only a brief existence, as they quickly became extensions of Montreal. Between 1905 and 1914, the city annexed twenty-six districts for a total of sixteen distinct municipalities.[25] After adding three more municipalities from 1916 to 1918, the city would not expand geographically until the 1960s.[26] Markedly enlarged due to all these annexations, Montreal was able to project an image of a city in constant growth.

But the accelerated growth of the city and multiplication of its suburbs obligated the municipalities to build or redevelop a multitude of infrastructures.[27] The linking of the aqueduct and sewer networks, the expansion of gas service, electricity, the telephone and public transportation were subjects of intense and politicized negotiations. At the same time, the city's real estate developers, public service contractors, and politicians sought to derive the maximum benefit from a unique period of growth. In the early 1920s, the provincial government pressured Montreal to annex four municipalities east of the city facing financially precarious situations. Now Montreal was ready to integrate these cities only if it could also incorporate the wealthy municipalities, namely Westmount and Outremont. Ferociously protective of their autonomy, they refused to join Montreal. The government finally decided to create the Montreal Metropolitan Commission in 1921. Including fifteen municipalities on the island, its mandate was to control the borrowing power of the suburban municipalities.

For mayors in the suburbs, the Metropolitan Commission appeared to be an efficient rampart against annexation to Montreal and a way to control its varied attempts at expansion. Moreover, the agency was likely to serve as a springboard for metropolitan-wide initiatives, such as the building of a highway running from east to west (Metropolitan Boulevard). Numerous local politicians and reformist circles wished that Montreal would take control of some municipal services and hoped for a harmonization of intermunicipal relations. Nevertheless, during the Second World War, the beginning of construction of a highway network by the provincial government and new housing policies that encouraged access to property ownership led to increasing separation of the suburbs.[28]

The Montreal Mosaic

Montreal's situation changed after World War II.[29] In the 1930s, the Depression hit the city's economy hard, harder than the more highly diversified Toronto economy. But the strong demand for Canadian goods during the war and the need, backed by the Canadian government, to rely on national industries sector and the Montreal transportation network to respond to the demand, enabled the city to maintain its position at the top of the Canadian urban hierarchy, at least for another decade. In Canada as across the Americas, the Depression hurt export sectors, challenging Montreal's long primacy. Then World War II turned every New World nation to attempting national development—in varied ways. Montreal and Canada revived economically, sustaining themselves and the Anglo-American alliance.

From Canadian to Quebecois Metropolis

Postwar reality caught up with the Montreal economy early in the 1950s. The steady shift of the gravitational center of the North American economy from the East Coast to the center of the continent and the development of the West Coast clearly favored Toronto, from then on at the center of Canadian economic activity. While the general prosperity of the 1950s and 1960s allowed the Montreal economy to maintain a considerable level of activity, the recession begun by the oil shock of the 1970s revealed the depth of the city's problems.[30] The two grueling decades that followed, while Montreal faced the turn to globalization, were marked by the need to restructure industrial activities. The aging structure that had sustained the Montreal economy since the middle of the nineteenth century corroded. The new international competition proved too strong for both heavy and light industries; many fell into decline, including footwear, textiles, and clothing.

The displacement of the industrial center of the economy also led to the dismantling of the railroad industry long concentrated in Montreal. The opening of the St. Lawrence Seaway in the middle of the 1950s permitted oceangoing vessels to reach the Great Lakes, freeing them from the need to stop in Montreal and transship merchandise. Increasingly competing with the port of Vancouver as trade became global, Montreal's kept 38 percent of maritime traffic in 1961, only 18 percent in 1977. The port authorities then rearranged Montreal's facilities into a container port, which advantageously resituated it on a continental scale. Though in 1950 slightly more than a quarter of the Canadian head offices were in Montreal, with a fifth in Toronto, since 1970 the latter has doubled its share as Montreal's declined. In addition, with the continentalization of the North American economy, U.S. investments in Canada dramatically increased, particularly in the natural resources sector but also in manufacturing. Ontario and especially Toronto profited, strengthening their positions in the Canadian economy.

What saved the Montreal economy from complete collapse was first the development of high-tech sectors such as aeronautical, pharmaceutical, and computer technology.[31] There was also an increasing concentration of companies in Montreal, focused on banking, food production, communications, and printing. As the metropolis of Canada for a long period of its history, Montreal had turned its back on the rest of the province. Of course, the links between the two were numerous and the interactions sustained, but until the 1950s, the Montreal economic elite focused on the entirety of Canada; its domination of the rest of Quebec was exercised only on the city's immediate hinterland.[32] From the 1960s onward, however, Montreal focused more on the province of Quebec, gradually becoming a regional— and international—metropolis.[33]

That shift came amid the ground swell of the Quiet Revolution beginning in 1960.[34] Fueled by a movement of national assertion, French-speaking elites worked toward the expansion of the provincial government. Increasingly defined as the national State of the Quebecois, the government became a tool for collective emancipation and improvement of living conditions. Strengthened by a new class of public servants, it proceeded to modernize the educational and health systems and develop social policies. The State also massively intervened in the economy to better control a sphere largely dominated by English-speaking interests. The Montreal economy greatly benefited from the positive repercussions of these transformations; important Quebec companies began or grew while help from the provincial government promoted the established of headquarters in the city.[35]

The postwar period was also marked by a wave of modernization of the built environment, a phenomenon that further stimulated Montreal's economy. This trend was most visible in three domains: the development of a new downtown, the building of highways and the widening of streets, and the construction of modern houses. During the Depression of the 1930s and the Second World War, urban development slowed considerably. This led to the aging of the real estate stock and an almost complete halt in the construction of residential units, which provoked a housing crisis. The situation became more critical after the war as the baby boom and new antibiotics combined to accelerate population growth. The surge of modernization swept over Montreal during this period, parallel to the drive for urban renewal and development Bryan McCann has detailed for Rio de Janeiro.

Municipal authorities proceeded to demolish older housing units and dismantle low-income neighborhoods, seeking simultaneously to solve sanitation and social issues planners and politicians associated with their populations. They worked to tear down slums and replace them with high-rise public housing complexes, separated from the rest of the city by green spaces. The urban renewal movement also addressed the problem of traffic, considered a key issue, by reconfiguring and widening streets and creating Montreal's highway network. Yet to minimize construction costs and to ensure profitability, planners decided that the main roads would be built through more run-down areas of the city, which had the dual "advantage" of reducing costs and demolishing old, dilapidated housing.

But starting in the 1960s, diverse voices began to speak up against this intensive development and the major transformations of Montreal's urban environment. In the beginning, the movement primarily focused on the preservation of architectural heritage. It also aimed to retake control of the city's urban development, which had become guided by the interests of private developers rather than Montrealers themselves. Rehabilitation, reappropriation, renewal: these words were used to signal the will of citizens to participate in the political life of their neighborhoods. In several areas of the city, opposition became organized with the creation of defense groups. Among these groups was the Citizen's Committee of Milton Park, which led a heated battle against the demolition of affordable housing units in downtown and managed to limit the development of an immense residential complex geared toward the middle class[36]. This battle, only one of many, led to the creation of Heritage Montreal in 1975, which has, since that time, played an important political and educational role in favor of the preservation of both the architectural and natural heritage of Montreal, while at the same time promoting the city's identity and unique characteristics.[37]

The Mosaic: An Urban Reality?

During this second period, Montreal benefited from the renewed international immigration flow to Canada that started after the Second World War. Though Toronto was now the principal destination for newcomers, Montreal continued to receive its share. From 1950 to 1970, the proportion of immigrants went from 15 percent to 25 percent of the city's population. New arrivals were still predominantly European. In first place were Italian nationals, moving ahead of the Jewish population as of 1961, as well as those from other southern European countries, such as Greece and Portugal (see table 5.2). In this period of strong economic growth—with Canadian national development intersecting with Quebecois national development—the integration of immigrants was not an issue because the need for workers was so great. In the early 1970s, with the liberalization of Canadian immigration policy, the countries of origin of immigrants started to shift. In the 1950s, 80 percent of new arrivals to Canada were from Europe; with the arrival of people from Asia, the Caribbean, and North Africa, this proportion fell to 17 percent in 1994.[38]

The city of Montreal acquired a truly mosaic character. The increase of the immigrant population created new ethnic enclaves while consolidating existing ethnic neighborhoods. New arrivals did not automatically settle in the traditional transition zone. Though Saint-Lawrence Boulevard remained the axis where immigrants entered Montreal, the countries of origin of its inhabitants changed. The Portuguese moved into the area previously occupied by Jews, who, in turn, moved to the northwest end of the city and founded the suburb of Côte-Saint-Luc. Likewise, many Greeks moved farther north. Immigrants reinforcing long-standing ethnic groups, namely Italians and Jews, immediately gravitated toward areas of the city where their counterparts were established. Their arrival reinforced the ethnic character of Jewish and Italian neighborhoods, now including two immigrant generations. Impoverished upon arrival, these newcomers benefited from the aid of their respective communities, allowing them to live in the same neighborhoods as more established community members.[39]

Italian Montrealers, constituting the largest minority group, tended to be highly concentrated, especially in Saint-Michel, Montreal North, and Saint-Leonard. With the influx of tens of thousands of compatriots, the community gained clout and created institutions such as the National Congress of Italian-Canadians, which aimed to defend community interests at the local and national level.[40]

A significant proportion of immigrants of northern European background immediately moved to wealthy neighborhoods in the west end of the city or to southwestern suburban areas near Lac Saint-Louis. This pattern underlines the necessity of nuancing the perception that all immigrants undergo considerable poverty and hardship. In this case, new arrivals were highly educated or skilled, and recruited to meet needs for manpower in rapidly expanding industries.

Thus, the creation of new enclaves and the reinforcement of old ones did not result in ghettos. Minority ethnic groups safeguarded their ethnic attributes, while also, as research has indicated, experiencing economic success. Ethnic-group attachment and the search for geographic proximity on the part of immigrants were not detrimental to advancement during this period marked by economic growth.[41] Some groups, such as the Jewish community, experienced great social mobility. The fact that many postwar arrivals chose to anglicize may have contributed to their material success. This was the case for the Jews, as it was for many Italians and Greeks. It is not surprising that these new immigrants anglicized, as the economic life of Montreal was dominated by and operated in English. However, such immigrant anglicization provoked much malaise on the part of the French-speaking majority, which would in time lead to a crisis. The limits to a societal model based on institutional networks dating back to the nineteenth century were revealed, especially in education.

The Explosion of Suburbia

The identity of Montreal was thus in a process of redefinition due the mix of massive postwar immigration, francophone political assertions, and national and provincial development projects. Meanwhile, the French-speaking population chose to relocate in the suburbs. This second push toward suburbanization, which started in the 1950s, is explained by the filling in of the last uninhabited districts in the city of Montreal. Suburbia was also an attractive option because land on the periphery was considerably cheaper than in the city.[42] Changing housing choices were also stimulated by new representation of the suburb as an ideal and idealized setting.

Suburbanization first spread on the island of Montreal, to then extend beyond the limits of the city toward Jesus Island (which became Laval in 1965). In the 1960s, the building of the Champlain Bridge encouraged the development of the south shore and notably Brossard.[43] On the north shore,

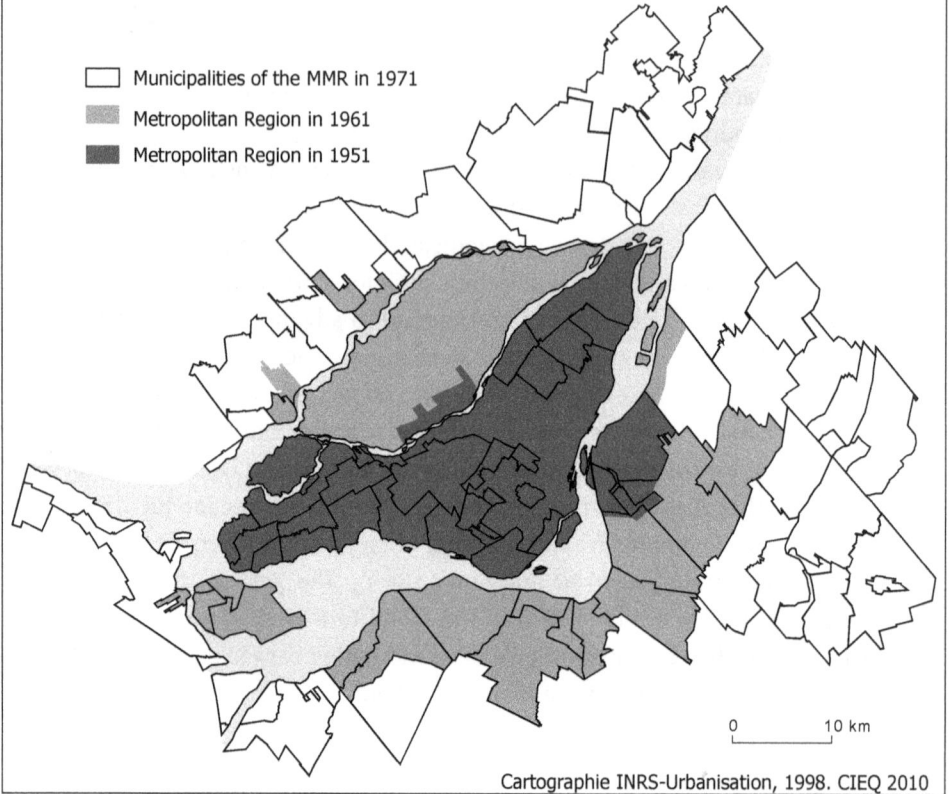

Evolution of the Montréal Metropolitan Region
in 1951, 1961 and 1971

Municipalities of the MMR in 1971
Metropolitan Region in 1961
Metropolitan Region in 1951

0   10 km

Cartographie INRS-Urbanisation, 1998. CIEQ 2010

MAP 5.4 Montreal metropolitan region. Credit: CIEQ (Interuniversity Center of Quebec Studies).

the construction of Highway 13 led to Saint-Eustache and that of Highway 25, to Mascouche. Thus, thanks to the car and the expansion of the highway system around Montreal, the urban expansion was discontinuous, leading to expensive land development (road construction, aqueducts, and sewers). Until recently, these costs were assumed by the municipalities that later reclaimed the investments through property taxes; real estate developers and builders had very little responsibility. They rushed to get involved in real estate development without having to worry about costs provoked by a leapfrog suburbanization, with residential clusters separated by vast zones of woods or fields.[44]

188   Michèle Dagenais

TABLE 5.2 Ethnocultural portrait of Montreal, 1901–1991

Year	Area	French %	British %	Jewish %	Italian %	European (Other Origins) %	Asian %	Other Origins %
1901	City	60.9	33.7	2.5	0.6	1.5	0.3	0.4
	Island	63.9	31.6	1.9	0.6	1.3	0.2	0.4
	CMA	—	—	—	—	—	—	—
1911	City	63.5	25.7	5.9	1.5	2.1	0.3	0.9
	Island	62.7	27.4	5.2	1.3	2.1	0.2	0.9
	CMA	—	—	—	—	—	—	—
1921	City	63.1	24.0	7.0	2.3	2.3	0.3	1.1
	Island	60.7	27.3	6.3	2.0	2.6	0.5	0.5
	CMA	—	—	—	—	—	—	—
1931	City	63.9	21.8	6.0	2.5	4.7	0.2	0.8
	Island	60.2	26.3	5.8	2.2	4.9	0.5	0.2
	CMA	—	—	—	—	—	—	—
1941	City	66.3	20.3	5,7	2.6	4.0	0.2	0.9
	Island	62.6	24.5	5.7	2.3	3.9	0.4	0.3
	CMA	—	—	—	—	—	—	—
1951	City	67.6	17.7	5.7	2.7	2.5	0.5	3.4
	Island	63.8	22.2	5.4	2.3	2.3	0.4	3.5
	CMA	64.6	22.0	5.1	2.2	2.3	0.4	3.4
1961	City	66.6	12.4	3.9	6.7	3.4	0.7	6.3
	Island	62.0	18.1	4.0	5.6	3.5	0.6	6.2
	CMA	64.2	17.9	3.5	4.8	3.2	0.6	5.8
1971	City	64.2	10.7	4.3	9.0	2.6	1.8	7.2
	Island	59.0	17.0	5.2	7.6	3.1	1.7	6.5
	CMA	64.3	16.0	4.7	5.9	2.7	1.4	5.6
1981	City	—	—	—	—	—	—	—
	Island	—	—	—	—	—	—	—
	CMA	65.7	11.4	3.2	5.6	6.6	2.7	2.4
1991	City	51.7	4.0	2.2	7.1	2.1	0.2	16.9
	Island	—	—	—	—	—	—	—
	CMA	58.3	5.3	2.5	5.3	1.6	1.6	13.2

Note: The data for the 1981 and 1991 censuses are not perfectly comparable with the previous ones, as they are based on a sample of only 20 percent of the population. Also, some respondents declared more than one ethnic origin. Finally, the 1991 data for the island is unavailable. Respondents were asked for mother tongue, not ethnic origin.

   Sources: Paul-André Linteau, *Histoire de Montréal depuis la Confédération* (Montreal: Boréal, 1992), 162, 318, 464, 473; Census of Canada, 1991.

The postwar period was therefore characterized by a process in which the city—thought of as a physical entity of unrestricted, contiguous growth—tended to disappear into a juxtaposition of less defined and less contiguous spaces. Contrary to the preceding period, when the city center attracted residents from the surrounding areas, it was now the periphery that benefited from population growth. Between 1941 and 1981, the population of the island of Montreal went from 1.11 million inhabitants to a little over 1.76 million. The population of the metropolitan region made an even more remarkable jump: from 1.14 million inhabitants in 1941 to 2.8 million inhabitants in 1981. By 2000, the island of Montreal counted 1.8 million inhabitants, while the metropolitan region consisted of nearly 3.5 million (see table 5.1).[45]

As elsewhere across the continent, the many problems generated by such rapid and dispersed growth were increasingly subjects of debate. From the 1960s, investigating committees explored intermunicipal problems on the island of Montreal and across the metropolitan region. They examined the local fiscal imbalances, economies of scale, and efficiency in the provision of municipal services, planning, and land settlement.[46] Amid struggles for better living conditions and rising environmental and legacy movements, a movement for urban rationalization encouraged town planning across all of Quebec.[47] In 1970, the Montreal Urban Community was founded to coordinate the island of Montreal's police force, public transportation, and drinking water supply. While the agency resolved certain problems, its power was limited on the geographical level since it could only exercise its authority on half the population of the metropolis. Little was accomplished in relations among the hundreds of small municipalities in the region, and the idea of creating metropolitan areas beyond the island remained a nonstarter in the face of political localisms often grounded in ethnic concerns.[48]

The explosion of suburbia had another important consequence. It favored the replication of the patchwork dynamic, long characteristic of the urban core, in the suburbs surrounding Montreal. In the west end of the city, the anglophone suburbs, some already established by the beginning of the twentieth century, continued to expand. As noted previously, they benefited from the arrival of northern European immigrants. Suburbs were also established in the northwestern part of the island, with many becoming increasingly ethnically diverse. Although not all were well-to-do, they were defined by comfortable standards of living. As early as 1971, the entire western half of the island was anglophone. In the northwest part of the island, new suburbs, such as Montreal-North and Saint-Leonard, included primarily workers of Italian- or French-Canadian origin.

In this context, the proportion of English-speakers in Montreal was maintained and even slightly increased, though the proportion of British origin was only 11 percent in 1971 (see table 5.2). The situation provoked much malaise among the French-speaking majority, as its weight in Montreal's population decreased from 1951 to 1971, going from 67.6 percent to 64.2 percent. The decline was partly attributable to falling birth rates in the French-speaking population. It is also explained by the relocation of families to the suburbs, a trend that has never stopped since the 1950s. As a result, the off-island, southern, and northern rims were becoming overwhelmingly francophone.

The Linguistic Crisis of the 1960s and 1970s

At the time, what most worried the French-speaking majority was the fact that a growing proportion of immigrants anglicized. This issue arose in the context of a rising French-speaking nationalism. Empowered by the enthusiasm of the Quiet Revolution, French-speaking Quebecois called on the provincial government to adopt language laws to protect the French language and increase its presence in the public space. The battle mainly played out over the language of instruction in the schools. The goal: to gallicize the children of immigrants who were increasingly attending English-language schools. This appeared to be the best strategy in the eyes of parents seeking to ensure the integration and successful future of their children. Conflict, which provoked a national crisis, exploded in the predominately Italian suburb of Saint-Leonard in the late 1960s.[49]

Worried as the demographic weight of French-speakers continued to decrease in Montreal, during a time of falling francophone birth rates, and increased anglicization of immigrants, more and more voices rose to insist that the government of Quebec mandate that children of immigrants attend French-languages schools. Feeling targeted by this demand, the Italo-Quebecois of Saint-Leonard set up an association to defend their right to educate their children in the language of their choice. They gained the support of the anglophone community of Montreal, in particular the small but prosperous core of British origin, concerned over the decline of their demographic weight. Anglo-Montrealers were very conscious of the advantages brought to their group by the anglicization of immigrants. In contrast, francophones perceived this anglicization as a threat to their very survival.

Beginning in 1968—just as middle-class protesters in Mexico City and across the world challenged established regimes—Quebec passed a series of laws reinforcing the use of the French language in all spheres of Quebec society. Finally, Bill 101 (Charter of the French Language) was adopted in 1977. It recognized French as the official language of the province. From then on, Montreal life gradually became more French, in the workforce, in stores, and public life in general. Montreal was increasingly defined as a French-speaking city.[50] Many hoped that French would become the common language of the entire population, regardless of ethnic origin. The use of French strengthened and spread, yet English remained quite present, not only because it was spoken by a significant minority, but also because much of economic life continued in English.

By the end of the postwar immigration wave, Montreal had been fundamentally transformed. Immigrant settlement patterns reinforced the existence of ethnic enclaves in the urban landscape, not only in the city core, but island-wide. The rest of the metropolitan area developed at an extraordinary rate due to the massive suburbanization of the francophone population. With the development of state-sponsored services, institutional networks based on language and/or religion were rendered obsolete. The adoption of French as the official language of Quebec led to the gallicizing of Montreal. Up until the early 1990s, many signs indicated that Montreal was in the process of becoming a multicultural and francophone city. The issue of increased ethnocultural diversity no longer threatened the francophone majority, while the city asserted its position as the French-speaking metropolis of Quebec and the Americas.

Toward a Pluralist City?

The assertion of Montreal as a multicultural and francophone metropolis began in times of dual national development—Canadian and Quebecois. It quickly faced difficult economic times. Begun in the 1980s, the shift from national development to globalization lived in Montreal as a reconversion of the city economy, persisted into the mid-1990s. In the end, the results were often positive once changes permitted a revival of economic activity. The recession period prompted companies to modernize their facilities, increasing their productivity through labor-saving technologies, to become more competitive—in Canada, in North America, and globally. In comparison to other North American metropolises, Montreal maintains a significant manufacturing sector, where 17 percent of jobs are found.[51] The implementation of the

North American Free Trade Agreement (NAFTA) in 1994 encouraged the exportation of goods south of border, benefitting Montreal-based companies. Besides, Montreal's labor and business costs were lower than in the United States.[52] The metropolitan economy also developed a strong tertiary sector, especially in high-tech services (financial services, insurance, and communications). The second half of the 1990s also brought a real estate boom that accompanied the revitalization of old neighborhoods and their gentrification.[53] Montreal in the later decades of the twentieth century shared much with other New World cities facing globalization: deindustrialization (though on a reduced scale), job losses in established sectors like the railroads, a turn toward a knowledge-based economy—and the rise of services.[54]

The increase of services included the marked growth of the cultural and recreational/leisure sectors. A new era of festivals was inaugurated (jazz, dance, theater, cinema, francophone music, etc.), which contributed to Montreal gaining an international reputation as a festive city.[55] Large sporting events such as the Formula One Grand Prix of Canada, the NHL hockey games of the Montreal Canadiens and the Rogers Cup of tennis also contributed to the transition toward a postindustrial economy. While clearly not the pillars of the Montreal economy, these sectors played a key role in branding Montreal with a unique personality, which in turn stimulated its tourism industry.

Montreal's branding as a festive city has been an important driving force for its sex industry. Montreal is now considered Canada's capital for prostitution, often described as the "sin city of Canada."[56] This reputation, which dates back to Prohibition,[57] continues to depict Montreal as a city of vice where access to all types of illicit activities is particularly easy. To what does the city owe this reputation? It is certainly due to more liberal alcohol laws, to the city's bustling nightlife, and to the diversity of leisure activities of all kinds. This reputation is also nourished by publicity campaigns that depict Montreal as a pleasure city in order to attract more tourists. One also has to take into account the prominence of the sex industry in the city, which is partly the result of high unemployment and poverty within Montreal's population—perhaps linked to globalization, deindustrialization, and the turn to the service sector for employment that is often informal and sometimes illegal.[58] However, there is a lack of research that systematically documents this sector. Studies of Montreal do not take account of the informal economy, which skews statistics, especially since the end of the twentieth century, a period marked by a slowdown in the growth of the formal economy. This trend, shared in so many cities, demands investigation.

While the Montreal economy struggled through the recession of the 1980s, a series of changes that were not immediately perceptible to the inhabitants of Montreal and Quebec took place. New tendencies would once again blur the identity of Montreal and call into question the arrangements adopted to ensure peaceful coexistence among the various groups in the city. Changes took place in the composition of the immigrant population and their settlement patterns in three ways:[59] first, there was a notable diversification of immigrants' countries of origin; second, the composition of immigrant neighborhoods diversified; and third, while the overwhelming majority of immigrants settled in the city center, some groups began to spread across the metropolitan space. Was Montreal going from a mosaic to a pluralistic city?[60]

Since the 1980s and 1990s, in Canada and elsewhere, immigration factors increasingly inscribed themselves in the global economic context and the growing internationalization of the workforce. The Canadian government redefined the selection criteria of immigrants to consider, even more than before, the country's economic objectives.[61] This encouraged the settlement of well-educated immigrants, who would presumably adapt more easily to economic fluctuations. These immigrants were selected on a point-based system whereby the level of education, age, and knowledge of the official languages are taken into consideration. Yet, for a range of reasons, including the difficulties immigrants experience in obtaining recognition for their expertise acquired abroad, compounded with the increase in unstable employment options, the strategy did not work as intended.[62] In addition to recruitment politics favoring skilled immigrants, new programs were funded for the hiring of temporary immigrant workers who tended to hold low-salaried jobs turned down by locals, such as those providing amenities to persons and manual work. In such a situation, it is not surprising to realize that the economic fortunes of immigrants fell, particularly in Montreal's metropolitan area.[63] By all means, the growing precariousness of immigrants is conducive to the development of an informal economy, but this remains to be documented.

Although Montreal receives fewer immigrants than Toronto, the places of origin of these newcomers are more diverse.[64] Moreover, their profile differs in comparison to those of other Canadian regions, because the Quebec government tends to favor immigrants who know French or who are likely to learn the language easily.[65] Montreal is noted for the large number of immigrants from North Africa, Lebanon, Haiti, and France, as well as immigrants from China, Romania, India, and Sri Lanka.

The situation differs by group, but overall the proportion of poor immigrants increased in recent decades, going from 29.3 percent in 1980 to 41.2 percent in 2000. The numbers reveal a disparity between recent immigrants and those who arrived during the 1950 to 1970 period. The degradation of living standard is particularly pronounced in the case of "visible minorities,"[66] whose unemployment rate in 2001, of 15.1 percent, is almost twice as high as that of the broader population (8.2 percent).[67] While their situation is not one of an "ethnic underclass," it is evident that immigrants identified as "visible minorities" have a more precarious existence, while immigrants of European origin have had better success.

As the origins of the immigrants diversified so did their ways of settling in the urban space. Though there remained a certain percentage along Saint-Lawrence Boulevard, the majority settled in the intermediary spaces between downtown and the suburbs. In 2001, very few neighborhoods on the island were without newcomers. Many settled in the west end of the city among anglophone majorities, others chose the more francophone east and northeast. Many neighborhoods long identified with one particular cultural community diversified. Others that stayed homogenous over the years were now transformed due to the influx of immigrants of various ethnic origins.

Contrary to previous years, immigrants did not form homogenous ethnic enclaves. Instead there was a rise in interethnic cohabitation—that is, neighborhoods where over 30 percent of the population is foreign-born and of diverse origins—in wealthy as well as poor areas. The situation worked against the formation of ghettos. However, certain multiethnic neighborhoods are among the poorest in the city, notably Côte-des-Neiges, in the west, Little Burgundy, in the southwest, and Saint-Michel, in the north.

In comparison to other large Canadian cities, like Toronto and Vancouver, Montreal is distinguished by a high concentration of immigrants within its territory: 70 percent of new arrivals live in Montreal, only 20 percent settle in the metropolitan region. Because fewer immigrants settle in Montreal, the situation, for the moment, appears to be a phenomenon of concentration rather than ghettoization.[68]

Even if over the past few years, immigrants have started moving to the Montreal suburbs located in the north, on the island of Laval, and on the south shore, in Brossard, they continue to opt for the city of Montreal and very rarely settle beyond it. Indeed, throughout Canada, immigrants generally choose to live in the country's big cities. In addition, statistics compiled by Statistics Canada indicate that from 1991 to 2001 94 percent of immigrants lived in urban centers, which means that only 6 percent settled in small towns or rural areas.[69]

In addition to the process of differentiation common to all Canadian metropolitan centers, in Quebec this reality is compounded by the linguistic question and the insecurity with regard to identity felt by the French-speaking majority. The statistics from the last censuses indicate that French is in decline in Montreal since the end of the twentieth century. The proportion of francophones has fallen from 53.2 percent in 2001, then to 48 percent in 2011. Thus, even the enactment of Bill 101, mandating the children of immigrants to attend French schools, did not compensate for the decline of francophones. There has been no massive linguistic transfer once the mandatory education was completed. Thus, 60 percent of allophones (those whose first language is neither English nor French) had chosen English by 1996, an improvement since 1971, when this choice was made by 74 percent.[70] Francophone families continue to prefer living in the southern and northern suburbs. These diverse dynamics have not contributed to an increase in anglophones; instead allophones have gone from 29.1 percent of the population in 2001 to 34 percent in 2011. Nine linguistic groups are responsible for 60 percent of the growth in allophone population, led by Arabic (22.4 percent), Spanish (13.4 percent), and Chinese (13 percent).[71]

This situation generates constant tensions between a cosmopolitan city and the rest of a more ethnically homogenous province. If until the end of the twentieth century the Quebec population was relatively favorable to immigration, in spite of its concern about the decrease in francophone clout, the advantages brought by this population influx, necessary to ensure the growth of its population, are no longer as evident. While it was hoped that learning the French language would help immigrants adapt, the process has not had the anticipated results. Instead of integrating immigrants into the dominant Franco-Quebecois culture, Montreal society is increasingly redefining and identifying itself as multicultural. The rift that separates Montreal from the rest of Quebec has heightened.

Metropolitan Management: An Identity as Well as a Social Issue

The metropolitan question resurfaced in this context. Numerous researchers sensitized the public authorities to the importance of new forms of urban management in order to confront a global and therefore more competitive economic reality. The period also led to a more coherent policy with regard to the provision of services in an increasingly sprawling urban area. Added to this were the challenges of dividing and sharing the costs of services and shared facilities previously assumed almost entirely by the city center. Meanwhile, peripheral suburban regions started to assert their economic, political, and cultural autonomy more and more.[72] Simultaneous centripetal and centrifugal pressures challenged the old center-periphery model.

On an economic level, since the 1970s the manufacturing centers that have remained relocated within the metropolis.[73] The suburbs have not grown as a result of people moving out from the city center. Instead, as of 1971, a growing proportion of the population has come from outside the agglomeration. Consequently, it has been the far south and north ends of the city that expanded the fastest. Today, "each part of the agglomeration is able to respond locally to the work, shopping, and leisure activity needs of its population."[74] In sum, the urban shape of Montreal is increasingly polycentric. As suburbs acquire urban characteristics, the historic heart of Montreal has lost centrality.

What are the consequences? Are we witnessing the breakup of the metropolis as calls for autonomy come from suburbs that are becoming autonomous and disparate? Yet Montreal—like the other cities of the Americas studied here—is increasingly the site of the economic growth that sustains the province and the nation. In this context of contradiction, should the vitality of metropolitan areas be left dependent on the ability of each component to make an interdependent profit? With these questions in mind, the government of Quebec initiated a municipal reform at the beginning of the twenty-first century. The Quebecois state wanted to establish decision-making bodies on a region-wide scale and reduce the excessive number of municipalities. In 2001, the Montreal Urban Community was abolished, replaced by a new Montreal Metropolitan Commission. Bringing together the sixty-four municipalities of the Montreal region, the organization is responsible for the strategic planning of the facilities and services (land settlement, economic growth, artistic and cultural development, waste management, public transportation, and arterial network). Few other New World cities have attempted such integrated governance—especially as Houston has expanded beyond the bounds of Harris County (see chapter 7).

In 2002, the government decided that it would amalgamate all the municipalities of the island of Montreal, balanced by a decentralized method of management. The new city would consist of an ensemble of boroughs, each granted considerable decision-making powers. Before finalizing this forced merging of the municipalities, the provincial government conceded a large margin of autonomy to former suburbs. Still, the maneuver failed to convince many, provoking such strong feelings of discontent that court suits tried, in vain, to have the decision overturned.

At the heart of these oppositions to the newly reconstituted city of Montreal were arguments related to identity. The main opponents were English-dominated municipalities that felt threatened by the amalgamation process. They asserted that their territorial integrity was essential to the survival of their cultural heritage and identity. The movement was also inspired by the desire to protect exclusive sites and the privileges that accompanied them.[75] During the 2003 provincial elections, the winning political party granted cities the right to de-amalgamate if they so chose. By June 2004, fifteen former municipalities, almost all situated on the west end of the island, de-amalgamated.[76]

Thus, instead of encompassing all former municipalities, the new city comprises only nineteen boroughs, corresponding to the cities that accepted the amalgamation. In order to administer the island of Montreal in this new context, an agglomeration council was created in 2006, consisting of the city's mayor, the representatives from the nineteen boroughs, and those of the fifteen suburban cities, designated as reconstituted cities. Montreal political life has become complex to the point where very few understand its organization. Local democracy, already stagnant, is at risk of becoming bloodless.[77]

In sum, while the metropolitan question in the Montreal region entails a multitude of political and social issues, common in city-regions of similar size, complex identity issues compound Montreal's difficulties. In contrast to large U.S. cities, the movement toward the autonomy of Montreal suburbs has yet to result in the creation of "edge cities." Montreal possesses a dynamic downtown in comparison to other large North American cities. Still, the Montreal region experiences many tensions, with a city center and many boroughs on the island very multiethnic; with suburban municipalities remaining jealous of their privileges and concerned about protecting their specific identities; and with the outer areas on each side of the island made up of overwhelmingly French-speaking populations.

New Ways of Appropriating and Demarcating
Montreal's Metropolitan Territory

Since the turn of the twenty-first century, questions of segregation/aggregation have been posed in new terms. To recap, during previous periods, immigrants tended to adopt a strategy of withdrawal within ethnic enclaves and from there established a feeling of belonging to the city. In neighborhoods where they represented a large proportion of the population, the space constituted a reference point from which they obtained political representation, on both a local and national scale. Thus, for example, Italians became fairly well represented at two levels.[78]

Yet, over the past ten years, the strategies used by a significant percentage of the new immigrant population have changed; they increasingly demand recognition based on cultural specificities. This has translated into new ways of appropriating and demarcating urban territory, as well as the means by which groups assert their existence and seek to acquire specific rights. The new strategies of recognition come from groups in which religious practices constitute a central component of culture and their identity. Instead of starting from a strategy of withdrawal before becoming part of the whole, these groups use the public space to assert their difference, constitute a social group, and demand a place in the political space of the city. Their demands for inclusion are therefore formulated on bases that differ from Montreal's traditional mechanisms of negotiation and arbitration. Instead of claiming rights stemming from their belonging within the mosaic of Montreal, as was the case in the past, demands now aim to obtain a right to the entire city and thereby express their allegiance to the latter.[79]

This situation has brought the multiplication of new places of worship all over Montreal, urban and suburban: synagogues, mosques, Hindu temples, gurdwaras, and Pentecostal churches. Though primarily destined for religious practice, they are also places of representation for these groups, in particular for Muslims. In the 1990s, the municipal authorities in Montreal and some suburban cities relatively easily issued construction permits for these places of worship, which were generally built in zones with available space. However, as requests increased with time, they led to greater opposition, whether for political or planning considerations. Conflicts have arisen especially since demands have spread involving other realities, notably about rules of access to municipal facilities, such as public pools.[80]

In the eyes of the majority, these demands seem contrary to the recent evolution of Quebec society, which, since the 1960s, has known an increasing secularization of the public sphere, and also of the public space. While new immigrant groups' strategies of affirmation in the urban space have brought greater visibility and dispersal across the territory, a growing proportion of the established population feels threatened and attempts to defend an increasingly rigid position, demanding that the public space remain "neutral." Perceiving any marking of the urban space with religious symbols as a refusal to integrate to the established society (with all its complexities), adherents to this reaction fight for uniformity across the Montreal landscape and practices facilitating the management of urban space.

Up until recent years, the people of Montreal seemed ready to accommodate different uses of the urban space, seeing the affirmation of different cultures as enriching. This translated into municipal policies promoting the pluralistic character of Montreal, considered a trait unique to this city of long-standing immigration, even an element of merit and distinction. Yet, fear of the loss of the collective francophone identity, in a context where its heritage and its specificity is under threat in an increasingly diverse world, has led to tense public debate around "the religious question."

The situation is far from unique to Quebec and Montreal, but debates are notably more animated and numerous. They have had the effect of relegating the socioeconomic problems faced by immigrants to the back burner, while several indicators demonstrate that this population is becoming more impoverished. Whereas in 1980, 29.3 percent of immigrants lived in situations of poverty, in 2000, this proportion rose to 41.26 percent, a major increase in only twenty years.[81] Thus, while the living conditions of immigrants become more precarious, questions surrounding identity dominate public debate, deflecting consideration away from the crucial questions of social equality. The risks seem great, especially among racialized minorities that feel more and more excluded and withdraw from the broader urban society. The new dynamic could lead to the formation of true ghettos.

The new ways of ethnic identification and mobilization cut across social cleavages defined by a very unequal distribution of wealth. Since the Second World War, suburban life has been made accessible to a growing proportion of the population. Yet it remains out of reach for many. Among the most socially and economically destitute are people who have never crossed either the major bridges or their municipal boundary. A "culture of poverty" has been transmitted from generation to generation in French-speaking neighborhoods hard hit by deindustrialization, notably in the center-south and east of Montreal. Meanwhile, many signs attest to the marginalization of immigrant youth, especially those concentrated in the poor neighborhoods of the southwest and northeast. Inequities thus plague the old linguistic majority underclass and the new immigrant groups seeking work and religious rights.

In a context of Quebec state disengagement, the city of Montreal has had to assume a large part of social costs, while with the most vulnerable segments of the urban population concentrated in its territory (young adults, single-parent families, unskilled workers, and migrants).[82] In the beginning of the twenty-first century, Montreal is confronted with an ensemble of issues that reveal that many of its problems remain unresolved: urban sprawl, the decentralization of economic activity, a high moving rate, the concentration of poverty, and linguistic cohabitation.[83]

Conclusion

During the twentieth century, Montreal underwent a series of transformations that are similar to those of other large cities of the New World whose destinies began linked to colonial empires. From those origins, Montreal's role in the international economy has shaped, but never determined, its complex history as a metropolis. First as a colonial city within the British Empire, then as Canada's hub of international commerce, Montreal was Canada's dominant metropolis for nearly a century, from the middle of the nineteenth century to the middle of the twentieth. But the rise and dominance of the United States during the mid-twentieth-century decades focused on national development, brought a repositioning of Montreal, pushed to second place by Toronto, Canada's new metropolis starting in the 1960s. These transformations demonstrate how the history of a medium-sized city such as Montreal has always been subject to influences that go far beyond its own borders.

If trends in the global economy continued to weigh on Montreal's destiny afterward, beginning in the 1960s and 1970s, Montreal settled into its role as Quebec's metropolis. This new status allowed the city to remain at the summit, if of a society considerably smaller than Canada. Thus, numerous Quebec companies established their head offices in the city, and new sectors linked to the knowledge-based economy emerged to respond to the needs of a predominantly francophone society. Yet, though Montreal is the second-largest city in Canada, its population has one of the lowest levels of education among cities of similar size in North America. Similarly, average salaries in Montreal are lower, notably because the economy today still includes a large number of industries with low salaries. That perhaps helped

Montreal to adapt and maintain some industry, as cheap labor became a comparative advantage in the new economy of globalization. Meanwhile, demographic growth has slowed (common among most cities shaped by the post-1950 population explosions), leading many to see a need to encourage international immigration to Montreal and to Quebec as a whole. That may help sustain the economy of low wages and spreading services (often marked by informality and illegality). Can it address persistent inequities, as it will certainly maintain challenging religious-ethnic interactions?

As a second-tier metropolis, Montreal evolves with the strain of two roles: the metropolis of Quebec and a North American metropolis in a changing world. This particular situation is demonstrated in the dual discourse that exists on Montreal today.

On the one hand, some are inclined to define Montreal as the metropolis of French-speaking Quebec, the largest city in a possibly sovereign Quebec. On the other hand, in particular for those who do not endorse sovereignty or are not proponents of Quebec nationalism, Montreal is perceived as a large, bilingual, and Canadian city, increasingly oriented toward the rest of the continent. Though neither discourse is necessarily erroneous, both paint only partial pictures of the reality. Indeed, the vitality of Montreal, its distinctive traits, and its assets hold to these two facets at once.[84] Because of its purpose as a French-speaking metropolis, Montreal developed its own distinctive personality and possesses a rich and original cultural life that distinguishes it from many other similarly sized North American cities. It is also thanks to the Quebec state and to the French-speaking capital that Montreal was able to maintain its key sectors and retain its head offices during the exodus of Anglo-Saxon capital to Toronto. That proved a key to Montreal and Quebec maintaining solid relative prosperities through the decades when national development policies faced the difficulties of debt and dynamism that led to the shift to globalization in the 1980s.

The bilingual nature of the city has been essential to its economic growth, yet its activities cannot be limited to the region or the province. Especially from the 1980s, they have had to extend to continental and international scales. Only that extension has enabled Montreal to fully exercise its role as locomotive of the Quebec economy. But because it accentuates the concentration of key resources in Montreal, this situation does not currently please the rest of Quebec, which feels crushed by the weight of Montreal. The promotion of bilingualism and pressures toward greater ethnic-religious diversity is seen as a threat to the survival of Quebec as the province-home of French-speaking North America.

What the tension between these two visions reveals in the end is also the unresolved problem of the insertion of an increasingly multicultural city within the whole of Quebec. Since the nineteenth century, as we have seen, successive immigration waves have diversified the composition of the Montreal population, while at the same time, they accentuated the difference between Montreal and the province. If during the height of the Quiet Revolution the city seemed to move closer to the rest of Quebec because of the gallicization of public life, recent immigration—itself a product of globalization—has again widened the gap between Montreal and Quebec.

Meanwhile, international immigration and the mobility of the population within the city, the metropolis, and the province redrew the map of jurisdictions at the metropolitan level. Since the 1950s, the city and the island of Montreal have experienced an evolution different from that of the suburbs of the north and south shores. The first became increasingly multicultural, even pluralistic. The second, in full development since then, retain relatively homogeneous, French-speaking populations. So while it would appear that the city's population was becoming more diverse, a new dividing line was drawn between the latter and the off-island population. In certain respects, the core of Montreal has become an ethnic enclave in relation to the rest of the province of Quebec—including the metropolitan suburbs.

Within Montreal, the incorporation of generations of immigrants during a large part of the twentieth century came through the process I identify as aggregation followed by integration. Now the question must be asked for the whole of Quebec: in the context of an ever more diverse population in the center of Montreal, does the success of its insertion in the province now depend on the integration of the multicultural and pluralist character of the city into the reality of all of Quebec? The question is pivotally important as multiculturalism is provoking heated debates in twenty-first-century cities across the Americas as well as in Europe. Montreal, with all its changing diversity, remains crucial to the economic prospects of Quebec in a globalizing world. When the core of that diversity set a francophone majority against a powerful anglophone minority in the 1960s, as Canada and Quebec faced new struggles of national development, francophone nationalism helped reinforce the economies of Montreal and Quebec, limiting the difficulties so common to cities and societies facing the turn to globalization. Now, as Montreal and Quebec live with deindustrialization and the shift toward services, along with diverse new migrants sent by the disruptive impacts of globalization elsewhere, can new accommodations of changing diversities keep the city and province economically strong and socially cohesive? Or will debates over multicultural rights deflect focus from the challenges of dealing with deepening inequities that cross both linguistic and ethnic lines?

The answers are important to Montreal, Quebec, and Canada—and to the Americas and the world. Montreal's previous successes incorporating diversity and abating economic difficulties offer hope. Its negotiation of the new challenges of globalization will tell much about the prospects of an increasingly urban and interdependent world going forward.

Notes

1. Jean-Pierre Collin and Jacques Léveillée, *Municipal Organization in Canada: Tradition and Transformation, Varying from Province to Province* (Montreal: Villes Régions Monde/Institut de Sciences Politiques et Socials, 2003), 29.

2. Heidi Hoerning and Margaret Walton-Roberts, "Immigration and Urban Change: National, Regional, and Local Perspectives," in *Canadian Cities in Transition. Local Through Global Perspectives*, ed. Trudi Bunting and Pierre Filion, 3rd ed. (Don Mills, ON: Oxford University Press, 2006), 408–418; Annick Germain and David Ley, "Immigration and the Social Geography of Large Canadian Cities," *Plan Canada* 40, no. 4 (2000): 29–32.

3. John Zucchi, *A History of Ethnic Enclaves in Canada* (Ottawa: Canadian Historical Society, 2007). On the idea of enclaves, albeit in another context, see Jordan Stanger Ross, "An Inviting Parish: Community without Locality in Postwar Italian Toronto," *Canadian Historical Review* 87, no. 3 (September 2006): 381–407.

4. The following definition will be used in this chapter when referring to the metropolitan region of Montreal: "[A] metropolitan region is defined as an urban core surrounded by urban and rural fringes with which there is a strong degree of social and economic integration: the area thus defined is identified especially by daily commuting patterns . . . . [T]he delimitation of a metropolitan region is likely to change from one census to another." Jean-Pierre Collin, Michèle Dagenais, and Claire Poitras, "From City to City-Region: Historical Perspective on the Contentious Definitions of the Montréal Metropolitan Area," *Canadian Journal of Urban Research/Revue canadienne de recherche urbaine* 12, no. 1 (Summer 2003): 21.

5. I tend to avoid using the word "integration" as it generally suggests that adaptation to a multicultural society is a one-way process which concerns only immigrants. In contrast, a word like "insertion" suggests that the encounter between immigrants and the host society is a dynamic process involving adaptation on both sides. See Annick Germain, "Les quartiers multiethniques montréalais: une lecture urbaine," *Recherches sociographiques* 40, no. 1 (1999): 11; see also Engin F. Isin and Myer Siemiatycki, "Making Spaces for Mosques: Struggles for Urban Citizenship in Diasporic Toronto," in *Race, Space and the Law: Unmapping a White Settler Society*, ed. S. Razack (Ottawa: Between the Lines, 2002), 185–209.

6. For an overview of Montreal's history, see Paul-André Linteau, *The History of Montreal: The Story of a Great North American City* (Montreal: Baraka Books, 2013), as well as Stéphane Castonguay and Michèle Dagenais, eds., *Metropolitan Natures: Environmental Histories of Montreal* (Pittsburgh: University of Pittsburgh Press, 2011).

7. Linteau, *The History of Montreal*, 79.

8. Similar to other large industrial cities, disparities in wealth were very pronounced in Montreal at the time. On this question see Bettina Bradbury, *Working Families: Age, Gender and Daily Survival in Industrializing Montreal* (Toronto: McClelland and Stewart, 1993).

9. Alvin Finkel and Margaret Conrad, *History of the Canadian Peoples, 1867 to the Present*, 2nd ed. (Toronto: Copp Clark, 1998), 118.

10. John Dickinson and Brian Young, *A Short History of Quebec*, 4th ed. (Montreal and Kingston: McGill-Queens University Press, 2008), 202.

11. Larry Gordon, "L.A. County Leads U.S. by Large Margins in Numbers of Latinos, Asians," *Los Angeles Times*, September 19, 1998, A24; Robin Fields, "Milestones of Growth and a New Ethnic Order," *Los Angeles Times*, March 30, 2001, U1; "Latinos: Four Counties See a Surge in Numbers," *Los Angeles Times*, March 30, 2001, U6.

12. Jim Simmons and Larry McCann, "The Canadian Urban System," in *Canadian Cities in Transition*, ed. Bunting and Filion, 54; Annick Germain and Damaris Rose, *Montreal: The Quest for a Metropolis* (Chichester, UK: John Wiley, 2000), 28–32.

13. Ronald Rudin, *The Forgotten Quebecers: A History of English Speaking Quebec, 1759–1980* (Quebec City: Institut québécois de recherche sur la culture, 1985).

14. Germain and Rose, *Montreal*, 217–219.

15. Roderick MacLeod and Mary Anne Poutanen, *A Meeting of the People: School Boards and Protestant Communities in Quebec, 1801–1998* (Montreal and Kingston: McGill-Queen's University Press, 2004).

16. On the notion of a third solitude, more specifically in relation to Canadian history and historiography, see Roberto Perin, "Clio as an Ethnic: The Third Force in Canadian Historiography," *Canadian Historical Review* 64, no. 4 (December 1983): 441–467.

17. Claire McNicoll, *Montréal: Une société multiculturelle* (Paris: Belin, 1993), 143–144.

18. Linteau, *The History of Montreal*, 330–332.

19. Jacques Langlais and David Rome, *Jews and French Quebecers: Two Hundred Years of Shared History* (Waterloo, ON: Wilfrid Laurier, 1991), 31–33.

20. Hugh MacLennan, *Two Solitudes* (Toronto: Macmillan, 1945), 295–296, quoted in Germain and Rose, *Montreal*, 213.

21. Paul-André Linteau, "La monté du cosmopolitisme montréalais," *Questions de culture* 2 (1982): 23–53.

22. Michèle Dagenais, *Democracy in Montreal from 1830 up to the Present* (Montreal: Ville de Montréal, 1992), 28.

23. On this specific issue, see Andrew Sancton, *Governing the Island of Montreal: Language Differences and Metropolitan Politics* (Berkeley: University of California

Press, 1985), as well as Harold Bérubé, *Des sociétés distinctes: gouverner les banlieues bourgeoises de Montréal, 1880–1939* (Montreal: McGill-Queen's University Press, 2014).

24. Many small suburban cities developed following the arrival of urbanites on vacation who colonized part of the Montreal region. For more on this, see Michèle Dagenais, "'Returning to Nature': Vacation and Life Style in the Montreal Region," in *Resources of the City: Contributions to Modern European Environmental History*, ed. Geneviève Massard-Guilbaud, Dieter Schott, and Bill Luckin (Aldershot, UK: Ashgate, 2005), 63–79.

25. Linteau, *The History of Montreal*, 202–203.

26. At the beginning of the 1960s, Montreal succeeded in annexing four additional suburbs, but this second wave of expansion did not last very long. Linteau, *The History of Montreal*, 499.

27. Jean-Pierre Collin and Michèle Dagenais, "Évolution des enjeux politiques locaux et des pratiques municipales dans l'île de Montréal, 1840–1950," in *Enjeux et expressions de la politique municipale (XIIe—XXe siècles)*, ed. Denis Menjot and Jean-Luc Pinol (Paris: L'Harmattan, 1997), 191–221.

28. In the 1930s and early 1940s, the construction of housing slowed to the point that by the late 1940s there was a dire need for facilities. The situation was such that the federal government had to develop policies in order to increase access to housing. The type of housing developments encouraged by the government, entrepreneurs, and the population were located in suburbia. See Germain and Rose, *Montreal*, 97 and following.

29. Mario Polèse, "Montréal économique, de 1930 à nos jours: Récit d'une transition inachevée," in *Histoire de Montréal et sa région, Tome II*, ed. Dany Fougères (Quebec: Presses de l'Université Laval, 2012), 972–977.

30. Linteau, *The History of Montreal*, ch. 12.

31. Polèse, "Montréal économique," 994 and following.

32. As Paul-André Linteau explains: "Cities like Sherbrooke, Trois-Rivières or Québec City each controlled their hinterland, with their commercial establishments, their distribution centers, their service industries . . . . But the important movement toward the concentration of francophone companies occurring in the 1970s and 1980s was often accompanied by the centralization of decision-making control in Montreal." *The History of Montreal*, 435.

33. The term is also justified by the importance of Montreal with regard to the cultural and intellectual life of the province. There had been an increased presence of radio and television networks, publishing houses, and artistic performances.

34. Dickinson and Young, *A Short History of Quebec*, 305–307.

35. That was the case of some of the larger francophone enterprises such as Provigo, Bombardier, or Quebecor and of public companies like Hydro-Quebec or the Caisse de dépôt et de placement.

36. Claire Heldman, *The Milton Park Affair: Canada's Largest Citizen-Developer Confrontation* (Montreal: Vehicule Press, 1987).

37. For more on this important group, go to http://www.heritagemontreal .org/en/.

38. Germain and Rose, *Montreal*, 234–235.

39. McNicoll, *Montréal*, 191.

40. Amanda Ricci, "From Acculturation to Integration: The Political Participation of Montreal's Italian-Canadian Community in an Urban Context (1945–1990)," M.A. thesis, University of Montreal, 2008.

41. McNicoll, *Montréal*, 243; Nadia Breimas-Assimopoulos, "Intégration sans acculturation: les Grecs de Montréal," *Sociologie et Sociétés* 15, no. 2 (1983): 129–142.

42. Germain and Rose, *Montreal*, 95–96.

43. Claire Poitras, "A City on the Move: The Surprising Consequences of Highways," in *Metropolitan Natures*, ed. Castonguay and Dagenais, 180.

44. Linteau, *The History of Montreal*, 498–499.

45. Collin and Léveillée, *Municipal Organization in Canada*, 29.

46. The socioeconomic impact of the power struggles over water management on the island of Montreal is analyzed in Michèle Dagenais and Claire Poitras, "Une ressource abondante et inépuisable? Urbanisation et gestion de l'eau dans le Montréal métropolitain aux XIXe et XXe siècles," *Histoire urbaine* 18 (April 2007): 97–123.

47. Gérard Beaudet, "Aménagement du territoire et urbanisme: le Québec a-t-il su relever le défi de la planification?" *Organisations et territoires* 14, no. 3 (2005): 8.

48. The municipal reform movement in Quebec at the end of the 1990s nevertheless resulted in a reduction of the number of municipalities in the province, going from 1,433 in 1995, to 1,147 in 2003. Collin and Léveillée, *Municipal Organization in Canada*, 9–10.

49. See Ricci, "From Acculturation to Integration," 58–68.

50. On this issue, see Marc V. Levine, *The Reconquest of Montreal: Language Policy and Social Change in a Bilingual City* (Philadelphia: Temple University Press, 1990).

51. Jean-Pierre Collin and Anne-Marie Séguin, *Une agglomération en changements: premiers éléments d'un bilan d'ensemble* (Montreal: Observatoire métropolitain de la région de Montréal, 1999), 15.

52. Montréal International, "Greater Montréal Takes Top Spot Again as Most Cost-Competitive City in North America," http://www.montrealinternational.com/en/blog/greater-montreal-top-spot-most-cost-competitive-city-north-america/.

53. Germain and Rose, *Montreal*, 184 and following. See also Linteau, *The History of Montreal*, 178.

54. Collin and Séguin, *Une agglomération en changements*, 6; Jean-Pierre Collin, "Montréal: Depictions of a Mid-size Metropolis," *Canadian Journal of Urban Research/Revue canadienne de recherche urbaine* 12, no. 1 (2003): 3.

55. Guy Bellavance and Christian Poirier, "Champ culturel et espace montréalais: une agglomération culturelle en transition," in *Histoire de Montréal et sa région*, ed. Fougères, 1354–1360.

56. "Montreal, Sin City of the North?" *Montreal Gazette*, July 15, 2008; see also "Montréal, plaque tournante du tourisme sexuel," *La Presse*, October 2, 2013.

57. On this topic, see Michael Hawrysh, "Une ville bien arrosée: Montréal durant l'ère de la prohibition (1920–1933)," M.A. thesis, University of Montreal, 2014.

58. According to the 2001 Census, 29 percent of Montreal's population lived below the poverty line, compared to 22.6 percent in Toronto and 27 percent in Vancouver. *Rapport sur la pauvreté à Montréal*, 8.

59. Germain, "Les quartiers multiethniques montréalais," 14–17.

60. Xavier Leloup, ed., *Les nouveaux territoires de l'ethnicité* (Quebec: Presses de l'Université Laval, 2008), 3.

61. Denise Helly, "La légitimité en panne? Immigration, sécurité, cohésion sociale et nativisme," *Cultures et Conflits* 74 (2009): 18.

62. Micheline Labelle, Anne-Marie Field, and Jean-Claude Icart, *Les dimensions d'intégration des immigrants, des minorités ethnoculturelles et des groupes racisés au Québec* (Montreal: Centre de recherche sur l'immigration, l'ethnicité et la citoyenneté, 2007), 34.

63. On the scale of large Canadian cities, Montreal has the highest poverty rate at 29 percent for the whole of the population, in comparison to 22.6 percent in Toronto and 27 percent in Vancouver. Labelle, Field, and Icart, *Les dimensions d'intégration des immigrants*, 28–29; Xavier Leloup, *Towards the Pluralist City? Distribution and Localisation of Visible Minorities in Montreal, Toronto and Vancouver in 2001* (Montreal, 2008), http://arminamartineau.tk/download/qov5DAEACAAJ-towards-the-pluralist-city.

64. In the Montreal metropolitan region, however, the proportion of immigrants is lower than in many other cities in Canada. In fact, in 1996, when immigrants represented 18 percent of the population in Montreal, in Toronto they equaled 42 percent of the population and in Vancouver, 35 percent. Germain and Rose, *Montreal*, 244. See also Andrew Heisz, *Trends and Conditions in Census Metropolitan Areas: Ten Things to Know About Canadian Metropolitan Areas: A Synthesis of Statistics Canada's Trends and Conditions in Census Metropolitan Areas Series* (Statistics Canada, 2005), http://www.statcan.gc.ca/pub/89-613-m/89-613-m2005009-eng.pdf.

65. Dickinson and Young, *A Short History of Quebec*, 348–349.

66. A term coming from immigration policy, it entered the lexicon of researchers and the media. By this one understands it to mean members of the black, Arab, Chinese, and South Asian groups.

67. Labelle, Field, and Icart, *Les dimensions d'intégration des immigrants*, 26.

68. Annick Germain, "The Montréal School: Urban Social Mix in a Reflexive City," *Anthropologica* 55 (2013): 3.

69. For a good overview of recent trends of the urbanization in Canada, see Pierre Filion and Trudi Bunting, "Understanding Twenty-First-Century Urban Structure: Sustainability, Unevenness, and Uncertainity," in *Canadian Cities in Transition*, ed. Bunting and Filion, 1–23. For an analysis of repercussions at the economic level, see Mario Polèse and Richard Sheamur, *The Metropolitanisation of Canada: Why Populations Continue to Concentrate in and Around Large Urban Centers and What it Means for Other Regions* (Montreal: INRS-Urbanisation, Culture et Société, 2003).

70. Linteau, *Histoire de Montréal depuis la Confédération*, 560.

71. Leloup, *Towards the Pluralist City*, 20. See also *Language Projections for Canada, 2011 to 2036* (Statistics Canada, 2017), http://veq.ca/wp-content/uploads/2017/03/Population-forecast-2011-to-2036.pdf.

72. Jean-Pierre Collin, "La dynamique intramétropolitaine dans l'agglomération montréalaise," in *Barcelona–Montréal: Desarrollo Urbano Comparado/Développement urbain comparé*, ed. Horacio Capel and Paul-André Linteau (Barcelona: Publicacions de la Universitat de Barcelona, 1998), 66.

73. For example, specialized poles have developed in the south shore, in the domain of transportation and, in Saint-Laurent, high-tech industry.

74. Collin, "La dynamique intramétropolitaine dans l'agglomération montréalaise," 75.

75. On this topic, see the report written by Paul-André Linteau for the Quebec government: *Groupes, identités et municipalités dans l'histoire de Montréal et de sa région* (Ministère des Affaires Municipales et de la Métropole du Québec, April 2001).

76. In addition, four municipalities from the south shore deamalgamated from the city of Longueuil. Linteau, *History of Montreal*, 192.

77. See the interview given by the former Québécois minister of municipal affairs, Louise Harel, in *La Presse*, February 17, 2009, A6.

78. At the municipal level, see, for instance, Amanda Ricci, "La participation des Italiens à la vie municipale montréalaise au cours des années 1950," *Cap-aux-Diamants* 102 (2010): 29–30.

79. Engin Isin, "Introduction: Cities, Democracies, Citizenship," in *Democracy, Citizenship, and the Global City* (New York: Routledge, 2002), 1–21.

80. Annick Germain, "La sociologie urbaine à l'épreuve de l'immigration et de l'ethnicité: de Chicago à Montréal en passant par Amsterdam," *Sociologie et sociétés* 45, no. 2 (2013): 99–113.

81. Jean-Luis Klein et Christine Champagne, eds., *Initiatives locales et lutte contre la pauvreté et l'exclusion* (Québec: Presses de l'Université du Québec, 2011), 48.

82. See the investigation done by Anne-Marie Séguin, "Les espaces de pauvreté," in *Montréal 2001: visages et défis d'une métropole*, ed. Claude Manzagol and Cristopher Bryant (Montreal: Presses de l'Université de Montréal, 1998); see also Philippe Apparicio and Anne-Marie Séguin, *Retour sur les notions de ségrégation et de ghetto ethniques et examen des cas de Montréal, Toronto et Vancouver: Rapport de recherche réalisé pour la Commission de consultation sur les pratiques d'accommodement reliées aux différences culturelles* (Montreal: INRS-UCS, 2008).

83. Jean-Pierre Collin, "Les arrondissements: le troisième pilier de la réforme municipale montréalaise," *Annuaire du Québec 2004* (Fides, 2003), 814.

84. In fact, it is the angle that Annick Germain and Damaris Rose have adopted in their book rightly named *Montréal: The Quest for a Metropolis*.

6 Generations of Segregation

Immigrant Dreams and Segregated Lives in Metropolitan Los Angeles

• •

GEORGE J. SANCHEZ

No person whose blood is not entirely that of the Caucasian race (and for the purpose of this paragraph no Japanese, Chinese, Mexican, Hindu, or any person of the Ethiopian, Indian, or Mongolian race shall be deemed to be Caucasian) shall at any time live upon any of the lots in said tract 15010.

A mimeographed sheet containing these words was handed to Julius Blue, an African American World War II veteran, and his wife when they inquired about purchasing a home in Allied Gardens, a new development of 392 single-family homes in Van Nuys, California, in August 1948. The couple had been drawn to the San Fernando Valley by an advertisement offering "wonderful terms" to G.I.s, giving them hope of improving their housing circumstances by moving from the central city to another part of the city of Los Angeles. The sheet, while reflecting long-standing housing practices by realtors and sellers in Southern California, came months after the United States Supreme Court had ruled in *Shelley v. Kramer* that racially restrictive covenants were discriminatory and could not be enforced by government or the courts. For decades following that May 1948 decision, however, realtors, homeowners, and organized associations worked together to ensure what they defined as the homogeneity of many Southern California neighborhoods. Cross burnings, threatening phone calls, property damage, and physical abuse were all parts of enforcing racial restrictions before and after the Supreme Court decision, as was open and organized opposition to blacks, Latinos, or Asian Americans moving into specific neighborhoods. From Kiwanis Clubs in Eagle Rock to Security First National Bank of Huntington Park, local institutions worked hard to keep preferred areas strictly limited to Caucasians.[1]

In May 1953, African American Korean War veteran Alfred Jackson, his wife Luquella, and their daughter Jacqueline moved into their new home on 2324 Reeve Street in Compton, to be met by a mob of white Compton homeowners yelling racial epithets. The confrontation came after months of clashes designed to keep Compton an exclusively white community. In February of that year, several white property owners were beaten for listing their properties with the South Los Angeles Realty Investment Company, one of the few companies that sold to both white and black buyers. City officials searched the city codes that year for a way to punish real estate agents who sold to blacks, finally sending the Compton police to arrest five real estate dealers under the law prohibiting solicitation within Compton city limits. It was only the Jacksons' own actions which kept them in their new home, since Compton police told the couple that they could not guarantee the safety of the newly settled African American homeowners. Alfred Jackson protected his family and their possessions with a pair of Colt .45 pistols, while a close friend stepped out of the house with a 12-gauge shotgun to disperse the white mob. In the days that followed, while Alfred was at work in the shipyards, Luquella took time off from work to guard their home and children with a shotgun in plain sight. Though verbal attacks continued for months, their armed self-defense appeared to have worked at keeping the mob at bay.[2]

In Los Angeles, a form of urban apartheid developed in the midst of widespread economic growth and development. By 1950, the city of Los Angeles had grown to over 4 million people, nearly all migrants from elsewhere in the U.S., Mexico, Latin America, and Asia, to become the nation's fourth-largest city. Spurred by agriculture, moviemaking, and World War II-era energy and defense industries, Los Angeles boomed through the Cold War decades. At the midpoint of the twentieth century, the city was in the middle of decades of unprecedented growth that would last until 1980. But economic boom and population expansion through in-migration only made the forces promoting an organized apartheid residential system more insistent on the necessity of keeping what they insisted were "the races" apart in Los Angeles.

These incidents of residential apartheid were not simply reflections of individual acts of racism or a time of particular racial strife in Los Angeles. They reflected a long-standing pattern of organized and systematic discrimination in housing that produced racial segregation in Southern California long before the Cold War era—a pattern that has changed, yet persists to the present. There are few areas of Southern California in which organized racial segregation did not fundamentally shape patterns of residential homeownership and rentals for a significant period during the past 140 years.

This wide pattern of segregated housing, of course, profoundly shapes all sorts of day-to-day opportunities and interaction among members of diverse groups long defined as "races": from access to employment to political participation, to access to schools. Since California citizens and legislators have fought all attempts to force public school integration through busing or other means, the segregated nature of housing in Southern California continues to affect the opportunity of children across the region to receive an equal education in integrated settings.

This chapter argues that residential segregation was a key way that city leaders and planners in Southern California managed the massive number of newcomers that defined Los Angeles for most of the past 140 years. It will also show how critical it was for newcomers to forge their own communities and to struggle for an expansive use of space in the public and private realms within the long segregated metropolis.

Dreams and Nightmares: Knowing Los Angeles

Many people in the United States and across the world believe that they "know" Los Angeles. As the site of the largest film, television, and music industry in the world, Los Angeles is one of the most visually represented places, competing with Manhattan for recognition around the planet. If you add the glamour and glitz of several sports team, many people have images of Los Angeles from its hyper-representation in popular and global media. Yet, the hyped images of Los Angeles often mask a very dark side of the city's history. Three major riots of the twentieth century, the zoot suit riots of June 1943, the Watts riots of August 1965, and the multiracial Los Angeles riots/rebellion of April–May 1992, have all also defined Los Angeles in starkly different terms—as a failed paradise of racial tensions and class uprising.

Indeed, the two best-known chroniclers of Los Angeles in the popular imagination reflect this contradictory impression of the city. Mike Davis's influential *City of Quartz* depicts Los Angeles in all its dystopian glory, focusing on its immense inequalities and the way in which white powerbrokers have structured and restructured the city and its architecture to keep the teeming immigrant masses of color at bay.[3] The late Kevin Starr in his magisterial series on the history of California has the direct opposite emphasis, emphasizing the creativity and accomplishments of city political and economic leaders. Starr's books chronicle how city officials translated an early Mediterranean imagery—or imaginary—into a city built by cultural creators who forged an industrial giant in Los Angeles.[4] For Starr, California and Los Angeles elites made the city a place of entrepreneurship, cultural diversity, and enduring accomplishment.

For more distant observers of Los Angeles, however, the contrasting images of a mostly white hyper-rich Hollywood world of Jack Nicholson and Meryl Streep, Denzel Washington and Salma Hayek and a desperate, largely African American South Central deflects understanding of the current demographic reality of the city and its metropolitan region. A contemporary study of immigrant integration in metropolitan Los Angeles emphasizes critical facts: one-third of the population in metropolitan Los Angeles today is foreign-born, one half of the workforce is immigrant, two-thirds of those under eighteen in the region are children of immigrants, and 90 percent of these children were born in the United States. These figures confirm something that the politics of the nation has yet to acknowledge: the economic and social fate of metropolitan Los Angeles and similar metropolitan regions are intimately tied to the future success of immigrant families and the capacity of cities to integrate new generations as full members of and contributors to the wider civil, political, economic, and cultural complex that shapes the burgeoning cities that increasingly define the nation and the world.[5]

The challenges are not new. Throughout the twentieth century and into the twenty-first Los Angeles has been a city becoming a metropolis caught in a seemingly endless cycle of boom and bust economies, almost always fueled by immigrant-driven demographic growth. Carey McWilliams could write in mid-twentieth century that, "half of the people you meet on the streets of Los Angeles have arrived less than five years previously." The fate of migrants from across the U.S. and immigrants from around the world in the city of Los Angeles has long determined the future of Southern California, be it the white newcomers from the rural Midwest of the early twentieth century, the post–World War II African American migrants from Texas, Louisiana, Mississippi and Arkansas, or the more recent immigrants from Latin America and Asia now dominating the newcomer class.

Partly because of the significance of in-migration to the fate of Los Angeles, city leaders have carefully attempted to manage the geography of the region by controlling the spread of the urban metropolis and the settling of new populations. Yet for a long time, residents, visitors, and historians of Los Angeles saw an unplanned city that spread from ocean to mountains in random, haphazard ways, giving the city its famous—or infamous—uncontrolled sprawl. But recent historical work has confirmed instead that metropolitan Los Angeles has been one of the most carefully planned regions in the twentieth century, its sprawl the result of an organized and deliberate residential pattern.[6] Moreover, a fundamental part of that management has been racial and class separation, intended to keep parts of Los Angeles reserved for white upper and middle classes, with other parts separated for racial and class others. The two images of Los Angeles, the glitzy Hollywood and the dystopian urban noir, actually have a systematic (or systemic) reality to them, grounded in a history of urban planning and residential restriction deeply embedded at the intersection of politics, geography, and culture.

Moreover, what appears to be a haphazard array of city and district boundary lines that lead most to not know exactly where they are in Southern California also has been revealed to be a systematic attempt for the city to grow in particular ways, including favored groups while excluding others from the benefits of incorporation, basic services, or reduced taxes.[7] As you fly into the Los Angeles basin or drive the ever-present freeways, it is almost impossible for most residents, let alone newcomers or visitors, to know if they are physically in the city or county of Los Angeles, or in some other incorporated city or county. Everyone in the metropolis is confronted with the enormity of the city, like other major cities, but the particular political geography of Southern California confuses newcomer and resident alike. This confusion across the great Southern California basin prompted the putdown that Los Angeles is "72 suburbs in search of a city." Unlike cities built upon islands and peninsulas (New York or San Francisco), or divided by major rivers (New Orleans) or set beside lakes (Chicago), Los Angeles' only major topological reference points are the ocean and the near and distant mountains. At some points, "the basin" can extend from fifty to two hundred miles, intersected by a few small mountain ranges that partially distinguish two massive valleys from a larger coastal plain.

But these topographical reference points have almost no bearing to how the city grew in the late nineteenth and early twentieth century. Instead, Anglo-American city leaders expanded the city from the original Spanish grid around the plaza to absorb areas where they anticipated new urban settlement, and then in conscious attempts to incorporate areas for infrastructural development. When city leaders wanted to make sure that the port of Los Angeles would be under city control, they incorporated a coastal area almost thirty miles from the center; they were forced to bind these area to the city by incorporating a narrow strip of land, no more than a mile wide at any point, because state rules of incorporation required a city's footprint to be contiguous and connected. When city officials secretly planned to steal Owens Valley river water for the burgeoning city two hundred miles away, leaders incorporated the San Fernando Valley into the city, since it would be the end deposit station of the Los Angeles–built statewide aqueduct.

Other areas would be excluded from the city of Los Angeles just as systematically and deliberately. Beverly Hills, iconic to the vision of a glitzy Hollywood, remains a separate city with its own police, fire department, and school system; so do Malibu and Santa Monica, the ocean havens of many of the Los Angeles elite. Hollywood, however, is not a separate city, but part of Los Angeles—and upon closer inspection dominated by poor Latino residents and a tacky tourist industry, with few residents tied to the movie industry. On the other side of town, almost all of East Los Angeles sits outside of the boundaries of the city as an unincorporated area of Los Angeles County, its residents never able to vote for the mayor or city council of Los Angeles. The largest community of Mexican-origin residents in the region is not counted in the city's population yet forms a critical part of the region's population and culture.

The County of Los Angeles, unlike the city, has almost no resonance outside the region—or in the consciousness of most Angelinos. Yet it plays a critical role in structuring metropolitan society. Los Angeles County includes a massive population, 10.4 million residents, larger than thirty-five states of the U.S. The county is also an economic powerhouse linked by finance and trade to key parts of the globe, standing as the eighteenth-largest economy in the world. In 1994, Los Angeles County passed New York as the nation's busiest trade center, utilizing one of the most important infrastructures in all the Americas. Los Angeles and Long Beach harbors together form the largest seaport in the United States and the fifth-largest in the world, while the Los Angeles International Airport is the number-one airport for origin or destination in the U.S., servicing 62 million passengers and 2 million tons of cargo in 2014. Over 50 percent of the cargo that comes into Chicago arrives from Asia via the ports of Los Angeles and makes its way by truck or rail to the Windy City, where it disperses to the east, north, or south across a wide expanse of North America. The infamous 1,200 miles of freeway in Los Angeles County report its history as the first large metropolis built for transportation by trucks and automobiles.

Most of the social services in the region, from health care to transportation, are controlled at the county level, not by the city or by higher regional or state authorities. Yet, a five-person board of supervisors with virtually no visibility in the local media or among residents governs the county. They tended to hold seats for life, once elected, until recently imposed term limits forced turnover. The board remains the most significant source of power and patronage in the region. The highly visible mayors of the city of Los Angeles, in contrast, have relatively little constitutional authority. As we shall see, in recent decades an African American and a Mexican American have served as mayor of the city—to much fanfare. Neither could do much to end the historic discriminations and segregations that afflict the city's large African American and Latino populations. The County of Los Angeles keeps no historical archives, regularly disposing of its most important documents even as it controls so much power and so many services. It is a key center of urban power with limited visibility and less accountability.

Indeed, when most historians and urban analysts consider Los Angeles, we include in the metropolitan area a district that encompasses at least five counties: Los Angeles, Orange, Riverside, San Bernardino, and Ventura. The great Los Angeles basin stretches through parts of all five and the history of the larger region tells us much about how metropolitan Los Angeles grew during the twentieth century. Until 1920, Los Angeles remained a city with fewer than a million people surrounded by a county that remained mostly agricultural—an emphasis that marked neighboring counties even more emphatically. Beginning in the 1920s and accelerating during and after World War II, the agricultural valleys saw landscapes dominated by vegetable and fruit production give way to towns and cities that grew to become part of the expanding suburban landscape of metropolitan Los Angeles. Indeed, before that suburban development, the outer valleys were marked with independent towns that had their own elites, often their own newcomer cultures transplanted from the eastern United States or directly from Europe, along with racialized communities of Asian and Latino cultivators and workers living on the other side of the tracks. When German immigrants were encouraged to migrate in the late nineteenth century to form a new agricultural colony in present-day Orange County, they chose to distinguish and identify their colony with a German name built on an existing Spanish-Mexican place name: Anaheim—"Ana" for the Santa Ana River, and "heim" meaning "home."

The result of such fragmented independence was that many of these regions, while clearly in the orbit of the metropolis of Los Angeles, framed their existence in opposition to the larger city, taking on a decided anti-urban ethos in their formation. Eventually this blended into a suburban disdain for the central city in the post–World War II era. Orange County, for example, originally part of Los Angeles County, split to forge a self-identity imagining life behind an "Orange Curtain," with many of its residents fleeing the city after the 1965 Watts riots to separate themselves from a multiracial Los Angeles.[8]

Today, however, non-Hispanic whites have become a minority of Orange County residents, contradicting the image that continues to prevail through television shows like *The O.C.* or *Real Housewives of Orange County*. In 1980, at the end of greater Los Angeles' deeply segregated World War II and Cold War booms, Orange County's population was 80 percent white. In the face of globalization, deindustrialization, and the rise of a new service economy, the county had a nonwhite majority in 2000. It is projected to have a Latino plurality by 2020, and a near Latino majority by 2040.[9] Its Latino population grew by 46 percent from 1990 through 2000 to 875,000, 28 percent of its total, giving Orange County the fifth-largest Latino population in any county in the nation as the new millennium began. Rapid demographic change in a city like Buena Park, for example, saw the white population drop from 71 percent to 38 percent in the 1990s. The ranks of Latinos rose by 48 percent in San Diego County since 1990, 45 percent in Ventura County, 72 percent in Riverside County, and 66 percent in San Bernardino County.[10] In all Southern California counties together, nonwhites outnumbered whites by more than 3 million in the year 2000. The world of postindustrial globalization has generated a new society of ethnic diversity. Yet while Mexican and Latino populations grow, new segregations have developed to maintain separations and inequities.

The Los Angeles metropolitan region makes up 60 percent of the total population of the state of California. In recent decades it has faced challenges of urbanization, globalization, and the accommodation of growing and diverse immigrant peoples—challenges that confront cities across the U.S., the Americas, and the world. As Los Angeles in many ways led the U.S. dream of national development from 1950 to 1980, it now leads in grappling with the challenges of urban globalization. In 2000, 36 percent of Los Angeles County's population was foreign-born, a larger foreign-born population than any of the leading nations in the world. Its only rivals trailed significantly: 18.8 percent of Canada's 30 million residents were foreign-born; Australia numbered 23.6 percent foreign-born among its 20 million residents.[11] Another 36 percent of Los Angeles County residents were born in the U.S. to parents or grandparents who were foreign-born. This means that Los Angeles has more people of Mexican descent than any city outside Mexico, the largest Korean population outside Seoul, the largest Filipino population outside Manila, and the largest Japanese population outside

Japan. The unfolding diversity of Southern California's population and the way it has been received and distributed—and too often segregated—over time have profound implications for the direction of urbanization and suburbanization in the United States and the world. Demographically, greater Los Angeles may define both the promise and the challenges of urbanizing globalization.

Segregated Foundations: Building the City of Dreams—for Whites

During its rapid growth from a small town to a large city in the late nineteenth and early twentieth century, Los Angeles became a leading innovator of methods of racial residential restriction in the United States. From the start, these efforts were produced by a combination of government officials, private real estate companies and realtors, and individual homeowners and associations. Indeed, Los Angeles city officials started down this path of restriction within months of the U.S. conquest of Mexico, when officials decided to sell off portions of the lands of the pueblo originally founded under the Spanish empire as *El Pueblo de Nuestra Señora la Reina de Los Ángeles* (the Town of Our Lady the Queen of the Angels) in order to raise revenues for the nascent local Anglo-American government. The selling of pueblo lands begun in November 1850 led several key city leaders in business, commerce, banking, and government to engage in land speculation by purchasing undeveloped lots with an eye to increasing profit after the city improved water rights and road development in the area. The speculative spirit brought west by gold-rush financiers, merchants, and prospectors, turned to real estate in Southern California, as Anglo-Americans bought up land with an eye to future development, while increasingly limiting Mexican American settlement to older pueblo dwellings near the original central plaza.[12]

It would take the rising influx of newcomers to Southern California in the 1870s and 1880s, however, prompted by the completion of transcontinental railroad lines linking Los Angeles to the rest of the United States, to accelerate the residential subdivisions on former pueblo property and the first wave of major profit-taking by land speculators. Three years of intense real estate speculation followed the arrival of the Santa Fe Railroad in Los Angeles in 1885, fueled by a city population that grew by 500 percent to total 50,000 by 1889. Indeed, as many as 130,000 people took advantage of lower railroad rates to explore Southern California in the late 1880s.[13] In this context, city officials and those involved in land speculation (often one and the same) worked assiduously to keep the Anglo newcomers away from both the poorer Mexican community that remained around the plaza, and the new and visible Chinatown that had established itself southwest of the plaza. The Chinese became the first targets of formal government attempts at exclusion and segregation when the new California constitution of 1879 allowed incorporated cities and towns to remove Chinese neighborhoods and prohibit the creation of new ones in the state. Newly appointed Los Angeles City Public Health Officer Walter Lindley, calling in 1879 for a new sewage system to extend the city's primitive sewage lines to new Anglo districts, contrasting them sharply with the city's Chinatown—"that rotten spot"—without proposing similar improvements for that district. In the 1870s, both Los Angeles and San Francisco passed "cubic air ordinances," which allowed officials to regulate crowded boardinghouses and apartments. While these laws should have applied to all dwellings, officials consistently targeted only the Chinese.[14]

While early efforts tended to be haphazard and idiosyncratic, the late nineteenth century saw land developers in many U.S. cities begin to take more systematic approaches to residential restriction. Although restrictive covenants had been used as early as the mid-eighteenth century in England by nobles seeking to subdivide but control their property, such contracts initially saw limited use in the United States, mostly by property owners seeking to preserve fashionable neighborhoods such as Boston's Lewisburg Square and New York's Gramercy Park in the nineteenth century. Until the 1880s, restrictive covenants almost always involved keeping unwanted business or behavior from a neighborhood rather than unwanted people. In the last decades of the nineteenth century, the U.S. Supreme Court and several state courts removed the remaining legal obstacles to covenants.[15] In California, Mr. Lee Sing sued the city of Ventura when it attempted to disallow Chinese residence in its jurisdiction; in response, federal courts ruled in 1892 that state and municipal governments could not themselves discriminate—but they could allow individuals to enter into residential contracts that would discriminate or prohibit selling property to members of certain racial groups. With this green light, the first racially restrictive covenant filed in Los Angeles came in 1902, using the all-inclusive term of "non-Caucasians" to define who could not purchase property. Within a few years, cities throughout Southern California applied restrictive covenants against Chinese, Japanese, Mexicans, African Americans, and sometimes Armenians, Jews, Italians, and others seen as racially undesirable.[16]

To say that individuals were given the right to discriminate by the California courts, however, would not do justice to the widespread collective action and interests of land developers and real estate agents in keeping most Southern California communities restricted. The Los Angeles Realty Board, founded in 1903, led regional efforts to organize the real estate industry, professionalize its membership, and institute racially restrictive covenants in as many established neighborhoods and new developments as possible. The board was also critical in mobilizing the Los Angeles city council to become the first city to pass an ordinance prohibiting industrial activities from a residential district. In 1908, Los Angeles led the national movement toward modern zoning by mapping out three large areas of the city in which almost all industrial operations would be forbidden, aiming to keep the majority of the city "a residential paradise of spacious homes in quiet, clean surroundings."[17] One effect of these ordinances was to enable city officials to solidify "the central role of race in the politics of acquiring and using space" by retroactively making it illegal for Chinese laundries to operate in all of these residential districts, even if they had been established before the passage of the laws. A differential policy based on race followed, as city officials regularly gave exemptions to the prohibition to Anglo-American launderers, while consistently prohibiting Chinese launderers in most parts of the growing city.[18]

The growing power of the Realty Board was also in evidence when the California state Supreme Court handed down a 1919 ruling in *Los Angeles Investment Co. v. Gary* that invalidated restrictive covenants against the *purchase* of property. With the help of the Los Angeles Realty Board and others in San Diego, Pasadena, and Laguna Beach, white developers, homeowners' associations, and realtors throughout the state quickly rewrote or added restrictive covenants against *occupancy* of homes by certain racial groups, a restriction that the Supreme Court allowed. By the mid-1920s, the typical deed of most houses bought or sold in California stated that "said premises shall not [be] . . . occupied or used by any person or persons other than those of the Caucasian race, provided, however, that the foregoing restriction shall not be construed to prohibit the keeping of domestic servants of any race."[19] Racial covenants coupled with other exclusionary measures were highly effective by the 1920s, in both affluent and working-class communities throughout Southern California. Few African Americans, Latinos, or Asian Americans lived outside of highly restricted areas. The affluent city of Beverly Hills, organized in the early twentieth century to the west of downtown, where the median value of a home was about $18,000, housed almost 5,000 families in 1930, but only one was African American and eight were of "other races." Working-class South Gate, south of downtown Los Angeles, where the median value of a home was less than $4,300, also only had one African American family among the 5,600 families residing there in 1930, with forty-one of "other races." And new suburban subdivisions put on the market in the 1920s, such as Palos Verdes Estates in south Los Angeles, had restrictions for each property which ran thirty pages, protecting against "encroachment by any possible developments of an adverse sort," prohibiting "undesirable neighbors" and selling or renting to an African American or Asian American family.[20]

What effect did this growing restriction against selling or renting to families of color have upon their choices for living in Southern California? Outside of a few outlying rural districts, the traditional downtown residential communities around the plaza and Chinatown remained a key starting point for Angelinos of color who first arrived in Los Angeles in the early twentieth century. In addition to those original "foreign districts," the neighborhoods remaining in industrial zones, particularly those along the railroad tracks and the industrialized Los Angeles River, became racially mixed ethnic neighborhoods, along with a growing eastside industrial district that stretched beyond the city limits to Whittier. New districts to the east and south that lay adjacent to these industrial zones or connected to them by rail lines, like Boyle Heights, Watts, and Belvedere, were relatively open to all. Each of these neighborhoods was racially and ethnically mixed in the early twentieth century, containing not only African Americans, Asian Americans, and Latinos but also disparate white ethnic groups such as Jews and Italians. There was a class element to early racial segregation—reserving neighborhoods of prosperity for whites, while allowing diverse others to mix in communities of labor and poverty. Even as these populations grew substantially in the wake of World War I and the growth of industrial labor in Southern California, these groups remained isolated and restricted to limited landscapes, resulting in overcrowding and deplorable housing conditions in much of the region.[21]

But these restrictions did not keep excluded minorities and the poor from trying to break the restrictions of power and individuals from trying to circumvent their reach. One case involved the Entwistle Tract, originally developed in 1905 by a woman named Lula Nevada Entwistle Hinton Letteau, well south of downtown around 41st Street, just east of Main Street. First developed as an all-white part of the city with restrictive deeds, including restrictions on occupancy, the covenants read that if the provision were violated, the property would revert back to the original owners of the development. Since the area was close to the growing African American community, some initial white homeowners sold homes to blacks without incident, so others came. By the mid-1920s, blacks made up half the neighborhood. In early 1924, William H. Long and his wife Eunice, an ordinary hardworking black couple, bought their first bungalow in the neighborhood at 771 East 41st Street, putting a down payment of nearly $2,000 on a property that had been bought and sold several times since 1905. Days later, however, the heirs of Mrs. Letteau brought suit against the Longs, arguing that the occupancy clause had been violated and that the title of the property should now revert to them. Although the NAACP took up the Long's defense, a superior court decision in December 1926 ruled in favor of the Letteaus, leading the heirs to sue every black homeowner in the Entwistle Tract, as well as the white owners who had been renting to African Americans. During the extended legal proceedings, Eunice Long saw her husband William deteriorate physically and mentally before tragically dying; she became a semi-invalid. Nonetheless, the Los Angeles County sheriff served her with an eviction notice and she lost what little she had left.[22]

Los Angeles' early boom development came as a railroad terminus and port city serving a surrounding region still primarily agricultural. Like Buenos Aires and Montreal in the first decades of the twentieth century, the emerging Southern California city grew by funneling sustenance to distant industrial centers—and by attracting immigrants to participate in an expanding economy in roles ranging from the fields to city processing plants to transport and trade, finance, and more. But all were not welcome to participate equally—and a key way to ensure inequality was through legal covenants enforcing residential segregation. People defined as white or Caucasian would rule and prosper and live together in select neighborhoods. Others defined as racial others—Chinese, Mexicans, blacks (the language of the time would have used the Spanish word, *negro*), and even people of European origins seen as "undesirable" were forced to live together in less desirable neighborhoods—often in or near polluted industrial zones. While a political and constitutional system that proclaimed democratic ideals insisted that state power could not enforce segregation, the highest courts repeatedly sanctioned the use of "private" contracts—which could only be enforced by public power—in mandating segregation. Los Angeles, the city of California dreams, was founded at an intersection of political power and economic interests that restricted prosperity to those defined as "us"—white

Caucasians—and imposed separation and inequality on those maligned as "them"—everyone else, in all their diversity. Modern Los Angeles was not born democratic.

Depression, War, and Boom: Segregating the Dream in Times of Challenge and Opportunity

Before the 1930s, the U.S. federal government had little interest in home-ownership, treating real estate transactions primarily as private decisions made by individuals or groups. The early segregation of Los Angeles was thus mostly a local affair. The collapse of the economy in the Great Depression and the spread of mortgage foreclosures, however, pushed the federal government to establish the Home Owners Loan Corporation (HOLC) in 1933 in order to refinance urban mortgages and provide a systematic approach to home appraisal. The goal was to stabilize the real estate market (still averaging 100,000 foreclosures a month in 1935) by adapting a nationwide approach. In order to do this, the HOLC recruited members of the National Association of Real Estate Boards to conduct appraisals of neighborhoods, rather than simply individual homes, as a basis for evaluating property. Not surprisingly, given realty boards' local prejudices, the racial makeup of a neighborhood came to be a significant part of evaluations. The appraisals fully utilized article 34 of the 1924 realty code of ethics, which stated, "A realtor should never be instrumental in introducing into a neighborhood a character of property or occupancy, members of any race or nationality, or any individuals whose presence will clearly be detrimental to property values in that neighborhood." In this way, the racial value system of realtors was codified into federal policy, which then reflected back into the private mortgage system for decades to come. If segregation developed in Los Angeles to control the benefits of growth before 1930, it carried on through the Depression—a time of declining property values—to limit the losses suffered in favored communities. The residential security maps produced by the HOLC became *the* standard by which all lenders evaluated mortgage applications, including those predicated on the guarantees of the newly established Federal Housing Authority (FHA).[23]

The repercussions were profound for the ethnically mixed neighborhoods of Boyle Heights, Watts, and others where African Americans, Latinos, Asian Americans, and others had lived together through the 1930s. In 1939, for example, the FHA gave its lowest possible rating to Boyle Heights specifically because its racial diversity supposedly made it a bad risk for housing assistance: "This is a 'melting pot' area and is literally honeycombed with diverse and subversive racial elements. It is seriously doubted whether there is a single block in the area which does not contain detrimental racial elements and there are very few districts which are not hopelessly heterogeneous."[24] For decades, it would be more difficult for prospective home buyers in Boyle Heights to obtain a federally guaranteed home mortgage, and they would be forced to pay a higher interest rate as a result of living in a "riskier" area. On the maps themselves, sections like Boyle Heights were outlined in red, leading to what the general public has come to know as "redlining." Over time, therefore, those who could leave the neighborhood did so because of the financial advantages involved. After World War II, that would mean that white ethnics such as Jews and Italians left the racially mixed neighborhoods, abandoning them to African American and Latino neighbors who continued to have few housing options in the Southern California.[25]

The other major housing activity of Roosevelt's New Deal was the passage of the Housing Act of 1937, which created the U.S. Housing Authority to support low-cost public housing projects by giving grants and loans to local housing agencies. In March 1938, the California state legislature passed bills to allow the creation of housing agencies in every city and county of the state. In June of that year, the Los Angeles City Council adopted a resolution authorizing the Housing Authority of the city of Los Angeles to operate. Most of Southern California's smaller, white-dominated towns refused to create such authorities in order to block public housing that would attract poor and minority populations into their locales. While the city of Los Angeles built ten multiunit public housing complexes in its jurisdiction in the early 1940s, white neighborhoods fought against their placement nearby. Consequently, all ten were built in or near eastside and southside areas that already had the highest concentration of black, Mexican, and other racial minorities. Poorer whites, especially those needed for wartime work, and, after the war, veterans would get priority in those public housing units until 1952, when the city of Los Angeles turned away from further public housing construction or upkeep. Then these "models of democracy" became rundown versions of the increasingly racialized communities they were already within.[26] New Deal federal housing programs, aimed to provide at least modest help to the less fortunate, in Los Angeles were implemented to reinforce the segregations that kept the less fortunate together in communities of contained others.

The onset of World War II created massive changes for the Los Angeles labor market. A profound labor shortage emerged as the region became the most important manufacturing location for weapons of war, particularly the building of ships, airplanes, and all the necessary steel, rubber, and mechanical components. The war made Los Angeles the city of unlimited growth—the standard for the California Dream that helped define a rising nation. Yet while Los Angeles officials enthusiastically accepted the moniker "Arsenal of Democracy" to describe the region, they failed to change the racial housing policies that severely limited the living options and social possibilities of black and Mexican war workers and their families. The population of African Americans in the city nearly doubled during the war, reaching 70,000 by 1946, yet blacks remained limited to finding housing in pre-war restricted areas. One exception was in the former Little Tokyo, renamed Bronzeville once its Japanese American residents were incarcerated in internment camps away from Los Angeles. The neighborhood quickly became notorious for substandard housing conditions and dangerous overcrowding. By 1944, 80,000 people lived in Bronzeville, a community that housed 30,000 before the war.[27] Howard Holtezendorff, a Los Angeles housing official testifying in 1944 before a congressional committee investigating the congested conditions, described Little Tokyo: "Our records . . . show families piling up . . . four, five, and six persons to a bedroom. In one case a family of five was living in a dirt-floored garage with no sanitary facilities whatsoever. In an abandoned storefront . . . twenty-one people were found to be living—and paying approximately $50 a month for these quarters."[28]

In contrast, white ethnics who had previously been segregated into the racially mixed neighborhoods of "others" in east and south Los Angeles began to move out in massive numbers during and after the war. The Jewish population of Boyle Heights plummeted by over 72 percent from 1940 to 1955, and made up less than 17 percent of the area's population by the mid-1950s. At the same time, the Mexican population grew to form almost half of Boyle Heights residents, and their numbers continued to increase dramatically over the next few years. Similarly, at the outbreak of World War II, Watts had approximately equal proportions of blacks, Mexicans, and whites, yet by 1958 blacks made up 95 percent of the Watts population. The multiracial population of Avalon, about 60 percent African American in 1940, was 95 percent black by 1960. Jews, Italians, and other white ethnics who had previously lived in these neighborhoods moved to the westside of Los Angeles and to the growing planned communities of the San Fernando Valley. In 1950, the *Valley Jewish Press* reported that there were about 22,000 Jewish families living in the Valley in a total population that had reached

400,000.[29] The Valley, however, contained fewer than 5,000 African Americans and other nonwhites in 1950; its growth was highly regulated on racial grounds. The war and its need for workers in defense industries shifted the lines of segregation. The new color line of the postwar era placed Jews and Italians decidedly into the "white race," but continued to exclude blacks, Asians, and most Mexicans.[30]

Meanwhile, the powers aiming to favor whites worked to reinforce the new color lines. Local white homeowners' associations in neighborhoods that immediately surrounded increasingly crowded black neighborhoods increased the legal and violent vigilance to keep blacks from buying or renting in their neighborhoods. Los Angeles African American attorney Loren Miller successfully represented many African American defendants in covenant cases, including Hollywood actors Louise Beavers and Hattie McDaniel (an Academy Award winner for *Gone with the Wind*), who had purchased homes in the fashionable Sugar Hill neighborhood. The city of Compton, meanwhile, was successful in rejecting a public housing complex during the war, rallying its citizens behind the slogan "Keep the Negroes North of 130th Street" and by harassing black motorists who crossed this boundary. As late as 1948, fewer than fifty African Americans lived in this city of 45,000 individuals. A 1947 Urban League study noted that Compton white homeowners utilized at least twenty-six different techniques to "scare off" prospective black home buyers, including vandalism, cross burnings, bombings, and death threats.[31]

These techniques became ever more important as a result of two landmark Supreme Court decisions. *Shelley v. Kramer* and *Barrows v. Jackson*, handed down in 1948 and 1953 respectively, effectively ended the ability of the judicial system to enforce racially restrictive covenants, the longstanding mode of preventing neighborhood integration, ruling them in violation of the Fourteenth Amendment. The Los Angeles Realty Board remained defiant in the wake of these rulings, urging "a nationwide campaign to amend the United States Constitution to guarantee enforcement of property restrictions."[32] More important, realtors encouraged the widespread use of "corporate contract agreements" and "neighborhood protective associations" as mechanisms through which homeowners could continue to regulate the sale of properties in their neighborhoods. Realtors increasingly saw themselves as the first line of defense of the color line after these rulings. But they were not alone. Banks were unwilling to break the racial lines set up by white homeowners and real estate agents, often setting higher interest rates for racial minorities, insisting they were a significant credit risk. Private developers intensified segregation by refusing to sell to blacks and other minorities in new tracts and subdivisions. The federal government continued to support the racial status quo, refusing to create institutional mechanisms to prevent racial discrimination, even with FHA and Veterans Administration (VA) home loans. Out of the 125,000 FHA housing units built in Los Angeles County from 1950 to 1954, only 3,000 (2.4 percent) were open to nonwhites.[33]

Yet real estate agents continued to be the most vocal and influential voices in widespread efforts to maintain racial segregation in housing in Southern California. Although the California Real Estate Association (CREA) in 1951 removed the specific section from their code of ethics prohibiting realtors from introducing "members of any race or nationality" whose presence would lower "property values in the neighborhood," realty boards continued to punish and expel members who violated agreed racial boundaries. In 1956, for example, a Downey broker was dismissed from the Southwest Realty Board after selling a house to a Mexican American family in Lynwood and refusing to pay the resulting fine imposed on him. The *Los Angeles Times* would only accept real estate listings from realtors affiliated with the Los Angeles Realty Board, maintaining through the 1950s a small section designated as "unrestricted" where racially integrated areas were listed. Despite numerous applications by black real estate brokers, in 1960 the Los Angeles Realty Board did not have a single African American among its more than 2,000 members. A report by the Los Angeles Commission on Human Relations found that, "It is indeed a startling fact that in the ten-year period ending in April 1960, only 1,437 additional Negro citizens, or 0.87 percent have found residences outside of the Central District of Los Angeles, and in San Pedro, Venice and Pacoima."[34] Despite this situation, a representative of the Realty Board, speaking before the U.S. Commission on Civil Rights in Los Angeles in 1960, declared racial discrimination in housing entirely nonexistent: "The inability of one to fulfill a desire is not discrimination: it is frustration which only the individual can overcome by personal improvement in his financial position."[35]

It is not surprising, therefore, when State Assemblyman William Byron Rumford convinced his colleagues to pass A.B. 1240 in 1963, a Fair Housing Act that prohibited discrimination in private housing financed by public sources, the California Real Estate Association (CREA) and its local affiliates led the effort to overturn the Rumford Act. Even though the act covered only about 25 percent of the nearly 3.8 million single family homes in the state, the real estate industry decided to make a stand against the growing proliferation of "open housing" laws spreading across the nation. CREA organized a campaign for Proposition 14, which appeared in 1964 on the statewide ballot; its purpose was to overturn the Rumford Act, and to invalidate components of other civil rights legislation banning discrimination in public housing, apartment rentals, and housing construction. The campaign was financed by a $10 assessment on all member realtors, and the self-named Committee for Home Protection took as their campaign motto "A man's home is his castle." Despite the fact that almost every California politician of both parties opposed Proposition 14 and California voters supported pro–civil rights Lyndon Johnson as president in a landslide in November 1964, the state's voters simultaneously approved Proposition 14 by a two-to-one margin. The political culture of segregation entrenched in Los Angeles in its earliest years of growth carried on even as national politics looked toward new integrations. A three-year legal battle ensued in which the U.S. Supreme Court eventually found Proposition 14 to violate the Fourteenth Amendment and reinstalled the Rumford Act.[36] But the electoral power of the forces against integration was strong and would be heard from again in the ballot box in California. In the difficult years of the Depression and then in the decades of boom defined the World War and then the Cold War, Los Angeles experienced intense migration and population growth. Yet the metropolis became more segregated, not less, carefully separating newcomers and long-term residents into newly racialized communities— ensuring that the "right people" gained the benefits of the boom.

From Boom to Globalization: Keeping Segregation in a New Los Angeles

Across the Americas, national development came with promises of gains for all—promises notably important in the United States as it mobilized a generation to face the risks of war. The decades from the 1930s through the 1960s were in many ways defined by promises of popular gains, contradicted by stubbornly enduring discriminations limiting the rights and opportunities of blacks, Mexicans, Asians, and women. Those contradictions came to a head in the 1960s, during another mobilization for war—the Vietnam conflict that many found of questionable legitimacy. While Los Angeles saw important fights for African American, Mexican American, and women's rights in politics and society, it also faced the challenge of the segregations that had so long enforced entrenched discriminations.

For most whites in twenty-first-century Los Angeles, the residential segregation of the pre–civil rights era seems long past. Given the major demographic transition of the Los Angeles population since 1965 in the era of legislated nondiscrimination, it appears that racial minorities, particularly recent immigrants from Mexico and Asia, now live throughout the Los Angeles basin in neighborhoods that opened to them long ago. With the non-Hispanic white proportion of the population falling below 50 percent in the five counties of Southern California, including Los Angeles County, appearances would indicate that racial minorities exist in any city or neighborhood in the region. Yet, most social scientists and demographers have concluded that residential segregation involving non-Hispanic whites has increased since 1960—as the privileged and prosperous have withdrawn into enclaves of self-separation. The self-segregation of the few has had profound effects for the housing options of racial minorities, both long-standing residents and more recent arrivals. One major study of segregation in Los Angeles in the twenty-first century, for example, has concluded that "despite the dramatic growth in diversity, white isolation from other groups has increased and become entrenched in socioeconomic stratification."[37] Moreover, the legacy of past racial discrimination has combined powerfully with continued racial discrimination in housing and lending practices, and with growing white resistance to antidiscrimination statutes, to reinforce the unequal nature of the Southern California housing market and segregation between the races in Los Angeles.

It is certainly the case that the overturning of Proposition 14 was only the first of many government attempts to right the wrongs of past housing discrimination. The assassination of Dr. Martin Luther King, Jr., in 1968 prompted the U.S. Congress to pass the first comprehensive fair-housing law in the nation's history. Title VIII of the Fair Housing Act authorized for the first time a government entity, the Department of Housing and Urban Development (HUD), to investigate complaints of discrimination. But like many of the antidiscrimination laws enacted then and since, a deep-seated "process of resistance, refusal, and renegotiation" met every attempt to enact open housing.[38] First, the act itself forbade HUD from initiating investigations, and gave people faced with discrimination only 180 days to file suit. Despite these weaknesses, the law provoked thousands of complaints of housing discrimination each year, but during the 1970s fewer than 30 percent led to mediation. As of 1980, only five victims of discrimination had received damages in excess of $3,500, and today experts estimate that more than

2 million cases of housing discrimination occur every year without any legal action being taken.[39]

During the 1970s, California voters passed two ballot initiatives by large majorities. They intended to block mandatory school desegregation measures that attempted to counter the segregated attendance that had resulted from discriminatory housing practices. In 1972, voters passed Proposition 21, also known as the Wakefield Amendment, championed by a fiery conservative from the L.A. suburb of South Gate, which prohibited all race-based assignments to public schools. In the early 1960s, South Gate emerged as a flashpoint for efforts to desegregate the Los Angeles School District because school officials regularly adjusted attendance areas to keep South Gate High School nearly 100 percent white, while nearby Jordan High School was almost entirely black, overcrowded, and in disrepair. In response, the American Civil Liberties Union (ACLU) filed a lawsuit to compel a change, which eventually expanded to *Crawford v. Los Angeles School Board* (1963). While Wakefield led a campaign against what he called "forced integration" and won with the voters in 1972, most of the amendment was invalidated by the courts as violating the Equal Protection Clause. In 1979, San Fernando Valley politician Alan Robbins successfully got voters to back Proposition 1, utilizing the growing mobilization of white parent activists whose program called BUSTOP fought against mandatory desegregation, worrying that the *Crawford* case would eventually include their schools. While BUSTOP leaders such as Bobbi Fiedler, Tom Bartman, and Roberta Weintraub all won spots on the Los Angeles School Board, the U.S. Supreme Court upheld Proposition 1, effectively ending any attempt at mandatory desegregation in *Crawford*. Both the courts and the school board embraced the concept of "voluntary measures" to achieve desegregation, including magnet schools and voluntary busing—mostly of minority children to relieve overcrowding and attend special programs.[40]

Both these efforts to counter school desegregation came from residential areas—South Gate and the San Fernando Valley—where white real estate agents and homeowner associations had historically restricted minority housing. Resistance to integration rested on the assumption that substantial benefits accrued to whites of all class backgrounds based on their ability to collectively keep their communities homogeneous. In the 1970s, Southern California witnessed an explosion in property values that would generate both a middle-class tax revolt and slow-growth protests led by homeowners associations. In the fall of 1973, home prices in Southern California were $1,000 below the national average; by the end of the decade they were over $42,000 higher and fifteen years later over $143,000 higher. Home prices increased almost three times faster than income in the late 1970s. White homeowners had benefited from decades of segregation that discriminated against racial minorities and created "exclusive" neighborhoods now gaining soaring property values—a major windfall of accumulated wealth they worked to protect at all cost.[41] The enormous and racialized disparity of wealth in Southern California contributed mightily to a national pattern; by the year 2000, the average white family had seven times the wealth of the average black family in the United States.[42]

The soaring rise of housing prices increasingly set homes in suburban white communities beyond the reach of most racial minorities in Southern California, despite the end of widespread formal—that is, contractual— housing discrimination. Instead, the city core, where African Americans and Latinos had developed neighborhoods before 1970, expanded dramatically in the late twentieth century; the inner ring suburbs and incorporated cities in Los Angeles County became a wide swath where racial minorities were in the vast majority. In greater Los Angeles, patterns of segregation changed to persist. As the leading geographers of the region acknowledged, "1990 settlement patterns of long-settled minorities, especially blacks, show clear effects of past exclusion."[43] Rather than an indication of preferences to live among one's own, the new pattern of residential segregation reflected the unavailability of low- or moderate-income housing in the region except in the inner core, whether for ownership or rental. In 2000, while two-thirds of families across the United States owned their own homes, only 48 percent of families in Los Angeles County did so, and only 39 percent in the city of Los Angeles could afford homeownership. Rents in Los Angeles broke the budgets of most low-income workers; the average rent of $1,220 per month for a two-bedroom apartment in the year 2000 left most renters to go without health insurance or childcare. Two out of every five renter households paid more than half their income in rent, while 30 percent lived in overcrowded conditions.[44] The housing crisis of the twenty-first century has been present in poor and working-class communities in Los Angeles for several decades—rooted in a long history of segregations, then exacerbated by the globalization that after 1980 left Los Angeles with a less dynamic and more polarizing economy. Housing was scarce, segregated, and expensive; incomes were low and ever more insecure. The California Dream faded— except for those withdrawing into gated and segregated communities.

Housing discrimination and unequal lending practices continued throughout the region in the post–civil rights era, with the federal and local government increasingly turning a blind eye to these inequities. William Bradford Reynolds, Ronald Reagan's appointee as director of the Justice Department's Civil Rights Division in 1981, filed only two housing discrimination suits in his first twenty months in office, a sharp drop from the Nixon, Ford, and Carter years. Sociologists Melvin Oliver and Tom Shapiro estimate that discrimination in the home loan industry costs black homeowners $10.5 billion in extra payments, depriving each black homeowner of nearly $4,000 as a result of the 54 percent higher rate they pay on home mortgages. According to a 1998 HUD study, high-cost loans were offered five times more often in black neighborhoods than in white neighborhoods, comprising nearly 51 percent of all loans in black neighborhoods as compared to 9 percent in white communities. And this discrimination exists only if blacks and other minorities can get mortgages. In 1992, the Federal Reserve Bank of Boston reported that black and Latino mortgage applications were 60 percent more likely to be turned down than whites, even when they shared similar employment and financial profiles. In Los Angeles, the patterns of discrimination are consistent and persistent, with blacks reporting housing discrimination three to five times more than any other group, and 10 percent of all native- and foreign-born Latinos reporting similar discrimination. Another study of Southern California found that black and Latino applicants are at greatest disadvantage securing conventional loans in suburban areas; when they gain mortgages, they are concentrated in long-segregated inner-core communities.[45]

The most disturbing part of the latest studies of housing discrimination, however, is not that it continues, but rather that fewer and fewer whites believe that it continues. While blacks, Latinos, and, to a lesser extent, Asians are still inclined to invoke structural barriers such as persistent discrimination in society to understand continued economic disparities in housing, whites increasingly blame minority-group disadvantage on supposed cultural deficiencies. Support for continued vigilance against housing discrimination, therefore, is waning in the general population, despite the fact that scientific studies continue to show its wide persistence. As more and more whites leave Los Angeles altogether, they believe that the wealth they claimed from segregated housing is a result of their own families' hard work and economic fortitude. The city of Los Angeles lost 200,000 white non-Latino residents in the 1990s, while the county lost almost one-fifth of its total white population.[46] Coupled with the continued limitations on housing equity for Latinos and African Americans in Los Angeles, this exodus reduces further the possibility of truly integrated neighborhoods in

Southern California. Once again in the era of accelerating globalization, segregation has changed to persist, still favoring the concentration of gains among whites and limiting the possibilities of African Americans, Mexicans, and other Latinos—and the generations of new immigrants that now sustain the Los Angeles metropolitan economy.

A Tale of Two Mayors: Political Openings and the Challenges of Globalization

As Los Angeles' decades of boom turned to uncertainties laced with polarization regarding the new economy of globalization, African American Tom Bradley served as mayor from 1973 to 1993. Later, as the city saw the dynamism of a new millennium crash in 2008 and its difficult aftermath, Mexican American Antonio Villaraigosa was mayor from 2005 to 2013. Their rise and governing of the city revealed new openings to political participation for long segregated peoples. But their celebrated eminence and the promise evoked by their rise to power should not mask the limits of what they could do as mayors of a city locked in a metropolitan region still defined by segregations. Both men surmounted exclusions to live the California Dream. Neither could erase the obstacles that limited the chances of so many others.

Born in Texas, the grandson of slaves and son of sharecroppers, Tom Bradley came to Los Angeles as a seven-year-old boy in the 1920s—part of the migration that built the burgeoning city. Raised in a segregated neighborhood, he attended public schools and UCLA and then joined the police, rising to the rank of lieutenant while earning a law degree in night school. With strong African American backing, he mobilized multiracial constituencies to win election to the city council in 1963, then to the office of mayor in 1973. His early career was marked by the Watts riots of 1965, making clear to all that the presence of a few blacks in office did not mean a lessening of racial challenges and economic exclusions in the city. As mayor, Bradley oversaw the final years of the boom fueled by defense industries as the United States withdrew from the conflict in Vietnam— the last of three Pacific wars that kept L.A. prosperous. The 1984 Olympics brought the city to the center of the world's attention—just as the decline of defense and energy industries left metropolitan Los Angeles to adapt to globalization while shifting to an economy of finance, services, and port transfers. Bradley worked to draw Japanese and other Asian investment to Los Angeles, to claim the best he could for his diverse constituents in a rapidly changing world and metropolitan economy.

Meanwhile, revolutionary conflicts in Central America and the collapse of the national development project in Mexico in the 1980s sent waves of new migrants to Los Angeles, reinforcing populations increasingly defined as Latino (to reflect the diversity among Mexicans and Central Americans, established residents and newcomers). In the 1980s and into the 1990s, the population grew, but economic opportunities proved limited and increasingly insecure (and often informal, to incorporate immigrants without documents). Meanwhile, communities across the metropolis faced new segregations. In 1992, when African Americans took to the streets to protest the acquittal of the white police officers who had beaten Rodney King during an arrest a year earlier, it was clear that Mayor Bradley did not control the police, who responded with sharp repression. Nor did his years in office end a deep sense of black exclusion and alienation in the city. He could not control the economic polarization that came with globalization or the segregations that persisted to keep limited prosperity within favored communities. Tom Bradley left office in 1993, a symbol of political possibilities amid constrained social opportunities.[47]

In 2005, Antonio Villaraigosa became Los Angeles's first Mexican American mayor since the nineteenth century—a victory that was evidence of both long exclusions and new possibilities. He too brought a compelling personal story. He was born Antonio Villar in Boyle Heights in 1953 to a Mexican immigrant father and Mexican American mother. Raised primarily by his mother, he mixed public school and college with part-time jobs and experience in César Chávez's United Farmworkers' boycotts. He earned a degree in history from UCLA in 1977, and a law degree from the People's College of Law in 1985. When he married Corina Raigosa in 1987, they merged names so that Antonio entered politics in the 1990s as Antonio Villaraigosa. He worked for the Los Angeles Teachers Union and the American Civil Liberties Union and was appointed to the Metropolitan Transportation Board in 1990, when Tom Bradley was mayor.

In 1994, Villaraigosa won election to the state assembly, rising to serve as speaker in 1998, until term limits returned him to Los Angeles in 2000. Losing a first bid for mayor to fellow Democrat James Hahn in 2001, Villaraigosa won a city council seat in 2003, then election as mayor in 2005—as the mortgage-driven Iraq War bubble soared toward a peak. He worked on school reform, environmental protection, and massive transportation expansion, until the crash of 2008 curtailed everything. Surviving economic collapse and fiscal austerity was the focus of his second term from 2009 to

2013.[48] The Mexican American, Mexican immigrant, and Latino immigrant populations expanded while facing residential exclusions—and for many newcomers, economic insecurity and marginality. Antonio Villaraigosa's rise to political leadership, like Tom Bradley's before him, announced the possibility of individual ascent and of political participation for African Americans and an increasingly complex Latino community. The challenges of social inclusion and shared prosperity in the era of globalization remained beyond the mayors' capacity to address in any transforming way. In that, the rise of the two mayors reveals Los Angeles, once the model for a California-driven American Dream, to be much like other cities across the United States and the Americas—places of dynamism mixing opportunities and exclusions in polarizations that have proven hard to shake.

Looking to the Future: Integrating a City of Diminishing Dreams

Over the past twenty years, I have had many opportunities to present my understanding of the historic multiracial community of Boyle Heights and the factors leading to its later racial segregation to former residents of the area, people who had experienced it firsthand as a unique multiracial residential enclave. In October 2003, I addressed about 150 people at the Jewish community center in Long Beach, over 70 percent elders who had grown up in Boyle Heights during the 1930s and 1940s. They were uniformly shocked by the 1939 FHA description of their community as "hopelessly heterogeneous" with "subversive racial elements" and perplexed by why government officials and the real estate industry did not want them to live with people of other races. Moreover, despite the fact that most had not lived in the community for over fifty years, they continued to refer to multiracial Boyle Heights as their home, instead of the various communities like Beverly Hills, Tujunga, Palm Springs, or Long Beach where they currently lived. Indeed, their social lives continue to revolve around friendships and relationships they developed as adolescents and young adults in Boyle Heights. The Roosevelt High School Alumni Club continued to draw more than 200 former "Rough Riders" to their fifty-year high school reunions into the 1990s, and many informal groups, such as the "Saxons" or the "Jasons" that began as clubs for young people in the neighborhood during the 1930s still meet weekly in communities throughout Southern California. The most active regularly turn out for the annual "Classic" football game each year between Roosevelt and Garfield High Schools, usually held at the Los Angeles Coliseum or the East Los Angeles College Stadium—the largest number of spectators in the nation to turn out for a high school football game.

These former Boyle Heights residents uniformly told me that they were never able to replicate the sense of community they experienced in Boyle Heights. They explained that they often don't know their neighbors in the towns and cities they moved to as adults or currently experience as elderly residents. As they moved up the economic ladder, they lost touch with the relationships that a working-class community like Boyle Heights promoted. There, personal connections often involved friendships and regular contact across racial lines, something they rarely experience in the suburbs of Los Angeles. The loss of interconnectedness they felt as they dispersed across greater Los Angeles reflects changes in the metropolitan region over the late twentieth century—a parallel to the splintering of life in greater Buenos Aires. The consolidation of new segregations underlies many of the problems they see now in the region, including in the much more segregated Boyle Heights of today.[49] Clearly the experiences of growing up in an integrated neighborhood and having regular contact with peers of diverse racial backgrounds had a profound and positive influence on their lives. They felt they were able to interact meaningfully with individuals from all backgrounds, and adjust successfully to the changing demographics of Southern California.

Of course, the old multiethnic Boyle Heights was segregated in the ways of the mid-twentieth century. Mexicans, blacks, Jews, and Italians mixed there as ethnic "others" inhibited from joining more prosperous white communities. Over the decades of boom and amid demands for rights from 1950 to 1980, Jews and Italians gained acceptance as "whites" and prospered enough to move to richer neighborhoods. Most blacks and Mexicans found themselves still in more segregated communities like Boyle Heights—where they engaged waves of new arrivals from Mexico, Central America, and beyond. Segregated communities are reappearing in metropolitan Los Angeles, but in ways that are new and sometimes not recognized. Koreatown, near downtown Los Angeles, is over 60 percent Latino residentially, and Korean-Latino interactions happen throughout the streets and businesses in the neighborhood. South Central Los Angeles has become close to 70 percent Latino and interactions between African Americans and Latinos have become commonplace in areas such as Watts, Compton, and

Inglewood, all districts that thirty years ago were overwhelmingly African American. Rebuilt residential segregations again contain and restrict opportunities for communities of "others" that are diverse except for their common poverty and definition as "others" by the powerful and the prosperous. As established African American and Mexican American families mix with immigrants from Mexico, Latin America, Asia, and the wider world, we are just beginning to learn about these new communities of segregation and the interactions within. Once again we see constrained communities operating as spaces of adaptation, bringing opportunity to some and limits to many; conflicts grounded in enclosed limitations create local frictions just as challenges and opportunities demand creative interactions.[50] Does Los Angeles change to stay the same?

As analysts look to the future of Southern California, many see a need to connect long segregated communities if the region is to prosper. Dowell Myers has written in *Immigrants and Boomers* that the future of the 78 million aging baby boomers in the United States is intimately tied to the fate of immigrants and their children—and nowhere is their future more intertwined than in metropolitan Los Angeles. He argues that the ratio of seniors to working-age residents in this country will be 67 percent higher in the near future, creating a situation in which "greater numbers of new workers will be required to replace retirees, new taxpayers will be needed to support senior benefits, and more home buyers must be found to buy all the homes that will be sold by baby boomer retirees."[51] He documents the rapid pace of immigrant advancement in Southern California and shows how important it is for the future of the region and the nation to invest in the opportunities for immigrant families and the successful integration of their children. The future social contract between generations in urban areas like Los Angeles will necessarily involve working across the racial and ethnic lines that long segregated residential communities and currently separate the elderly and youth, aging baby boomers and an emerging diverse work force. New patterns of interaction—residential, social, and cultural—among immigrants and natives, newcomers and established residents, can create an urban society of greater shared opportunity as we adapt to the promise and limits of globalization. Continuing segregations will keep polarizations, limited opportunities, and potential conflict in our urban future. The world and its cities face great challenges in the twenty-first century; worsening them with segregations and other exclusions is not the path to opportunity and prosperity in Los Angeles—or other cities across the Americas.

Notes

1. See George J. Sanchez, "'What's Good for Boyle Heights Is Good for the Jews': Creating Multiracialism on the Eastside During the 1950s," in *Los Angeles and the Future of Urban Cultures: Special Issue of the American Quarterly* 56, no. 3, ed. Raul Homero Villa and George J. Sanchez (2004): 634–640.

2. "The Story of Reeve Street, United States of America," *California Eagle*, Los Angeles, May 14, 1953, 1, 8; Josh Sides, *L.A. City Limits: African American Los Angeles from the Great Depression to the Present* (Berkeley: University of California Press, 2003), 126–127; Sides, "Straight into Compton: American Dreams, Urban Nightmares, and the Metamorphosis of a Black Suburb," in *Los Angeles and the Future of Urban Cultures*, ed. Villa and Sanchez, 583.

3. Mike Davis, *City of Quartz: Excavating the Future in Los Angeles* (London: Verso, 1990).

4. See the "Americans and the California Dream" series from Oxford University Press, especially Kevin Starr, *Inventing the Dream: California Through the Progressive Era* (New York: Oxford University Press, 1985) and *Embattled Dreams: California in War and Peace, 1940–1950* (New York: Oxford University Press, 2002).

5. Manuel Pastor and Rhonda Ortiz, "Immigrant Integration in Los Angeles: Strategic Directions for Funders" (Program for Environmental and Regional Equity and Center for the Study of Immigrant Integration, University of Southern California, 2009).

6. Greg Hise, *Magnetic Los Angeles: Planning the Twentieth-Century Metropolis* (Baltimore: Johns Hopkins University Press, 1999); see also Dana Cuff, *The Provisional City: Los Angeles Stories of Architecture and Urbanism* (Cambridge: Massachusetts Institute of Technology Press, 2000).

7. For a full exploration of these issues, see Michan Connor, "Creating Cities and Citizens: Municipal Boundaries, Place Entrepreneurs, and the Production of Race in Los Angeles County, 1926–1978," Ph.D. dissertation, University of Southern California, 2008.

8. See Lisa McGirr, *Suburban Warriors: The Origins of the New American Right* (Princeton, NJ: Princeton University Press, 2001).

9. Nancy Cleeland, "Great Diversity in Expectations," *Los Angeles Times*, September 28, 1998, A1, A20.

10. Larry Gordon, "L.A. County Leads U.S. by Large Margin in Numbers of Latinos, Asians," *Los Angeles Times*, September 19, 1998, A24; Robin Fields, "Milestones of Growth and a New Ethnic Order," *Los Angeles Times,* March 30, 2001, U1; "Latinos: Four Counties See a Surge in Numbers," *Los Angeles Times,* March 30, 2001, U6.

11. Dowell Myers, *Immigrants and Boomers: Forging a New Social Contract for the Future of America* (New York: Russell Sage Foundation, 2007), 39.

12. John D. Weaver, *El Pueblo Grande: A Non-Fiction Book About Los Angeles* (Los Angeles: Ward Ritchie Press, 1973), 23–24; Douglas Monroy, *Thrown Among Strangers: The Making of Mexican Culture in Frontier California* (Berkeley: University of California Press, 1990), 222–232; Richard Griswold del Castillo, *The Los Angeles Barrio, 1850–1890: A Social History* (Berkeley: University of California Press, 1979),

30–61. William Deverell goes so far as calling the 1850s part of "the unending Mexican War." Deverell, *Whitewashed Adobe: The Rise of the Los Angeles and the Remaking of Its Mexican Past* (Berkeley: University of California Press, 2004), 11–25.

13. Starr, *Inventing the Dream*, 49.

14. *Hearings Before the United States Commission on Civil Rights, Los Angeles, 1960* (Washington, DC: United States Government Printing Office, 1960), 207–278; Christopher Jimenez y West, "More than My Color: Space, Politics and Identity in Los Angeles, 1940–1973," Ph.D. dissertation, University of Southern California, 2007, ch. 2; Natalia Molina, *Fit to Be Citizens? Public Health and Race in Los Angeles, 1879–1939* (Berkeley: University of California Press, 2006), 15–31.

15. Robert M. Fogelson, *Bourgeois Nightmares: Suburbia, 1870–1930* (New Haven, CT: Yale University Press, 2005), 43–59.

16. *Hearings Before the United States Commission on Civil Rights*, 207–278; Jimenez y West, "More than My Color," ch. 2.

17. Mansel G. Blackford, *The Lost Dream: Businessmen and City Planning on the Pacific Coast, 1890–1920* (Columbus: Ohio State University Press, 1993), 84, 92–93; Jon A. Peterson, *The Birth of City Planning in the United States, 1840–1917* (Baltimore: Johns Hopkins University Press, 2003), 309.

18. Natalia Molina, *Fit to be Citizens*, 35–43.

19. Douglas Flamming, *Bound for Freedom: Black Los Angeles in Jim Crow America* (Berkeley: University of California Press, 2005), 218–219.

20. Fogelson, *Bourgeois Nightmares*, 5–19, 137.

21. Mark Wild, *Street Meeting: Multiethnic Neighborhoods in Early Twentieth-Century Los Angeles* (Berkeley: University of California Press, 2005), 18–56.

22. Flamming, *Bound for Freedom*, 221–225.

23. Jimenez y West, "More than My Color," ch. 2; C. L. Neir, "Perpetuation of Segregation: Toward a New Historical and Legal Interpretation of Redlining Under the Fair Housing Act," *John Marshall Law Review* 32 (1999); Kenneth T. Jackson, *Crabgrass Frontier: The Suburbanization of the United States* (New York: Oxford University Press, 1985).

24. Home Owners Loan Corporation City Survey Files, Area D-53, Los Angeles, 1939, National Archives, Washington, D.C., p. 7. Also quoted in George Lipsitz, *Time Passages: Collective Memory and American Popular Culture* (Minneapolis: University of Minnesota Press, 1990), 137.

25. See Sanchez, "'What's Good for Boyle Heights Is Good for the Jews,'" 634–640.

26. Jimenez y West, "More than My Color," ch. 2; Flamming, *Bound for Freedom*, 354–355; Don Parsons, *Making a Better World: Public Housing, the Red Scare, and the Direction of Modern Los Angeles* (Minneapolis: University of Minnesota Press, 2005).

27. Sides, *L.A. City Limits*, 44–45.

28. Quote in Lawrence B. de Graaf, "Negro Migration to Los Angeles, 1930–1950," Ph.D. dissertation, University of California, Los Angeles, 1962, 189.

29. Letter from Morris J. Kay, Publisher, *Valley Jewish News* to John Anson Ford, February 9, 1950, John Anson Ford papers, Box 75, Folder B IV 5i cc(15), Huntington Library.

30. Sanchez, "'What's Good for Boyle Heights,'" 634–38; Sides, *L.A. City Limits*, 109.

31. Kevin Allen Leonard, *The Battle for Los Angeles: Racial Ideology and World War II* (Albuquerque: University of New Mexico Press, 2006), 265–266; Sides, "Straight into Compton," 584–586.

32. *California Real Estate Magazine*, September 1948.

33. Daniel Wei HoSang, "Genteel Apartheid: Racial Propositions in Postwar California," Ph.D. dissertation, University of Southern California, 2007, ch. 3; Sides, *L.A. City Limits*, 106–108.

34. "Population and Housing in Los Angeles County: A Study in the Growth of Residential Segregation," published by the Los Angeles Commission on Human Relations, March 1963, in Box 2, Folder 1, "California: Housing 1959–1964," Democratic Leadership Council papers.

35. *Hearings Before the United States Commission on Civil Rights*, 275; HoSang, "Genteel Apartheid," ch. 3; Jimenez y West, "More than My Color," ch. 2.

36. HoSang, "Genteel Apartheid," ch. 3.

37. Philip J. Ethington, "Segregated Diversity: Race-Ethnicity, Space, and Political Fragmentation in Los Angeles County, 1940–1994," final report to the John Randolph Haynes and Dora Haynes Foundation, September 13, 2000, 4. For a similar analysis across U.S. metropolitan areas, see Douglas S. Massey and Nancy A. Denton, *American Apartheid: Segregation and the Making of the Underclass* (Cambridge, MA: Harvard University Press, 1993).

38. I take the use of the term "process of resistance, refusal, and renegotiation" from George Lipsitz, *The Possessive Investment in Whiteness: How White People Profit from Identity Politics* (Philadelphia: Temple University Press, 1998), 29.

39. Lipsitz, *Possessive Investment*, 28–29.

40. HoSang, "Genteel Apartheid," ch. 4; see also Becky M. Nicolaides, *My Blue Heaven: Life and Politics in the Working-Class Suburb of Los Angeles, 1920–1965* (Chicago: University of Chicago Press, 2002), 272–327, for a wider discussion of South Gate's efforts at racial exclusion.

41. Davis, *City of Quartz*, 168–186.

42. See *Race: The Power of an Illusion*, Episode 3, "The House We Live In," executive producer Larry Adelman (PBS, 2003).

43. James P. Allen and Eugene Turner, *The Ethnic Quilt: Population Diversity in Southern California* (Northridge: Center for Geographical Studies, California State University, Northridge, 1997), 44.

44. Robert Gottlieb, Mark Vallianatos, Regina M. Freer, and Peter Dreier, *The Next Los Angeles: The Struggle for a Livable City* (Berkeley: University of California Press, 2005), 100–101.

45. Lipsitz, *Possessive Investment*, 32; "Uncle Sam Lends a Hand: Did the Government Racialize Housing and Wealth?" PBS Go Deeper website for *Race: The Power of an Illusion*, http://www.pbs.org/race/000_About//002_06-godeeper.htm; Camille Zubrinsky Charles, *Won't You Be My Neighbor? Race, Class, and Residence in Los Angeles* (New York: Russell Sage Foundation, 2006),120; Carolyn B. Aldama and Gary A. Dymski, "Urban Sprawl, Racial Separation, and Federal Housing Policy,"

in *Up Against the Sprawl: Public Policy and the Making of Southern California*, ed. Jennifer Wolch, Manuel Pastor Jr., and Peter Dreier (Minneapolis: University of Minnesota Press, 2004), 113.

46. Charles, *Won't You Be My Neighbor*, 120–121; Lawrence Bobo, "Racial Attitudes and Relations at the Close of the Twentieth Century," in *America Becoming: Racial Trends and Their Consequences*, ed. Neil J. Smelser, William Julius Wilson, and Faith Mitchell (Washington, DC: National Academy Press, 2001); Davis, *City of Quartz*, rev. ed. (London: Verso, 2006), xiv.

47. The details of Bradley's life and political career are available at https://www .mayortombradley.com/what-we-do/ and "Tom Bradley, Mayor in Era of Los Angeles Growth, Dies," *New York Times*, September 30, 1998, https://www.nytimes.com /1998/09/30/us/tom-bradley-mayor-in-era-of-los-angeles-growth-dies.html. The interpretation is from this larger analysis of segregation in the context of John Tutino's analysis of the city's economic trajectory in chapter 1.

48. The details of Villaraigosa's career are in www.britannica.com, "Antonio Villaraigosa," again interpreted in the context of this chapter and Tutino, chapter 1.

49. For a vivid compilation of these attitudes and experiences, see "Crossroads: Boyle Heights," a documentary compiling life histories, conducted with former residents for the museum exhibition, "Boyle Heights: The Power of Place," presented at the Japanese American National Museum, produced by the Frank H. Watase Media Arts Center, 2002.

50. See, for example, the work of Abigail Rosas, "On the Move, and in the Moment: Community Formation, Identity, and Opportunity in South Central Los Angeles, 1945–2008," Ph.D. dissertation, University of Southern California, 2011.

51. Myers, *Immigrants and Boomers*, 263.

7 Energy Capital and Opportunity City

Houston in the Twentieth Century

• •

JOSEPH A. PRATT AND MARTIN V. MELOSI

This chapter focuses on Houston, Texas, the last of our six New World cities to become a major metropolis—and among them, the city with the most dynamic twentieth-century economy. Houston's global leadership in the production, transportation, processing, and consumption of oil and natural gas has propelled its long-term, sustained economic success. For more than one hundred years this region has adapted to the cycles of booms and busts in the world petroleum industry. While adjusting to its changing role in the world economy, the Houston region has expanded from the center of the emerging oil center of Texas and the southwestern United States, to the capital of oil and natural gas in the U.S., and more recently into the generally accepted—if self-proclaimed—"energy capital of the world." Houston's effective management of the economic challenges of building a diversifying economy around its oil-related core of industries marked it as an exception to the record of other regional economies strongly tied to energy. While expanding employment and improving infrastructure, it has had a more difficult time in managing the inevitable social, political, and environmental challenges that have accompanied oil-led development.

Energy Capitals Defined

We define energy capitals as cities/regions shaped by energy-led development, with strong roles in energy production, energy distribution, and/or energy technology. Key examples of such cities in the Americas include Houston, Texas, USA; Calgary, Alberta, Canada; Villahermosa, Mexico; Caracas, Venezuela; and San Fernando, Trinidad. In the past, the production, transportation, and intensive use of energy also strongly influenced such cities as Pittsburgh, Pennsylvania; Tampico, Mexico; and Los Angeles, California. Among numerous energy capitals, Houston emerged as *the* energy capital of the late twentieth century. Major companies with strong ties to the city hold central roles in organizing global energy production and trade. The Houston region's development has been inextricably intertwined with oil and natural gas and with the waves of new urbanites they attracted. As William Cronon and others have demonstrated, the urbanization process entails the connection of city and hinterland which often extends the impact of urban development beyond politically constructed borders, while creating interdependence between built and natural features.[1]

Industrial expansion marked by mass migration to cities from rural areas has transformed major regions around the world in the last two centuries. This process reshaped the global economy; population in many traditional agricultural areas declined sharply as people in search of broader opportunities moved in mass to urban regions. It is important to note that oil-led development is a special case of urban-industrial growth that embodies a particularly intense form of globalization due to the central role of oil in the modern economy. The oil industry expanded rapidly and steadily through time, shaped in part by the growth of automobile-related industries and other major enterprises such as steel, glass, and rubber that grew in response to the rise of the automobile and other forms of gasoline- and diesel-dependent transportation. Oil is a liquid fuel easily transported and widely distributed geographically. Its use also has been made available and promoted by well-organized and technologically advanced corporations in both the private and public sectors. Another often-neglected attribute of the petroleum industry is its central importance to national defense, as demonstrated in both World Wars I and II.

Houston's close historical ties to this vital global industry also presents a special case. The modern oil industry was born ninety miles east of the city of Houston in 1901 when the discovery of the giant Spindletop gusher near Beaumont, Texas, accelerated the rapid growth of the use of oil as an energy source. Modern Houston was born at the same place and time, and oil and the city grew together throughout much of the twentieth century. The boom after Spindletop drew entrepreneurs, capital, and an expanded workforce to the region. These resources were used to explore for oil in other parts of Texas and in surrounding states. For a time in the years from 1901 to the 1920s, it seemed that every hole drilled in the southwestern states of the U.S. produced oil, and the resulting glut of oil led to the emergence of this broad section of the nation as the center of the world oil production into the 1960s. As the established transportation, commercial, financial, and legal center of the upper Texas Gulf Coast in the late nineteenth century, Houston was well situated to serve the needs of this booming new regional industry. As large oil fields in this broad region sought broader markets for their crude, Houston emerged as the hole at the end of a funnel of pipelines from oil companies in the interior of the southwestern U.S. seeking access to deep water for shipping. Extraordinary long-term economic benefits accrued to the city as a result of its location, its resource base, and the luck of the timing of the Spindletop boom.

Oil was a mixed blessing for Houston, bringing both the jobs that made it a city of opportunity for migrants and the social costs that often made it a difficult place to live. Houston is not unique in its transformation from a small city to a major metropolis due to the impact of energy-led growth. Indeed, many regions of the world have been greatly affected by the production and transportation of large amounts of energy, a process often accompanied by the introduction of advanced technologies by large companies based outside the region. The long-term impacts have included the transformation of regional economies, population growth fueled by mass migration to the opportunities presented by growth, fundamental changes in labor markets and educational infrastructure, high social costs in the areas of environmental quality and health, the shaping of regional infrastructure and the transformation of urban space, and changes in cultural attitudes.[2]

Houston's sustained economic growth provided jobs and capital that at times masked mounting societal problems. The contrast with our other cities is striking. Mexico City, Buenos Aires, and Montreal have long struggled with energy dependence. Los Angeles was a major energy center for a time in the mid-twentieth century—a role that faded along with much of its once-celebrated prosperity. And Rio de Janeiro, for most of the twentieth century the city that defined urban difficulties, now sees a greatly expanded petroleum industry as a way forward. Can late development as an energy capital help resolve entrenched challenges in a teeming metropolis of inequality and marginality? Perhaps. When Houston finally moved to ameliorate long-slighted social costs in the late twentieth century, its sustained oil-led development helped generate resources that could be used to improve quality of life.

The results of the region's sustained growth are impressive. Houston is currently the fourth-largest U.S. city in population and one of the largest in area. It sits at the center of the tenth-largest metropolitan area in the United States. It is home to over one hundred racial and ethnic groups, making it one of the most diverse cities in the nation. Although incorporated in 1836, the Bayou City is a product of oil-led development in the twentieth century, when the modest southeast Texas town blossomed into a full-scale metropolis. As the petroleum industry expanded throughout the global economy during the twentieth century, the city's thriving economy connected it to national and world petroleum markets. On the negative side of the equation, however, pollution problems mounted, largely unaddressed until the late twentieth century, as the energy capital produced and processed petroleum products for expanding world markets. Long-festering social tensions generated by deeply embedded racial attitudes and a Jim Crow racial order with legally sanctioned segregation could not be swept under the carpet forever. A business elite with close connections to oil and related industries dominated the city's politics, resisting social and environmental change under the banner of states' rights. In the cases of stricter control of environmental issues and desegregation, only federal intervention in the form of new laws finally brought these issues to the fore in the 1960s and 1970s.

Energy capitals are historically significant because of the roles they play and have played in both production *and* consumption of energy. Concentration of human and material resources for purposes of survival, construction of infrastructure, and the production and consumption of goods and services are essential characteristics of communal living. Energy-led development shaped the evolution of many cities and regions, influencing metropolitan growth while changing patterns of energy consumption and concentrating the environmental impacts of energy production locally as well as in areas of consumption far removed from production facilities. Our emphasis on energy and urbanization intersects with and revises recent thinking on global cities.[3]

Saskia Sassen has noted that, "Economic globalization, accompanied by the emergence of a global culture, has profoundly altered the social, economic, and political reality of nation-states, cross-national regions, and . . . cities."[4] The focus on transnational networks of cities and "transnational spaces for economic activity" in Sassen's work and elsewhere focuses on the general integration of the global economy, an encompassing perspective that may be too general to fully understand the trajectories of particular cities with particular rules in their home regions and the world. Our emphasis also intersects with the work on "the resource curse" or "the oil curse," which emphasizes the difficulties of emerging oil-producing nations as they seek to develop by exporting oil produced primarily by foreign companies.[5] More comparative work on energy-led development over time and place can provide a broader context for understanding the resource curse.[6] Though oil has brought its share of difficulties, it has not cursed Houston.

Instead it has brought a combination of economic benefits and social costs that has influenced the city's evolution.

Here we focus on the case of Houston in the comparative context of five other New World cities with different historical origins and different relations to the essential question of energy. The following questions focus our analysis of Houston as the energy capital of the Americas and the world:

- What economic benefits and costs have accrued to the region over time?
- How has migration of workers to the jobs in energy-related manufacturing altered the demographics and spatial organization of the region, expanding the influence of the urban center out into its hinterland?
- How have the needs of the energy industry shaped urban infrastructure, particularly industrial and municipal demand for water supply and wastewater systems, transportation and communication networks, disposal facilities, and scientific and technical educational systems? Such infrastructure not only relates to the direct needs and wants of energy industries but also plays a major role in urban development per se.
- What have been the most obvious social and physical costs? In particular, what have been the primary environmental impacts on the region of the specialized technology used in energy production and processing?
- What has been the impact of oil-related growth on the political system as it sought to make public policy about the costs and benefits of energy-led development?
- What has been the impact of the interaction between urbanization and energy development on culture, including labor, education, race and ethnicity, gender, and a variety of other social concerns?

Each of these queries generates a large subset of related questions for analysis of the rise of Houston in the twentieth century and for comparative analysis for other energy capitals. The same questions might be profitably used to compare urban development among all the cities analyzed in this volume. This project challenged our authors to explore the twentieth-century trajectory of an important New World city with a perspective chosen as especially revealing. The focus on Houston as an energy capital is our contribution to that comparative conversation.

The Physical Setting

While Houston and its history have been shaped by human forces that created an energy-intensive metropolis, geography and climate cannot be ignored. At their bases, globally linked urban histories remain environmental histories. Houston is foremost a product of the Texas coastal zone, an area of approximately 20,000 square miles with about 2,100 square miles of bays and estuaries, 375 miles of coastline, and 1,425 miles of shoreline.[7] Texas has two shorelines—one along the Gulf of Mexico and another along the bays. Bolivar Peninsula, Galveston Island, and Follets Island are grass-covered barrier flats and sandy beaches that separate the bay areas from the Gulf of Mexico.[8] Nature's design provides a measure of protection from hurricanes for the industrial sites and refinery towns that grew along the shores of Galveston Bay and of the ship channel that connected the bay to the city of Houston.

The entire Galveston Bay drainage basin covers 33,000 square miles of land and water from the Dallas-Fort Worth metroplex to the Texas coast. Above the bays two major river valleys—the Trinity and the San Jacinto—and several minor valleys of headward-eroding streams cut into the coastal plain. The Brazos River and Oyster Creek flow through the western portion of the Texas coastal zone.[9] From these rivers and bayous came the abundant fresh water that played an important role as cooling water for the region's growing refining complex after 1920. Within the Houston-Galveston map area are approximately 2,268 square miles of land—a broad area of flat coastal plain between marshes and the areas of pine and hardwood forests along the Trinity River and north of present-day downtown Houston.[10] Situated approximately forty-nine feet above sea level on prairie some fifty miles from the Gulf of Mexico, the city of Houston is linked geographically, geologically, and climatically to the Texas coast. The coastal plain of which Houston is a part comprises gently dipping layers of sand and clay, favorable for artesian water. The city historically has drawn water from the large Chicot and Evangeline aquifers running through the city.[11]

Surface water from Houston drains into the Gulf of Mexico via an elaborate network of bayous. With an average yearly rainfall of forty-two to forty-six inches from torrential rains, the area is subjected to frequent flooding. Since urbanization removes much of the filtering capacity of the soil, runoff has exacerbated Houston's tendency to flood as the city continued to expand. Since the city also is susceptible to hurricanes and tornadoes, water and the pollutants it carries have been the greatest natural threats to Houstonians and its neighbors.[12] Besides its extensive waterways, Houston also is a heavily vegetated city. Large portions of the region are forested, with substantial tree growth along the bayous, and to the south, the area is covered with a combination of prairie, marsh, forest, and abandoned agricultural lands. At the highly developed city center, the ground and canopy cover has diminished markedly. A "heat island" effect is most pronounced in this area, with temperatures higher there than along the city's periphery.[13]

In many respects, Houston's climate is one of its most identifiable features. An ill-fated publicity campaign once used the phrase "Houston is Hot!" to promote the city. Indeed, Houston's climate is subtropical and humid, with prevailing winds bringing heat from the deserts of Mexico and moisture from the Gulf. The sun shines for much of the year, with an annual growing season of almost 300 days.[14] As one geologic study noted, "The attributes that make the Texas Coastal Zone attractive for industrialization and development also make it particularly susceptible to a variety of environmental problems."[15]

The deepwater ports, intracoastal waterways, good water supplies, large tracts of arable land, and relatively mild climate have been valuable assets. In addition, the region has a variety of other exploitable resources, including timber, sulfur and salt, sand and gravel, shells for lime, abundant wildlife and sea life, and petroleum reserves.[16]

The agricultural, commercial, industrial, and recreational possibilities for the region, however, have come with a price due to natural and human impacts.[17] Extensive dredging of channels and passes resulted in discharge of sediment into bays, ultimately modifying circulation patterns, and affecting water quality and estuarine plants and animals. Because of increased cultivation, the construction of irrigation and drainage canals and urban paving results in streams accelerating the transport of sediment into bays as well as increasing nonpoint pollutants, including pesticides and herbicides. Straightening and lining streams with concrete—as in the case of several bayous in Houston—encourage flash flooding. Thermal effluent from manufacturing processes and power generation can be lethal to fish. Aggressive withdrawal of groundwater causes land subsidence, saltwater intrusion, and fault activation. Discharge of organic materials and trace metals too numerous to mention—including oil production, pipelines, spills, and chemical production—adds significantly to the pollution load of all watercourses. Other actions also have had significant impacts on oyster reefs, submerged aquatic vegetation, intertidal marsh vegetation and animal life, and freshwater wetlands.[18]

Several aspects of the region's physical environment played key roles in shaping oil-led urbanization and industrialization. The first of these was the extremely flat topography for almost one hundred miles from the coast. When Houston began its rapid expansion outward into the undeveloped land on its periphery, it became the largest city in area in the United States. Its system of circles within circles of freeway tying suburbs to central city took advantage of the flatness of the land and the lack of previous development to build an efficient—yet often crowded—automobile-centered transportation system. The lack of major mountain ranges and the flat land reaching into the city's hinterlands facilitated the construction of the pipelines from the Texas coast to the oil fields in the interior. Deepwater in the Gulf of Mexico provided ample opportunities to transport large volumes crude and refined oil to distant markets. Abundant fresh water was available in the region to fulfill the needs of the large refineries that grew to process oil. Central to the economy that fostered the development of the highway system was a final gift from nature to the region: the vast deposits of oil and natural gas underneath the surface all along this section of the Gulf Coast.

Houston and Oil-Led Development

For decades, the region remained a major producer of oil and natural gas—and much more. It also became the hub of long-distance pipelines and a preferred site for the construction of large refineries. Oil production tended to boom when new fields opened only to decline when years of production depleted these fields, devastating regional economies as oil producers moved on to search for other new fields. Refineries and pipelines could not be moved; the large permanent investments in these facilities represented sunk costs that tied companies to the Houston region while attracting and training workers for permanent industrial jobs. Several oil companies founded in the region ultimately grew into important international concerns. Many jobs also grew in new industries that supplied goods and services to the owners of these facilities. Once local companies such as Hughes Tool Company (a leader in the development of drill bits) and Cameron Iron Works (key innovator for blow-out preventers) grew with the regional economy before moving into broader markets and becoming leading international companies. As a result, the regional oil industry became much more than a producer of oil. Indeed, around the central function of oil exploration and production steadily grew a dynamic and diversified core of oil-related industries unrivaled in its size and complexity.

The Spindletop strike near Beaumont in 1901 signaled the establishment of the oil industry in the Southwestern United States. It produced a new group of rivals to challenge Standard Oil's control of the industry—Gulf, Texas (Texaco), Shell, Sun, and others. Because of its size and the other large oil fields soon discovered on the Gulf Coast, Spindletop helped fundamentally alter the demand for oil; by encouraging the use of refined petroleum for fuel, these giant new reserves paved the way for the rise of the gasoline powered automobile. Along with the discovery of oil at Spindletop, the construction of the Houston Ship Channel made Houston the center of the oil and gas industry.[19] While Beaumont was close to the major oil fields, it did not have the railroads, banking system, or port facilities that Houston had already developed as a cotton port.[20]

Fundamental changes in the national and international energy industries shaped the subsequent growth of Houston into a major metropolis. Since the late nineteenth century, fossil fuels ultimately supplanted wind, water, and animal power; in the process, local sources of energy have been replaced by sources provided by an increasingly specialized and concentrated energy economy. Oil and natural gas surged forward over coal during the twentieth century to become the dominant energy source in the industrial world. More than any other U.S. city, Houston benefited economically from this development. It became synonymous with oil much as Pittsburgh was with coal and steel or Detroit was with automobiles.

Many aspects of Houston's growth as an oil capital are instructive for other regions. The Houston area benefited from the good timing of the discovery of nearby massive new oil fields at the turn of the twentieth century, when the petroleum industry emerged as the favored new supplier of energy. As the earliest refining center in the southwestern United States, pipelines quickly connected the upper Texas-Louisiana Gulf Coast with the large oil fields across Texas, Louisiana, Oklahoma and other southwestern states. By the 1930s, half of the world's production of oil was located within 600 miles of Houston, and the region surrounding the city could boast of 4,200 miles of pipeline reaching outward to hundreds of fields. At that time more than fifty refineries and other energy businesses operated along the channel.[21]

Houston and its region benefited greatly from large and permanent investments in giant refining complexes, a spiderweb of pipelines, and modern oil shipping facilities. While oil fields might come and go in boom-towns in West Texas and Oklahoma, the permanent investments in refineries, pipelines, and ports in Houston remained. Even with the decline of oil production in the southwestern U.S., the major manufacturing plants continued to thrive because of their excellent location with access to deep water for shipping oil to major markets in the northeastern U.S. and Europe, and later for receiving crude oil imports from the large oil fields of Mexico, Venezuela, and the Middle East. The United States remained one of the largest producers and consumers of oil in the world for much of the twentieth century, and with the nation's largest refining complex, the Houston region remained a major part of the global oil economy well after regional oil extraction declined.

The rapid construction of oil refineries along the Houston Ship Channel altered the trajectory of the regional economy. From the early days of Texas oil to at least the 1960s, Houston had a national identity as a major refining center, and these giant plants hiring work forces in the 3,000 to 5,000 range remained powerful magnets attracting people and resources to the area. While the Gulf Coast refining region, writ large, extended from New Orleans to Corpus Christi (with almost 35 percent of the nation's refining capacity in 1970 and providing a substantial share of refined goods going to the Northeast), its historical and geographic center was the 100-mile coastline from Houston to Port Arthur, which contained the greatest concentration of refineries in the United States. Houston itself was at the center of the extensive expansion of refining, which further enhanced its reputation as a major energy center. Most of the large, integrated oil companies with operations in the United States chose this prime location for a major refinery. By 1927, eight refineries with a capacity of approximately 125,000 barrels of crude a day were operating in the Houston area,[22] and the region from Lake Charles, Louisiana, to Houston remains today one of the largest combined refining and petrochemical producing areas in the world.

Unlike many regions both blessed and cursed by the discovery of large oil fields, Houston proved well prepared by its late nineteenth-century history to absorb the benefits of oil-led development. At the time of the Spindletop discovery, the region enjoyed the oversight of a well-established democratic government located within a mature federal system of government. Before the discovery of oil, being a regional center of cotton commerce and shipping with well-developed transportation, legal, and financial ties to the national and global economy gave it a leg up on regional competitors. The city's aggressive civic/business elite hastened growth by pushing development—in particular, the expansion of the key innovation in transportation of this era, the completion of the Houston Ship Channel. The state political system made the choice to encourage competition in the region's booming oil industry. A final important asset in turn-of-the-century Texas was a well-developed framework of laws enforced by a strong court system. Thus a combination of timing, natural endowments, new technology, and public choices nurtured Houston's evolution into an energy capital. As will be discussed later, these circumstances enabled Texas and migrants to Texas from other oil regions to control the development of the state's oil. Regions less prepared for the effective management of vast oil reserves proved much less fortunate.

When the oil boom gripped the Houston region in the first two decades of the twentieth century, the region captured most of the permanent benefits. Most significantly, the city became the headquarters for a variety of oil-related companies that later grew into important global concerns. Specialized oil-related manufacturing located in the city quickly grew to include such products as drill bits, equipment for managing the control of oil from oil wells, and specialized instruments needed to find and produce oil. Houston also became home to companies that specialized in refinery and pipeline construction, and many others in a general business characterized as "oil tools and supplies." Timing again proved important for the region. As Houston emerged as a center of international oil-related businesses, other companies originally from outside the region (notably oil tool and service companies such as Halliburton and Schlumberger) established large regional offices in the city. These companies were among the first to create specialized technical products and services for oil production. As their businesses spread around the globe, Houston benefited from both job growth and capital accumulation.

By World War I, Houston had a large, vigorous core of oil-related business, finance, and law. The opening of the Houston Ship Channel (HSC) in 1914 cemented the region's growing leadership in all things oil. The HSC used extensive dredging to transform an existing stream, Buffalo Bayou, and a channel through Galveston Bay into a deep-water channel to the Gulf of Mexico.[23] Before the discovery of oil, Buffalo Bayou had provided a major commercial conduit for cotton, timber, and other commodities.[24] The need to transport oil and other petroleum-related goods added incentive for additional waterway improvements. These went forward in the early years after the discovery of oil.

With the opening of the HSC, the land along its banks became a vast center for petroleum refining; an equally large complex of petrochemical production followed in later decades.[25] Between 1929 and 1945, oil and related industries replaced cotton as the central feature of the Houston economy. In 1935, almost half of all Texas oil was shipped through the Port of Houston. *Fortune* asserted that, "Without oil Houston would have been just another cotton town."[26] Today, petroleum remains the top import and export, along with other petroleum products, crude fertilizers and minerals, and organic chemicals.

World War II brought significant changes to the oil industry as it cooperated with government to meet the need for the high-octane aviation fuel, synthetic rubber, and other petroleum-based products needed to win a global war.[27] The emergence of petrochemicals as a major, fast-growing industry enhanced the economic impact of the region's oil-related core. This dynamic new industry made extensive use of oil and natural gas in its manufacturing processes, and its plants were often constructed near oil refineries and owned by oil companies.

During World War II, giant shipbuilding facilities sprang up along the HSC, as did steel plants and a petrochemical complex financed cooperatively by the federal government and private business. The Port of Houston also grew as a major employer in those years.[28] The Houston region prospered greatly from war-related spending on refining and petrochemicals; in fact, half of the synthetic rubber used in the war came from Texas. Houston, in particular, was at the heart of petrochemical production, especially because the Gulf Coast refineries were a major source of the raw material (the feedstock) for the manufacture of petrochemicals. By 1950, there were twenty-seven chemical plants along the ship channel. Chemicals remained one of the fastest-growing industries in the postwar era, and by the 1980s, the Houston area had more than half of the petrochemical capacity in the country.[29]

An additional economic impact of oil on the region came during and immediately after the World War II era with the emergence of Houston as the U.S. center of the booming natural gas industry. Government funding for the construction of two of the earliest long-distance oil pipelines for transporting crude and refined products from the giant oil fields and refineries in the Southwest to staging areas on the East Coast for shipments to Europe came in response to the sinking of large numbers of oil tankers by German submarines in the Gulf of Mexico. After the war, the U.S. government sold these two pipelines at auction with the stipulation that they be converted to the shipment of natural gas. In the years that followed, Houston became the headquarters of many of the major gas transmission companies and their suppliers. In terms of ownership and control of supplies, Houston gradually became the natural gas capital of the United States.[30]

The oil-related core of industries centered in Houston grew in size and complexity as layer after layer of industrial activities followed oil, gas, and petrochemicals into the region. In the long postwar boom from 1945 into the 1960s, the HSC area became the largest center of chemical manufacturing in the world. Specialized construction firms such as Brown & Root Industrial Services were major participants in the rapidly growing offshore industry in the Gulf of Mexico and then around the world. More and more administrative offices for the oil-related core of industries moved to Houston. Oil tool and supply companies for onshore and offshore production also helped create a broader oil-related complex of businesses. During the 1960s and 1970s, additional technical work of the industry came to the region, with growing oil and gas research centers, specialized legal and financial services, growing training in engineering both in the companies and the region's universities, and management centers. The city hummed with activity and optimism in this era, as the oil boom sparked by dramatically higher prices for oil in global markets seemed destined to go forward for decades. The bubble burst in the mid-1980s when a sharp drop in oil prices devastated the region's oil-driven economy. The lesson was clear. Despite the complexity and depth of the oil-related core of industries and its past success in generating jobs, the regional economy remained vulnerable to sharp changes in the oil and natural gas industries. Concerned about this vulnerability, Houston's business and civic leaders acknowledged the need to diversify the regional economy.[31]

Much of the "new, non-oil economy" that emerged in Houston after the bust of the 1980s had indirect ties to the oil industry. For example, the building of the Johnson Space Center in 1962 in nearby Clear Lake was orchestrated by an alliance of George Brown of Brown & Root, the president of Humble Oil, and Vice President Lyndon Johnson. In 1925, oilman and philanthropist George H. Hermann donated the funds for a charity hospital for Houston's poor. Hermann Hospital was the first medical building in what eventually became the Texas Medical Center (TMC). The trustees of the M. D. Anderson Foundation conceived the idea for the TMC in the early 1940s. The foundation planned the first units to be the University of Texas Hospital for Cancer Research and the Baylor University College of Medicine. In 1944, city-owned property of 134 acres adjacent to Hermann Hospital passed to the foundation after a popular vote authorized the sale in 1943. The Texas Medical Center received the title to the land in 1945. The board of directors of the TMC then sought to attract institutions related to health education, research, and patient care to the new site.[32]

The philanthropic support of many Houstonians who had made their original fortunes in oil fostered the growth of the TMC, which became a major employer in Houston by the 1980s. By 2012, it had more square footage than downtown Houston—the equivalent of the seventh-largest central business district in the United States. Today, the Texas Medical Center is the world's largest medical complex, including twenty-one hospitals, thirteen support organizations, three medical schools, two pharmacy schools, several other academic and research institutions, nursing programs, public health organizations, and a dental school.[33]

Even the real estate development industry that built the Houston suburbs had strong ties to the oil industry. For example, Friendswood Development, a major regional developer that built much of Clear Lake (southeast of Houston) and Kingwood (northeast of the city), originally was affiliated with Exxon and named after one of its important regional oil fields. To the north, the Woodlands grew into a substantial city inspired by the efforts of oilman George Mitchell. The impact on the infrastructure of Houston and the surrounding area was massive and made even more complex by such diversity of economic growth—including new forms of land use and the growing need for expansion of city services.[34]

The oil industry in Houston did not, of course, vanish after the oil price bust in the early 1980s. The oil economy rebounded through the application of new technologies and the consolidation of operations through mergers. Houston benefited from both of these trends. Time after time, the consolidation of companies produced a move of their headquarters to Houston, making the city a net gainer of jobs as the industry shed positions. This was clearest in the 1990s, when changes and cutbacks in offshore production in the Gulf of Mexico led to substantial relocations of employees from New Orleans to Houston. The need for improved technology brought new jobs to the region with the expansion of the many oil-related research laboratories already in the city and with the growth of new research. One symbol of Houston's leadership in technological issues was the massive international Offshore Technology Conference, annually held in the city since 1969.[35] This annual meeting of tens of thousands of visitors from around the world to compare notes on developments in offshore oil is a fitting symbol of the central role of Houston in the global petroleum industry.

Few in the industry argue with the city's status as the generally acknowledged "energy capital of the world," a title justified by its unique concentration of petroleum-related activities and likely to remain apt for as long for as oil and natural gas remain the world's dominant fuels. But it should be noted that the region's standing in global energy has changed significantly in the decades since the 1970s as other regions and nations have asserted a stronger role in the development and management of energy industries.

Two key changes in global energy have altered the current and future standing of Houston. The energy crisis of the 1970s and 1980s led to a wave of nationalizations of Western oil companies and the creation and strengthening of national oil companies in the major producing nations. This change had immediate and far-reaching impacts on the control of oil. In effect, companies with strong historical ties to Houston lost decision-making authority over giant oil reserves in many of the largest oil-producing nations in the world. The second key change in global energy—the emergence of international efforts to understand and manage the impacts of climate change—has long-term implications for Houston's primary industries that could limit their expansion.[36]

Among our six New World cities, Houston is exceptional for its expansive sustained economic growth throughout much of the twentieth century and beyond. In this sense, it has remained a city of opportunity for most of its modern history—opportunity in this sense of job creation and capital accumulation. Many of the world's other energy capitals have lived life cycles of rapid growth, maturity, and decline. An early stage of rapid growth has repeatedly brought a boomtown atmosphere after the introduction of advanced technologies increased the regional production of energy destined for national and international markets. If a region succeeded in absorbing the economic growth generated by energy development, it often enjoyed an extended period of maturity in which the growth of demand for its products encouraged economic expansion. Sooner or later, however, the era of growth gave way to times of decreased demands for the city's energy-related products, leading to a period of economic decline unless the region found the will and the resources to diversify its economy.

Cycles of boom and bust in global oil prices have proven to be some of the most significant social costs of oil-led development. Economies dependent on oil are vulnerable to changes in energy supply and demand beyond their control, especially in the era since the 1970s when a global market for oil brought extreme swings in prices due to new discoveries and geopolitical forces. In some cases, regions have been successful in absorbing new technologies and building economies capable of diversifying in the face of fundamental changes in the energy industries. Why have some regions been able to absorb the technologically advanced processes needed for energy production and some have not? And why have many lived through times of boom and maturity to face difficult eras of decline?

Houston is a revealing focus for such essential analysis. It has grown as the historical and geographical center of a region shaped by oil-led development for more than a century. It has adapted to a recurring cycles of booms and busts in the oil industry by gradually building a more diverse regional economy. To date the region has surmounted extreme dislocations from sharp declines in oil prices during busts in the 1900s, 1920s, 1930s, 1980s, 1990s, and 2010s. Generally, the industry has responded by innovating new technologies to reduce earlier costs and by consolidating through mergers and acquisitions. For its part Houston often has emerged stronger from these busts; it has benefited from many mergers, since the consolidated company frequently has taken this opportunity to move various functions to Houston to place them more firmly in the heart of the activities of the industry. As the oil-related core has grown larger and more diverse with the expansion of natural gas and petrochemicals, the city has made an effort to defend its established global leadership in refining, petrochemical production, and the transportation of natural gas, while developing stronger presences in other industries ranging from medical services to space-related industries to higher education.

Migration, Demographic Change, and Urban Sprawl

Energy production and consumption affected not only Houston's growth patterns and infrastructure but its population as well. A good example was the influence of the burgeoning refining and petrochemical industries on patterns of in-migration and demographic change. These giant plants processed crude oil and natural gas into a variety of products, in the process creating tens of thousands of industrial jobs that attracted generations of workers to the region. The manufacturing jobs in these and other oil-related facilities gave the region a distinctive industrial working-class tone; this was a place where people from the rural hinterland of Texas and Louisiana and Mexico came in search of greater opportunities for themselves and their children.[37] Bringing with them the racial attitudes inherited from the strict and violent segregation practiced in the small-town rural South, they helped make Houston the largest Jim Crow city in the nation by 1950. But despite segregated housing and public services and segregated work forces in the area's refineries and factories, these workers—black and white—also brought the migrants' faith that those who worked hard could create a better future for their families in Houston.

They also brought firsthand knowledge of the hard life on the farm during the agricultural depression of the 1920s and 1930s; factory work was a step up for them. A fundamental optimism that the city held opportunities for those willing to work hard floated in the air of Houston along with the fumes from the refineries. Jobs, not air pollution, remained the primary concern for millions of people who migrated to the region in the twentieth century. While Jim Crow Houston faded after the rise of the civil rights movement, racism did not die completely or uniformly. The city's ghettos and barrios persisted—if not as large, expansive sites, as multiple enclaves throughout the burgeoning metropolitan area. Environmental justice reformers in the predominantly black community of Northwood Manor, for example, fought the placement of a toxic waste facility there beginning in 1979. In other parts of east Houston, several protests arose over neighborhoods threatened by Superfund sites.[38]

While not the only source of Houston's economic growth, oceanic shipping, oil refining, and petrochemical production were central in turning the area's regional markets into national and international ones. As national markets grew, fossil fuels helped expand the size and economic reach of Houston by stimulating the transportation and communication systems that tied ever-larger sections of the nation's hinterlands into its urban-centered economy. The resulting urban growth pushed the effective boundaries of the city out into surrounding areas, creating the standard metropolitan area that now defines urban life there.

From the refining boom on the Houston Ship Channel in the 1920s forward, poor white and black tenant farmers and family farmers from east Texas and western Louisiana flocked from the depressed agricultural conditions in the interior and went to work in the factories along the ship channel in search of improved lives for themselves and their children. They were joined during and after World War II by growing numbers of Mexican nationals and Mexican Americans who also made the journey from rural to urban lives. Cajuns from south Louisiana moved to the urban-industrial centers to the west at about the same time, and many found their way to the industrial jobs in the Houston area.[39]

In the early years, many of these jobs as pipefitters, welders, and common laborers did not require the completion of a high school education, but over time the region also attracted highly educated engineers, accountants, and managers. As time passed, regional universities such as the University of Houston and Rice University came to offer specialized technical degrees in great demand in the oil and petrochemical industries, and graduates—sometimes the children or grandchildren of refinery workers—also found jobs as technicians in the oil-related complex.[40] Individual and family success stories about climbing the economic ladder in the dynamic Houston economy held out hope for intergenerational mobility with a path up into the lower middle class.

Yet, for many years there was not a commensurate change in city leadership—white elites with strong business ties made most of the decisions about Houston's future. Ultimately, ethnic, and to some degree, class politics would influence the city's aspirations and objectives well beyond decades of white elite rule. Segregation would not die easily, as already stated, and even the city's emerging diversity bred multiple—and sometimes conflicting—goals for white, black, and brown Houstonians.[41]

Sustained growth over the course of the mid- to late twentieth century brought a range of challenges. Where would those who flocked to the city live? How would the urban services needed by a growing population be provided? Transportation was a key issue facing the booming region. A prototypical "Sunbelt city," Houston grew with the automobile. With no widespread investment in public transit before the coming of oil in 1901 and the opening of the Houston Ship Channel, the city expanded rapidly just as cars came into general use. It is symbolically fitting that the decade of the city's fastest growth in the twentieth century was the 1920s, when car use took off in the region and around the nation and the ship channel refining complex boomed. In that decade, the first substantial suburbs connected to the central city by jobs and roads were the refinery towns east of the city in the industrial corridor along the ship channel—Pasadena, Galena Park, Baytown, Deer Park, and Texas City.[42]

In subsequent decades, the city expanded in every other direction. Favorable state laws such as the Municipal Annexation Act (1963) allowed the city to aggressively capture adjoining areas and thus further enlarge its territory. By 1999, this generous annexation policy had allowed Houston to reserve approximately 1,289 square miles for future absorption.[43] Land surrounding the city offered living space for the millions of migrants to the region; cheap gasoline provided the fuel needed to commute longer and longer distances; inexpensive electricity produced primarily by abundant and low-cost natural gas allowed for the air conditioning that made the city livable during its long, harsh summers. Local, state, and federal governments responded to the demand of citizens to build more and more roads reaching farther and farther out from the city. Individuals responded by amassing the funds to acquire cars, and, if possible, homes in the suburbs. The city sprawled outward, driven by the relatively inexpensive housing out in working-class suburbs. The region as a whole moved easily and with little public debate toward a "mass transit" strategy of more highways filled by more cars, with one driver per vehicle.[44]

The Houston region grew from a frontier town in the early nineteenth century to a regional center of almost 125,000 in 1900, and finally to an expansive metropolis of more than 5 million in 2005. Urban growth has been a core objective of the city from its modest start spearheaded by John Kirby and Augustus Chapman Allen in 1836 until this day. Shipping, rail, and especially automotive and truck transportation helped push Houston's borders and Houston's influence beyond its initial location along Buffalo Bayou.[45]

The booming new industry and the growing use of the automobile greatly accelerated the city's expansion out into the surrounding countryside in the twentieth century. By the turn of the twenty-first century, "Houston"—as defined by economic and commuting ties, not by political boundaries—had become one of the world's largest cities in area, spanning more than 600 square miles in its political boundaries and perhaps 1,500 square miles that stretched thirty or forty miles from downtown Houston in every direction over a broad area of the Texas Gulf Coast. Much of this area had been farmland in the early twentieth century, but by the year 2000 from Katy to Conroe to Baytown to Galveston to Sugar Land, each exit looked much the same, the homes in each subdivision merged into several generic floor plans, and all roads led into and out of Houston. The city exhibited the worst kind of urban sprawl—pattern-less, unplanned, and highly decentralized. Houston remains the largest city in the United States without zoning, creating both flexibility for developers and uncomfortable combinations of mixed-use areas. In the postwar years, the city had half the population density of Los Angeles and extended into ten counties. For practical, but not political, purposes, this large area reaching out from the central city via a well-developed highway transportation system and jobs increasingly located throughout the region in a series of mini-downtowns became Houston.[46]

MAP 7.1 Houston. Credit: Jose Mario Lopez, School of Architecture,
University of Houston.

Energy and Urban Infrastructure

Over decades of sustained outward urban growth, both energy and environmental costs became embedded in regional transportation systems. Once
infrastructure for the transportation of both goods and people has been
built, change was most difficult, in spite of shifting political calculations of
economic and environmental costs. By the end of the twentieth century,
most people living in a thirty-mile radius of the central city had become

TABLE 7.1 Population of Houston metropolitan statistical area
(Houston-Baytown-Sugarland), 1837–2005

Year	Population	Year	Population
1837	1,500	1930	439,226
1850	14,773	1940	627,311
1860	29,801	1950	908,822
1870	42,962	1960	1,364,569
1880	63,729	1970	1,903,192
1890	76,959	1980	2,753,155
1900	122,785	1990	3,342,247
1910	176,589	2000	4,715,407
1920	256,023	2005	5,280,077

Sources: Proximity One, "Metropolitan Area Characteristics and Trends," http://www
.proximityone.com/metros.htm#top10, "Houston Facts, 2000," Greater Houston Partnership Research Department, http://www.houston.org/tophoustonfacts/houstonfacts
2000; Houston Metropolitan Population and Components of Change, Real Estate Center,
Texas A&M University https://www.recenter.tamu.edu/data/population; David McComb,
"Houston," *Handbook of Texas*, https://tshaonline.org/handbook/online/articles/hdh03.

"Houstonians" who were tied into the economic and cultural life of the city
primarily through a sprawling system of roads and freeways.[47] The specialized transportation system of pipelines, tanker trucks, railroads, barges, and
oceangoing tankers used by the region's petroleum-related core of industries
bound together the region's economy and tied it into national and global
markets.

Cities and regions that reap the long-term economic benefits of energy
production are often physically transformed—or at least modified—by the
burgeoning energy industries and, at times, pay high social and physical
costs, as if they were a sacrifice zone. Demands for water, wastewater systems and solid-waste disposal systems, communication, transportation networks and facilities, and external sources of power (particularly electricity)
put pressure on cities to expand their infrastructure, and in some cases, energy industries compete directly with municipal infrastructure needs.

Houston's growing population needed water, as did its large industrial
complex, and the city sought creative ways to fill both of these needs. The
transformation of Houston's water-supply system from one largely dependent on groundwater to one increasingly reliant on surface water is a good
example of how energy-led industrial development influenced urban infrastructure and urban services.[48] Houston established its first public water-

TABLE 7.2 Area of Houston city limits, 1910–2000

Year	Square Miles	Year	Square Miles
1910	17.4	1960	328.1
1920	36.5	1970	433.9
1930	71.8	1980	556.4
1940	72.8	1990	539.9
1950	160	2000	617

Sources: U.S. Bureau of the Census, "Population of the 100 Largest Urban Places," 1910–90, http://www.census.gov/population/www.documentation /twps0026.html; Houston Facts 2000, Greater Houston Partnership Research Department, http://www.houston.org/tophoustonfacts/houston facts2000.

supply system in 1876. By national standards, the Bayou City's commitment to a centralized water source and distribution network was typical for a city of its age, size, and location. The system, however, was unique in that the city relied on groundwater from countless wells from 1887 until the 1940s.[49] Until it turned to surface water prior to World War II, Houston was the largest city in North America to rely exclusively on well water.

In the nineteenth and early twentieth centuries, Houstonians believed that their source of water was clean and never-ending.[50] Theoretically, the underground supply was abundant for many future generations; realistically, demand on the system increased so rapidly that productive wells were depleted or ceased to be free flowing. Population growth accounted for much of the escalating demand, but agricultural and industrial uses also were important. After the opening of the Houston Ship Channel, pressure on the aquifer from industrial use rose dramatically.[51] The immediate response to growing demand was to sink new wells, to add pumps to existing wells, to build new pumping plants, and to extend distribution lines.[52]

Contentment with the water supply tended to mask structural deficiencies in the system. By the mid-1930s, it was essentially a collection of water plants and distribution mains pieced together by expansion into subdivisions along the fringes of the city and through modest annexation.[53] The challenges to the water system eventually eroded the city's confidence in the groundwater supply. Artesian well pressure had begun to decline as early as 1910, and for several years the water level dropped by an average of five feet annually. With increased industrial pumping along the ship channel for cooling and other purposes the depth to retrieve water increased.

MAP 7.2 Houston area surface water. Credit: Jose Mario Lopez, School of Architecture, University of Houston.

The deterioration of the wells—and the lack of a wholesale rate for water—led many industries and owners of commercial buildings to drill more of their own wells. By 1941, the public supply furnished less than 40 percent of the total demand of the metropolitan area.[54]

The decline in well productivity—and growing independent action of commercial and industrial enterprises—led several experts to view the problem as nearing a critical stage. In the 1930s and early 1940s, almost forty reports on the water supply's condition were written, but they were often contradictory or inconclusive.[55] Alvord, Burdick & Howson, a Chicago engineering firm retained by the city, issued a report in February 1938 that favored the use of the San Jacinto River as a single, inexpensive, and reliable water source.

The San Jacinto was the nearest surface supply with a large drainage area above the ship channel. A reservoir site was available only fifteen miles from the city's industrial district.[56] The study painted a poor picture of the existing water supply system, adding that it "is virtually a group of small town supplies without the distribution facilities or interconnections essential to the delivery of water for either fire or domestic use." In addition, the city's investment in the system was less than one-third that of the average city of its size.[57]

In May 1937—before the Alvord, Burdick & Howson report was made public—the engineering staff recommended filing an application with the State Board of Water Engineers to appropriate water from the San Jacinto River to complement groundwater withdrawal. G. L. Fugate, chief engineer of the water department, pursued the combined well/surface water program into the 1940s, viewing the damming of the San Jacinto as a source principally to supply industrial demand.[58]

The onset of World War II finally pushed Houston toward surface supply. On September 10, 1941, the city filed an application with the Federal Works Administration for financial support to improve the water-supply system and to obtain a supplemental supply from the San Jacinto River. Wartime exigencies directed the federal government's interest in the project to the eastern portion of the city around the ship channel, designated as a "defense area." The industries there would employ an estimated 90,000 workers during the war.[59] In July 1942, the War Production Board authorized the San Jacinto River Conservation and Reclamation District to build a dam and other facilities on the San Jacinto to supply water for war industries along the ship channel and in the Baytown area.[60]

Because of the urgent need for water, the War Production Board declared in August 1942 that the agency best showing the ability to deliver water to industries in the Baytown area would be favored. Neither the city nor the water district would permit a grant to the other, so the federal government announced its intention to construct the facility itself. Ironically, since the city's preliminary plans and surveys were well advanced, the Federal Works Agency adopted Houston's program, and in November 1942, it employed the city as its architect-engineer with Fugate as contract engineer.

Actual construction of the dam began in December 1942 by Brown & Root for delivery of water to industries at Baytown and in the Pasadena area in 1943. Two open canals from the river were constructed to serve the ship channel: the West Canal leading to Pasadena and the East Canal terminating at the Humble Refinery in Baytown. Despite the increase in available supply from the San Jacinto, distribution facilities still did not reach remote sites along the ship channel, and as a result wells served the rising demand from new industries.

In June 1944, Houstonians voted for a $14 million bond issue to increase groundwater supplies and for more mains, and also to buy the West Canal from the federal government, to build another dam across the San Jacinto River, and to construct a filtration plant. Because of the need for additional funding, Lake Houston Dam on the San Jacinto was not in operation until 1954. The new public water supply provided water for the city of Houston and the industrial complex from Houston to Baytown; it also supported irrigation for various crops, including rice.[61]

The debate over water in the 1930s, coupled with the rise of wartime industries along the ship channel, began Houston's transition from a city totally dependent on wells to one dependent on a dual supply, and eventually to primary reliance on surface water. The ability of the new surface supply to save the city from its dependence on shrinking groundwater resources did not grow out of some enlightened city policy. Indeed, the requirements of the refining and petrochemical industries in particular dictated the change. And for a time, the new surface supply benefited industry much more than the city. Without industrial demand for water, Houston's transition to a surface supply may have been much farther in the future than World War II.

Environmental Costs

Economic development has long been a byword of Houston's success as a modern city. However, the most visible social and physical costs of energy-led development have been the concentration of environmental and health risks from refining much of the nation's fossil fuels and producing great quantities of its petrochemicals. Houston and other energy capitals often have been forced to absorb substantial local costs for producing energy sold in national and international markets. The response to such costs has been slow and difficult, in part because investment in the technology of pollution controls lagged behind investment in the technology of energy production.

Only after decades of neglect of mounting problems from oil pollution did the region get more serious about pollution control, and then only after the federal government stepped in to take charge with a wave of stricter air, water, and land use standards. The political and legal processes for negotiating societal solutions to such problems have shaped regional responses to social and physical costs.[62]

Despite the Houston area's capacity to "absorb" the economic benefits of oil industry, using its oil wealth to sustain long-term economic growth, one significant part of the "curse of oil-led development" proved most difficult: the management of the environmental impacts of the production and use of petroleum and other commercial and industrial development. The sustained expansion of a massive oil-related complex of industries gave Houston a unique identity within the national economy while also creating distinctive levels and forms of air, water, and ground pollution. Because petroleum was both the major industry and the major fuel for modern Houston, it has been the de facto "oil pollution capital of America."[63] In December 2012, *Forbes* ranked Houston thirteenth among America's twenty dirtiest cities. It stated that the oil refineries and chemical plants along the Houston Ship Channel discharged more than 20 million pounds of toxic materials each year into the air of the greater Houston metropolitan region. Because of its dependence on automobiles, trucks, and buses for transportation (and because of temperature inversions), Houston ranked eighth in ozone and twenty-third in annual particle pollution.[64]

Although the strong and complex connections between energy use, urban growth, and environmental issues are intuitively obvious, they are rarely analyzed. Houston may serve as an exemplary case.[65] Cars commuting around the rambling city, trucks delivering innumerable goods, and buses transporting locals combined with the refineries and petrochemical plants produced serious air and water pollution. Adding to the city's environmental woes, it is susceptible to severe weather conditions such as tornadoes and hurricanes, "heat island" effects, and a propensity to flood often and intensely. Volumes of water exacerbate nonpoint pollution problems as all kinds of toxic materials—from lawn fertilizers to heavy metals—run into the city's extensive network of bayous draining the city and ultimately spill into the Gulf of Mexico. Severe pollution problems arose from the transportation of the millions of barrels of crude oil and refined products per day that flowed through these plants on their way through the global oil economy. In this sense, the Houston region served not only as the nation's refining center but also as one of the national economy's primary dumping grounds for oil and petrochemical-related forms of pollution.[66] Altogether, the region suffered the triple dilemma of dealing simultaneously with mounting oil-related pollution from both the exhausts of gasoline-powered automobiles, the production of oil and chemical products from local plants, and myriad urban pollutants.[67]

Oil, Politics, and Pollution

Efforts to find a politically acceptable balance between the costs and benefits of petroleum processing and petroleum pollution proved challenging. For much of the region's history a broadly shared societal consensus that included a majority of the population, rich and poor, favored oil development largely unrestrained by pollution controls. "Opportunity" and "economic growth" were the twin tenets of the local religion of "boosterism," and the church did not have much tolerance for doubters who voiced concerns about the quality of life.

Those who called for stricter controls of pollution had to overcome more than regional attitudes favoring growth. Politics and civic leadership were dominated by businessmen and businesswomen whose idea of a "healthy business climate" included low taxes, weak unions, and very limited regulation. Scholars have provided the useful label "free enterprise city" to describe the dominance of Houston's political and civic cultures by conservative businessmen.[68] Granted such business power is hardly unique among cities in capitalist America, and further granted that much of the power and the behavior of the local elite can be explained with reference to their commitment to segregation as easily as to their dedication to free enterprise, the fact remains that business and civic leaders in Houston historically represented a strong and consistent barrier to the passage and enforcement of effective pollution controls.

Political realities also included the entrenched power in the governance process at the state and federal levels of the well-organized interests of the major industries that produced the bulk of the region's industrial pollution. Private corporations strong in the global energy economy made many of the basic decisions about Houston's oil-related development. In Houston, as around the world, price dictated the key decisions on energy use and, to an extent, the approach to pollution control. But the political process played pivotal roles in channeling government promotion of energy businesses and blocking government regulation. The economic importance of oil in the state of Texas and in the city of Houston, in particular, skewed political decisions toward policies that promoted the oil industry and away from policies that constrained it. This was true at least until the federal government preempted much of the traditional authority of states over pollution control after the 1960s. The state's one-party political system through the 1960s also proved to be a barrier to change, as those who defended Jim Crow had strong incentives to support the "states' rights" arguments of those who fought against federal government involvement in pollution control.[69]

An important part of the economic/environmental history of the region has been the ongoing efforts by some to create more effective pollution controls while also encouraging continued economic growth. Only recently have segments of the American public—including some civic leaders and grassroots organizations in Houston—recognized that high levels of pollution were not only a threat to public health and the quality of life but also can become a barrier to economic growth and the creation of jobs in the region and the nation. For most of Houston's history—in politics and in practice—there was little effort to balance energy and environmental needs, since pollution control was treated as distinctly secondary to economic growth. Yet, there are at least tentative signs in recent years that a new balance, with greater concern for environmental quality, is politically possible. Although far from a comprehensive solution, the creation of the Bureau of Pollution Control and Prevention in 2010 was a sign of change at least in public awareness of a variety of environmental problems that the city faced. The bureau is located within the Environmental Health Division of the Houston Department of Health and Human Services. Previously called the Bureau of Air Quality Control, it underwent organizational changes leading to the integration of several environmental programs.[70] A variety of nongovernmental environmental organizations also have spearheaded change over the years, many under the banner of the Citizens' Environmental Coalition.[71]

Beyond Oil Growth and Environmental Challenges: Medical Houston

While business and political leaders promoted the oil and energy industries and worked to limit environmental regulations, and working people negotiated to hold good jobs, deal with desegregation, and keep pollution at bay—Houston saw the rise of a new industry that flourished at the intersection of its prosperity and its challenges. While there is no evidence that it was planned for such reasons, the rise of a major medical industry could tap the wealth of energy development and provide solutions to the health challenges linked—or not—to the city's little-regulated pollution. By the 1960s, Houston's hospitals were famed as centers of cardiac and cancer care. Multiple medical schools trained new generations of professionals. Not only did the people of Houston have access to cutting-edge medical services, people with resources came from across the Americas and the world to seek its famed benefits.

In the process, medical care became Houston's second major industry and a leading source of professional and service employment for its growing population. Houston weathered the energy downturn of the 1970s and 1980s in good part thanks to the steady growth of medical services and related employments. It is important to remember that if Houston's rise to metropolitan eminence was led by the energy sector, its endurance depended in important ways on the dynamic success of its second industry—medicine—and the related economic and service activities in spawned and sustains.

Oil and Cultural Change

"Traditions, customs, beliefs, and folklife" define a sense of place, and the area along Buffalo Bayou and the Houston Ship Channel has distinctive values that reflect its history.[72] As the birthplace of Texas independence from Mexico and as a region that contributed greatly to the military efforts of the United States in World War I and World War II, this area wears patriotic pride on its sleeve. Although to outsiders, this sense of patriotism often appears to be conservative and exclusive, a closer look at the region's history shows a strong commitment to economic opportunity for people from all walks of life. This is a working-class region filled with people who came in search of better futures for themselves and their children; it contains a population that has grown increasingly diverse over time. A key element of the region has been the coming together of people from different backgrounds and places in the workplaces, schools, and towns along the ship channel into a diverse society gradually producing a distinctive culture.

Migration created a very diverse population both within the industries on the ship channel and in Houston as a whole. Over the years people came from everywhere—adjacent states, Mexico, Central America, the Caribbean, Europe, Asia, Africa, and the Middle East. Because of the obsession with issues of black and white in Jim Crow Houston, until at least the 1960s questions of race and ethnicity neglected the status of other groups in the region. Mexican Americans, Cajuns, and the region's steadily growing Asian population were considered white in terms of voting rights, schools, and civil rights and non-black in social status.[73]

In recent years, racial and ethnic diversity has increased. Based on data from 2008 to 2012, 28.31 percent of Houstonians were foreign born. Of those, 20.51 percent were born in Latin America, 5.34 percent in Asia, 1.11 percent in Europe, 1.08 percent in Africa, 0.19 percent in North America, and 0.07 percent in Oceania.[74] Another trend is the dramatic reduction in the percentage of the white population and the historic increase in Latinos. In 1980, the white population stood at about 52 percent; in 2010 it was only 26 percent. Black or African American population also declined from about 27 percent to 23 percent. Latino population surged from about 18 percent to almost 44 percent. Asians grew moderately from 0.02 percent to 0.06 percent.[75] The figures reflect changes in the city's municipal core, not the extended metropolitan region. In a major recent demographic shift, white Houston has suburbanized; the core city remains diverse while becoming Latin American in ways reminiscent of Los Angeles.

In the industrial workplaces along the ship channel until the late 1960s, most jobs were designated as black or white. The major refineries, for example, had all-black labor gangs; this meant that blacks who came to work were laborers forever, while non-blacks moved into more skilled positions such as electricians, pipe-fitters, and machinists. When independent unions were established in the 1930s and 1940s, there were separate black and white unions. The largely successful campaign to unionize the manufacturing plants on the HSC marked one great social movement in the region; efforts to desegregate these factories marked another. The two movements were often at odds with each other, and the playing out of the societal dramas of both the coming of unions and desegregation in the workplace are important parts of the history of the Houston Ship Channel area in particular.[76]

Desegregation did not mean integration; the presence of a diverse workforce did not guarantee that different groups would come to share similar values and cultures. But the creation of a regional culture that embraced many aspects of diversity while enabling different groups to retain much of their distinctiveness went forward on numerous fronts in the region. The first of these was in the workplace and in the union halls, where workers from different backgrounds forged common bonds. Most of those who worked in the refineries, the petrochemical plants, and other factories along the ship channel shared one common characteristic: they had been attracted to the region by the promise of steady work with decent wages and benefits and job security.

In the boom years after World War I, the major oil companies along the ship channel avoided the growth of independent unions through different variants of what historians have called "the American Plan," which used the improvement of working conditions and the creation of company-dominated workers' organizations to block the growth of independent unions. In the 1920s in new refinery towns such as Baytown, this meant housing built by the companies for their workers, medical care provided inside the refineries for workers and their families, and a variety of sponsored activities such as sports leagues, Christmas parties, and hunting and fishing "camps" owned by the companies and made available to their workers.[77]

In the 1930s and afterward, the company unions gradually disappeared in most of the refineries, as workers organized to secure wages and benefits through the collective action by their unions and through organized voting campaigns in what passed for the progressive wing of the Democratic Party, which dominated Texas politics into the 1970s. Long nights spent working and talking and eating on the graveyard shift created unity, as did the shared experiences of long, hard strikes and occasional success in electing pro-labor politicians such as Senator Ralph Yarborough (Dem.) and local mayors and sheriffs.[78]

The union hall became a meeting ground outside of the factories, and participation in union activities reminded individuals within this diverse workforce of their common economic bonds. Labor Day parades and related festivities produced a shared sense of pride. The success of the Oil Chemical and Atomic Workers (OCAW) made the towns along the ship channel centers of union activity in a region and a state where unions previously had little presence.[79]

More significant in forging a common social identity among workers' families were the local schools. Refinery towns such as Pasadena, Galena Park, Deer Park, Baytown, and Texas City sprang up along the ship channel in the 1920s and 1930s. These were among the first suburbs of Houston, and they were shaped by the presence of the plants in the region. Baytown, one of the first new towns to emerge after the opening of the ship channel, was founded in the early 1920s as a company town for workers at the new Humble Oil (now ExxonMobil) refinery.[80] Baytown and most of the other refinery towns were independent cities with their own school districts, and the refineries and chemical plants gave them a distinctive student body and an unusual form of financing that provided resources to create good schools. Diversity in the workplace was reflected in diversity in the classrooms, especially after the desegregation of most of these school districts in the 1960s. In lieu of high property taxes, the refineries generally negotiated direct payments to the schools, thus avoiding annexation to Houston. Payments were often substantial; many companies also became partners with the school districts in supplying equipment such as computers and providing volunteers. The educational and social life of the schools created a common ground for the families of those who worked along the ship channel.[81]

Educational programs were obviously a big part of the common experience of students and their families, but during and after the civil rights movement, conflict in the schools also became a part of school life. The desegregation of the Jim Crow school systems throughout the region brought anger and confusion along with legal and political struggles over approaches to desegregation. At the same time, tensions grew in predominantly Latino schools over the issues raised by bilingual education. Confrontations over these issues defined an era of chaotic change in public schools from elementary schools to college campuses.[82]

Extracurricular activities played a role in building a measure of community amid this chaos. Foremost among such activities in the lives of the refinery towns were sports, especially high school football. Even by the standards of football-crazy Texas, the refinery towns closed ranks with uncommon passion for Friday night football. The teams on the field—as well as the members of the bands and drill teams—became an expression of the unity of the diverse collections of families and students on the field and in the stands. Football and other high school sports gave players the experience of working for a common goal with classmates from a variety of backgrounds. When it all came together, particularly when the local high school made a run deep into the state playoffs in December, entire communities forged common bonds through the high school football team, in a sense establishing a new, shared cultural tradition. When Texas finally desegregated competitions in the 1960s, it created single state championships in high school sports to replace the tradition of separate black and white championships. The coming of desegregation in high school sports—and in high school student bodies—was an important, highly visible, and eventually unifying part of the contested process of desegregation.[83]

The diverse cultural traditions that the various groups of migrants brought to the region did not, of course, disappear. Some basic differences in the refinery towns remained quite visible. The French-based Cajun dialect and the Spanish language of Latino migrants gave these groups a distinctive "cultural marker"—at least as long as children and grandchildren continued to speak these languages. The Catholic religion embraced by many Cajuns and Latinos remained at odds with the Protestant traditions shared by many of the white and black migrants from the South. In language and religion, the members of the various groups at times kept their distance.[84]

But in two other areas, food and music, traditions fused to give the region distinctive new hybrids. Food from the various migrant groups quickly spread to others; it could be smelled and tasted, and it was good. Country boys, black and white, brought foods ranging from barbeque to fried chicken to chicken-fried steaks. Mexican foods found a new expression in the Tex-Mex dishes that could be found in the refinery towns and later all over the Houston region. Cajuns created new variations on the old theme of fried shrimp and blackened fish, in the process creating a distinctive Gulf Coast version of a variety of seafood dishes. These "working-class" foods became an important part of Houston's culinary identity; even after the oil boom of the 1970s brought new Asian and Italian foods and restaurants to the region, they remained dependable staples of the diets of Houstonians.

The fusion of the different cultural traditions represented in the refineries created a rich regional music that gives new life to the often debunked notion that America was a melting pot for new immigrants. It was in the case of music in the Houston Ship Channel area. Over time, music with roots in rural life in the interior of Texas and Louisiana, Mexico, and south Louisiana merged to create several distinctive strains of urban music. Cajun music burst onto the scene in Houston during World War II, and Houston record companies produced several of the records by artists such as Clifton Chenier; they became classics of a new form of Cajun music influenced by western swing bands such as Bob Wills and the Texas Playboys. From the Creole tradition of Louisiana, Cajun and Creole migrants created in Houston a new sound known as Zydeco.[85]

White rural southerners brought to Houston the country ballads of the Scots-Irish tradition, but they also helped create the harder-driving honky-tonk variant of country music, which thrived in the night spots along the ship channel, including Gilley's, the bar made famous by the movie *Urban Cowboy* (1980). The most prominent regional embodiment of the varied traditions of country and honky-tonk was the music of George Jones, who grew up near Beaumont but regularly performed in the region. Houstonian

Rodney Crowell, who grew up in the refinery town of South Houston, continued the tradition.[86] Rural blacks brought the region the traditional country blues sounds of artists such as Huddie Ledbetter and Lightnin' Hopkins; they also helped create the new rhythm and blues as played by artists such as Bobby Blue Bland, laying bricks for the foundation of rock and roll and, later, hip-hop.[87] Over time, a fine tradition of Tex-Mex music also developed in the region. Few American regions have a musical heritage as rich and varied as the Gulf Coast from New Orleans to Houston. The migrants along the ship channel—and in the region as a whole—listened to, supported, and sang and danced to music that reflected the influence of elements from a variety of musical traditions.[88]

This music and the clubs where it was performed came to symbolize Houston as a working-class city where people worked and played hard. The culture of the ship channel did not, however, neglect key parts of the rural tradition of the migrants who came to work in the industrial plants. A shared remnant of the rural roots of many white, black, Latino, and Cajun migrants was a passion for hunting and fishing. Those who worked hard in industrial plants saw good reasons for going "home" to the farming towns, where they could take to the woods and lakes and return to their country-boy roots for a time. Such trips highlighted the ever-stronger pull of the industrial coast as deteriorating conditions in the interior continued to push many of the few remaining farmers off the land. Communities that once supported family farms became dependent on jobs that serve hunters and fishermen who grew up in the interior and moved to the coast; they also provide an inexpensive option for displaced country boys to retire.

By the last decades of the twentieth century, the pace of migration to the Houston Ship Channel area slowed, as automation took a toll on the number and quality of factory jobs. During the middle of the century, Labor Day parades and festivities celebrating the important role of workers in the American economy drew good crowds in the region. In more recent times, Houston has held well-organized celebrations of Cinco de Mayo and Martin Luther King Day to mark an important Mexican historic event and an important African American life, affirming the important place of Mexican Americans and African Americans in the region's history. Cultural impacts of all types—not to mention a glorious variety of food, and the influence of hip-hop and Tejano music—have exploded locally.

Although oil was a pervasive force in the region's economy, a variety of forces shaped its culture, including the rural roots of many of the migrants to the Houston area and the racial mores of the southern United

States as a whole. Oil provided many of the jobs that drew a diverse working class to the region, tossed them together in the refineries and the schools, and produced a new mix of music, food, and entertainment. The working-class foundation of the region's culture began to change after the 1960s, when automation in the refineries greatly reduced the number of industrial jobs and the enlargement of white-collar professionals from inside and outside the region began to move the city toward a more metropolitan culture.[89]

The decline of industrial employment and the rise of new racial and ethnic diversity in the city gradually altered local politics and culture, and no doubt will continue to do so in the future. The growing numbers of Latinos, mostly of Mexican and Central American origins, and the declining numbers of whites and African Americans promise to reshape regional politics, while the energy industries will continue to rule Houston's economic life. What this means for the destiny of an energy capital shaped by work, culture, and politics long defined by tensions between white and black of traditional Jim Crow society remains to be seen.

Oil Capital of the Americas

As the Houston metropolis area absorbed broad areas on the city's periphery and increasingly diverse migrant populations, a specialized oil, natural gas, and petrochemical-related infrastructure reached out to build a larger economically important region that stretched from the Houston Ship Channel to New Orleans. Sharing similar technologies and markets and a specialized transportation system, this large area with a giant complex of oil-related production, refining, and manufacturing held a specialized role in the national and global economy that was generally fruitful for the region and powerfully beneficial to Houston.

Houston's role as "Oil Capital of the Americas" illustrates its importance in the world. Companies and experts with strong ties to the Houston region played important, evolving roles in the development of oil in Mexico and Venezuela. The oil industries in Texas and Mexico emerged at the same time around 1900. The Texas industry, centered in Houston, absorbed much of the capital generated by "foreign" investment (that is, from the financial centers in the U.S. East Coast) and quickly developed a local oil elite that owned substantial amounts of the region's oil-related businesses. Several major international oil companies had roots in Houston and its region; most had major offices and research centers.

In contrast, from the 1900s forward the development of Mexico's Golden Lane oil boom centered around the city of Tampico. Foreigners, many representing Houston-area interests, quickly dominated the business. Much less of the profit generated by outsiders' investment stayed in the Tampico regions, and fewer people from the region—or elsewhere in Mexico—gained leading positions in the development of its industry. Oil production from the Golden Lane rose rapidly beginning in 1913—while war in Europe stimulated demand and revolutionary conflicts in Mexico threatened destruction or expropriation. Production survived to reach a peak in the postwar years, but not surprisingly the foreign companies that dominated the fields expanded their plants on the U.S. Gulf Coast to refine Mexican output, avoiding large permanent investments in the Tampico region. After decades of tense negotiations in which postrevolutionary needs for energy and revenues crossed revolutionary aspirations for sovereign control, when production began to decline in the 1930s, the Mexican government nationalized the foreign concerns in 1938, banning them from future participation in Mexican oil fields, refining, and distribution. It is little noted, however, that PEMEX, the Mexican national oil company, continued to maintain strong ties with specialized financial, legal, and oil tool and service companies in the United States, many based in Houston.[90] Having lost direct control, Houston firms used their financial and technical advantages to continue to facilitate and profit from Mexican national petroleum and petrochemical production.

The Venezuelan experience began in much the same way but evolved in a different direction. As in Mexico, foreign companies ruled early Venezuelan oil development; they left little permanent mark on the nation's economy other than the enrichment of a small elite of political and business allies. Spurred on by the emergence of an opposition political party in Venezuela and the example of Mexican nationalization, in the 1930s Venezuelan authorities began to demand and receive higher prices for crude oil. Knowing that a labor conflict had been the final stimulus to Mexico's nationalization, the foreign companies took more seriously the need to improve life for their Venezuelan workers, including better wages and working conditions and technical training. Here again, companies with strong ties to the Houston region managed much of this process of change; they gradually became more comfortable making major permanent investments in refineries in Venezuela.[91]

When nationalization came in 1976, these Houston-based concerns remained indirectly involved in the development of PDVSA, Venezuela's

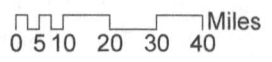

MAP 7.3 Houston area energy infrastructure. Credit: Jose Mario Lopez, School of Architecture, University of Houston.

— Crude Oil, HGL, and Other Petroleum
Product Pipelines

● Oil Refineries

0 5 10   20   30   40 Miles

MAP 7.4 Houston area pipelines. Credit: Jose Mario Lopez, School of Architecture, University of Houston.

major national oil company; they were invited back into the country in the 1990s. Throughout the last half of the twentieth century, the technical expertise needed to build and operate run the modern petroleum industry in Venezuela and elsewhere became widely dispersed, creating a technical "brotherhood" that transcended geographical boundaries. In 2002, the managers and technical leaders of PDVSA faced off against President Hugo Chávez: he demanded a turn to a "socialist" orientation that would take revenues in the near term but make long-run viability uncertain; they insisted that their professional engineering and technical values rule the nation's energy sector. Chávez ended the political showdown by firing thousands of PDVSA workers.[92] Many of the fired workers soon relocated to Houston and Calgary.

In Mexico and Venezuela, as across much of the world, oil production began financed and controlled by companies based primarily in the U.S. and Europe. As production, profits, and revenues rose, nationalisms—whether revolutionary as in Mexico or populist as in Venezuela—rose to demand local sovereign control. A long struggle ensued, often framed as pitting international capital against resource producing nations, yet financial and especially engineering and technical capacity remained focused in and near Houston. A stark symbol of the recognition of the centrality of the global energy capital was the purchase of Houston-area refining plants by both PEMEX and PDVSA. They recognized the need to utilize Houston technology to access U.S. markets while continuing to seek independence from foreign control in their own nations. Houston with its well-developed array of oil-related industries and services has benefited from all stages of the development of oil across the Americas. The Houston region remains at the center of a growing web of technical knowledge and specialized services for the global oil industry, even as national political struggles over the control of oil in an increasingly global industry have created competing centers of control and expertise around the world.

The Formal and Informal in Houston

As an economically pivotal and notably prosperous city of the Global North, Houston rarely receives attention from the vantage point of the formality/ informality construct—key themes in various essays in this study of New World cities. Still, Houston's twentieth-century rise remains marked by contradictions that in complex ways reveal that formality and informality—

even legality and illegality—are challenges in cities of prosperity as well as in cities marked by greater poverty and marginality.

One key contradiction shaped this study: the promotion of the energy businesses that shaped Houston's prosperity and global importance came largely though formal activities made legal by government policy. Generous tax breaks granted by the federal government to the oil industry in the 1920s and again in the early 1950s and justified as necessary for national security proved long-lived and financially important for the oil companies, as did quotas on imported oil. The same general observation applies to the long history of Jim Crow-style segregation in the region: state and local laws provided the formal framework for legally sanctioned segregation that also was supported also by the informal traditions of racism and lynching and other forms of violence in support of these laws.

Growing oil pollution long flourished as an accepted informality, as government agencies with potential authority to impose stricter standards looked the other way for decades as the oil companies practiced a form of self-regulation that addressed the most visible forms of pollution while allowing the broader problems to grow. The environment and many citizens paid a price, but until the passage of much stronger federal and state environmental standards and the creation of more powerful environmental regulatory agencies in recent decades, there was little legal sanction. Now that much long-accepted pollution has become illegal, we can only wonder how much continues informally, thus illegally.

Houston's history is also grounded on key political relationships driving urban growth, primarily as they relate to public/private approaches to decision making. In some respects, the moniker of "Free Enterprise City" suggests the central role of private-sector action vividly observed in the historic role of private elites in managing the city's affairs. Although "formal" easily equates with "governmental," "private" does not necessarily mean "informal." Much of Houston's physical growth occurred as a result of fusing public and private interests, making it little different from most large North American cities. Yet the so-called 8F crowd who met regularly in Houston in the mid-twentieth century was composed of political and economic leaders who by and large did not hold municipal office, but helped direct the future of the city for decades. The pro-business climate of Houston gave substantial license to promote the economic development of key industries without imposing serious restrictions. The Houston Chamber of Commerce—and later the Greater Houston Partnership—also wielded great influence over the planning of the city. Did such relationships among the powerful move beyond formality and perhaps create enduring informal ways of asserting power? Certainly. But the more confounding question, and one needing to be explored more fully, is whether such action operated within a recognizably legal setting or not. We can only speculate whether the massive demographic changes taking place in the Bayou City as Mexicans and other Latinos approach majority status will unravel the semiformal elitist approach to government—or replace it with similar variant, perhaps by inviting key Latino leaders into the semiformal halls of power. And what changes to the community's labor force and its very culture have been shaped by undocumented immigrants has yet to be fully studied.

Meanwhile, as the twentieth century ended and Houston held its advantageous position in the world economy, it began to face in at least limited ways some of the key challenges lived in other, less fortunate New World cities. The economy boomed, but new technologies limited the steady industrial employment that had earlier drawn so many to the region. The economy shifted toward a service orientation ranging from technical and engineering specialties, through medical care and education, to burgeoning retail and household service sectors. Much prosperity remained, but a population that increased by nearly 2 million from 1990 to 2005 created inevitable challenges—often gaps that were filled in part by the informalities of diverse ways of self-employment, and too often by the illegalities of gangs, drug cartels, and various criminal elements that operated widely in the city (as elsewhere). Houston, with its prosperity, has not been immune to the challenges of late-twentieth-century urbanization—not to crime, not to congestion and air pollution, not to calamitous flooding, not to economic and social inequality among its citizens.

The establishment of myriad ethnic and racial enclaves in the largest city in North America without zoning laws raises questions about the effective hold of municipal authority on Houston and Houstonians. In his study *Metropolitan Migrants*, Rubén Hernández-León explores the migration of workers from Monterrey, Mexico, to Houston since the 1990s. His close analysis details how Houston remains favored, even as it shares challenges with other struggling cities. Most notably, Houston has become the favored destination of migrants from Monterrey—Mexico's most technologically advanced industrial city. When NAFTA undermined much production there, the most educated and skilled of workers headed to Houston, where they often found work in the energy and medical industries. Yet their migration remained illegal and thus had to proceed through informal channels. Migration networks are well known—historically facilitating relocations across the globe. Hernández León found that in the Monterrey to Houston exodus, "migration entrepreneurs"—recruiters, smugglers, and couriers— came to the fore. They often began to operate at the intersection of illegality and informality, but many developed businesses that came out of the shadows to operate publically and largely legally. "Combined," he states, "migrant networks and migration entrepreneurs have successfully channeled *regiomontanos* (Monterrey skilled workers) to Houston, a global city for the oil industry with an increasingly diversified economy, where these Mexican urbanites have formed settlements and occupational niches."[93] Hernández León raises questions worth exploring for Houston. To what extent do networks of informality and illegality constitute activities central to the city's evolving economy? Are such networks a brief episode reflecting the fall of Monterrey and the growth of Houston? Will they continue to evolve into formal businesses and perhaps reinforce Houston's prosperity? How will new migrants and new entrepreneurs emerging from informality influence future generations of local politics and social life?

Houston the energy capital and Houston the bastion of free enterprise might be closer to cities in the developing world than we think. What some see as corruption of the political system with the rise of 8F or the role of the chamber of commerce, others view as elite noblesse oblige. What some see as an illegal immigrant invasion, others see as skilled and entrepreneurial newcomers seeking chances in the opportunity city. With such disparities of vision, it may be useful to explore more deeply to what degree public/ private associations and interactions might be better understood in the context of formalities and informalities, legalities and illegalities. Raising such questions will lead to interesting conclusions.

Conclusions

Houston's ability to reap long-term economic benefits from oil-led development and then successfully bring a measure of diversity to its economy after the oil bust of the 1980s make it a symbol that a major city can be built on a foundation of oil. Due to good luck in the timing and location of the first major oil discoveries on the upper Texas-Louisiana Gulf Coast and the growing size and complexity of the oil-related core over time, the region became a city of job opportunity for generations of migrants who came in search of better lives for themselves and their children.

Such opportunities came with a high environmental price—including considerable and as yet not fully understood health costs—and an array of urban problems. However in many cases, they also involved trading rural poverty for a lower-middle-class home in Houston's sprawling suburbs, a trade easily criticized by those who have never lived a life of squalor. In the Houston area, the migrants found for their children far superior schools than those in the hinterland, and they also found greater options in almost all parts of their lives. All in all, Houston's ascent as first a regional center of oil production and refining, then a national oil and natural gas capital, and finally the self-proclaimed energy capital of the world, has helped shape the evolution of a large section of the city and its hinterland. While far from perfect in the eyes of many who live in older, more mature cities, Houston remains a dynamic place where people still come for opportunity and still may find it—often in an oil-related job.

This judgment has been called into question in recent years by two factors: the cycle of boom and bust in the shale oil and gas industry that seemed to promise resurgence of the U.S. oil industry in the global economy, and the rising concern about climate change and the widely recognized need to reduce the emissions of greenhouse gases such as carbon dioxide and methane from the burning of fossil fuels. The recent signs of recovery by the U.S. shale oil and gas industries with the gradual rise in oil prices suggests that the Houston economy might rebound and remain an important contributor of oil and gas for the national economy for decades into the future. No such "quick fix" seems likely for the long-term dilemma presented by global warming, which poses very difficult dilemmas for a regional economy long focused on oil and natural gas. Houston has meant opportunity for many people—essentially in the form of job opportunity for some and capital accumulation for others. All urban problems are not resolved by jobs alone, however, and thus the ultimate measure of Houston's success as a twenty-first century city will depend on how able its leaders and citizens will be in harnessing the best of its past in the face of a challenging future.

Epilogue: An Unwelcome Visit from Harvey

Despite its history of economic vibrancy, Hurricane Harvey—possibly more than any of Houston's "natural" disasters—exposed some of the Bayou City's most serious liabilities. Semi-tropical East Texas has experienced hurricanes, tornadoes, and heavy rains for generations, and thus weather has been a central player in its history. Houston's rampant growth led to a topography heavily laden with concrete and asphalt—a perfect terrain for rapid and fierce runoff. Real estate development with only modest public and private attention to developing safeguards in a massive flood-prone region added to potential risks.

In 2015, 2016, and 2017, Houston experienced three 500-year floods in succession, most likely exacerbated by climate change. On August 25, 2017, the city was hit by a Category 4 storm, Hurricane Harvey, that despite is apparently less-than-ominous name took the lives of 88 people and caused billions of dollars in damages. Ultimately that storm affected 13 million people in Texas, Louisiana, Mississippi, Tennessee, and Kentucky. Harvey made landfall three times in six days, and at its peak (September 1, 2017) put about one-third of Houston under water. In some spots, neighborhoods experienced more than 50 inches of rain. Hurricane Harvey damaged 203,000 homes, 12,700 of which were destroyed. The scale of this "rain event" was of a kind almost too vast to comprehend.[94]

In characteristic fashion, the people of Houston showed remarkable resilience in the face of an almost unfathomable catastrophe. Despite the city-wide resolve, people were left wondering if this could happen again and what steps would be necessary to combat it. Could the can-do attitude that made Houston an opportunity city push back against its vulnerabilities?

Notes

1. William Cronon, *Nature's Metropolis: Chicago and the Great West* (New York: Norton, 1991); Kathleen Brosnan, *Uniting Mountain and Plain: Cities, Law, and Environmental Change Along the Front Range* (Albuquerque: University of New Mexico Press, 2002).

2. The following are examples of useful energy histories relevant to the study of energy capitals: Ibrahim M. Al-But'hie and Mohammad A. Eben Saleh', "Urban and Industrial Development Planning as an Approach for Saudi Arabia: The Case Study of Jubail and Yanbu," *Habitat International* 26 (January 2002): 1–20; Saud Al-Oteibi, Allen G. Noble, and Frank J. Costa, "The Impact of Planning on Growth and Development in Riyadh, Saudi Arabia, 1970–1990," *GeoJournal* 29 (February 1993): 163–170; William Beaver, *Nuclear Power Goes on-Line: A History of Shippingport* (Westport, CT: Greenwood Press, 1990); Henry F. Bedford, *Seabrook Station: Citizen Politics and Nuclear Power* (Amherst: University of Massachusetts Press, 1990); Rómulo Betancourt, *Venezuela: Oil and Politics* (Boston: Houghton Mifflin, 1979); Brian Black, *Petrolia: The Landscape of America's First Oil Boom* (Baltimore: Johns Hopkins University Press, 2000); Howard I. Blutstein, *Venezuela: Politics in a Petroleum Republic* (New York: Praeger, 1984); Jonathan Brown, *Oil and Revolution in Mexico* (Berkeley: University of California Press, 1993); Craig E. Colten, ed., *Transforming*

New Orleans and Its Environs (Pittsburgh: University of Pittsburgh Press, 2000); Michele Stenehjem Gerber, *On the Home Front: The Cold War Legacy of the Hanford Nuclear Site* (Lincoln: University of Nebraska Press, 2002); Mustapha Ben Hamouche, "The Changing Morphology of the Gulf Cities in the Age of Globalisation: The Case of Bahrain." *Habitat International* 28 (December 2004): 521–540; Tony Hodges, *Angola: Anatomy of an Oil State* (Bloomington: Indiana University Press, 2004); Augustine A. Ikein, *The Impact of Oil on a Developing Country: The Case of Nigeria* (New York: Praeger, 1990); Pauline Jones Luong and Erika Weinthal, "Prelude to the Resource Curse: Explaining Oil and Gas Development Strategies in the Soviet Successor States and Beyond," *Comparative Political Studies* 34, no. 4 (2001): 367–399; Paul Sabin, *Crude Politics: The California Oil Market, 1900–1940* (Berkeley: University of California Press, 2004); Jorge Salazar-Carrillo and Bernadette West, *Oil and Development in Venezuela During the 20th Century* (Westport, CT: Praeger, 2004); Myrna I. Santiago, *The Ecology of Oil: Environment, Labor, and the Mexican Revolution, 1900–1938* (Cambridge: Cambridge University Press, 2006); Lee Scamehorn, *High Altitude Energy: A History of Fossil Fuels in Colorado* (Boulder: University of Colorado Press, 2002); Joel A. Tarr, ed., *Devastation and Renewal: An Environmental History of Pittsburgh and Its Region* (Pittsburgh: University of Pittsburgh Press, 2003); Robert Vitalis, *America's Kingdom: Mythmaking on the Saudi Oil Frontier* (Stanford: Stanford University Press, 2007); James C. Williams, *Energy and the Making of Modern California* (Akron, OH: University of Akron Press, 1997).

3. See, for example, Saskia Sassen, *Cities in a World Economy*, 2nd ed. (Thousand Oaks, CA: Pine Forge Press, 2000); Sassen, *The Global City: New York, London, Tokyo* (Princeton, NJ: Princeton University Press, 1991); Sassen, ed., *Global Networks, Linked Cities* (New York: Routledge, 2002); Arturo Almondoz, *Planning Latin American Capital Cities, 1850–1950* (London: Routledge, 2002); Mark Abrahamson, *Global Cities* (New York: Oxford University Press, 2004); Malcolm Cross and Robert Moore, eds., *Globalization and the New City: Migrants, Minorities and Urban Transformation in Comparative Perspective* (New York: Palgrave, 2002); David L. A. Gordon, *Planning Twentieth Century Capital Cities* (London: Routledge, 2006).

4. Sassen, *Cities in a World Economy*, xvi.

5. Short discussions of many oil-producing regions are found in Augustine A. Ikein, *The Impact of Oil on a Developing Country: The Case of Nigeria* (New York: Praeger, 1990). See also Hodges, *Angola*.

6. For our efforts to contribute to this broader context, see Joseph Pratt, Martin V. Melosi, and Kathleen Brosnan, eds., *Energy Capitals: Local Impact, Global Influence* (Pittsburgh: University of Pittsburgh Press, 2014).

7. W. L. Fisher, J. H. McGowen, L. F. Brown, Jr., and C. G. Groat, *Environmental Geologic Atlas of the Texas Coastal Zone—Galveston-Houston Area* (Austin: Bureau of Economic Geology, University of Texas at Austin, 1972), 1.

8. David G. McComb, *Galveston: A History* (Austin: University of Texas Press, 1986), 6–8. See also Houston Geological Society, *Geology of Houston and Vicinity, Texas* (Houston: Houston Geological Society, 1961), 3,7; Robert R. Lankford and John J. W. Roger, comps., *Holocene Geology of the Galveston Bay Area* (Houston: Geo-

logical Society, 1969), vii, 1; Fisher et al., *Environmental Geologic Atlas*, 7. Jim Lester and Lisa Gonzalez, eds., *Ebb and Flow: Galveston Bay Characterization Highlights* (Galveston, TX: Galveston Bay Estuary Program, 2001), 12; Joseph L. Clark and Elton M. Scott, *The Texas Gulf Coast: Its History and Development*, vol. II (New York: Lewis Historical Publishing, 1955), 14–16; Houston Geological Society, *Geology of Houston and Vicinity, Texas*, 3.

9. Fisher et al., *Environmental Geologic Atlas*, 7.

10. Fisher et al., *Environmental Geologic Atlas*, 7; G. L. Fugate, "Development of Houston's Water Supply," *Journal of the American Water Works Association* 33 (October 1941), 1769–1770.

11. Planning and Development Department, *Public Utilities Profile for Houston Texas* (Summer 1994), III-15; Fugate, "Development of Houston's Water Supply," 1769–1770. The geologic formations from which Houston obtains groundwater supplies are upper Miocene, Pliocene, and Pleistocene in origin. See Nicholas A. Rose, "Ground Water and Relations of Geology to Its Occurrence in Houston District, Texas," *Bulletin of the American Association of Petroleum Geologists* 27 (August 1943): 1081.

12. See "Houston," *Twentieth Century Cities*, part 4 of Association of American Geographers, *Contemporary Metropolitan America*, ed. John S. Adams (Cambridge, MA: Ballinger, 1976), 109, 121–124; Houston Chamber of Commerce, *Houston Facts '82*.

13. U.S. Environmental Protection Agency, *Heat Island Effect*, https://www.epa .gov/heat-islands.

14. U.S. EPA, *Heat Island Effect*; Visit Houston, Houston Weather, https://www .visithoustontexas.com/travel-planning/weather/.

15. Fisher et al., *Environmental Geologic Atlas*, 1.

16. Fisher et al., *Environmental Geologic Atlas*, 1, 7.

17. Espey, Huston, and Associates, prep., Archival Research: Houston-Galveston Navigation Channels, Texas Project—Galveston, Harris, Liberty, and Chambers Counties, Texas, April 1993, 8, 10; McComb, *Galveston: A History*, 121–149; David Roth, "Texas Hurricane History," National Weather Service, Lake Charles, Louisiana, 2004.

18. Fisher et al., *Environmental Geologic Atlas*, 15, 20; Robert R. Stickney, *Estuarine Ecology of the Southeastern United States and Gulf of Mexico* (College Station: Texas A&M University Press, 1984), 247–280; Lester and Gonzalez, eds., *Ebb and Flow*, 9–11.

19. Marilyn M. Sibley, "Houston Ship Channel," *Handbook of Texas*, Texas State Historical Society, https://tshaonline.org/handbook/online/articles/rhh11; Sibley, *The Port of Houston* (Austin: University of Texas Press, 1968), 102–145; Garvin Berry, "Promoters, Politicians Turned Shallow Bayou into Seaport," *Houston Business Journal*, November 22, 1982; Lynn M. Alperin, *Custodians of the Coast: History of the United States Army Engineers at Galveston* (Galveston, TX: United States Army Corps of Engineers, 1977), 95–101.

20. See Joe Feagin, *Free Enterprise City: Houston in Political-Economic Perspective* (New Brunswick, NJ: Rutgers University Press, 1988), 61.

21. Barry J. Kaplan, "Houston: The Golden Buckle of the Sunbelt," in *Sunbelt Cities: Politics and Growth Since World War II*, ed. Richard M. Bernard and Bradley R. Rice (Austin: University of Texas Press, 1983), 197; Walter L. Buenger and Joseph A. Pratt, *But Also Good Business: Texas Commerce Banks and the Financing of Houston and Texas, 1886–1986* (College Station: Texas A&M University Press, 1986), 73, 109; Walter Rundell, Jr., *Early Texas Oil: A Photographic History, 1866–1936* (College Station: Texas A&M University Press, 1977), 136; David G. McComb, *Houston: A History* (Austin: University of Texas Press, 1981), 78–79.

22. Joseph A. Pratt, *The Growth of a Refining Region* (Greenwich, UK: JAI Press, 1980), 3–7, 33. See also Feagin, *Free Enterprise City*, 62, 65–66; David G. McComb, *Texas, A Modern History* (Austin: University of Texas Press, 2014), 125: Kaplan, "Houston: The Golden Buckle of the Sunbelt," 197; Sibley, *The Port of Houston*, 161; James J. Parsons, "Recent Industrial Development in the Gulf South," Geographical Review 40 (1950):74.

23. "Buffalo Bayou," *Handbook of Texas*, Texas State Historical Society, https://tshaonline.org/handbook/online/articles/rhb28. See also Martin V. Melosi, Thomas McKinney, and Terry-Tomkins-Walsh, "Historical Significance of Buffalo Bayou, Houston, Texas," National Heritage Area Nomination (Washington, DC: U.S. Department of Interior, National Parks Service, 2005).

24. "Historical Significance of Buffalo Bayou, Houston, Texas," 52–56.

25. "Historical Significance of Buffalo Bayou, Houston, Texas," 58.

26. Quoted in Beth Anne Shelton et al., *Houston: Growth and Decline in a Sunbelt Boomtown* (Philadlephia: Temple University Press, 1989), 15.

27. Pratt, *Growth of a Refining Region*; Paul Levengood, "Houston at War: The Creation of a Major City," Ph.D. dissertation, Rice University, 2001.

28. Pratt, *Growth of a Refining Region*; Levengood, "Houston at War."

29. Texas State Historical Society, "Petrochemical Industry," *Handbook of Texas*, http://www.tshaonline.org/handbook/online/articles/dop11; Louis P. Galambos, ed., *The Global Chemical Industry in the Age of Petrochemicals* (Cambridge: Cambridge University Press, 2006).

30. Christopher J. Castañeda, *Regulated Enterprise: Natural Gas Pipelines and Northeastern Markets, 1938–1954* (Columbus: Ohio State University Press, 1993); Castañeda and Clarence Smith, *Gas Pipelines and the Emergence of America's Regulatory State: A History of Panhandle Eastern Corporation, 1928–1993* (Cambridge: Cambridge University Press, 1996); Castañeda and Joseph A. Pratt, *From Texas to the East: A Strategic History of Texas Eastern Corporation* (College Station: Texas A&M University Press, 1993).

31. For the impact of the oil price bust on a major oil company with a strong presence in Houston, see Joseph A. Pratt, *Exxon: Transforming Energy, 1973–2005* (Austin: University of Texas Press, 2013).

32. "Texas Medical Center," *Handbook of Texas*, Texas State Historical Society, http://www.tshaonline.org/handbook/online/articles/kct23.

33. Ben Koush, "The Buildings of the Texas Medical Center Through the Years," September 5, 2012, *OffCite*, http://offcite.org/the-buildings-of-the-texas-medical-center-through-the-years/.

34. See Martin V. Melosi and Joseph A. Pratt, "The Energy Capital of the World? Oil-Led Development in Twentieth-Century Houston," in *Energy Capitals*, ed. Pratt, Melosi, and Brosnan, 30–57.

35. "Photos: OTC Through History," FuelFix, https://fuelfix.com/blog/2014/05/04/photos-the-offshore-technology-conference-through-the-years/.

36. Joseph A. Pratt, "Exxon and the Control of Oil," *Journal of American History* 99, no. 1 (2012): 145–154. For sweeping views of the rise of producer power, see Anthony Sampson, *The Seven Sisters* (New York: Viking, 1975); and Daniel Yergin, *The Prize* (New York: Free Press, 2008). For an overview of the rise of climate change and its impact on oil, see Daniel Yergin, *The Quest* (New York: Penguin, 2012), 419–520.

37. As the economy diversified in Houston, and medicine ultimately became the largest employer in the metropolis, the nature of the workforce changed dramatically. Yet, this economic diversification was built on the back of the energy industry, thus never retreating from its influence on the Bayou City.

38. See Robert D. Bullard, "Dumping on Houston's Black Neighborhoods," Elizabeth D. Blum, "The Gunfighters of Northwood Manor," and Kimberly A. Youngblood, "Voices of Discord: The Effects of a Grassroots Environmental Movement at the Brio Superfund Site," in *Energy Metropolis*, ed. Melosi and Pratt, 207–240, 260–273.

39. General patterns of migration are discussed in Pratt, *Growth of a Refining Region*. See also Bernadette Pruitt, *The Other Great Migration: The Movement of African Americans to Houston, Texas, 1900–1941* (College Station: Texas A&M University Press, 2013); Herbert Winthrop, *Negro Employment in Basic Industries—A Study of Racial Policies in Six Industries* (Philadelphia: University of Pennsylvania Press, 1970); F. Ray Marshall, *The Negro and Organized Labor* (New York: Wiley, 1965); Robert D. Bullard, *Invisible Houston: The Black Experience in Boom and Bust* (College Station: Texas A&M University Press, 1987); Thomas Kreneck, *Mexican American Odyssey* (College Station: Texas A&M University Press, 2001).

40. Patrick Nicholson, *In Time: An Anecdotal History of the University of Houston* (Houston: Gulf, 1977); Fredericka Meiners, *A History of Rice University: The Institute Years, 1907–1963* (Houston: Rice University Press, 1982).

41. For discussions of changes in Texas politics, see George Norris Green, *The Establishment in Texas Politics: The Primitive Years, 1938–1957* (Westport, CT: Greenwood Press, 1979); Mary Beth Rogers, *Barbara Jordan: American Hero* (New York: Bantam, 1998); Chandler Davidson, *Race and Class in Texas Politics* (Princeton, NJ: Princeton University Press, 1990).

42. For a general overview, see David Brody, *Workers in Industrial America* (New York: Oxford University Press, 1993); for a case study in the Houston region, see Henrietta M. Larson and Kevin Wiggins Porter, *History of Humble Oil and Refining Company: A Study in Industrial Growth* (New York: Harper, 1959).

43. Martin V. Melosi, "Community and the Growth of Houston," in *Effluent America: Cities, Industry, Energy, and the Environment*, ed. Martin V. Melosi (Pittsburgh: University of Pittsburgh Press, 2001), 194–195.

44. See, for example, Tom Watson McKinney, "Superhighway Deluxe: Houston's Gulf Freeway," in *Energy Metropolis*, ed. Melosi and Pratt, 148–172.

45. Melosi and Pratt, "Introduction," in *Energy Metropolis*, ed. Melosi and Pratt, 8.

46. See Diane C. Bates, "Urban Sprawl and the Piney Woods: Deforestation in the San Jacinto Watershed," in *Energy Metropolis*, ed. Melosi and Pratt, 173–184; Melosi, "Community and the Growth of Houston," 190–205.

47. Melosi, "Community and the Growth of Houston," 190–205.

48. This section is drawn from Martin V. Melosi, "Houston: Energy Capital," *New Geographies* 2 (2009): 101–102.

49. Planning and Development Department, *Public Utilities Profile for Houston, Texas* (Summer, 1994), III-15.

50. City of Houston, *Public Water Supply System* (January 1948), 4.

51. Fugate, "Development of Houston's Water Supply," 1768–1769.

52. "Report of Water Committee," City of Houston, *Annual Report, 1909*, 24.

53. "Report of Water Commissioner," *City Book of Houston, 1914*, 106; "Mayor's Annual Message," *City Book of Houston, 1914*, 80–81; *City Book of Houston, 1925*, 41; Bud A. Randolph, "The History of Houston's Water Supply," *Texas Commercial News* (June 1927): 43.

54. Fugate, "Development of Houston's Water Supply," 1770–1771.

55. "Spending $4,000,000 to $6,000,000 on Water System Urged," *Houston Chronicle*, September 2, 1937.

56. Fugate, "Development of Houston's Water Supply," 1772–1774.

57. Alvord, Burdick & Howson, "Report on an Adequate Water Supply for the City of Houston, Texas," February 1938, 1–3, 75–76.

58. "New Plan for Water Supply to Be Offered," *Houston Chronicle*, February 3, 1939.

59. J. M. Nagle, "Houston Gets Needed Water," *American City* 60 (February 1945): 77.

60. William W. McClendon, "The San Jacinto River Conservation and Reclamation District's Proposed Plan of Full Scale Development," *Slide Rule* (March 1945): 11; "Water Supply Dam to Be Built on San Jacinto," *Houston Post*, July 14, 1942; City of Houston, Utilities Department, *Engineering Report for Water Works Improvements*, January 17, 1944.

61. Houston Water Department, *Report of Director for Year 1942*, 16; "Houston's Greater Water Supply Near," *Houston* 23 (August 1952): 8–9; Water Supply and Conservation Committee, Houston Chamber of Commerce, *Water for the Houston Area*, December 1954, 3; U.S. Department of the Interior, U.S. Geological Survey, "Characteristics of Water-Quality Data for Lake Houston, Selected Tributary Inflows to Lake Houston, and the Trinity River Near Lake Houston, August 1983–September 1990," *Water-Resources Investigations Report 99-4129* (1999), 2, 4.

62. For examples of energy pollution studies with an industrial focus, see: Barbara L. Allen, *Uneasy Alchemy: Citizens and Experts in Louisiana's Chemical Corridor Disputes* (Cambridge: Massachusetts Institute of Technology Press, 2003); Joan Norris Booth, *Cleaning Up: The Costs of Refinery Pollution* (New York: Council on Economic Priorities, 1975); Craig E. Colten, "Chicago Waste Lands: Refuse Disposal

and Urban Growth, 1840–1990," *Journal of Historical Geography* 20 (April 1994): 124–142; Colten, *Industrial Waste in the Calumet Area, 1869–1970: An Historical Geography* (Springfield: Illinois Department of Energy and Natural Resources, 1985); John T. Cumbler, "Whatever Happened to Industrial Waste? Reform, Compromise, and Science in Nineteenth Century Southern New England," *Journal of Social History* 29 (Fall 1995): 149–171; Neil Cunningham, Robert A. Kagan, and Dorothy Thornton, *Shades of Green: Business, Regulation, and Environment* (Stanford: Stanford University Press, 2003); Hugh S. Gorman, "Manufacturing Brownfields: The Case of Neville Township, Pennsylvania, 1899–1989," *Technology and Culture* 38 (July 1997): 539–574; Gorman, *Redefining Efficiency: Pollution Concerns, Regulatory Mechanisms, and Technological Change in the U.S. Petroleum Industry* (Akron, OH: University of Akron Press, 2001); Andrew Hurley, "Creating Ecological Wastelands: Oil Pollution in New York City, 1870–1900," *Journal of Urban History* 20 (May 1994): 340–364; James E. Krier and Edmund Ursin, *Pollution and Policy: A Case Essay on California and Federal Experience with Motor Vehicle Air Pollution, 1940–1975* (Berkeley: University of California Press, 1977); Steve Lerner, *Diamond: A Struggle for Environmental Justice in Louisiana's Chemical Corridor* (Cambridge: Massachusetts Institute of Technology Press, 2005); Martin V. Melosi, *Coping with Abundance: Energy and Environment in Industrial America* (New York: Knopf, 1985); Stephen Mosley, *The Chimney of the World: A History of Smoke Pollution in Victorian and Edwardian Manchester* (Winwick, Cambridgeshire, UK: White Horse Press, 2001); Joseph A. Pratt, "Letting the Grandchildren Do It: Environmental Planning during the Ascent of Oil as a Major Energy Source," *Public Historian* 2 (Summer 1980): 28–61; Joel A. Tarr and Bill Lamperes, "Changing Fuel Use Behavior and Energy Transitions: The Pittsburgh Smoke Control Movement, 1940–1950, A Case Study in Historical Analogy," *Journal of Social History* 14 (1981): 561–588; Jeffrey K. Stine and Joel A. Tarr, "At the Intersection of Histories: Technology and the Environment," *Technology and Culture* 39 (1998): 601–640.

63. For a pioneering study of energy, growth, and environment in a region, see James C. Williams, *Energy and the Making of Modern California* (Akron, OH: University of Akron Press, 1997). For an excellent account of the early politics of oil-led development in California, see Sabin, *Crude Politics*.

64. Christopher Helman, "America's 20 Dirtiest Cities," *Forbes*, July 16, 2012, http://www.forbes.com/sites/christopherhelman/2012/07/16/the-worlds-25 -biggest-oil-companies/.

65. There is as yet no comprehensive economic history of Houston. For a general political history, see McComb, *Houston: A History*. See also Sibley, *Port of Houston* and Alperin, *Custodians of the Coast*.

66. See Melosi and Pratt, "Introduction," and Joseph A. Pratt, "A Mixed Blessing," in *Energy Metropolis*, ed. Melosi and Pratt, 7–13, 21–51.

67. Joseph A. Pratt, *Birth of a Refining Region* (Greenwich, CT: JAI Press, 1980), 72–75, 105. See also Shelton et al., *Houston: Growth and Decline in a Sunbelt Boomtown*, 16–17; Parsons, "Recent Industrial Development in the Gulf South," 76–77; Randolph B. Campbell, *Gone to Texas: A History of the Lone Star State* (New York:

Oxford University Press, 2003), 407–408; Kaplan, "Houston: Golden Buckle of the Sunbelt," 198; Feagin, *Free Enterprise City*, 66, 71; McComb, *Houston*, 81, 128–129; Clark and Scott, *Texas Gulf Coast*, 234; Warren Rose, *Catalyst of an Economy: The Economic Impact of the Port of Houston, 1958–1963* (Houston: University of Houston, 1965), 7; and several sections of Melosi and Pratt, eds., *Energy Metropolis*.

68. See Feagin, *Free Enterprise City*.

69. On the national level, see Robert Engler, *The Politics of Oil, Private Power and Democratic Directions* (New York: Macmillan, 1961). For Houston, see Feagin, *Free Enterprise City*. For Texas, see Green, *Establishment in Texas Politics*. For Houston, see also Joseph A. Pratt, "8F and Many More: Business and Civic Leadership in Modern Houston," *Houston Review of History and Culture* 1, no. 1 (Summer 2004): 2–7, 31–44.

70. Health and Human Services, City of Houston, "BPCP-About Us," http://www .houstontx.gov/health/Environmental/bpcp_aboutus.html.

71. Citizens' Environmental Coalition, http://www.cechouston.org/. See also Terry Tomkins-Walsh, "'A Concrete River Had to be Wrong': Environmental Action on Houston's Bayous, 1935–1980," Ph.D. dissertation, University of Houston, 2009.

72. On the occasion of the 100th anniversary of the opening of the Houston Ship Channel in 2014, *Houston History* magazine published a special issue on its history, *Dredged to Excellence: 100 Year on the Houston Ship Channel* (Fall 2014 issue). See "What a Deep-Water Channel to Houston Created," https://houstonhistorymagazine .org/2014/10/what-a-deep-water-channel-to-houston-created/.

73. For over thirty years, the impact of the growing diversity of Houston's population on the city's evolution has been recorded and analyzed by a team of researchers under the leadership of sociologist Stephen Klineberg at the Kinder Institute for Urban Research, Rice University.

74. "Houston, TX Population and Races," USA.com, http://www.usa.com/houston -tx-population-and-races.htm; See also "Harris County Leads as Share of Foreign-Born Texans Grows," *Houston Chronicle*, January 2, 2014.

75. City of Houston, Planning and Development Department, "Race/Ethnicity, 1980–2010," July 5, 2012, http://www.houstontx.gov/planning/Demographics/docs _pdfs/Cy/coh_race_ethn_1980-2010.pdf.

76. Michael R. Botson, Jr., *Labor, Civil Rights, and the Hughes Tool Company* (College Station, TX: Texas A&M University Press, 2005. See also Ernest Obedele-Starks, *Black Unionism in the Industrial South* (College Station: Texas A&M University Press, 2000); Tyler Priest, "Labor's Last Stand in the Refinery: The Shell Oil Strike of 1962–1963," *Houston History* 5, no. 2 (2008): 7–15.

77. Brody, *Humble*.

78. Patrick L. Cox, *Ralph W. Yarborough: The People's Senator* (Austin: University of Texas Press, 2002).

79. There is not yet a good history of the Oil, Chemical, and Atomic Workers. For information, see Pratt, *Growth of a Refining Region*, 153–188; Harvey O'Connor, *History of the Oil Workers International Union* (Denver: Oil Workers International

Union, 1950); Ray Davidson, *Turmoil and Triumph: the First 50 Years of Local 4-376, Oil, Chemical, and Atomic Workers Union* (1983).

80. See Henrietta M. Larson and Kevin Wiggins Porter, *History of Humble Oil & Refining Company* (New York: Harper, 1959).

81. Frank R. von der Mehden, ed., *The Ethnic Groups of Houston* (Houston: Rice University Press, 1984). Gradual assimilation through education was accelerated during World War II, as women entered the refinery work forces in unprecedented numbers. See Gary J. Rabelais, "Humble Women at War: The Case of Humble's Baytown Refinery, 1942–1945," *Houston Review of History and Culture* 2, no. 2 (2005): 33–36, 58.

82. Amilcar Shabazz, *Advancing Democracy: African Americans and the Struggle for Equity in Higher Education in Texas* (Chapel Hill: University of North Carolina Press, 2004); William H. Kellar, *Make Haste Slowly: Moderates, Conservatives, and School Desegregation in Houston* (College Station: Texas A&M University Press, 1999); Guadalupe San Miguel, "The Fight for Bilingual Education in Houston: An Insider's Perspective," *Houston History Magazine* 9, no. 1 (2011): 48–51.

83. The best source to gain a sense of the intensity of Texas high school football and its important place in the life of many Texans is H. G. Bissinger, *Friday Night Lights: A Town, a Team, and a Dream* (Boston: Da Capo, 1990).

84. Von der Mehden, ed., *Ethnic Groups of Houston*, ch. 2–3, 11.

85. Roger Wood, *Texas Zydeco* (Austin: University of Texas Press, 2006).

86. George Jones with Tom Carter, *George Jones: I Lived to Tell It All* (New York: Random House, 1996); Rodney Crowell, *Chinaberry Sidewalks* (New York: Vintage, 2012).

87. Roger Wood, *Down in Houston: Bayou City Blues* (Austin: University of Texas Press, 2003); Alan Govenar, *Lightnin' Hopkins: His Life and Blues* (Chicago: Chicago Review Press, 1996).

88. Guadalupe San Miguel, *Tejano Proud: Tex-Mex Music in the Twentieth Century* (College Station: Texas A&M University Press, 2002); Manual Peña, *Musica Tejana: The Cultural Economy of Artistic Transformation* (College Station: Texas A&M University Press, 1999).

89. Sethuramen Srinivasan, Jr., "The Struggle for Control: Technology and Labor in Gulf Coast Refineries, 1913–1973," Ph.D. dissertation, University of Houston, 2001.

90. Myrna Santiago, *The Ecology of Oil: Environment, Labor, and the Mexican Revolution, 1900–1983* (Cambridge: Cambridge University Press, 2006); Ognen Stojanovski, "Handcuffed: An Assessment of Pemex's Performance in Gridlock," in *Oil and Governance: State-Owned Enterprises and the World Energy Supply*, ed. David G. Victor, David R. Hults, and Mark Thurber (Cambridge: Cambridge University Press, 2012), 280–333.

91. Salazar-Carrillo and West, *Oil and Development in Twentieth-Century Venezuela.*

92. Terry Lynn Karl, *The Paradox of Plenty* (Berkeley: University of California Press, 1997); Tina Rosenberg, "The New Nationalization: Where Hugo Chavez's 'Oil Socialism' Could be Taking the Developed World," *New York Times Magazine,*

November 4, 2007, 45; David Hultz, "Petroleos de Venezuela, S.A.: From Independence to Subservience," in *Oil and Governance,* ed. Victor, Hultz, and Thurber, 418–477.

93. Rubén Hernández-León, *Metropolitan Migrants: The Migration of Urban Mexicans to the United States* (Berkeley: University of California Press, 2008), 4.

94. Kimberly Amadeo, "Hurricane Harvey Facts, Damage and Costs: What Made Harvey So Devastating," March 1, 2018, *thebalance.com,* online, https://www .thebalance.com/hurricane-harvey-facts-damage-costs-4150087, accessed March 19, 2018.

Epilogue

Spatial, Temporal, and Institutional Influences in New World Cities

· ·

MARTIN V. MELOSI

"The global scale and impact of urban settlements and cities will determine the course of the emergent twenty-first century." So predicted experts from the Population Institute in Washington, D.C., in a 1999 paper.[1] By 2030, almost 5 billion people will live in cities, with the pace of urbanization especially accelerating in the developing world.[2] Dramatic processes of urbanization and unprecedented challenges of city life became global phenomena in the twentieth century, and they will continue to shape the future. Fathoming the twentieth century without placing cities at the center (or near the center) is a historical distortion. This fact is particularly true in our understanding of the history of the Western Hemisphere and its place in the globalization process. As John Tutino suggested, the Americas have a common history, but different experiences. That being said, the cities discussed in *New World Cities* nonetheless demonstrate many common qualities and tensions over time.

Among its goals, *New World Cities* stresses the central role of major cities in shaping the history of the Western Hemisphere in the twentieth century. On this palette, the essays in this volume attempt to connect globalization, urbanization, and inequality as interrelated issues. Obviously, a variety of other relevant topics for discussion range beyond this emphasis. We recognize, for example, that megacities specifically and most large cities in general suffer from a litany of environmental problems that directly influence the lives of their citizens and the hinterlands beyond.[3] As world historian J. R. McNeil asserted, "Twentieth-century urbanization affected almost everything in human affairs and constituted a vast break with past centuries. Nowhere had humankind altered the environment more than in cities, but their impact reached far beyond their boundaries. The growth of cities was a crucial source of environmental change."[4] While *New World Cities* does not operate on that scale of discourse, each essay in the book—to a greater or lesser degree and with greater or lesser intensity—gives primary attention to the place of its city in the global economy; the effect of popular participation through politics of adhesion, division, or survival; and the roles of formality and informality, legality and illegality in shaping city life.

New World Cities is meant to open a dialogue over urbanization in the Western Hemisphere to see where that discussion might lead. We recognize our essays have aggregated many diverse and complex factors that influence urban expansion in each city. In so doing, we also hope to generate comparisons among cities in the Americas that rarely get compared. Future studies may wish to integrate an analysis of urbanization in the region more broadly, not only for a better appreciation of cities in the twentieth century but to deepen understanding of the twenty-first century. To set some parameters for the book, the editors provided a geographic frame— the Western Hemisphere—and a temporal limit—the twentieth century. They were intrigued to see what the authors would place in and draw out of this evocative container. Valuable analyses, perspectives, and evaluations resulted. Particularly insightful was the use of key spatial, temporal, and institutional markers to address the themes of the book. Such markers helped to contextualize globalization, urbanization, and inequality for our cities and provide bases for comparison. First, several of the essays build their narratives and analyses on the importance of space and place—that is, how the dynamics of growth and power are shaped by land uses and physical segregation and separation. Second, all of the essays place globalization in a time sequence to emphasize what has changed and when. And third, formality and informality are treated in some fashion, especially to ascertain their impacts on structural and institutional factors that govern city growth and political participation.

Spatial Influences

Spatial analysis of cities and urbanization in general is not new, but it can be usefully applied as a way of determining growth patterns and dynamic social and political change not always found in many existing studies of the urban Americas. In an attempt to grasp the broad features of the urban environment, sociologists and geographers in particular developed theories of urban ecology over the years. The origins of the ecological approach to spatial and social organization can be traced to nineteenth-century concepts and principles conceived by plant and animal ecologists. Urban sociology, however, was founded at the University of Chicago during World War I by

Robert E. Park and Ernest Burgess. Some refer to the Chicago school as the "subsocial school," because, as Gideon Sjoberg stated, its members had been intent upon studying humans in their "temporal and spatial dimensions and explaining the resulting patterns in terms of subsocial variables." The fundamental subsocial variable was "impersonal competition," a concept borrowed from nineteenth-century social Darwinism and classical economics, which emphasized laissez-faire doctrine and the operation of the marketplace. Those committed to the ecological perspective of the Chicago school concentrated on factors determining urban spatial patterns and their social impacts. The spatial arrangement of cities, proponents argued, was dependent on competitive economic and social forces.[5]

Less interested in the larger ecological overlay of spatial analysis, authors in *New World Cities* utilized spatial arrangements to emphasize political and social change over time, to define relationships especially between urban cores and peripheral communities, and to determine how they shaped the history of those cities. Such an approach highlights social and political tensions driving urban growth in the twentieth century, and demonstrates the vital influence of spatial arrangements on urbanites both north and south. Bryan McCann explicitly concentrated on land use in his study of Rio de Janeiro, emphasizing how formal and informal settlement "pushed the periphery outward," but also demonstrated the city's long history of "conjoined" formal and informal growth. For example, while the formal transportation sector influenced spatial change as it has done in most cities, informal growth of the favelas was "a key component" in Rio's modernization, not simply an anomaly. McCann presented the relationship of the formal and the informal, which shaped the interactions of the citizenry, in terms of patterns of housing and the physical proximity of Rio's communities. In so doing, he made visible and more concrete a history of a city with a reputation as a "laboratory for urban trial and error."

Mark Healey's essay also relied on land use and a spatial perspective to understand the growth and development of Buenos Aires. He considered the transformation in the role of the urban core and of the periphery, largely in terms of power and politics. Peripheral development around Buenos Aires changed from its role as a "crucible for transforming national politics" and as a "key to social ascent" to "a space of relegation and abandonment." The periphery, once a "zone of contested opportunity" in the beginning of the twentieth century, decayed into the "domain of difficulty and marginality." The devastation of the industrial suburbs during the military regime of the late 1970s and early 1980s turned the city inward away from the vibrant periphery. The deindustrialization that arrived with globalization, and which devastated the periphery, graphically showed the political implications of the city's changing fortunes. Political and social tensions represented in spatial terms are an effective way to validate the deep impact of changing societal objectives and the impact of various approaches to decision making.

In George Sanchez's Los Angeles, racial segregation is graphically demonstrated by the physical separation generated by "a long-standing pattern of organized and systematic discrimination in housing." In this case, Sanchez utilized a spatial argument to illustrate long-standing practices influencing division of the races. Complicit were not only the city government but land developers and realtors who bought into the policy. In Sanchez's mind, Los Angeles was an "innovator" in methods of racial residential restriction. The impact of residential and neighborhood segregation was more than an observable metaphor for political and social exclusion. It was a real-world method of cordoning off people from the acquisition of power or political action—the formalization of "urban apartheid."

In Montreal, Michèle Dagenais argued that ethnic enclaves were a means of "spatial and social organization" for majority and minority groups, but that tensions could arise between city-center and suburban restructuring. Overall, since the 1950s, the city and island of Montreal were multicultural, while its suburbs were more homogenous, housing an essentially French-speaking population. While economic changes were influential in recasting the city, ethnolinguistic questions clearly influenced urban/suburban patterns. As in McCann, Healey, and Sanchez's essays, space is a reference point for observing urban change. Land-use patterns and practices are essential in all of these essays at getting to the heart of the changing functioning of the cities and how they reflect larger questions of politics, economics, and social change. The essays avoid orthodox treatment of cities and suburbs as opposing forces, and instead concentrate on how spatial changes demonstrate real shifts in power and influence as actors and as communities acted upon. Divisions between north and south are much less prevalent here. What stands out are functional change and the forces that produce it. Even in Mexico City, Tutino gave attention to the central city's dependence on "sustenance from outside" in the form of food and other supplies. Joseph Pratt and Martin Melosi made the physical setting of the city a central player in Houston's economic development. Giving spatial influences agency in all of the essays is a powerful analytical tool, which helps to bridge differences among the cities.

Globalization and Urbanization

Common interests in population, growth, economics, labor, infrastructure, and politics—rather than a common approach—shaped the essays in *New World Cities*. However, these issues are not presented in a vacuum. As John Tutino explained in chapter 1, while all the cities experienced growth and change in different ways, "urban prospects have been shaped in fundamental ways by their differing experiences of rapid population growth as the hemisphere turned from national development to globalization."

Each essay, as one might expect, takes account of the globalizing economy in light of its city's modern history, but in every case the timing of the changes also is quite similar. Tutino concentrated on the impact of a population crush and deindustrialization in modern Mexico City, which experienced few benefits from a globalizing economy for its non-elite citizenry. Mexico's remaining industry moved north toward the U.S. border to serve export markets through low-wage workers, often young single women. In the capital, an emerging service economy based on government, finance, and commerce benefited the few over the many, while enterprise for those on the lower rungs of society took the form of informal self-employment or street vending. Rio de Janeiro, McCann observed, deindustrialized like Mexico City, and jobs disappeared from the industrial sector in the face of "the new globalization" to be replaced in part by sporadic work in a growing informal sector. McCann's emphasis deals less with the desperation of the underclass, as Tutino emphasized, and more with a variety of changes in the informal sector, including the evolution of favelas, global tourism, and rising drug trafficking. Both, however, see creativity in poor people's use of informality to find income and build neighborhoods.

Healey explored how Buenos Aires prospered longer into the twentieth century than did Mexico City or Rio, then faced new challenges that limited popular participations and gains as Argentina's military regime ruled as what can only be seen as a plunge into globalization. In Buenos Aires, an important outcome of the earlier Peronist promotion of national development was the growing significance of political influence shifting to the industrial suburbs over the core city—sustaining a shared if ever more fragile prosperity into the 1960s. With the turn to globalization, the promise of revived prosperity never materialized in a way that the military leaders and then democratizers hoped—or at least promised. Buenos Aires joined Mexico City and Rio as a metropolis of rising underemployment with many people locked in "a vast urban periphery of marginality."

The stories told by Dagenais, Sanchez, Melosi, and Pratt as we move north seem different. After sustaining its prosperity during and after World War II (like Buenos Aires), Montreal faced economic challenges from the 1960s onward while joining a movement for francophone rights within Canada. Yet rather than severely deindustrializing, Montreal (at first) restructured its industries and its overall economic activities to meet the new challenges of globalization. It also turned to new forms of urban management, especially in the provision of services, to address changes demanded in a new economic setting. Dagenais discussed Montreal's bilingual heritage to demonstrate, in part at least, how unresolved issues of a dual vision of the city's future did not disappear with the changing economic landscape. Like elsewhere in the Americas, Montreal's economy was and continues to be intertwined in regional and international dynamics.

For Los Angeles, Sanchez set as context "a world of postindustrial globalization" that produced "a new society of ethnic diversity." In such a setting, he argued, separation and inequality were maintained rather than halted. Sanchez stated, "As Los Angeles in many ways led the U.S. dream of national development from 1950 to 1980, it now leads in grappling with the challenges of urban globalization." Houston's trajectory in the new global setting has been shaped in large measure by oil. As such, the city economy continues to be based on a vital resource that powers much of the global economy. Houston's industrial prowess in the refining of petroleum, supplying natural gas, and manufacturing petrochemicals remains a central feature of a worldwide economic engine—and one that will continue to be influential until (if?) alternative energy sources replace fossil fuels in the foreseeable future. However, fracking and new oil discoveries in recent years, plus the rise in importance of natural gas, already have impacted Houston's economy, but toward what ultimate end is uncertain. That Houston underwent a substantial economic transformation, especially in the 1980s, helped to ensure that it will not fall into severe boom and bust cycles it faced in the past. Not surprisingly, Melosi and Pratt's chapter placed primary emphasis on the role of Houston in the global economy, but with a different set of outcomes than in other cities in this study.

None of our essays gives full attention to all aspects of globalization as it affects the respective cities. Still, our varying emphases reveal an instructive range of influences. One thing is clear: the impact of globalization on these Western Hemispheric cities is not neatly divided between Global South and Global North. Los Angeles and Montreal faced challenges of social and economic integration of its citizens in similar ways as Mexico City, Buenos

Aires, and Rio. Were there scales of differences? Of course. But a neat division of impacts is not apparent. Collectively, our essays demonstrate a shared need for growing cities to accommodate to a postindustrial era. The abstract hope of a more unified planet and common human bonds was not easily fashioned in the twentieth-century emergence of globalization. Indeed, the rising tide of nationalism, particularly expressed in Brexit and the election of Donald Trump, is a strong reaction to globalization but in less expansive ways than demonstrated in the essays in this volume. What should not be lost in the various discussions in *New World Cities* is the role of globalization as a significant turning point in all the cities in the Americas under discussion. The common bond is temporal, and the bigger question needing to be addressed is: how do we gauge the timing of globalization trends more precisely in contributing to changes in urban politics, the economy, and social relationships?

Structural and Institutional Change: Formality/Informality

Among the most important results of putting together *New World Cities* was the dialogue it created among the authors about questions and concerns over structural and institutional changes in the cities with respect to governance and public participation. Concepts such as formality/informality and legality/illegality have been most commonly used in studies of the Global South in discussing structural and institutional issues, but the premises behind them apply equally well in a variety of situations in the Global North. From the first workshop, Bryan McCann's paper on Rio de Janeiro stimulated a conversation that became an ongoing dialogue about formality and informality, and how they might relate to any and all of the cities under study. Tutino's introductory chapters were written for our second gathering, and aimed explicitly to follow McCann's lead. The dichotomy resonated in Mark Healey's analysis of Buenos Aires, and opened a broad discussion about contrary, parallel, or even distinctive ways of thinking about urban organization in the U.S. and Canada. The relationship among legal, illegal, and extralegal community activity emerged as concerns in all of the papers. Other possible pairings such as corporate/bureaucratic and individual/collective actions were touched upon if not fully developed. In the respective papers, the authors most often equated urban formality with government action or sanction reinforced by law and/or practice, while informality rarely implied private action—even in northern cities. There was nothing in our discussions—or even our papers—that was meant to force a common understanding or application of formality/informality. The overall impact, however, and the value of further pondering about questions of formality/informality was to break the old mold of viewing the structural and institutional makeup of cities as static or assuming that power and policy making only reside in duly constituted government entities and their servants, labor unions, nongovernmental organizations, and so on. The formality/informality construct is a valuable tool for rethinking how structural change occurs in cities.

As "constructed opposites," formality and informality have been part of the social science discourse about development economics since the 1940s. The gulf between capitalist elites and peasant households was an area of growing concern in developing countries, especially in Latin America. By the 1970s, assessments of formal/informal dichotomies influenced policy making. Yet, the schema met with considerable debate in scholarly and policy literature, as did efforts to "formalize" what had been considered "informal" associations or institutions. Some scholars argued that the discourse needed to move to what actually constituted economic activity in poor countries. Others asserted that formal and informal are actually metaphoric concepts rather than representing actual conditions.

There is no single definition or interpretation that universally characterizes what formal and informal mean. According to scholars studying conditions in India and elsewhere in the developing world, two dimensions are particularly noteworthy: the actual reach of official governance on local or national levels and the extent to which a particular activity is structured "according to a predictable framework." This is a structural and operational model that attempts to get at the heart of how the formal and the informal actually function.[6] In his chapter on Mexico City, Tutino was very much in tune with this line of thought when he discussed notions of "structural informality" and "sanctioned illegality." We begin to see that urban organization and interactions built around formal/informal dichotomies are not simply impulsive or reactive; they are linked ways of governance, economic activity, and participation.

In 2008, researchers in Mexico, the United States, and Canada who all had been working on a variety of "informal" practices in an urban context formed the Continental Research Network on Informality in Metropolitan Spaces (RECIM). It adopted a "socio-anthropological" approach to analyzing "social facts." "Under what conditions do informal practices become illegal and punishable under the law?" The researchers had the sense that "tolerance of informality will vary across places and that managing urban space is a key element to maintaining a balance between informality and formality."[7] These assertions suggest that informal arrangements are essentially grassroots and strongly linked to specific locations.

The RECIM's initial queries broadened into discussions of potentially new forms of informality emerging in a global context and the degree to which states may change their tolerance for such activity. Discussion went beyond looking at the content of existing laws and regulations that may influence informal activity, and raised questions about how laws are utilized and enforced. *"Who* is the law, rather than solely *what* is the law" proved significant.[8] Such a question shifts attention to issues of power and decision making, and away from informal networks as insular entities. Our studies in *New World Cities* integrate the question of power defined broadly—who is the law?—and the question of neighborhood action—how do people work within, against, or around the law?—often in domains of informality.

In the recent past, much of the scholarship on the informal tended to stress questions of marginality, equating informality with poverty. Janice Perlman in discussing squatter settlements criticized the "myth of marginality" as too narrowly conceived to understand the internal workings of the settlements and the relation of those settlements (and the poor) to the state itself.[9] In a similar way, Ananya Roy questioned the idea of informality as "an extra-legal domain" which required policy interventions to integrate the informal into "the legal, formal, and planned sectors of political economy." Roy was skeptical about the division between law and informality, arguing that, "legal norms and forms of regulation are in and of themselves permeated by the logic of informality." In this case, the "structural nature of informality" is "a strategy for planning." Roy saw informality as "a deregulated rather than unregulated system."[10] Her query brings to the table the important question about the intention of the state vis-à-vis informal institutions. And at the very least it reinforces what the RECIM scholars and others have done to connect state law and action to informal institutions, making clear the importance of the reciprocal relationship between them.

New World Cities does not take up the long-standing debates over the nature of formal/informal, and does not speak directly to the policy implications of the coupling. Our emphasis on informality is decidedly historical. We view this perspective as complementary to ongoing discussions and debates over formal/informal rather than competitive or contradictory. For example, Tutino's analysis of Mexico City and McCann's history of Rio emphasize the interplay of formality and informality, while Healey's piece on Buenos Aires stresses state action and the political participation of popular groups in the formal politics of Peronism. Are the differences a matter of diverging interests and perspectives? Perhaps. But Healey's analysis of the Argentine metropolis, read alongside the studies of Mexico City and Rio de Janeiro, suggests important comparative questions: Did Peronism's reach to incorporate urban popular communities extend beyond what political powers were willing or able to do in Mexico and Brazil? Did it hold much urban political action in Buenos Aires within the domain of the formal (until the coming of military rule and the turn to neoliberalism)? We cannot answer these questions now, but asking them matters.

Healey's essay bypassed the formal/informal construct, not because informality was rare or unimportant in Buenos Aires, but because for much of the twentieth century it did not focus on the key domain of urban power and politics. Our studies of U.S. and Canadian cities do not explicitly address formality and informality in any detail, perhaps because that perspective is atypical of traditional historical scholarship there. Sanchez on Los Angeles, Dagenais on Montreal, and Melosi and Pratt on Houston tend to work with an implicit dichotomy between the public and the private, an approach deeply established in the Global North. Yet we have been led to ask if the continuing importance of thousands of noncitizen Mexican workers in Los Angeles and Houston, often captured in debates about whether they should be defined as illegal or undocumented, might make questions of legality/illegality and formality/informality useful for analyzing key aspects of urban life in more northerly cities. Sanchez's deep discussion of realtor practices in Los Angeles' segregated housing market fits the model well. In Houston, the importance of private business influence in governance—through the famous 8F Crowd for example—was not discussed in the Pratt/Melosi essay, but clearly demonstrates substantial informal influence in the Bayou City at one time.[11] Echoes of the formal/informal paradigm everywhere helped to create a dialogue among participants, raising questions about power relationships, social order, and regulatory authority in all six cities.

Sociologist Louis Wirth's now seventy-plus-year-old emphasis that urbanization could no longer be viewed simply as a process whereby people were attached to a place, but instead were bound by systems of social relationships, characterizes several studies in *New World Cities*.[12] This might seem to be an aging concept, a relic from another era, yet Wirth connected cities with people in such a way to help us move beyond viewing urban areas as fundamentally fixed and local, if on a large scale. Where formal/informal dichotomies and relationships are highlighted in *New World Cities*, emphasis is placed on social actors, the forms of social organization, and the role of the state. Questions of migration and immigration, governmental policies of segregation, and shared concerns with urban politics as they relate to popular communities emphasize social interactions. Of course, there is much more to the study of cities and urbanization than questions of social order, social relationships, and the politics they sustain. But all of the essays in the book converged in viewing social organization and related political action at the center of urban challenges ranging from economic development to environmental change.

Emphasizing social and welfare impacts, Aprodicio LaQuian, director emeritus of the Centre for Human Settlements at the University of British Columbia, argued that "Mega-cities have more in common with each other than with their rural hinterlands whether they are located in developed or developing countries."[13] This assessment held true with respect to (1) "the rapid spread of urbanism as a way of life despite the decline in metropolitan growth; (2) further impoverishment of the urban poor in most mega-cities; (3) erosion of the capabilities of metropolitan governments to plan, finance, and manage urban development; (4) increase in social ills and urban pathologies; and (5) changing demographic structures, including aging, of large city populations."[14] What holds true for megacities is applicable for the variety of cities in our book.

Rio, Mexico City, and Los Angeles fit several of the trends that LaQuian suggested, but not necessarily in the same way. The advantage (disadvantage?) of a historical analysis is to make complex what appears to be simple. Patterns of informality bring into question the role of central government versus local action in the two Latin American cities, whereas government appears to play a different (possibly a more coercive and central) role in Los Angeles. "Urban pathologies" such as crime and drugs clearly have had serious negative impacts on all three cities. Demographics have changed, but common metrics for determining levels of impoverishment among the urban underclass are highly dependent on careful evaluation of the role of favelas and barrios in these cities and what they return to the locals in terms of livelihood and security.[15] Also, what does "opportunity" mean in these major cities of the Western Hemisphere and elsewhere? Is it strictly an economic term or one that also includes more or less regulation of daily activities or something as basic as a choice in where to live and work? As several of our essays suggested, informality is both a limit and an opportunity.

In his study of modern Rio de Janeiro, McCann describes a roller-coaster ride of a rising formal sector until the 1960s, and an intensifying informal sector especially in the 1980s and beyond. For decades, development in the formal sector "triggered growth" in the informal sector. In this setting, favelas that perhaps began as squatter settlements became places where the dynamics of informality grew and were nurtured. None of this denies problems of poverty and crime. Indeed, the late-century weakening of the formal sector came as relatively new and more violent criminal networks disrupted the formal/informal relationships that had evolved, threatening the lives and welfare of so many who so long had worked to build the favelas. These growing criminal networks exposed the limits of the viability of the informal sector in areas such as security, where the role of the state seems essential. Indeed, there always were limits to informality in the same way that the formal sector began to realize its own limited reach into the favelas. Informality, as others have argued, cannot be divorced from questions of legal constraints and legal protections. Property rights, for example, demand some legal framework even to sustain the informal sector's hold on favelas. From the government's perspective, how much informality was acceptable and what kind? McCann's essay effectively uses the formal/informal model to explain changes in Rio's growth and development in the twentieth century; it also utilized the historical case-study approach to demonstrate not only the dynamics of informality as expressed in the favelas but the limits and pitfalls of a changing relationship between the formal and informal sectors. A lingering question is whether condoning some level of informality was a viable tool for urban—or even national—governments.

Tutino's essay on Mexico City took a somewhat different slant on the role of informality. His emphasis, decidedly economic and social, is clearly on marginality. Tutino makes clear that, as several studies of global urbanization suggest, a major attraction of in-migration to Mexico City was the potential for economic, educational, and cultural opportunity. But he also suggested that while "opportunities are legion" and cities "are poles of attraction for people seeking new life chances," they also are "defined by dependencies." In such a setting, as Mexico City grew "explosively," structural dependencies reinforced the existing power base, and that combination moved people at the bottom toward "self-help and a limited politics of services and survival." In setting such a context, Tutino sought the rationale for informality, a different emphasis from McCann's effort to identify the institutionalization of informality in sustaining the favelas.

Both stress informality as a by-product of the necessary functioning of emerging megacities in economic environments that limited formal employment, housing, and services and political environments that condoned (or at least acquiesced in) such informality. Tutino emphasized that the formal economy did not generate the resources, jobs, or revenues necessary to sustain the burgeoning city on a broad scale. Given what was available, its leadership was incapable of (or possibly unwilling to) effectively provide the needs of its growing population without informal, extralegal, and illegal means used equally among the powerful, privileged, and poor. Instead, the city leaders may have preferred to invest in profitable economic sectors and wealthy neighborhoods at the expense of those people farther down the ladder.[16] Yet the imbalance in the power relationship between the formal and the informal produced a middle ground where services and economic opportunity leaked out slowly to the margins.

The story told here is one of persistent growth under a range of regimes and over the course of many years. But in the face of rampant population growth, the power structures did not change fundamentally. Mexico City continued to be run by elites tethered tightly to the national government. Resources were invested in production and profit more than infrastructure and services—à la geographer David Harvey and several of his intellectual compatriots.[17] Little room could or would be made for greater public participation in the realities of the growing metropolis or attention to the substantial needs of the expanding population. With respect to housing and community, development of new subdivisions was sanctioned but the necessary infrastructure and services were not forthcoming. "Sanctioned illegality," as Tutino described it, became an accepted policy.

While McCann discussed informal institutions as compromise solutions to Rio's problems, Tutino treated them as a default mechanism in a place where economic growth and opportunity were restricted to elites, and where basic services and infrastructure—like the poor and dependent majorities—were marginalized rather than prioritized. As Mexico City began to relinquish its role as an industrial center in the 1980s, and as new and relocated industries increasingly served a global export market, the gap between formal and informal sectors widened rather than narrowed. As in Rio, crime in the city and drug cartels in the periphery worsened conditions, making it difficult to consider revising an entrenched system. Even the brief oil boom of the late 1970s did not act as a positive change agent, as it created the debt crisis that made the 1980s Mexico's "lost decade." Not everything, however, moved farther down a desperate slope. Better medical care, educational opportunity, some infrastructural improvements, and even a less aggressive in-migration were indicators of improving life in the 1990s—especially in older neighborhoods, often built by decades of self-help. But little of this came from the top down without pressure from the bottom up.

Tutino's faith in the grassroots in Mexico City is not unlike McCann's image of the dynamic favelas. Tutino, as stated earlier, chose to build his discussion of informality much more around an economic framework in which he emphasized the inability of the formal sector to produce jobs in the wake of constant population pressure. Tolerating informality was a way out for elites, a way to defer certain costs and responsibilities without giving up production and profits. An important consequence was increased marginality of poorer sectors of the population. Such an approach contrasts with McCann's effort to demonstrate the value of the informal sector vis-à-vis the favelas, the possibility of absorbing informal institutions into the formal structure, and the unfortunate consequences of the rise of drug cartels there in the decades of globalization.

In the case of Buenos Aires, Healey stressed the relationship between governance and citizenship, emphasizing the central role of the formal sector in its relationship with the periphery of the city from the late nineteenth through the twentieth century. Unlike the papers on Rio and Mexico City, Healey's study placed greater emphasis on the symbiosis between core and periphery. This is true, particularly on the impact of outward growth manifest through industrialization, and ultimately on how changing national regimes responded to the dynamics of growth in the capital and its suburbs. His concentration is on the turn from the populist rule of Juan Perón to the later military regimes and subsequent conservative democratic governments that oversaw a difficult shift to globalization with limited employment.

The state government is a primary actor in this story, even as Healey made clear the important role that popular movements in the periphery played in the changing nature of Buenos Aires' development. We see more emphasis too on transportation, urban infrastructure, and urban planning than in the other papers, as well as some discussion of housing. The essay is broader in scope if not deeper in exploring informality and its role along the city's frontier. Unlike Tutino's essay, where population growth and economic change are central to driving Mexico City's evolution, or in McCann's essay, where informality continually undermined—or balanced in some way—an "arc of formality," Healey stressed the mutual push/pull of the core/periphery relationship. Taken as a whole, the three essays open up a range of important questions about formality/informality and their links to diverse modes of politics as ways to analyze urban development.

Sanchez placed Los Angeles at a crossroads in the Western Hemisphere. Given its demographic fluidity, its geographic and demographic connections to the Latin American world, its serious contrasts between rich and poor, and its graphic reminders of marginality, the City of Angels seemed ready for a penetrating appraisal of informality. Sanchez analyzed state-condoned, state-supported, and state-sanctioned segregation, especially through the lens of housing and neighborhood formation. Yet he made clear that those most active in perpetuating housing segregation included not only several formal governmental entities on the city, county, state, and federal level, but also included important players from the private sector—particularly real estate agents and associations. Segregation was drawn clearly across racial/ethnic lines and often class lines. The place of Latino populations in the racial mix is less murky in Sanchez's story than in studies of other cities where that population can be counted among Caucasians or simply lumped into the amorphous category of "nonwhite." Sanchez's story of segregation is a familiar one, but presented as much more deeply entrenched than others have argued. Has he shown us "constrained formality" as an alternative way to incorporate the poor? He definitely has raised important questions about the "informal" influence of local realtors, although he may not have stated it in that way.

Sanchez devoted the bulk of his essay to how the formalities of law and other regulations, the informal influence of realtors, and habitual racist practices acted upon a population delineated by the powerful as a racial/ethnic other. There is less discussion of the responses by those acted upon, however. When the less powerful and the ethnic other appear, they are often challenging authority through the legal system. Yet even with this limitation, we see in Los Angeles a city struggling under many of the same problems of in-migration, rapid growth, crowding, and marginality being experienced south of the border.

Montreal, argued Dagenais, was defined by "multiple, quite unique tensions." The city, however, underwent rapid growth at the end of the nineteenth century, and also faced local/regional, national, and international challenges on its path to becoming a regional metropolis in the twentieth century that made it not so unlike other cities in *New World Cities*. Indeed, the city redeveloped and redefined itself in such a way to change from an essentially bicultural city into a multicultural center distinctive from the megacities of the hemisphere, but with a smaller global footprint. Dagenais focused especially on the city's identity as a metropolis long divided between French-speakers and English-speakers—a bipolar history unique among all the other cities in the book. Defined by its bicultural character—the city of "two solitudes"—Montreal "became multicultural and French after the Second World War, and then multiethnic and partially multilingual at the turn of the twenty-first century."

The self-conscious efforts to create ethnic enclaves, an existing culture of poverty, the marginalization of immigrants, and a degree of state disengagement all seemed to replicate experiences of the informal sector that we have seen especially in Rio and Mexico City. Yet these developments were of a far more limited scale in Montreal, for the most part resolved politically, and usually brought back to the formal sector. Thus a comparison with Los Angeles, rather than Rio and Mexico City, may be most appropriate. In some respects, the public identity of Montreal as the French-speaking capital of Canada, and the center of tensions between French-speaking and English-speaking Canadians, tends to cloud the growing reality of an emerging multicultural city, where groups have utilized a degree of informality to place themselves within the larger Canadian culture and survive intact.

Dagenais does not place her evaluation explicitly in the formal/informal debate, relying instead upon a more traditional framework emphasizing ethnic politics and the intersection of public and private power to analyze the growth of a city in the developed world. Still, she offers an important opportunity to think about Montreal's push to multiculturalism in a way compatible with cities in the developing world, while also facilitating comparisons with other North American cities. This is not so far-fetched given that informality can be found in Canada's past in some interesting ways. For example, prior to the Great Depression, Quebecois—derided as "Mexicans of the North"—entered the United States illegally (or informally) to work in agriculture, textiles, and lumber in New England.[18] Montreal's story, therefore, might fit interestingly (if not completely) with the cities of the Global South. Like Los Angeles, whatever extralegal and informal movements emerged to shape Montreal, most eventually worked through the formal and legal political system to find consolidation in a city of relative prosperity.

As emphasized in Melosi and Pratt's chapter on Houston, the city often has been referred to as "Free Enterprise City." The common way to evaluate its history was to highlight its growth and development as an emerging metropolis while private-sector elites ruled and pulled the strings of its economy.[19] The chapter discussed the development of public services common to most American cities, especially water and transportation, and emphasized the overriding impact of the twentieth-century oil boom as the central factor creating Houston's persona as an "energy capital"—perhaps the global energy capital. This interpretation placed heavy emphasis on private-sector action, without the conspiratorial tone of studies that view local economic titans as manipulating handpicked political leaders.

While "formal" easily equates to "governmental," "private" does not mean "informal." Much of what is private in the politics and social development of Houston is defined by legal sanctions ranging from incorporation to nonprofit status, and thus is almost always formal. But "private" has been used in so many ways and in so many contexts that its derivation is not always clear. Is organized crime, for example, private? No rules of incorporation or legal status sanction it. And "legal" and "illegal" (or extralegal) remain murky areas. As RECIM scholars have queried, "*Who* is the law, rather than solely *what* is the law" may be the most pertinent issue here—as in all of the case studies in the book. How Houston political leaders interpreted their relationship with private industry and other government entities, for example, may go a long way in explaining what appears to be a freewheeling approach to urban development—that was officially condoned. Although Houston's growth may be more conventional than some have stated, the fusing of the public and the private is particularly intense and influential. Perhaps the key question from Melosi and Pratt's history of Houston, pertinent to all our cities, is "Who is the power and how is it organized and exercised?"

Looking at institutional arrangements in Houston, there is no debate that the government condoned and enforced segregation in the city for many years, and that the city through its state-mandated annexation powers controlled its periphery with a vengeance. But when one ventures into the public/private relationships that have existed in Houston for generations, one has to speculate about what in this relationship is public and legal, and what might be construed as informal and extralegal. It appears that the privatization of power—or the development of public/private partnerships—remained mostly in the domain of the formal and legal. When it gets out of hand, in Houston it is treated as corruption. Defining that boundary deserves continuing analysis for all our cities. Meanwhile, a recent and rising flow of migrants from Mexico to Houston, and their importance to sustaining the city's continuing boom, may open more traditionally "Latin American" questions about legality, formality, and their opposites.

One tentative conclusion is to suggest that North American cities with their generally greater economic resources have limited or frustrated the development of the informal sector, and by doing so given primacy to formal institutions. This may be true in some sense, but often we are dealing with problems of semantics. Informal structures by other names are at work (see realtors or undocumented immigrants). What also is true in some cases is that the powers that promote formal sectors in many North American cities, rather than condoning informal arrangements, simply ignore problems they choose not to address rather than openly ceding their control to informal networks. The specter of homelessness in the United States, especially since the 1980s, is a good example of a problem largely ignored by the public sector but yielded to private shelter programs and related organizations. In any event, Sanchez's paper left us with a lingering sense that Los Angeles may reside in that netherworld or limbo between a society with all the elements necessary to produce significant informal networks, yet one still ruled by dominant and in large part legitimate government and legal structures that distinguish between its citizens—and alien residents—in emphatic ways. What seems absent—or at least limited—in Los Angeles and other north-of-the-border cities are sustained movements where those without sanctioned legal rights build homes, neighborhoods, and movements to defend and ultimately legalize them. Or maybe we are not looking hard enough to identify them?[20]

Our studies of Los Angeles, Montreal, and Houston together have examples of how formality/informality can be a useful construct for understanding how the more prosperous cities operate in the twentieth century, but such analysis could be teased out better with greater attention to groups or movements that clearly qualify as informal. While examples of informality do exist in northern cities, it is more typical for scholars to think in terms of public/private schemes, governmental/nongovernmental approaches, and so forth, as stand-ins for the formality/informality framework. Aside from realtors and land developers, greater discussion of a range of groups from NGOs to drug cartels, from worker protest groups to city gangs, could broaden our understanding of the functioning of northern cities. Perhaps the importance of the labor market shaped by undocumented workers—a sector influenced in large part by roots in Mexico and Latin America—can be understood in more innovative ways than as a persistent social problem. Disparate phenomena like Hoovervilles, other squatter communities, street markets, and vigilante groups are sprinkled throughout the history of North America, but rarely discussed as part of the informal urban network.

While the discussion of formality/informality across the Americas remained a bit messy, with terminology still underdefined or unclear, all of the authors in *New World Cities* are keenly aware of the importance of structural and institution changes taking place in their cities. And all of the essays, in some way, treated those changes with an eye toward questions of formality/informality despite the contrasting terminology utilized to express it.

Another key component of structural and institutional change is the role of popular participation in setting societal priorities. Easily discernible forms of popular participation in our cities are obvious on one level, yet much less so on another. A clear gap remains between the few haves and the many have-nots. The nature and extent of that gap is a little more complex. The Mexico City that Tutino writes about suffered from increasing concentration of power and limited participation linked to structural elements in the urban governing and economic systems. Local councils and courts historically offered a voice to non-elites, but this was intermittent. Informal activities and ad hoc neighborhood movements, however, regularly militated against the excesses of the system. Production in the postindustrial era, which brought great wealth to the rich and fewer job opportunities to the poor, was built upon a contradiction "that brought explosive urban growth with unparalleled riches and unprecedented proliferations of marginality after 1950." From the 1990s, with the full turn to globalization under NAFTA, the coastal and border regions of Mexico became enmeshed in the violent repercussions of drug trafficking, a form of economic opportunity no more advantageous to the underclass than the promises of globalization. In perhaps an ultimate contradiction, Mexico City has been spared most of the violence, capital accumulation, and limited employment brought by the global drug economy.

Popular participation and popular mobilization centered in the favelas of McCann's history of Rio. There, as in Mexico City, midcentury times of national development mixed limited economic gains with informalities that both constrained rights of citizenship and enabled families to find some opportunities to build homes and neighborhoods in the space. With the turn to globalization and the decline of formal employment and state-provided infrastructures and services, many favelas saw spaces of informality become places of violent illegality as havens for drug lords and others wishing to escape the hand of government. McCann's essay is interested in questions of formality/informality, especially in treating the relationship between the core and the periphery, highlighting the demands of working-class residents in Rio looking for inclusion and eschewing marginality. The discussion of favelas in the larger context of Rio's recent history offers a resolute approach to the discussion of popular participations, showing contradictions also evident in Tutino's broader discussion of the social and economic divisions and participations in Mexico City.

Healey emphasized the importance of labor-based popular politics that forced accommodations by the powerful, first during times of export boom, then under Peronist national development. He examined especially the evolving politics of neighborhoods, and the growing reality of population decentralization. For wealthy neighborhoods the promise of economic progress remained bright; for those in less affluent and working-class neighborhoods, the story was different. With globalization, Buenos Aires saw the rise of *villas miserias*—towns of misery—that brought marginalities and political exclusion long common elsewhere in Latin America to once-favored Buenos Aires.

Dagenais emphasized Montreal's historic division between anglophone elites and a francophone majority, the nationalism pressed by the latter across Quebec just as the city lost leadership in Canada's national economy, and the challenges of incorporating new immigrant communities under late-century globalization. Such factors brought a politics of popular participation, defined broadly, into view even as she discussed how an expanding metropolis built outward to incorporate new diversities. Her discussion of the arrival of new immigrants emphasized the location of various groups in the city matrix, and thus is more implicit than explicit about opportunities to benefit from the city's economic institutions. The broader brush here provides an opportunity to explore the ways in which citizens involved themselves in city affairs. Building on her work, others may wish to explore questions of participation and marginality more fully.

Sanchez, like Tutino, offered a more generalized critique on how the underclass fared in Los Angeles. It is clearly linked to ethnicity, the question of marginality tied to persistent segregation. Barriers, in this case, are not so much derived from a changing economy, but exacerbated by the emergence of the postindustrial world. Implicit here is the notion that true popular participation is limited by the stranglehold of segregation—a physical dividing line with political and social implications. Melosi and Pratt connect a discussion of the job opportunities afforded the working class in Houston to its heyday as an energy capital. Like Sanchez and Dagenais, there is less direct attention to popular participation in the affairs of the city, but marginality historically has been linked to segregation in "Jim Crow Houston." The environmental implications of the oil and gas economies in Houston—pollution in its many forms—fell heavily if not exclusively on working-class and poor neighborhoods. The essay provides a departure point to explore more fully what economic success meant for the working class in the long term, and to what degree a postsegregation era, racially and ethnically diverse Houston offered an even playing field for its citizens.

Among the six histories presented here, the three on Latin America deal directly with questions of popular participation and marginality, and the three on Canada and the United States emphasize changing combinations of opportunity and inequality. In part, this may reflect different historiographical traditions. Does it also derive from greater economic and social exclusions in Latin American cities, leading to more independent and assertive movements that often operate outside formal political channels? There is some truth to that, but it is worth remembering that Buenos Aires was a city of shared economic gains and active political inclusions long into the twentieth century. And there, the rise of marginalities came with new political exclusions. In the years after 1950, the greater economic gains in the Global North by no means promoted equitable distribution of wealth, and have widened gaps between rich and poor, but the northern cities were hardly as bottom-heavy as their neighbors to the south. Global South cities, where globalization often exacerbated economic gaps, and where (outside Buenos Aires) marginality seems historically more widespread, found themselves creating neighborhoods of exclusion. And while popular participation continued—focused more on neighborhood rights and services in the south, more on linguistic, ethnic, and racial rights in the north, and making gains in both—nowhere did they find the ways and means to change the course of urban development in the globalizing world.

Final Thoughts

Every essay in *New World Cities* has an explicit or implicit tip of the hat to the debate over formality and informality, often with respect to questions of growth and social order. The lesson to take away from the book is not whether the formal/informal model should guide our understanding of major cities in the twentieth and twenty-first centuries, particularly in the Western Hemisphere. Rather, the questions raised by each of the essays suggest the need to rethink the measures we use to define modern cities, their social organizations, their political contests, and their growth patterns. Along with attention to the formal and informal, there is a clear need to rethink questions of public/private enterprise, governmental/nongovernmental action, legal/illegal/extralegal constructs, corporate/bureaucratic questions, and individual versus communal relationships. Reevaluating the role of power—governmental and corporate, public and private, national and local, elite and popular—and the implications of the existing institutions that foster change will require substantial effort.

Starting out on this project, all of the participants assumed certain things about their cities and possibly about the cities that others were studying. Some were uncertain as to what a hemispheric approach to urbanization might produce. Others assumed that great differences existed between North and South America, between cities in developed or developing countries. Like any good analytical exercise, the cumulative work of the authors has produced insightful and useful scholarship, but left us with many more questions than answers. In the broadest sense, comparative history should take us outside of our set perceptual boxes, and help us consider alternative ideas and concepts. Yet, the authors in *New World Cities* have found common ground in not simply addressing formality and informality, but in taking a serious look at how our cities fit within the global economy and the degree to which daunting transformations in our cities in the late twentieth century inspired popular participation in addressing the quandaries of such change and the persistence of the limits to democratic decision making. Common ground clearly was struck with collective attention to our cities in terms of place and space, the timing of globalization, and changes in the institutions and structures of the cities.

Did our labors cover all the ground necessary to address our choice of subject? Of course not. But *New World Cities* makes clear that ending such a project with an eye on fundamental, shared concepts—rather than by intent or dumb luck—can break down intellectual barriers of geography and culture, and provide a departure point for raising deeper questions about urbanization in the Americas, and cities in general. Like any venture into something new, much was learned, and much research and analysis, local and comparative, still needs to be pursued.

Notes

1. Werner Fornos, Desikan Thirunarayanapuran, and Harold N. Burdett, "Population and the Urban Future," in *Time-Saver Standards for Urban Design*, ed. Donald Watson (New York: McGraw-Hill, 2003), 1.1-1.

2. Caroline Ash et al., "Reimagining Cities," *Science* 319, no. 5864 (2008): 739.

3. See Jim Motavalli, et al., "Cities of the Future: Today's 'Mega-cities' Are Overcrowded and Environmentally Stressed," *E: The Environmental Magazine* 16 (September/October, 2005): 26–36.

4. J. R. McNeill, *Something New Under the Sun: An Environmental History of the Twentieth-Century World* (New York: Norton, 2000), 281–82.

5. From Martin V. Melosi, *The Sanitary City: Urban Infrastructure in America from Colonial Ties to the Present* (Baltimore: Johns Hopkins University Press, 2000), 4. See also Andrew C. Isenberg, ed., *The Nature of Cities: Culture, Landscape, and Urban Space* (Rochester, NY: University of Rochester Press, 2006), xii–xiii.

6. Basudeb Guha-Khasnobis, Ravi Kandur, and Elinor Ostrom, "Beyond Formality and Informality," *Linking the Formal and Informal Economy*, September 2006, Oxford Scholarship Online Monographs, 1–7, 16, https://global.oup.com/academic /product/linking-the-formal-and-informal-economy-9780199237296.

7. "Rethinking the Political: Informality, Governance and the Rule of Law in an Urban World," RECIM 4th meeting, Mexico City, March 23–25, 2011, http://ciesas.files .wordpress.com/2011/01/4th-recim-meeting-march-20111.pdf.

8. "Rethinking the Political."

9. For instance, see Janice E. Perlman, "Marginality: From Myth to Reality in the Favelas of Rio de Janeiro, 1969–2002," in *Urban Informality: Transnational Perspectives from the Middle East, Latin America, and South Asia*, ed. Ananya Roy and Nezar AlSayyad (Lanham, MD: Lexington Books, 2004), 105–146.

10. Ananya Roy, "Why India Cannot Plan Its Cities: Informality, Insurgence and the Idiom of Urbanization," *Planning Theory* 8 (2009): 76, 82–85. See also Nezar Al-Sayyad, "Urban Informality as a 'New' Way of Life," in *Urban Informality*, ed. Roy and AlSayyad, 7–30.

11. The 8F Crowd, or Suite 8F Group, was an informal association of politically active businessman in Texas during the 1930s to the 1960s. The name comes from a room in Houston's Lamar Hotel where they met and sought to influence the management of the city.

12. Louis Wirth, "Urbanism as a Way of Life," *American Journal of Sociology* 44 (July 1938): 1–24.

13. Aprodicio LaQuian, "Social and Welfare Impacts of Mega-City Development," in *Mega-City Growth and the Future*, ed. Roland J. Fuchs et al. (New York: United Nations University Press, 1994), 192.

14. LaQuian, "Social and Welfare Impacts," 193.

15. There is good evidence that workers in urban areas tend to be more productive and earn more than their counterparts in rural areas—thus a correlation between populations living in urban areas and the level of income. However, there is no good evidence that the level of urbanization affects the rate of economic growth. Poverty persists. See David E. Bloom, David Canning, and Gunther Fink, "Urbanization and the Wealth of Nations," *Science* 319, no. 5864 (2008): 772–775.

16. For more on the idea of the urban growth machine, see Andrew E. G. Jonas and David Wilson, eds., *The Urban Growth Machine: Critical Perspectives Two Decades Later* (Albany: State University of New York Press, 1990).

17. See Noel Castree and David Gregory, *David Harvey: A Critical Reader* (New York: Wiley-Blackwell, 2006).

18. Aristide Zolberg, "A Century of Informality on the United States-Mexico Border," *SSRC*, August 17, 2006, http://borderbattles.ssrc.org/Zolberg/.

19. See Joe R. Feagin, *Free Enterprise City: Houston in Political-Economic Perspective* (New Brunswick, NJ: Rutgers University Press, 1988).

20. Useful examples come from the burgeoning literature on American suburbanization, such as Andrew Wiese, *Places of Their Own: African American Suburbanization in the Twentieth Century* (Chicago: University of Chicago Press, 2004), which discusses how individual black families built homes on marginal land outside central cities well before suburban tract development.

Contributors

MICHÈLE DAGENAIS is professor of history at the Université de Montréal. A specialist in the urban and environmental history of Quebec and Canada, she has published numerous books and articles in French, notably *Faire et fuir la ville. Espaces publics de culture et de loisirs à Montréal et Toronto aux XIXe et XXe siècle* (Presses de l'Université Laval, 2006). She has published in English, notably *Montreal, City of Water: An Environmental History* (UBC Press, 2017). She also coedited with Stéphane Castonguay, *Metropolitan Natures: Environmental Histories of Montreal* (University of Pittsburgh Press, 2011).

MARK HEALEY is an urban, environmental, and political historian of Latin America and the author of *The Ruins of the New Argentina: Peronism and the Remaking of San Juan after the 1944 Earthquake* (Duke University Press, 2011). He teaches at the University of Connecticut and is currently writing an environmental history of water and wine in drylands Argentina.

BRYAN MCCANN is professor and chair of the history department at Georgetown University and president (2016–2018) of the Brazilian Studies Association. He is the author of *Hello, Hello Brazil: Popular Music and the Making of Modern Brazil* (Duke University Press, 2004), *The Throes of Democracy: Brazil since 1989* (Zed Books, 2008), *Hard Times in the Marvelous City: From Dictatorship to Democracy in the Favelas of Rio de Janeiro* (Duke University Press, 2014), and *Getz/Gilberto* (Bloomsbury, 2018).

MARTIN V. MELOSI is Cullen Emeritus Professor of History and founding director of the Center for Public History at the University of Houston. His research specialties include urban and environmental history, energy history, and the history of technology. Among many works, he is the author of *The Sanitary City: Urban Infrastructure in America from Colonial Times to the Present* (Johns Hopkins University Press, 2000), *Effluent America: Cities, Industry, Energy, and the Environment* (University of Pittsburgh Press, 2001), and *Precious Commodity: Providing Water to Americas Cities* (University of Pittsburgh Press, 2011), past president of the American Society for Environmental History, the Public Works Historical Society, the Urban History Association, and the National Council on Public History, he is currently completing an environmental and political history entitled *Fresh Kills: The Dilemma of Consuming in New York City* with Columbia University Press.

JOSEPH A. PRATT is Cullen History and Business Emeritus Professor at the University of Houston, where he served as chair of the history department and interim dean of the College of Liberal Arts and Social Sciences. A leading historian of the petroleum industry, he is the author and coauthor of numerous books, including *But Also Good Business: Texas Commerce Banks and the Financing of Houston and Texas, 1886–1986* (Texas A& M University Press, 1986), *Baker and Botts in the Development of Modern Houston* (University of Texas Press, 1991), and *Exxon: Transforming Energy, 1973–2005* (Briscoe Center for American History, University of Texas at Austin, 2013), and co-editor with Martin V. Melosi of *Energy Metropolis: An Environmental History of Houston and the Gulf Coast* (University of Pittsburgh Press, 2007) and co-editor with Martin V. Melosi and Kathleen Brosnan of *Energy Capitals: Local Impact, Global Influence* (University of Pittsburgh Press, 2014).

GEORGE J. SANCHEZ is professor of history and American studies and ethnicity at the University of Southern California, where he also serves as director of the Center for Diversity and Democracy. He is the author of *Becoming Mexican American: Ethnicity, Culture and Identity in Chicano Los Angeles, 1900–1945* (Oxford University Press, 1993), and coeditor of three other books, including *Los Angeles and the Future of Urban Cultures* (Johns Hopkins University Press, 2005). Born in Boyle Heights to two immigrant parents from Mexico, he was a first-generation college student, receiving his BA in History and Sociology from Harvard University and his Ph.D. from Stanford University.

JOHN TUTINO is professor of history and international affairs and director of the Americas Initiative at Georgetown University. He is the author of *Making a New World: Founding Capitalism in the Bajío and Spanish North America* (Duke University Press, 2011), *The Mexican Heartland: How Communities Shaped Capitalism, a Nation, and World History, 1500–2000* (Princeton University Press, 2018), and *Mexico City, 1808: Power, Sovereignty and Silver in an Age of War and Revolution* (University of New Mexico Press, 2018). He recently edited *New Countries: Capitalism, Revolutions, and Nations in the Americas, 1750–1870* (Duke University Press, 2016).

Index

Buenos Aires (cont.)
urbanization in, 5, 146–47, 161, 297; urban planning, 155–56, 160, 165–66, 301; *villeros,* 158, 160, 161–62; wealth and power in, 3
Building Code for Rio de Janeiro (1937), 122–23
Burgess, Ernest, 296–97
Bush, George W., 103–4
BUSTOP program, 230

Cabral, Sérgio, 138
Cadíz Constitution (1812), 75
Caldeira, Theresa, 59
California, 47, 59. *See also* Los Angeles
California Real Estate Association (CREA), 227–28
Câmara, Helder, 127
Cameron Iron Works, 249
Canada, 4, 7, 24, 44–45, 53, 56, 177, 315. *See also* Montreal
Canada-United States Free Trade Agreement, 56
Capital in the Twenty-First Century (Piketty), 3
capitalism: agricultural, 7, 26–27, 28; commercial, 2, 33–34; contract, 81; global, 6, 8, 11, 12–13, 33, 81, 106; industrial, 2–3, 7, 21–23, 24, 28, 34, 36, 42, 51, 70, 103; inequities of, 17; medical, 7, 26, 56–57, 103; national, 36, 39, 43, 45, 54, 69–70, 103; and population growth, 28; silver, 34–38, 69, 72; vs. socialism, 6, 11
Caranza, Venustiano, 83
carceral state, 59
Cárdenas, Cuauhtémoc, 93–94
Cárdenas, Lázaro, 36, 83–84, 86
Chávez, Hugo, 280
Chenier, Clifton, 274
Chicago, population, 7, 48
Chinese exclusion, 219–20
Citizen's Committee of Milton Park, 185
City of Quartz (Davis), 212
Ciudad Juárez, 32

Ciudad Nezahualcóyotl, 90–92
Codesco, 131
coffee trade, 13, 38
Cold War, 6, 7, 22, 23, 45, 51–52, 211
Compton, 210–11, 226
Confederate secession (1861), 49
Constitution (Mexico, 1857), 75
Continental Research Network on Informality in Metropolitan Spaces (RECIM), 302–3, 311
Córdoba model, 159
cotton production, 21, 22, 25, 35
Crawford v. Los Angeles School Board, 230
CREA. *See* California Real Estate Association
Crowell, Rodney, 274–75
Cruzada São Sebastião, 127
Cuba, 72
Cuban Revolution (1953–1959), 23

Davis, Mike, 8–9, 24, 212
Department of Housing and Urban Development (HUD), 229, 232
desegregation, 230, 245, 271, 273
development programs: failure of, 8, 9; transformation through urbanization, 9–10. *See also* urban planning
Díaz, Porfirio, 76, 81, 82
drug trafficking, 14, 58, 60, 101, 103–4, 134–35, 140, 282, 299, 307–8, 313
Duhalde, Eduardo, 163

East Los Angeles, 215
elections, 60–62
employment: dependence on state for, 85, 89; in formal sector, 58, 113, 115, 118–19, 138, 306–7, 313; globalization, effect on, 13, 20, 29, 34, 41, 56–57, 60, 308, 313; and green revolution, 7; illegal, 57–58, 282, 299; under industrial capitalism, 42; labor-saving production, effect on, 24, 26; under neoliberalism, 100; and privatization, 93; secure, scarcity of,

10–11, 23, 28, 30, 45, 52, 55, 60, 77–78, 79, 81, 85, 91, 276, 282, 313; in security, 59; self-employment sector, 57–58, 94, 282, 299; in service sector, 193, 270; and transit, 95, 97; of visible minorities, 195

energy industry, 13, 16, 242–46, 256. *See also* oil industry

Engelke, Peter, 11

Entwistle Tract, 221–22

Equal Protection Clause, 230

Estado Novo (Vargas regime), 113, 122–24, 140

Estatuto da Cidade (Brazil, 2001), 136

Estrada de Ferro Dom Pedro II (railroad), 119–20

ExxonMobil, 255, 272

Fair Housing Act (1968), 229

Federação de Associações de Favelas do Estado de Guanabara (FAFEG), 128–29

Federal Housing Authority (FHA), 223–24, 227, 235

FHA. *See* Federal Housing Authority

Fiedler, Bobbi, 230

Financial Crisis (2007–2008), 104

Findlay, Ronald, 2

formal/informal sectors, 301–16; employment in, 58, 113, 115, 118–19, 138, 306–7, 313; in Houston, 280–83; in Mexico City, 71, 72, 77–81, 90, 100; in Rio de Janeiro, 112–18, 119, 301

Fox, Vicente, 103–4

Franco, Marielle, 139–40

francophone nationalism, 15, 53, 56, 60–61, 203, 300, 314

Frankfurt, 8, 30

Friendswood Development, 255

Fugate, G. L., 265

General Agreement on Tariffs and Trade (GATT), 93

Glaeser, Edward, 10

Global City, The (Sassen), 2

globalization: acceleration of, 6–7, 10, 11, 14, 20, 28, 39, 41; capitals of, 30; challenges of, 15, 203–4, 217–18, 233–35; concentrated power from, 16–17; deindustrialization under, 114, 193, 298; democratic openings from, 60–61; and energy industry, 16; foundations of, 23; and Global South, 8; and immigration, 203; inequities of, 20, 29–30, 59–61, 295–96, 314–15; integration of, 8; job loss due to, 10–11; and labor-saving production, 8, 24–29, 34; via NAFTA, 94, 95, 101, 103, 313; and national development, 1–2, 6, 23–24, 28, 45, 51–57, 59, 192; neoliberal, 70, 95, 132, 161; networks of cities in, 20–32; and oil industry, 243; participatory representation, lack of, 102; persistence of, 3, 8; pivot of, 34–38, 41, 43, 45, 93, 101, 166, 183, 202, 203, 308; and popular movements, 14–17, 62–63, 113; promise of, 20, 29; and segregation, 228–33, 237; transitions in, 6; in 20th century history, 21–24; uncertain, 47–49; and urbanization, 1–3, 7, 8, 10, 12–17, 21, 34, 62–63, 70, 106, 295–96, 299–301

Global North, 9, 11–12, 300

Global South, 8, 9, 11–12, 30, 32, 112, 300

gold trade, 13, 15, 38

Gonçalves, Daniel, 126

Gorelik, Adrián, 146

Great Acceleration, The (McNeill/ Engelke), 11

Great Depression (1930s), 6, 14, 15, 21, 22, 36, 39, 42, 47, 51–52, 54, 83, 87, 165, 183, 223–28

Great War. *See* World War I (1914–1918)

green revolution, 7, 27, 36–37, 86–87, 94

Guanabara experiment, 128–29, 130

Gulf Oil, 250

H1N1 swine flu, 104

Hahn, James, 234

of WWII on, 224–25; energy industry, 13, 242; future of, 235–37; and
globalization, 234, 237; growth of,
15, 47; housing prices, 230–31;
housing segregation in, 210–12,
218–33, 298, 304, 309; immigrant
population, 213, 216; in-migration to,
213–14, 309; knowing, 212–18;
migration to, 49; national development in, 54, 59, 300; original name,
218; population, 7, 47–48, 51, 52, 53,
55, 217, 225–26; public housing, 224,
226; race riots (1992), 212; service
economy of, 55; suburban subdivisions, 221; urbanization in, 5; urban
planning, 213–14; U.S. acquisition of,
34; war industries, 47; Watts riots
(1965), 49, 53, 212, 216–17, 233;
wealth and power in, 3; zoot suit
riots (1943), 47–48, 212
Los Angeles County, 215–18
Los Angeles Investment Co. v. Gary,
220
Los Angeles Realty Board, 220, 226

Magarinos Torres, Antoine, 126
Maia, César, 135
Malibu, 215
Manila, 71, 72
Martínez del Río banking group,
75–76
Marx, Karl, 22
Maximilian I (Holy Roman Emperor),
73–74
McDaniel, Hattie, 226
McNeill, John, 11, 295
McWilliams, Carey, 213
M. D. Anderson Foundation, 254
medical advances, 24, 27, 57, 85–86,
103
Menem, Carlos, 162–63
Metropolitan Migrants (Hernández
León), 282
Metropolitan Revolution, The (Katz/
Bradley), 10

Mexican-American War (1846–1848),
34, 36
Mexican Revolution (1910–1920), 6, 21,
22–23, 27, 36, 70, 82–85, 86
Mexican War of the Reform (1858–1860,
73–74, 76
Mexica (Aztec) state, 35, 70–71
Mexico, 6, 13, 21–22, 27–28, 35–37, 49,
52, 60
Mexico City, 2, 5, 32, 69–106, *74*, 298;
barrios, 24, 58, 72, 76, 88, 90; as
capital of Mexica, 35–36, 71; as
capital of Mexico, 72–73; as capital of
New Spain, 71; concentration and
marginality in, 105–6; council, 83;
crime and violence in, 10; diversity
in, 3, 99–100; early history, 69–71;
earthquake (1985), 37–38, 92–93,
106; earthquake (2017), 106; effect of
revolution on, 82–85; elections in, 61,
62, 101; food riots (1692), 72;
globalization of, 70, 92–103; green
revolution in, 27–28, 36–37, 86–87,
94; illegality and informality in, 71,
72, 77–81, 90, 100, 307–8; and
indigenous republics, 72; in-
migration to, 306; labor-saving
production around, 27; liberal
development in, 73–82; lost decade
of, 307–8; middle class in, 77;
national development of, 85–92, 93;
parcialidades, 75; Paseo de la
Reforma, 77, 81–82, 99, 105, 106;
pivot to globalization, 34–38;
population, 4, 7, 23, 36–38, 52, 55,
69, 85–86, 98, 308; privatization in,
75–76, 77, 93; railroad connections,
76–77; and revolution, 82–85; service
economy, 102; silver economy, 13,
33–34; Tepito barrio, 77–78; in
21st century, 103–5; urbanization in,
5, 70–73, 85–103; water problems,
80–81; wealth and power in, 3
Miller, Loren, 226
Mitchell, George, 255

privatization, 75–76, 93, 311
Proposition 1 (California), 230
Proposition 14 (California), 228
Proposition 21 (California), 230

Quebec, 45, 56, 61. *See also* Montreal
Quiet Revolution (1960–1970), 184, 191, 203

RECIM. *See* Continental Research Network on Informality in Metropolitan Spaces
Renting Law (1942), 123–24
Revista Brasileira de Estatística (journal), 127
Reynolds, William Bradford, 232
Rio de Janeiro, 2, 32, 33, 38–41, 112–41; Bairro Peixoto neighborhood, 121–22; *bairros,* 135–38; Borel favela, 125–28; Brás de Pina neighborhood, 131–32; Building Code (1937), 122–24; as capital, 13, 38; coffee trade, 13, 39; criminal turf occupation, 118, 134–35, 140, 299, 307; diversity in, 3; elections in, 62; Estado Novo regime, 113, 122–24, 140; favelas, 14, 24, 54, 55, 58–59, 112–14, 117, 122, 124–25, 129, 135–38, 140, 297, 299, 313; formal/informal sector, 112–18, 119, 301, 305–6; globalization in, 113–14, 299; gold trade, 13; Guanabara experiment, 128–29, 130; housing projects, 123, 130–32; irregular subdivisions in, 118–19, 124, 132–33, 134, 137; map, *116*; migration to, 114; mobilizations in, 114–15, 128, 139–40; modernity/tradition in, 120–21; Morro dos Cabritos favela, 121; plantation economy, 34; police brutality in, 118, 126, 139, 140; population, 4, 7, 13–14, 23, 36, 38–41, 51, 52, 54, 55, 127; Praia do Pinto favela, 129; redemocratization in, 132–33; regularization in, 133–34; Renting Law (1942), 123–24; slave trade in, 38, 118; state violence in, 138–39; streetcars and railways in, 118–20; titling programs, 117, 133, 135–36; tourism economy, 114, 119, 140–41, 299; urbanization in, 5; Vidigal favela, 132; wealth and power in, 3
Riverside County, 216
Robbins, Alan, 230
Rockefeller Foundation, 27, 86–87
Roosevelt, Franklin D., 224
Rostow, Walt, 22
Rousseff, Dilma, 41, 137–38
Roy, Ananya, 303
Russia, 6, 21, 22
Russian Revolution (1917), 6, 21, 22

Saint Domingue, 38. *See also* Haitian Revolution (1791–1804)
Saint Lawrence Seaway, *172*
Salinas, Carlos, 92–93, 97
San Bernardino County, 216
sanctioned illegality, use of term, 307
San Fernando, 242
Santa Fe Railroad, 218
Santa Monica, 215
São Paulo, 4, 7, 38–41, 54–55, 59
Sassen, Saskia, 2, 8–9, 24, 29, 245
Scobie, James, 150
segregation: and globalization, 15, 228–23, 237; in housing, 210–12, 218–33, 298, 304, 309; persistent, 53, 228–33; self-, 229
Serviço Especial de Recuperação das Favelas e Habitações Anti-Higiênicas (SERFHA), 127
Shapiro, Tom, 232
Shelley v. Kramer, 210, 226
Shell Oil, 250
Sierra de Ajusco, 95–97
Silva, Luiz Inácio da, 41
silver economy, 13, 33, 35, 36
Sing, Lee, 219
Sjoberg, Gideon, 297

Weintraub, Roberta, 230
Welcome to the Urban Revolution
 (Brugman), 9–10
welfare programs, 3, 9, 29, 141
Wirth, Louis, 304
World War I (1914–1918), 6, 21, 22,
 42–43
World War II (1939–1945), 6, 22–23, 27,
 36, 47, 51, 223–28

Yarborough, Ralph, 272
Yucatán peninsula, 26–27, 36

Zapata, Emiliano, 27, 82. *See also*
 Mexican Revolution (1910–1920)
Zonas Especiais de Interesse Social
 (ZEIS), 136
zoot suit riots (1943), 47–48, 212
Zydeco, 274